JUAN LUIS VIVES

ARCHIVES INTERNATIONALES D'HISTOIRE DES IDEES

INTERNATIONAL ARCHIVES OF THE HISTORY OF IDEAS

34

JUAN LUIS VIVES

CARLOS G. NOREÑA

JUAN LUIS VIVES

MARTINUS NIJHOFF / THE HAGUE / 1970

ISBN 90 247 5008 3

PRINTED IN THE NETHERLANDS

To Maria, my Wife

CONTENTS

ABBREVIATIONS

Adv. Ps-D. *Adversus pseudo-dialecticos*
DD.   *De disciplinis* (Part, Book, Chapter)
De IFC.   *De Institutione feminae Christianae* (Book, Chapter)
De OM.   *De officio mariti* (Chapter)
De pac.   *De Pacificatione*
De RD.   *De ratione dicendi*
De RSP.   *De ratione studii puerilis*
De SP.   *De subventione pauperum* (Book, Chapter)
De VFC.   *De veritate fidei Christianae* (Book, Chapter)
EE.   *Erasmi Epistolae*, eds. P. S. and H. M. Allen
ELL.   *Exercitatio linguae Latinae* (Number of dialogue)
LC.   *Litterae ad Franciscum Craneveldium*, ed. Henry de Vocht
M   *Vivis Opera Omnia*, ed. Gregorio Mayans y Síscar
R   *Vives. Obras Completas*, trans. Lorenzo Riber

ACKNOWLEDGMENTS

I want to express my sincere gratitude to the following publishers for granting me permission to quote from books covered by their copy-rights: Clarendon Press (*Opus Epistularum Des. Erasmi Roterodami*, P.S. and H.M. Allen editors), Gregg Press (*J. L. Vivis Opera Omnia*), and Librairie Universitaire of Louvain (*Litterae ad F. Craneveldium*, ed. Henry de Vocht).

INTRODUCTION

Humanism has constantly proclaimed the belief that the only way to improve man's life on earth is to make man himself wiser and better. Unfortunately, the voice of the humanists has always been challenged by the loud and cheap promises of scientists, by the inflammatory tirades of politicians, and by the apocalyptic visions of false prophets. Material greed, nonsensical chauvinism, racial prejudice, and religious antagonism have progressively defiled the inner beauty of man. Today's bankruptcy of man's dignity in the midst of an unparalleled material abundance calls for an urgent revival of humanistic ideals and values. This book was planned from its very start as a modest step in that direction.

It is not my intention, however, to attempt, once again, a global interpretation of Humanism in general, or of Renaissance Humanism in particular. I have been dissuaded from such a purpose by the failure of contemporary scholars to agree on such basic issues as whether the Renaissance was a total break with or a continuation of medieval culture, whether it was basically a Christian or a pagan movement, whether it was the effect or the cause of the classical revival. Instead, then, of discussing the significance of sixteenth century humanism, this book concentrates upon the life and the thought of a single humanist. The choice of Juan Luis Vives was the result of several circumstances, some of them rather personal in character. As a Spaniard living in a self-imposed exile, I have always felt a profound admiration for this lonely countryman of mine who had the temper to entertain noble and serene visions of man's future in spite of torturing doubts, constant betrayals, tempting radicalism, personal failures, and international chaos. Vives' books, on the other hand, convinced me that his thought had been grossly misrepresented by a large section of Spanish scholarship and unduly neglected by foreign, especially English, writers. As a rule Vives has been depicted by his own countrymen as a man of the counter-Reformation. In the decades which followed the Spanish Civil War this trend reached almost ridiculous proportions: Vives' name was associated with those of Ignatius of Loyola, the American Conquistadores, Trent, and Lepanto, as a symbol of the religious and political role which Spain was supposed to play in world history. My interpretation of Vives as a cosmopolitan European, indifferent to religious sectarianism, vulnerable to doubt, of secular and worldly ideas, is a radical departure from those provincial misconceptions. The primary purpose of this book is to support with solid evidence this novel characterization of Vives' thought. Furthermore, I decided to write in English to make up for the surprising shortage of English studies on the subject.

The understanding of Vives' intellectual performance demands a complete familiarity with the cultural reality of Spain, France, the Low Countries, and England in the first half of the sixteenth century. Although I do not claim to be a specialist in each one of those extremely complex and rich fields of historical research, the first part of this book attempts to relate Vives' mental development to its historical and cultural environment. More than a history of Vives' life, Chapters Two through Seven intend to be an intellectual *curriculum vitae*. As far as I know this is the first biography of Vives which makes full use of the rich correspondence of Vives from and to Erasmus, Cranevelt, Thomas More, and Budé. There is a certain parallelism between the two parts of the book. Chapters Seven through Twelve are disposed in such a way as to correspond roughly to the stages of Vives' life. Vives' critical ideas are the reaction to his own experience of medieval education in Paris; Vives' Erasmianism covers the early years of Bruges and Louvain; English Humanism helped Vives to develop his political and educational theories; finally, the last years of poverty and loneliness in Flanders brought to its full maturity the philosophical thought of our Humanist. In this second part I have tried as much as possible to give a fresh impression of Vives' own style by inserting frequent and long quotations from his books. I have, nevertheless, translated the original Latin text to make this book more acceptable to a larger number of readers. The Renaissance specialist will find the original Latin text in the footnotes. Besides quoting the classical Latin edition of Mayans y Síscar, I have added in the footnotes a reference to the Spanish translation of Lorenzo Riber, whose exhuberant and classical elegance might be more accessible to some students of Spanish culture than the beautiful but prohibitive Latin original.

I am strictly obliged to express my thanks, first of all, to my wife who made this effort not only possible, but meaningful and enjoyable. I am particularly in debt to Professors Jason Saunders, Richard Popkin, Américo Castro, Herbert Marcuse, Carlos Blanco, and Claudio Guillén – all of them members of the faculty at the University of California at San Diego – for their encouragement and suggestions. I also feel very grateful to all the employees of the Interlibrary Loan at the San Diego and Santa Cruz campuses of the University of California whose patient work made it possible for me to reach the large number of bibliographical apparatus which a book of this kind necessitates. Finally, I want to thank all those who helped me to cleanse the impurities of my English diction: Dorothy Wells, Bonnie Zimmerman, Victoria Kroyer, Audrey Schlegel, Paul Manners, Eleanor Hall, and last but not least, my own daughter Victoria.

Santa Cruz, December 1968

CHAPTER 1

THE VICISSITUDES OF VIVES' FAME

During his life and in the first hundred years after his death (1540-1640) Vives enjoyed tremendous prestige. At the age of thirty the Humanist from Valencia was well known all over Europe. The Pope, Adrian VI, was his personal friend; Charles V, Henry VIII, Catherine of Aragon, and Ferdinand of Austria lavished their royal patronage upon him; Mary Tudor, the Archbishop-elect of Toledo, and the daughters of Thomas More were at one time or another his private pupils; the Universities of Valencia, Paris, Louvain, and Oxford were proud of their relation with him; the University of Alcalá was eager to obtain his services; the greatest scholars of the day – men such as Erasmus of Rotterdam, Thomas More, Linacre, Fisher, Budé, Juan De Vergara, Alfonso Valdés, and many others – were his close friends. The wealthy patrons of that time sought to have Vives under their generous wings: Busleyden in Louvain, Cardinal Wolsey and Lord Mountjoy in England, Doña Mencía de Mendoza in Breda. Erasmus himself was absolutely convinced that Vives' fame would some day overshadow the reputation of any of his contemporaries.

An inventory of Vives' editions gives us an impressive idea of his fame. If we leave aside Erasmus (who, in spite of his humble forecast, obviously relegated Vives' memory to the background) and Ramus, whose popularity at the end of the century is still an enigma to the historian of philosophy, it is almost certain that Vives shares with Melanchthon the glory of being the most read Humanist of northern Europe in the second half of the sixteenth century. The exhibition organized by the French National Library on the fourth centennial of Vives' death included over five hundred different editions of Vives' works.[1] In the field of education alone the *Repértoire* of Buisson con-

---

[1] A catalogue of this exhibition was published by J. Estelrich, *Vivés. Exposition organisée à la Bibliothèque Nationale* (Paris, 1941).

tains the following statistics: Erasmus, three hundred and eighty different editions; Ramus, one hundred and five; Melanchthon, one hundred and four; Vives, ninety-one; Valla, seventy; Budé, forty-eight; Lipsius, twelve.[2] In the short period of two years (1538-1540) there were more than one hundred different editions of his books.[3] In the second half of the sixteenth century the *Exercitatio linguae latinae* was printed forty-nine times; the *Institutio feminae Christianae*, thirty-two; the *Introductio ad Sapientiam*, forty-six. The printing locations were spread throughout Europe: Paris, London, Basel, Cologne, Lyon, Antwerp, Augsburg, Nüremberg, Leyden, Ingolstadt, and a surprisingly small number of Spanish cities like Zaragoza and Valencia.[4]

The most important books of Vives were soon translated into the main European languages, English, French, and Spanish more extensively, but also into German, Dutch, and Italian. The *Institutio feminae Christianae* was translated in 1528 into Spanish by Justiniano and printed eight times before the end of the century; the same book was translated into English by Hyrde in 1540 and printed four times in the same period; the book was translated into French by Changy in 1542, by Tyron in 1579, and by an anonymous writer in 1587. Between 1540 and 1612 there were more than forty French translations of Vives' works.[5]

These statistics, which are certainly incomplete, suffice to prove that Vives' books were well known and easily available in all the European libraries by the end of the sixteenth century. The result of this amazing record was to extend Vives' reputation throughout European cultural life. Vives' prayers were incorporated into the *Book of Common Prayer* of Edward VI; the Socinians in the Netherlands also used the devotional writings of Vives.[6] For two hundred years the *Civitas* Dei was almost invariably printed in Vives' text and with Vives' critical footnotes; the *Exercitatio lingua latinae* was widely used as a textbook for Latin instruction; the programs of the treatise *De subventione pauperum* were adopted by the city officials of Bruges and in many towns of Flanders and Brabant; Vives' philosophical and rhetorical books were an integral

---

[2] Ferdinand Buisson, *Répertoire des ouvrages pédagogiques du XVI siècle* (Paris, 1886).
[3] The three most popular books of Vives were the *Introductio ad Sapientiam, Exercitatio linguae Latinae,* and *De institutione feminae Christianae.* See Adolfo Bonilla y San Martin, *Luis Vives y la filosofía del Renacimiento,* 3 vols., 2nd ed. (Madrid, 1929), III, 224-239.
[4] See Appendix I.
[5] See Estelrich, *Vivés,* "Diffusion de Vivés en Français," pp. 127-139.
[6] These facts will be solidly documented in different parts of this book.

part of the Ramist controversy; Vives' educational theories were imitated by the Jesuits and Protestant reformers alike.[6] In Spain a powerful group of scholars and writers drew their inspiration from Vives' works. Although they never organized themselves into a school, their names are closely related to our Humanist: the philosopher Fox Morcillo, the Humanists Lorenzo Palmireno and Simon Abril, the grammarian Sánchez de las Brozas, and the pedagogue Bonifacio. Huarte, Gracian, Melchor Cano, and García Matamoros admired Vives and recognized the significance of his work.[7]

The first biographical information about Vives after his death is found in the memoirs of Ludovico Guicciardini and Nicolaus Cleynaerts. The German physician, Conrad Gesner, put together the first (and incomplete) bibliography of Vives.[8] In the first half of the seventeenth century we find abundant testimonies to Vives' reputation. In the first two decades of the century the Jesuit Andreas Schott of Antwerp and his disciple Valère André praised Vives with enthusiasm in their reports about the academic life of Louvain.[9] Another Jesuit, Antonio Possevino, registered the objections of the theologians of Louvain to Vives' remarks on Saint Augustine's *Civitas Dei*.[10] A few years later the Protestant historian Lucas Osiander classified Vives among the secret admirers of Luther, a view which was made popular again in the middle of the eighteenth century by the classical history of philosophy by Jacob Brücker.[11] Perhaps on account of these sectarian appraisals of Vives' religious attitudes the second half of the sixteenth century and the first two decades of the eighteenth century were much less generous with the Spanish Humanist. Nevertheless, we cannot forget the isolated enthusiasm of Nicolas Antonio, and the short but fair references in the *Poly-*

---

[7] Bonilla, *Vives*, "Las doctrinas de Vives en España y el extranjero," II, 329-339.

[8] Ludovico Guicciardini, *Descrittione di tutti i Paesi Bassi* (Anvers, 1568), p. 294. N. Cleynaerts, *Super hospitiis et moribus Hispanorum epistolae* (Rotterdam, 1705). I have not been able to find this book, quoted by Estelrich, *Vivés*, p. 241. Conrad Gesner, *Bibliotheca Universalis* (Tiguri, 1545), pp. 430-434. Missing from Gesner's catalogue are *Exercitatio linguae Latinae, Adversus pseudo-dialecticos*, and *De prima philosophia*.

[9] André Schott, *Hispaniae Bibliotheca* (Frankfurt, 1608), pp. 604 ff. Valère André, *Bibliotheca Belgica sive virorum in Belgio vita, scriptisque illustrium catalogus* (Bruxelles, 1739), 2 vols., II, 679-682. André writes: "Vulgatum praeloquium tres vires eo tempore reliquis omnibus anteferre, Budaeo ingenium, Erasmo dicendi copiam, Vivi nostro judicium laudem adjudicando." (*Ibid.*, p. 679).

[10] Antonio Possevino, *Apparatus sacer* (Cologne, 1608). Possevino complements Gesner's catalogue of Vives' works but adds others which modern scholarship does not recognize any more, like *De prosperis et adversis*, and *Libellum de charitate Dei et proximi*.

[11] J. Brücker, *Historia critica philosophiae*, 4 vols. (Leipzig, 1763), I, 3; IV, 86-88. Estelrich, *Vivés*, p. 147 mentions also Lucas Osiander, *Epitomes historiae ecclesiasticae* (Tübingen, 1608).

histor of Morhof, the *Historia Philosophica* of Georg Horn, and the *Bibliothèque Critique* of Richard Simon.[12]

In 1732 the Valencian Humanist Gregorio Mayans y Síscar, under the patronage of the local Bishop Fabian y Fuero, undertook the difficult task of printing the complete works of Vives. Unfortunately Mayans died in 1781, one year before the publication of the book which was finished by his brother Juan Antonio.[13] This edition, which is the only one easily available today and was, therefore, chosen to serve as reference in this book, was far from perfect. First of all, it is incomplete: missing are the *Commentaries on Saint Augustine,* most of Vives' correspondence, and some minor works. Critically Mayans' edition does not add anything to the *editio princeps* of Basel (1555) upon which it was founded. At the end of the first volume, Mayans included a biography of Vives which is the classical point of departure for all later writings on the subject. By contemporary standards, however, the *Vita Vivis* of Mayans is not a reliable source of information. The genealogy of Vives which precedes the *Vita* is today recognized as a fantastic fabrication by the author.[14] Nevertheless, Mayans y Síscar deserves full credit for having revived the memory of Vives at the end of a century which had been, as a whole, quite cool to the Spanish Humanist.

The effect of Mayans' edition was soon felt by the intellectual elite of Europe. In Spain, two philosophers of some interest, Juan Pablo Forner and especially Andrés Piquer of Valencia, relied heavily upon Vives' ideas. In 1839, a Spanish scholar, Ricardo Gonzalez-Múzquiz, published a rather superficial book with the pompous title *Vindication of the illustrious Spanish philosopher J. L. Vives, the first reformer of European philosophy.*[15] Much more significant to the history of said

[12] Nicolas Antonio, *Bibliotheca Hispana nova* (Rome, 1672), I, 723.
Georg Horn, *Historiae philosophiae libri septem* (Leyden, 1655), p. 320: "Omnia quae tanta cum pompa Ramus philosophis proposuit totidem verbis reperias in L. Vives commentariis."
Georg Morhof, *Polyhistor* (Lübeck, 1708), I, 337. Two other works deserve special menton here. The first is J. M. Pacquot's *Mémoires pour servir à l'histoire litteraire des Pay-Bas.,* 14 vols. (Louvain, 1765-1770), II, 34-60.
Also Jean Pierre Niceron, *Mémoires pour servir a l'histoire des hommes ilustres,* 27 vols. (Louvain, 1780-1785), XXI, 173-180.
[13] Gregorio Mayans y Síscar, *J. L. Vivis Valentini Opera omnia,* 8 vols. (Valencia, 1782). At the end of the first volume there is a short biography of Vives, *Vivis Vita.* Missing are the following writings of Vives: *Philalethae Hyperborei* (1533) – a pamphlet against the divorce of Henry VIII whose authenticity is still in doubt – and, *Descriptio temporum et rerum Romanarum* (1534).
The first edition of *Vivis Opera omnia* was made by Nicolas L'Evèsque, Basel, 1555. See Bonilla, III, 179.
[14] See below, p. 18, note 9.
[15] Ricardo Gonzalez-Múzquiz, *Vindicacion del ilustre filósofo español Juan Luis Vives, primer reformador de la filosofía en Europa.* (Valladolid, 1789).

European philosophy was indeed the impact of Vives' thought upon the leaders of the Scottish School of Common Sense. In the first half of the nineteenth century Thomas Reid and Dugald-Stewart confessed their deep admiration for the Spanish thinker; William Hamilton, in the second half of the century, followed the same tradition and gave a modern interpretation of Vives' syncretism.[16] A group of Barcelona intellectuals, under the influence of the Scottish philosophers, went back to Vives' moderate but progressive ideas as an antidote against the radical thought of Spanish Hegelians and Krausists.[17]

The privilege of initiating modern research into the life and the writings of Juan Luis Vives was reserved for two Belgian scholars, A. J. Namèche, a professor of rhetoric at Louvain, and Emile Van den Bussche, the archivist of the city of Bruges. In 1841, Namèche wrote a memoir on Vives at the request of the Academie Royale de Bruselles; in 1871 Van den Bussche complemented Namèche's work with some "eclaircissements et rectifications." [18] These two reports provide the bulk of bibliographical information for most of the Vives' research. We will carefully point to any significant contribution made after them. On the other hand, it is only fair to emphasize that neither scholar attempted a serious analysis of Vives' thought although Namèche presents an intelligent and fair sketch of Vives' most important writings. The decisive work of these two Flemish scholars was complemented by the interesting information provided by the historians C. Fonteyn, P. F. A. Ram, A. Henne, Altmeyer, and especially F. Nève in his memoires about the Trilingue College.[19]

From the work of Namèche and Van den Bussche, at the end of the nineteenth century, to our own days, the number of articles, books, and dissertations on Vives has reached the massive proportions characteristic of twentieth century scholarship. I shall attempt here to classify the material according to languages and to give a general evaluation of its

[16] See below, pp. 282-283.
[17] See below, p. 283.
[18] A. J. Namèche, "Mémoire sur la vie et les écrits de Jean-Louis Vives," *Mémoires couronées par l'Academie Royale des sciences et belles-letres de Bruxelles,* XV (1841), première partie; Emile Van den Bussche, "Jean Louis Vives, Eclaircissements et rectifications biographiques," *La Flandre. Revue des Monuments d'Histoire et d'Antiquités,* VII (1876), 291-328.
[19] P. F. X. Ram, *Analectes pour servir a l'histoire de l'Université de Louvain* (Louvain, 1859).
Alexander Henne, *Histoire du règne de Charles-Quint en Belgique* (Bruxelles, 1858-1860).
J. J. Altmeyer, *Les précurseurs de la Réforme aux Pays-Bas.* (Paris, 1886).
Felix Néve, *Mémoire historique et littéraire sur le collège des trois langues à l'Université de Louvain* (Bruxelles, 1856).

content. Naturally, the most extensive bibliography on Vives is written in Spanish. In the last three decades of the nineteenth century Carlos Mallaina and Octavio Marticorena wrote on Vives without adding any significant information to the classical biographies of Mayans, Namèche, and Van den Bussche.[20] The man who organized in great style the triumphant home-coming of Vives into the ancestral mansion of Spanish culture was the indispensable Marcelino Menéndez y Pelayo. Although he never wrote a book on Vives, Menéndez y Pelayo's huge critical work – which spreads through twenty solid volumes – includes almost a hundred pages on the subject. In *La Ciencia Española* (1880) the author tries to outline Vives' system of thought and its kinship with the permanent traditions of Spanish philosophy (?); some pages of the seven volumes of *Historia de los heterodoxos* (1880-82) attempt to draw a clear distinction between Erasmus' less Catholic attitudes and the spotless orthodoxy of Vives, "superior to Erasmus in almost every consideration," and "the most pious of all the Humanists"; in *Historia de las Ideas estéticas* (1882) Menéndez y Pelayo makes a fair evaluation of Vives' literary merits; finally, in *Los precursores españoles de Kant* (1892) – a very revealing title – the author, himself an enthusiastic admirer of William Hamilton's eclecticism, sets forth to prove in a few pages that Vives was a forerunner of Bacon, Descartes, and of Kant, and was, in short, "the initiator of modern school." [21]

Unfortunately, the obvious provincialism and religious rigidity of Menéndez y Pelayo's grandilocuent generalizations are not valuable commodities in today's scholarly market. The brilliance of the author's literary criticism is seldom matched by the depth of his philosophical insights. Menéndez y Pelayo's puzzling mixture of serious research and rhetorical enthusiasm is at least partly responsible for the banality of some Spanish biographers of Vives whose patriotic and religious zeal was not accompanied by the encyclopedic erudition of their master.

The most valuable exception to this trend is Adolfo Bonilla y San Martín, a disciple of Menéndez y Pelayo, who inaugurates the twentieth century with three volumes entitled *Luis Vives y la Filosofía del Renaci-*

---

[20] Carlos Mallaina, *Estudio biográfico de Luis Vives* (Burgos, 1872). Octavio Marticorena, "Filósofos españoles: Luis Vives," *Revista de España*, XXV, (1872), pp. 60-80.
[21] Marcelino Menéndez y Pelayo, *Obras completas,* 19 vols. (Madrid, 1911-19). *La ciencia española,* II, 208. *Historia de los heterodoxos,* IV, 52-53, 73; *Historia de las ideas estéticas,* 2nd ed., 9 vols. (Madrid, 1856), III, 217-233. *Ensayos de crítica filosófica,* "De los orígenes del criticismo y del escepticismo y especialmente de los precursores españoles de Kant," IX, 167-178.

miento (1903).[22] Although Bonilla's book is itself based upon the work of Mayans, Namèche, and Van den Bussche, its third volume, especially, contains a large number of footnotes with a wealth of original information and references, a detailed description of three hundred and forty-one different editions of Vives' works, and a rich bibliography. Except for recent investigations based upon Vives' correspondence – which Bonilla only partially knew – this book is still the most reliable and complete source of information on Vives' life and writings. The second volume, however, dealing with Vives' thought, is the weakest section of the book. This part is burdened with long and irritating digressions, an impressionistic accumulation of irrelevant testimonies, and an excessive emphasis upon tradition. Moreover, Bonilla seems reluctant to draw all the conclusions from the less orthodox passages of Vives. Menéndez y Pelayo's pages, together with Bonilla's book, have had an excessive impact upon Spanish research on Vives and have prevented in many cases a frank and realistic appraisal of his merits. Neither man mentions the mere possibility of Vives' Jewish ancestry.

A considerable proportion of Spanish writings on Vives since the publication of Bonilla's book is neither original nor profound. However, the studies of S. Cuevas Zcqueira, B. Calatayud, L. Getino, Mateu y Llopis, and A. de Fornet on the local background of Vives' childhood and on the impact of his thought upon some Spanish thinkers are of significant interest to the historian of Spanish culture.[23] The first important event of this period was the official establishment of a permanent Vives-Chair in the University of Valencia in 1926. The Chair has been privileged to count among its occupants such scholars as A. Torró, Alcaydc Vilar, Vicente Losada, and especially Mariano Puigdoller, who in 1940 published a study of Vives under the deceiving title *La filosofía española de Juan Luis Vives*. The fourth centennial of Vives' death brought a new intensification of Vives' research. Mateu y Llopis' catalogue of the exhibition organized by the city of Barcelona complements

---

[22] See above, note 2. Also, "Clarorum Hispaniensium epistolae ineditae," *Revue hispanique*, VIII (1901), 181-308. This collection of letters, together with those published by Bonilla himself (*Luis Vives*, III, 129-165), considerably increased the correspondence published by Mayans y Síscar.

[23] Santiago Cuevas Zequeira, *Luis Vives, Fox Morcillo y Gómez Pereira* (Habana, 1897).

B. Calatayud, *Luis Vives, Feijoo, y Panduro* (Madrid, 1925).

Alonso Getino, *Vitoria y Vives* (Madrid, 1931).

Felipe Mateu y Llopis, *Vives, el expatriado* (Barcelona, 1941).

A. de Fornet, *Blanca March y Valencia, Las madres de Luis Vives.* (Madrid, 1942).

the similar work of Estelrich in Paris.[24] The Chair of Luis Vives in Valencia and the *Collection Occident* in Paris published in this year two anthologies of articles on Vives by such scholars as Eugenio D'Ors, Carreras y Artau, Zaragüeta, and Gregorio Marañón.[25] The last and most important development in the historiography of Vives was signaled by the publication of Américo Castro's writings in 1948. For the first time, the thought of Vives was presented as an integral part of the Spanish Jewish tradition.[26] The publication in 1964 of the processes of the Valentian Inquisition against the parents of Vives by Miguel de la Pinta y Llorente and José M. de Palacio and the publication in 1929 of Vives' intimate correspondence with Cranevelt have profoundly shocked the more alert and open-minded intellectuals of contemporary Spain.[27] Under the dramatic title "Hecatombe de Luis Vives," a well-known journalist from Barcelona has recently published an editorial attacking Spanish scholars for having perverted the image of Luis Vives for more than four hundred years.[28] Although the accusation might be slightly exaggerated, it is a fact that Lorenzo Riber, writing in 1947 the intro-duction to his otherwise magnificent translation of Vives' works, still shuddered in horror at the very thought of Vives' imputed Jewish ances-try.[29] A few years later, in 1954, B. Monsegú published a book on Vives which earned the "National Award Menéndez y Pelayo" without even alluding to such possibility.[30] The same Monsegú included in the book

---

[24] For more details on the Chair of Luis Vives, see Estelrich, *Vivés*, pp. 171-172. Mariano Puigdollers, *La filosofía española de Juan Luis Vives* (Barcelona, 1940). F. Mateu y Llopis, *Catálogo de la Exposicion Bibliográfica celebrada con motivo del IV centenario de la muerte de Luis Vives* (Barcelona, 1940).

[25] V. Alcayde et alii, ed. *Ofrenda de los antiguos Amigos en su IV centenario,* Universidad de Valencia, Cátedra de Luis Vives (Valencia, 1940). J. Estelrich, ed. *Vivès, humaniste espagnol,* Collection Occident (Paris, 1941).

[26] Américo Castro, *España en su Historia. Cristianos, Moros y Judíos* (Buenos Aires, 1948). "Un aspecto del pensar Hispano-Judío," *Hispania* XXXV, (1952), 161-172. "Lo Hispánico y el Erasmismo," *Revista de Filología Hispánica* (Buenos Aires), II (1940), 1-34; IV (1942), 1-66. There is an English translation of Castro's main writings, revised and augmented by the author himself, *The Structure of Spanish History,* trans. E. L. King (Princeton, 1954).

[27] Manuel Pinta y Lorente and José M. de Palacio, *Procesos Inquisitoriales contra la familia judía de Luis Vives,* Consejo Superior de Investigaciones Científicas, (Madrid, 1964). For Cranevelt's correspondence, see below, note 46.

[28] José Plá, "La hecatombe de Luis Vives," *Destino* (Barcelona, Dec. 3, 1966) writes: "¿Cómo es posible que los eruditos no hayan encuadrado la figura de J. L. Vives en su tiempo, en su raza, en las circunstancias de su vida y en su manera de ser? ¿Porqué tanta mentira?"

[29] Lorenzo Riber, *Juan Luis Vives. Obras completas,* 2 vols. (Madrid, 1947).

[30] Bernardo Monsegú, *Filosofía del humanismo de Juan Luis Vives* (Madrid, 1961).

a chapter on Vives' conception of logic which does not even mention the names of Rudolph Agricola or Peter Ramus.

It would be unfair, however, to close this short summary of Spanish research on Vives with this pessimistic note. On the positive side one needs to add the erudite and sensitive studies of Escosura, Carriazo, Valle, and Gomis on his social theories; Díaz Jimenez, Blanco, Garmendia, and Urmeneta on his psychology; Zaragüeta and Ferrer on the pedagogy of our Humanist; and finally, the short but enlightening lines of Ortega y Gasset on Vives' significance in the history of European culture.[31]

Next to the Spanish bibliography of Vives, we have to mention the German publications, which are amazingly large in number and of fine scholarly quality. Unfortunately, the large majority of these studies concentrate on Vives' pedagogical ideas. The leaders of this tradition – which began at the end of the nineteenth century – are Heine and Dilthey with their fine studies, and Wychgram, F. Kaiser, and F. Kuypers with their editions and translations of Vives' pedagogical writings.[32] The German Universities reacted to this intellectual challenge with a large number of doctoral dissertations, inaugural speeches, well-documented articles, and monographs. Hause, Nebe, and Bohlen explored the relations between Vives and Comenius; Meisser and Hofer studied the influence of Quintilian upon the Spanish Humanist; Wychgram investigated the possible influence of Vives upon Fenelon. Wolf did the

---

[31] Pablo de la Escosura, "La beneficencia en el siglo XVI: consideraciones sobre el opúsculo de J. L. Vives, *Del socorro de los pobres*," *Revista de España*, IX (1876), 193-210, 339-356, 462-481.
José Maria Carriazo, *Las ideas sociales de J. L. Vives* (Madrid, 1927).
F. del Valle, "La mendicidad y el paro en el *Socorro de los pobres* de J. L. Vives," *Razón y Fé*, CXXV (1942), 78-95.
Enrique Díaz-Jimenez, *Los fundamentos éticos, religiosos y psicológicos de la pedagogía de J. L. Vives* (Madrid, 1929).
Ricardo Blanco, *Luis Vives: la pedagogía científica y la instruccion de la mujer* (Madrid, 1935).
H. Garmendia de Otaola, "Luis Vives: ensayo de pedagogía comparada." *Razón y Fé*, CXIX (1940), 130-139.
J. Zaragüeta, *Las directrices de la pedagogía de J. L. Vives* (Madrid, 1945). José Ferrer and Ricardo Garrido, *Luis Vives y la psicología educativa* (Valencia, 1944).
José Ortega y Gasset, *Vives-Goethe*, (Madrid, 1961).
[32] Heinrich Heine, *Vives' Schriften über Erziehung und Unterricht* (Leipzig, 1881).
Wilhelm Dilthey, *Gesammelte Schriften* (Göttingen, Stuttgart, 1960): "Weltanschauung und Analyse des Menschen seit Renaissance und Reformation," Band II, 422-429; Pädagogik, Band IX, 158.
Jacob Wychgram, *Johan Ludwig Vives: Pädagogische Schriften* (Wien, 1891).
Franz Kaiser, *Juan Luis Vives' pädagogische Schriften* (Freiburg, 1896).
Franz Kuypers, *Vives in seiner Pädagogik* (Kiel, 1897).

same with relation to Johan Sturm.[33] Eulitz wrote a solid dissertation on Vives' correspondence with Budé, and finally, O. Bürger probed the personal relations between Vives and Erasmus of Rotterdam.[34] In comparison with this inpressive study of Vives' educational theories, the number of writings dealing with his philosophical ideas is rather disappointing, in spite of the brilliant suggestions by Schaumann, Lange, and Dilthey at the turn of the century.[35] In some cases at least, Schaumann's original attempt to count Vives among the precursors of Kant has prevented rather than fostered an objective and intelligent appraisal of Vives' thought, especially among the many young Kantian authors of doctoral dissertations. Nevertheless, some of these publications deserve an honorific mention here. Pade, G. Hoppe, Siske, and Ilg are the authors of illuminating studies of Vives' psychology; the social ideas of Vives have been investigated by Wurkert, Weitzmann, and Thürlemann; Graf wrote on Vives' apologetics; while Kater and Günther searched into Vives' dependence upon Aristotle and his influence on Bacon's thought.[36]

French scholars have also specialized in Vives' pedagogy. The extensive studies of Compayré and Rousselot in their general histories of

[33] August Nebe, *Vives, Alsted, Comenius in ihrem Verhältnis zu einander* (Elberfeld, 1891).

Paul Hause, *Die Pädagogik des Spaniers J. L. Vives und sein Einfluss auf Amos Comenius* (Erlangen, 1890).

Jan L. Bohlen, "Die Abhängigkeit J. A. Comenius von seinen Vorgängern," doct. diss. (Erlangen, 1906).

J. M. Hofer, *Die Stellung des D. Erasmus und des J. L. Vives zur Pädagogik des Quintilian* (Erlangen, 1910).

[34] Adolphus G. Eulitz, *Der Verkehr zwischen Vives und Budaeus* (Chemnitz, 1897).

Otto Bürger, *Erasmus von Rotterdam und der Spanier Vives: eine pädagogische Studie* (München, 1917).

[35] I. Chr. Schaumann, "De J. L. Vive Valentino philosopho, praesertim anthropologo ex libris eius 'De anima et vita,' " doct. diss. (The Hague, 1792). This dissertation was published by Bonilla, *Luis Vives*, III, 143-160.

Friedrich A. Lange, *Luis Vives*, trans. Menéndez y Pelayo (Buenos Aires, 1944).

[36] Roman Pade, *Die Affektenlehre des J. L. Vives* (Münster, 1893).

Gerhard Hoppe, *Die Psychologie des J. L. Vives* (Berlin, 1901).

G. Siske, "Willens- und Charakterbildung bei J. L. Vives," doct. diss. (Langensalza, 1911).

Paul Ilg, "Die Selbstätigkeit als Bildungsprinzip bei J. L. Vives," doct. diss. (Langensalza, 1931).

Georg Wurkert, *Ludwig Vives' Schrift der Armenpflege* (Pirna, 1901).

W. Weitzmann, *Die soziale Bedeutung des Humanisten Vives* (Leipzig, 1905).

Inés Thürleman, *Erasmus von Rotterdam und L. Vives als Pazifisten* (Freiburg, 1932).

Paul Graf, *L. Vives als Apologet* (Freiburg, 1932).

T. G. A. Kater, *Vives und seine Stellung zu Aristoteles* (Erlangen, 1908).

R. Günther, *Inwieweit hat L. Vives die Ideen Bacons von Verulan vorbereitet* (Freiburg, 1932).

education (1879 and 1881) and Massabieaus' enthusiastic review in 1873 of Vives' Latin dialogues were followed by considerable research.[37] In 1888 two Latin dissertations of the University of Paris dealt with Vives' program of education for boys and girls.[38] In 1897 Parmentier examined the impact of Vives upon English educators.[39] The philosophy of Vives was first explored in France by Vadier (1892), who wrote on Vives' ethics; a few years later, in 1898, Lecigne wrote another Latin dissertation on Vives' political philosophy.[40] Indirectly, the large number of French studies on the University of Paris, the French Renaissance, Erasmus, Budé, Ramus, and Montaigne have helped to clarify important aspects of Vives' philosophical career. The most important of these related studies is undoubtedly the work of M. Bataillon on Spanish Erasmianism, a book which is absolutely indispensable to place Vives in his proper place within the Spanish intellectual and religious life of the sixteenth century.[41]

Italian scholarship has been less interested in Juan Luis Vives. For many years there were only two minor monographs on Vives' educational and psychological ideas, written by Piazzi (1891) and Rivari (1922).[42] The more interesting writings of Faggi in 1938 opened, however, a new era of Italian bibliography on Vives.[43] Nulli in his Erasmian studies and Garin in his penetrating essays on the philosophical aspects of Italian Humanism have recognized the exceptional importance of Juan Luis Vives.[44] In the last two decades, the books of Papagallo,

[37] Gabriel Compayré, *Histoire critique des doctrines de l'éducation en France depuis le seizième siècle* (Paris, 1879).
Paul Rousselot, *La pedagogie feminine* (Paris, 1881).
Louis Massabieau, *Les Colloques scolaires du seizième siècle* (Paris, 1878).
[38] Charles Arnaud, "Quid de pueris instituendis senserit L. Vives," doct. diss. (Paris, 1887).
Francis Thibaud, "Quid de puellis instituendis senserit L. Vives," doct. diss. (Paris, 1888).
[39] Jacques Parmentier, *Histoire de l'éducation en Angleterre* (Paris, 1896).
[40] Berthe Vadier, *Un moraliste du XVIe siècle. J. L. Vives et son livre de l'Education de la femme chretiènne* (Genève, 1892).
Charles Lecigne, "Quid de rebus politicis senserit J. L. Vives," doct. diss. (Lille, 1898).
[41] I have used the Spanish translation of A. Alatorre, *Erasmo y España* (México, 1950), an edition revised and augmented by the author himself, Marcel Bataillon. See also, "Du nouveau sur J. L. Vives," *Bulletin Hispanique*, XXXII (1930), 97-114.
[42] Enrico Rivari, *La sapienza psicologica e la pedagogia di G. L. Vives da Valenza* (Bologna, 1922).
A. Piazzi, "Luis Vives, pedagogista del Rinascimento," *Rivista Italiana di Filosofia*, IX (1891), 113-179.
[43] A. Faggi, *Studi filosofici e letterari* (Torino, 1938).
[44] S. A. Nulli, *Erasmo e il Rinascimento* (Rome, 1955).
Eugenio Garin, *L'Umanesimo Italiano: Filosofia e vita nel Rinascimento* (Bari, 1952). Also, *La cultura filosofica del Rinascimento Italiano* (Firenze, 1961).

Sancipriano, and Manzoni have brought Vives' research to the front line of Italian scholarship.[45]

Nevertheless, the most important advance in the field was achieved, once again, by a Flemish scholar, the Louvain professor Henry de Vocht. In 1929 de Vocht published the personal correspondence between Vives and Cranevelt with a rich critical apparatus, abundant footnotes, and magnificent introductions.[46] This edition, together with de Vocht's long and detailed history of the foundation of the Trilingue College, as well as a short but solidly documented monograph on Vives' visits to England, has enriched Vives' biography with revealing new data totally unknown to the biographical tradition of Vives up to Bonilla y San Martín.[47] De Vocht's scholarly investigation with its higher standards of accuracy and documentation was very similar to the superb edition of Erasmus' correspondence patiently prepared by P. S. Allen, a masterpiece of modern research without which it is impossible to attempt a clear understanding of Vives' life and thought.[48]

Allen and de Vocht (who for some reason, unknown to me, wrote in English) invite us to cast a quick glance at the contribution of British and American scholars in the field of Vives' studies. Twentieth century British scholarship was introduced to Vives by W. R. Woodward's classical history of Renaissance education which places Vives' chapter (thirty pages) between Sadoleto and Melanchthon.[49] Most of the British literature on Vives, however, was written by a single man, Foster Watson, whose entire life was dedicated to the composition of six books in English, two books in Catalan, and several articles dealing mainly with Vives' local background and his life in England.[50] Although Watson's

[45] A. Papagallo, "La pedagogia di G. L. Vives," doct. diss. (Torino, 1955).
Mario Sancipriano, *Il pensiero psicologico e morale di G. L. Vives* (Firenze, 1957).
Bruno Manzoni, *Vives, Umanista Spagnolo* (Lugano, 1960).
[46] Henry de Vocht. ed. *Litterae virorum eruditorum ad Franciscum Craneveldium, 1522-1528* (Louvain, 1929).
[47] H. de Vocht, *Monumenta Humanistica Lovaniensia*, "Vives and his Visits to England,' pp. 1-59. Also, *History of the Foundation and the Rise of the Collegium Trilingue Lovaniense (1517-1550)* (Louvain, 1951).
[48] P. S. and H. M. Allen, ed. *Opus Epistularum Desiderii Erasmi Roterodami*, 12 vols. (Oxford, 1906-1958). Also, "Ludovicus Vives at Corpus," *Pelican Record*, (1902), 156 ff.
[49] William Harrison Woodward, *Studies in Education during the Age of the Renaissance 1400-1600*, 2nd ed. (New York, 1965), first published in 1906, pp. 180-209.
[50] Foster Watson, *Vives and the Renascence Education of Women* (New York, 1912); *Vives on Education* (Cambridge, 1913); *J. L. Vives, a Scholar of the Renascence* (London, 1920); *Luis Vives* (Oxford, 1922); *Luis Vives, el gran Valenciano* (Valencia, 1923). *Les relacions de Joan Lluis Vives amb els anglesos i amb l'Anglaterra* (Barcelona, 1918). "J. L. Vives and St. Augustine's Civitas Dei," *Church*

efforts have considerably increased our knowledge of Vives' relations with his English friends, his books exaggerate the importance of Catherine of Aragon and Vives' himself upon the educational reform of Tudor England and fail to show the philosophical foundations of Vives' pedagogy. Moreover, Watson was obviously misled by his touching Hispanofilia into an overestimation of Vives' Valencian heritage.

In sharp contrast to the altogether extensive and rich research on Vives carried out by European scholars, Americans so far have been unbelievably sparing in their attention to the Spanish humanist. Besides the translation of Vives' *Fabula de homine* in Kristellers' anthology of humanist philosophy, and a short article of Thorndike, the only book on Vives published in the United States was Daly's doctoral dissertation of 1929.[51] Nevertheless, American specialists in Renaissance studies show today an increasing interest in Vives. Kristeller in his books on Renaissance philosophy, W. Ong in his Ramus research, N. Gilbert in his magnificent book on the Renaissance concept of method, Adams in the study of the London reformers, and many others speak of Vives with admiration and recognize his importance.[52] As a whole, however, American intellectuals have not yet become aware of Vives' significance in the history of European thought. Books dealing with the Renaissance are still written without a single mention of Vives' name. Very recent scholarly works spell his name in Italian (Ludovico Vives), and educated people still confuse the Spanish Humanist of the sixteenth century with the Italian philosopher of the eighteenth century, Giovanni Battista Vico. General histories of philosophy make unflattering remarks about the triviality of humanistic thinking.[53] I sincerely hope that the pages to

---

Quarterly Review, LXXVI (1913), 154-157. "The influence of Valencia on Vives," *Aberystwyth Studies* XI (1927), 47-103.

[51] E. Cassirer, P. O. Kristeller, and J. II. Randall, eds. *The Renaissance Philosophy of Man*, (Chicago, 1948). See chapter 13, note 42.
    Lynn Thorndike, "John Luis Vives," *Essays dedicated to J. H. Robinson* (New York, 1929).
    Walter Daly, "The educational Psychology of J. L. Vives," doct. diss. (Washington, 1924).

[52] Paul O. Kristeller, *Renaissance Thought* (New York, 1961).
    Walter Ong, *Ramus, Method, and the Decay of Dialogue* (Cambridge, 1958).
    Neal W. Gilbert, *Renaissance Concepts of Method* (New York, 1960).
    Robert P. Adams, *The Better Part of Valor* (Seattle, 1962).
    The brilliant study of James K. McConica, *English Humanists and Reformation Politics under Henry VIII and Edward VI* (Oxford, 1965), reveals the author's profound interest in Vives.

[53] Myron P. Gilmore, *The World of Humanism 1453-1517*, 2nd. ed. (New York, 1962) does not even mention Vives' name. The same is true with Wallace K. Ferguson's book *The Renaissance in Historical Thought* (Cambridge, 1948) and Douglas Bush, *The Renaissance and English Humanism* (Toronto, 1939).

follow will give Vives the familiarity and acclaim among English speaking people which he so justly deserves.

J. J. Scarisbrick, in his otherwise magnificent book *Henry VIII* (Berkeley, 1968), does not dedicate to Vives a single line. To make things worse, he spells his name in Italian (Ludovico) − a small but highly misleading mistake.

CHAPTER 2

THE LEGACY OF VALENCIA (1492-1509)

Juan Luis Vives was born in Valencia, Spain, the sixth of March, 1492, a year Spanish scholars refer to as the *annus mirabilis*. And indeed amazing was this year in which the Catholic Kings conquered Granada, Roderigo Borgia became Pope Alexander VI, the Jews were expelled from Castile and Aragon, Columbus discovered America, and Nebrija published the first European grammar of a vernacular in his *Arte de la Lengua Castellana*.

The capture of Granada by the combined troops of Ferdinand and Isabella put an end to the territorial control of the southernmost region of the Peninsula by a political power ethnically and religiously different from all the kingdoms south of the Pyrenees. The 700-year-old effort of the Christian *Reconquista* was thus crowned with a flattering success. The community of purpose symbolized in the military victory of the Christian sovereigns over the troops of Boabdil gave to the recent dynastic union of Castile and Aragon a badly needed political sanction. Indeed, the process of political consolidation had hardly started. Not only were Portugal and Navarre independent Crowns, Castile and Aragon themselves were under different administrations. In fact, the only political institution common to both kingdoms since 1487 was the Royal Council of the Inquisition. The geography, the historical background, and the social organization of Castile and Aragon were radically different. Castile was pastoral, nomadic, and central. Aragon was urbane, cosmopolitan, mercantilistic, and peripheric. In Castile the Crown had to compete with a proud nobility, the big landowners of the rough and endless plateau. In Aragon the Royalty had to cope with the privileges and *fueros* of an energetic patriciate and the tight setup of the guilds.[1]

---

[1] For a further study of Castilian and Aragonese characteristics, see Salvador de Madariaga, *A Modern History*, 2nd ed. (New York, 1960), pp. 19-26; also, José Ortega y Gasset, *España Invertrebrada*, 12th ed. *Revista de Occidente* (Madrid,

The frenzied enthusiasm which followed Granada's surrender was sadly misdirected into different channels. Ferdinand's means of achieving nationhood and political unity was typically masculine and aggressive. The victims of the King's expansionistic imperialism were the Roussillon and Cerdagne in 1493, North Africa in 1494, Naples in 1495, and Navarre in 1512. As for Isabella, her uncompromising and demanding religious faith was far from satisfied with the vigilance exercised over the New-Christians by the tribunal of the Inquisition. Only three months after the end of the Muslim power and less than three weeks before the capitulations with Columbus, the Catholic Kings ordered the expulsion of all non-converted Jews from the Kingdoms of Castile and Aragon. Among the hundred and fifty thousand people who fled the country there were some of the most influential men in the world of finance and administration. The crime was punished by its own consequences: the loss of so many Jewish careerists and entrepreneurs caused a serious economic crisis in the years ahead. Those who remained, after a more or less sincere conversion, had to live in constant fear and suspicion.[2] The expulsion of the Jews and the end of the Muslim Kingdom of Granada brought to an end a glorious tradition of 700 years of tolerance in a society where three races, three religions, and three castes lived in creative harmony and peace. The American conquista and the Counter-Reformation on the other hand produced a new Spanish national consciousness from which, as we shall see, Juan Luis Vives was totally alienated.

The city of Valencia where Vives was born and where he spent the first seventeen years of his life was at that time the most prosperous metropolis of the Crown of Aragon. The Kingdom of Aragon was the name of a confederation which included Catalonia, Valencia, and Aragon proper – its oldest but least important member. For many years Catalonia had played the preponderant role by reason of its military conquests in Italy, the amazing expansion of its trade, and the intelligent balance of royal power and local privilege embodied in its political constitution. Nevertheless, the accession of a Castilian dynasty in 1412, the horrors of the Black Death, and the destruction brought about by the civil war of 1462 weakened Catalonian power and made possible

1962), pp. 44-45; Rafael Altamira, *A History of Spanish Civilization*, trans. P. Volkor (London, 1930), pp. 110-116.

[2] See José Amador de los Ríos, *Estudios históricos, políticos, y literarios sobre los judíos de España y Portugal*, 3 vols. (Madrid, 1873-76), pp. 176-200. In spite of its apparent objectivity Amador describes the Jewish nation as "a people destined to crawl on the surface of the earth hopelessly trying to escape the immutable decree of God." (III, 189).

Valencian leadership. Although Valencia never reached the constructive dynamism of Barcelona, Vives' home town was for many years the proud heir to the Catalonian legacy of enterprising cosmopolitanism, administrative skill, and intense cultural life. The Valencians had many good reasons to be proud of their city. How reluctant its inhabitants were to leave Valencia can be seen from the behavior of Jews and Moriscos. Most Valencian Jews preferred to become Christians rather than to go into exile after the decree of 1492. As for the Moriscos, more than a hundred thousand of them decided to stay in Valencia even after the collapse of Granada.

Although Vives left Valencia at the age of seventeen, and probably never returned to it, the delight in his native town, the "garden of Spain," remained forever a cherished, nostalgic remembrance. All the books of Vives, but especially his dialogues, sparkle with priceless, detailed memories of the early stage of his life, the house where he was born, the elementary school which he attended, the lavish plenty of Valencia's renowned fruit and flower market, the river Turia which "meanders through roses and all kinds of flowers," and above all the blue transparentness of the Valencian sky which, by contrast, made Paris, Louvain, and Oxford cold, gray, and unfriendly.[3] The dedication of his book *Somnium Scipionis* (1521) to Everard de la Marck, Bishop of Liège and Archbishop-designate of Valencia, begins with a highly poetical eulogy of his home town:

> The people of Valencia are by nature joyous, alert, facile, and yet tractable and well disciplined . . . The members of the nobility are more numerous in that city than in any other, of marvelous magnificence, affability, and humanity. So fertile is the soil that there is hardly a fruit or a vegetable or a medical plant which it does not produce and pour forth in richest measure. It is so beautiful that there is no time in the year in which both the meadows and abundant trees are not clothed and painted with foliage, flowers, verdure, and a variety of colors.[4]

There was no chauvinism in this frank loyalty and affection for the local environment of his youth. Valencia's name deserves to be insepara-

---

[3] The local references of Vives can be found in M, I, 387; R, II, *ibid.,* 957 (*ELL.,* dialogue *Leges ludi*) and M, I, 287; R, II, 886 (*ibid.,* dialogue *Euntes ad ludum*). Also, M, V, 62-65; R, I, 603-605 (*SS.,* dedication).

[4] M, V, 63; R, I, 604. (*SS.*)

[5] Practically all the early editions of Vives' books carried the Latin name Joannes Ludovicus Vives Valentinus. Thus, e.g., the Antwerp edition of the *Declamationes Syllanae* (1520), the Basel edition of the *Somnium Scipionis* (1521), the Antwerp edition of *De Concordia* (1529), and, finally, the Basel edition of Vives' *Opera omnia* (1555). See the pictures of the title pages of those editions in Mateu y Llopis, *Catálogo,* pp. 17, 61, 63, 73.

bly linked to that of Vives with much more reason that Rotterdam is associated with the name of Erasmus, a man without a home or a past.[5] Nevertheless, it would be a great exaggeration to say with some of his biographers that Valencia's background had a decisive influence upon Vives' thought; it might be true, however, that Valencia's sensual exuberance had something to do with Vives' Baconian spirit, or that Vives' attention to the vernacular could be partly explained by the Valencians' pride in their own dialect against the Castilian expansionism of Isabella's tutors and grammarians.[6]

Of much greater importance for the understanding of Vives' individuality is the determination of his ancestry and home education. His books are a clear proof of the deep impact left upon him by the harmony of his parental home, the exemplary virtues of his especially beloved mother, "matronarum omnium pudicissima," and the severity of the early training which strongly emphasized patriarchal authority, feminine monasticism, and filial obedience.[7] The personal touch of those momentos finally irritated Erasmus, a man who was neither proud of nor especially attached to his own parents. It is even probable that in compliance with Erasmus' policies, some of these familiar remembrances were left out in the Basle edition of Vives' books.[8]

Modern scholars have clearly proved that Mayans' genealogy was nothing but a free and fantastic arrangement of different and unrelated individuals by the name of Vives who lived in the kingdom since the days of James I, the Conqueror.[9] Nevertheless, Namèche in 1841, Mallaina in 1872, and even Bonilla y San Martin in 1929 merely repeat Mayans' fancies without even considering the possibility of Vives' Jewish ancestry, although Amador de los Ríos had, already in 1842, expressed the suspicion that Juan Luis Vives was the son of Jewish converts.[10] It is true that the arguments of Ríos were not very persuasive. Against him, Mateu y Llopis convincingly proved that the name Abraham Aben Vives, found by Ríos in a document of the thirteenth century, was only

---

[6] Watson, the enthusiastic admirer of Vives, overplays the impact of the local circumstances upon his intellectual career. See *El Gran Valenciano*, pp. 4-8. Other scholars, some of them Spanish, frankly admit that it is difficult to find any trace of regionalism in Vives' character. See, e.g., Juan Ríos Sarmiento, *J. L. Vives* (Barcelona, 1940), p. 15.

[7] The references to Vives' parents are found in M, IV, 207; R, I, 1099 b (*De IFC.*, II, 5); also M, IV, 263, 264; R, I, 1144 b (*ibid.*, II, 11) and M, IV, 372; R, I, 1314 b (*De OM.*, 3)

[8] See below, p. 134.

[9] See, e.g., Angel Losada, "Luis Vives en la actualidad internacional," *Revista de Filosofía*, VII (1952), 151.

[10] *Estudios históricos*, p. 14.

one of the mutually independent branches of Vives existing at that time in the Kingdom of Valencia.[11]

The suspicion of Vives' semitism was a shock to a large section of Spanish scholars who were extremely reluctant to admit that the "catolicísimo Vives" (Menéndez y Pelayo) was a member of the "deicide nation." As late as in 1947, Lorenzo Riber, a respectable member of the Spanish Royal Academy of Language and translator and editor of Vives' works, wrote the following incredible words: "We indeed feel an instinctive repulsion toward the alleged Jewish origin of Vives' parents... We deeply regret to see the most Christian of all humanists spotted with this *ancestral blemish*." [12] Menéndez y Pelayo, on the other hand, does not even care to discuss the issue in any of his books. Soon, however, more serious and high-minded scholars were pressing the question to its solution. In 1948 Américo Castro defended the Jewish extraction of Juan Vives as a "reasonable speculation" based on the following evidence. First, the name of Vives was very frequent among Spanish Jews; secondly, Vives' real reason for staying away from Spain apparently was the fear of the Spanish Inquisition; thirdly, Vives' personal bitterness had all the characteristics of the Jewish converts; and, finally, Vives' perfect knowledge of the Rabbinic traditions as revealed in his apologetic works betrays a Jewish education.[13] In 1952, Abdon Salazar, a disciple of Salvador Madariaga in London, informed Professor Castro of his intention to publish some documents found in the archives of Valencia which, according to him, totally confirmed Castro's conjectures of 1948.[14] Unfortunately such documents were not published until 1964, and then not by Abdon Salazar but by two other Spanish scholars, Miguel de la Pinta y Llorente, a specialist in the history of the Inquisition, and by José María de Palacio y Palacio, a Valencian archivist. These documents, published under the title *Procesos Inquisitoriales contra la familia judía de Luis Vives* (Madrid, Investigaciones Científicas) prove beyond the shadow of any doubt the following facts: first, Juan Luis Vives was Jewish by both the paternal and the maternal lines. His father was Luis Vives Valeriola, his mother Blanquina March y Almenara. Juan Luis had one brother, Jaime, and three sisters, Beatriz who joined him in Bruges in 1531, Leonor, and Ana whose husband was also later persecuted by the Inquisition. Secondly, Juan Luis' mother, Blan-

---

[11] Mateu y Llopis, *Vives, el expatriado,* pp. 6-8.
[12] Introduction to the Spanish translation of Vives' works, p. 15.
[13] *España en su Historia,* Apéndice X, pp. 682-685.
[14] Castro himself uses this information in "Un aspecto del pensar Hispano-Judío," 161-172.

quina, became a Christian in 1491, one year before the decree of expulsion. She died in the pest of 1509 in a little village south of Valencia. Thirdly, Luis Vives, the father of Juan Luis, was probably the son of Jewish converts but at the age of sixteen had already some troubles with the Valencian Inquisition. A second and much longer process (1522-1524) ended in a fatal sentence: Luis Vives was "delivered to the secular arm," a somber expression which means that he was burned at the stake. Fourthly, in 1525 the sisters of Juan Luis regained in a legal process the property of their father previously confiscated by the Inquisition. Fifthly, in 1528, twenty years after the death of Vives' mother, a new process was opened to clarify her behavior after the conversion. Witnesses testified that she had visited the synagogue as a Christian; consequently, her earthly remains were removed from the Christian cemetery and publicly burned. The sisters of Vives were forever deprived of any right of inheritance to the paternal and maternal property. Three years later Beatriz, the only one who never married, joined her brother Juan Luis in Bruges. Vives' private correspondence reveals the sadness, the confusion, and the despair which those brutal facts caused in his soul. We shall return to those, until now, mysterious and unexplained passages of Vives' letters because they help to understand one of the critical turning points of his life in Louvain.[15] The collapse of the traditional views on Vives' background bewildered many educated Spaniards. In a rather dramatic editorial entitled *La Hecatombe de Luis Vives, el Humanista*, the well known journalist José Plá asks the following questions: "Why have we accumulated so much respectable falsehood? What is the excuse for so many biographies on Vives entirely based on ignorance and malevolent fantasy?"[16] Indeed the time has arrived to reexamine the accepted image of Juan Luis Vives with honest objectivity.

There is no doubt that Vives' Jewish ancestry gives us a much deeper understanding of his life and his mind.[17] Not that this fact alone could provide a master key to explain all the facets of his thinking. After all, the victims of the Inquisition were in many cases no more Jewish than the Inquisitors themselves. In fact the three first General Inquisitors were Spanish Hebrews and the best known anti-semitic writers, Ramon Martí, Pedro Alfonso, and Jerónimo de Santa Fé were, like Vives himself, Christians of Jewish parentage.[18] Nevertheless, the number of Jews

---

[15] See below, pp. 72-74.

[16] *Destino,* Barcelona, 3 December 1966.

[17] Castro has repeatedly emphasized this aspect of Vives. See, e.g., *Structure of Spanish History,* pp. 577-584.

[18] Bataillon, *Erasmo y España,* pp. 60-66. Castro maintains also that the pro-

who turned against the members of their own race was comparatively small. Most of them were undoubtedly self-respecting members of a well-defined ethnical group with a dramatic past and a typical bent of mind. The great achievement of the Spanish Jew throughout the Middle Ages had been to impose upon the Christian monarchs and the Muslim authorities a policy of tolerance and even privilege against the religious fanaticism of the lower classes. Recognition and persecution in constant fluctuation burdened the lives of the Jews with an insufferable feeling of insecurity. The slight discrimination of the early monarchs of the *Reconquista* was followed by the horrible massacre of thousands of Jews in Granada (1066). The great reign of Alfonso VI was blemished by the destruction of the *aljama* of Toledo in 1108, and the incredible bloodshed of Seville in 1391 stood in sharp contrast with the enlightened attitude of Alfonso X the Learned (1252-1284). In spite of these atrocities, the Spanish Jew, powerfully enriched by his contact with Islam, rose to a high level of creativity unparalleled in the history of medieval Europe. Characteristically enough, the apogee of the Jewish creative genius coincided exactly with the golden era of Cordova's Caliphate. Abraham ibn Ezra (1093-1167), Shelomo ibn Gabirol (1021-1052), Yehudah ha-Levi (1080-1140), and especially Maimonides (1135-1204), startled the medieval thinkers of central Europe with their Arabic books written in Hebrew characters. The Spanish Hebrews were also mainly responsible for the employment of Castilian in books of learning during the reign of Alfonso X in the thirteenth century. In medicine, in specialized trade, in public administration, and in financing the well-educated Jews played a decisive role both in the Christian and the Arabic zone of the Peninsula. The increasing number of converts in the fifteenth and sixteenth centuries tended somehow to conceal their Jewish origin. The literature of these centuries is full of distinguished converts: Don Santob, Alonso de Cartagena, Juan de Mena, Rodrigo de Cota, Hernando de Pulgar, Fernando de Rojas, Fray Luis de Leon, and Mateo Alemán. In the Spanish Levant, Valencia in particular, the number of converts was relatively higher than in Castile or northern Spain. The parents of Vives were typical Valencian Jews: urbane, well educated, prosperous, and respected. From them Vives inherited the Jewish concern and skill in matters of public administration, social legislation, education, and dispensation of justice. Vives' idea on welfare, not as an ecclesiastical work of charity but as a publicly financed assistance, reveals a secular

cedures and the hatred of the Inquisition was mostly inspired by Jewish converts. See, *Structure of Spanish History*, pp. 52-54.

conception of social ethics totally foreign to the Christian feeling of that age.

Together with this practical bent, Vives also carried in his veins all the subtle and even self-contradictory idiosyncrasies of a persecuted minority: a tendency to withdraw from the hostile outside world into the tortured intimacy of a free individuality; a vital, almost existentialistic contact with life as a problem, as a challenge or a threat rather than a purely theoretical acceptance of abstract concepts and schemes; a secret enticement to take revenge on the antagonistic society with a radical and independent criticism of traditional ways of thinking and venerable institutions; and, finally, a mood of bitter scepticism toward the basic beliefs of the self-complacent majority. This is the true background of the somber tradition of Don Santob and Juan de Mena, Rodrigo de Cota and Fernando de Rojas, the picaresque literature and the escape from the world in the mysticism of the *alumbrados*. Vives' concrete introspection of the self, his increasing isolationism from friends and society, the startling mixture of his biting scepticism and comforting religious faith are tokens of the rich Jewish heritage which was his.

As for his religious education at home, there is little doubt that from the beginning Vives was given an intense Christian training. He was probably baptized as an infant, a practice which he would eventually question.[19] It is very reasonable to suspect that since his parents decided to stay after the decree of March, 1492, the child was given the only religious affiliation which would make possible his future life in a Christian society.

In 1508 Vives attended the Gymnasium of Valencia. The school itself, founded in 1501 by a Valencian Pope, Alexander VI, and confirmed in 1502 by Ferdinand of Aragon, was an eloquent testimony to the glories and the struggles of early Spanish Renaissance.[20] Both Castile and Aragon had felt very strongly the impact of the Italian quattrocento. The Courts of Juan II of Castile and of the Catholic Kings had slowly become centers of high education and learning where famous humanists like the Mialenese Pietro Martire and Lucio Marineo Siculo where "shedding the lustre of letters" over the young Spanish nobility. In Naples until 1458 the Court of the last king of Aragon, Alfonso the

---

[19] The baptism of Vives is shrouded in mystery. Mayans does not mention it, and Bonilla is satisfied with an obscure document found in the Church of Saint Donatian, Bruges, by the Belgian scholar Van den Bussche. See Bonilla, *Luis Vives*, III, 7, note 10.

[20] For a short history of the Valencian gymnasium, see Bonilla, *Luis Vives*, I, 26-31.

Magnanimous, had competed with the Medicis and the Papal Court of Leo X in patronizing the very elite of Italian Humanism: Poggio, Valla, Filelfo, and Aeneas Sylvius Piccolomini. If the Castilian tongue fully triumphed in *La Celestina,* the theater of Juan de la Enzina, and Gil Vicente, Valencia was privileged to see the first Spanish printing press (1473) and to open the first of the twenty new universities of that century (1501). Compared to Salamanca or Lérida, the young University of Valencia was only a provincial, second-class institution. Vives' description of the place is not very enthusiastic: "The entrance to the school was frequently muddy because of the rain, the dust, and the large number of students . . . The hall is rather dark although the portal itself is not unpleasant." [21] However, in spite of its modest beginnings, the University of Valencia was not unaware of the novelties and conflicts of Spanish Renaissance. The controversy between the grammarians of old and the more liberal humanists played an important part in the academic life of Valencia. The new tendencies were represented by Petrus Badía; the conservative party was led by Amiguet, "homo insigniter barbarus," as Mayans calls him.[22] Soon the rivalry between the two teachers was a matter of lively discussion among the students. Gaspar Escolanus in his *History of Valencia* reports a fascinating anecdote about the school days of Vives.[23] In the class of Rhetoric, Amiguet, well aware of Vives' sharp wit, ordered him to write a speech against Nebrija, the leader of the more liberal Spanish Humanists. In my opinion most biographers of Vives have missed the importance of this apparently insignificant anecdote. Vives was at that time fourteen years old, probably mature enough to realize that the quarrel between Amiguet and Badía was much more than an academic dispute about the methodology of teaching grammar as Mayans naively implies.[24] Behind Badía was Antonio de Nebrija whose *Introductiones Latinae* had just been published in Valencia in 1505. Nebrija might not have been, as Bataillon claims he was, a forerunner of Erasmus in the Spain of Cardinal Cisneros.[25] But Nebrija had been in close contact with the Valla-inspired

[21] M, VII, 127; R, I, 273 b. (*Virginis Dei parentis ovatio*).
[22] M, I, 20 (*Vivis Vita*).
[23] I have not been able to find this book, quoted by Mayans, I, 10. (*Vivis Vita*).
[24] M, I, 12; "Caspar Escolanus, *Lib. 5 historiae Valentinae,* cap 23., narrat Antonium Nebrissensem transtulisse humaniores litteras ab Italia in Hispaniam, eiusque *Artem Grammaticae Iatinae* invectam fuisse in Academiam Valentinam anno millessimo quingentesimo septimo . . ." (*Vivis Vita*).
[25] *Erasmo y España,* pp. 25-37. In the introduction to the Spanish translation, Bataillon recognizes that his book had been widely criticized for labelling as "Erasmian" any liberal Christian of the Spanish Renaissance. The author explains that such denomination includes Erasmus' way of thinking and "similar attitudes."

movement which prevailed in Bologna in the last decades of the fifteenth century and was profoundly impressed by the new trends of tradition-free criticism of the Scriptures, the rejection of scholasticism and Papal territorial ambitions which he had learned in the *Annotationes in Novum Testamentum* and *De Donatione Constantini*. As a matter of fact, Nebrija never adapted himself completely to the clericalism of Cisneros and Alcalá. The first Latin and Greek scholar of the sixteenth century in Spain collaborated for only one year in the monumental work of the *Biblia Polyglota Complutensis* when the book was about to be printed (1514). Nebrija became suspect by the Inquisition because of his friendship with Pedro de Osma, the professor of Salamanca who dared to deny the sacrament of penance in 1478. When Nebrija made public his intention to publish a grammar of the Bible, the General Inquisitor, Fray Diego de Deza, initiated a process against him in 1504. Nebrija's *Apology* is one of the most important documents of Spanish Humanism: it could have been written by Colet in London or Erasmus in Paris.[26] The *Apology* was written a year before Vives was asked by his teacher to write, as a practice of rhetoric, an "oratio contra Antonium Nebrissensem." We do not know for sure whether Vives actually wrote it. But we know that in violent reaction against the education being imposed upon him, Vives went to the opposite extreme: Nebrija was practically the only Spanish scholar he ever recommended and admired.[27]

Vives remained in the *Estudio General* of Valencia only a year or two. Basically his time was dedicated to Latin grammar which he took with Jerónimo Amiguet and Daniel Sisó. Of lesser importance were the Greek classes of Bernardo Navarro, some secondary disciplines like poetry and rhetoric with Juan Parthenio Tovar, and a few rudiments of logic.[28] Surprisingly enough, Juan Luis Vives was instructed in the *Institutiones* of Justinian by his uncle Enrique March who no doubt was very eager to keep the venerable legal traditions of the maternal side.[29] In 1509 Juan Luis left Valencia for Paris. The choice was indeed a

[26] The complete title was *Apologia earum rerum quae illi objiciuntur*. It was probably written between 1504 and 1506, but was not published until 1507. Some important paragraphs are quoted by Bataillon, *Erasmo y España*, pp. 28-30; the Apology of Nebrija basically coincides with the thoughts of Erasmus in his letter to Christopher Fisher (*EE.*, I, 182; March, 1505).

[27] Vives praises Nebrija twice in his book *De ratione studii puerilis* (M, I, 264, 276; R, II, 322, 332) and twice in *De Disciplinis* (M, I, VI, 325, 326; R, II, 601, 602). For other quotations, see M, I, 16-18. (*Vivis Vita*).

[28] Bonilla, *Luis Vives*, I, 31-36.

[29] M, I, 24. (*Vivis Vita*) Vives himself mentions this study in the Commentaries on Saint Augustine's *Civitas Dei*, book 19, chapter 21 (Eng. trans. Healey, 2nd ed. [London, 1620], p. 747).

very fashionable one at the beginning of the sixteenth century: as we shall see, Paris was invaded by Spanish professors and students, especially from Catalonia, Aragon, and Valencia. At first hand it seems amazing that Italy apparently was not even considered as an alternate possibility. After all, the Aragonese' presence in Naples was a strong link between Italian culture and Valencia. Perhaps the aristocratic rather than the educational humanism of Italy was more attractive to famous scholars than to young students. It is also possible that the belligerent attitudes of Julius II in those years were a threatening sign of the sad events which eventually took place. In the case of Vives – who never visited Italy – we do not even detect the Italian nostalgia which quivers in so many Northern Humanists. Moreover, Vives – the cosmopolitan Humanist who made Bruges his second home and loved France with tender affection, who praised the importance of Germany as a bulwark against the threats from the East and who had in England his closest friends – in most of his writings betrays a slight touch of animosity against Italy. In the first decades of the sixteenth century Vives considered the Italian Renaissance as a thing of the past: "In the days of our grandfathers there was a great revival of letters in Italy." [30] The great Italians of his own generation were completely ignored by Vives: Leonardo da Vinci, Michelangelo, Macchiavelli, Pomponazzi. Vives tried to convey the impression that Northern Humanists had overshadowed the achievements of the Italians: "Our Budé with his De Asse has humiliated all the Hermolaos, Picos, Politians, Vallas, and Italy as a nation." [31] He deeply disliked the excessive formalism and the paganizing trend of Italian Renaissance.[32] For Italy itself, "the incentive of all greed and the cause of all our evils," he had, together with rare words a praise, a slight contempt. According to Vives Italians would be wise to invite a Frenchman or a Spaniard to take over their political leadership; [33] nowhere could one find more false doctors than in the city of Rome; [34] the cruelty of Spanish soldiers was only outdone by that of the Italian mercenaries.[35]

---

[30] M, VI, 171; R, II, 468 a. "Memoria avorum et patrum coeptum est in Italia revocari studium linguarum." (DD., I, 4, 4).

[31] EE., IV, 1108, vv. 110-115. Letter from Vives to Erasmus. "Philosophiae quum esse illum peritissimum clamant volumina quinque De Asse ... Quod opus eius Hermolaos omnes, Picos, Politianos, Gazas, Vallas, cuntancque Italiam pudefecit."

[32] See De Disciplinis, part 1, book 4, chapter 4: "De auctorum imitatione." (M, VI, 171-181; R, II, 468-475).

[33] M, VI, 465; R, I, 49 a. "Itali ipsi illi ... iis digressiis, altero die Alpes transirent, ut aliquem vel Hispanum accirent, vel Gallum, qui in se dominarentur ... Modo iras suas ulciscantur, canem aliquem nedum hominem quemvis, principem ac dominum reciperent ..." (De Europae dissidiis).

[34] M, VI, 73; R, II, 396. (DD., I, 1, 10).

Altogether a picture which does not fit too well into some traditional schemes about the History of the Renaissance.

Although there is nothing surprising in the choice of Paris for his university studies, Vives' constant refusal to return to Spain after their completion was a meaningful decision which cannot be ignored or minimized. Some Spanish scholars have emphasized the civic order and prosperity of the Low Countries as the main reason for Vives' determination to establish his residence there in 1512. Accordingly, they have presented an extremely somber picture of the calamities which afflicted the Kingdom of Valencia in the first decades of the century.[36] It must be noticed, however, that the plague did not strike Valencia until 1519 and that the social revolution of Juan Llorenç and the Germanias – in which some of Vives' relatives were tragically involved – did not start until 1521. Furthermore, Vives was not only reluctant to return to Valencia in particular, but in general to Spanish territory. In 1522, at the instigation of one of his powerful friends, Juan de Vergara, Vives was invited by the University of Alcalá to take over the chair of Humanities left open by the death of Nebrija. The otherwise flattering invitation did not tempt Vives for a moment. After the tragic execution of his father, Vives felt indeed impelled to visit his destitute sisters in Valencia. Nevertheless, although some scholars believe that he paid a short visit to the city in 1523, it is much more probable that the trip was canceled because of a well-justified fear and an instinctive reluctance to sacrifice his own intellectual freedom.[37] I am convinced that Vives never returned to Spain for exactly the same reason which has kept many Spanish intellectuals in a self-imposed exile: Vives' free, tolerant, and open-minded attitude demanded a wider horizon than his country could offer him. The plain truth is that Vives had a very poor idea of Spanish culture. Raymond Lully and Sabiunde are totally absent from his work in spite of the fact that the reputation of both had been widely spread by Lefèvre d'Etaples, by Nicholas Cusanus, and by other humanists.[38] Even the work of Saint Isidore of Seville is belittled by Vives. The *Etymologies,* he says, 'are nothing in comparison with the contributions

---

[35] M, VI, 463; R, I, 47 b. "Etsi merent sub Hispanis ducibus Itali quidam, qui crudeliora in suos edunt facinora, quam ulli Hispanorum." (*De Europae dissidiis*).

[36] Such is the attitude of Mateu y Llopis, *Vives, el expatriado,* pp. 2-30; also, Marticorena, "Filósofos españoles," p. 67.

[37] See below, p. 27.

[38] See Carreras Artau, *Historia de la filosofía española* (Barcelona, 1931), pp. 177-239. The author shows how Lully's disciples were particularly numerous and enthusiastic in the Kingdom of Aragon during Vives' lifetime.

of Budé'.[39] The well-known biblical work of Cardinal Cisneros and his team of scholars at Alcalá was completely ignored by Vives. But he did not forget to make clear that Spanish scholars were mostly responsible for the corruption of scholastic philosophy at the University of Paris.[40] The fate of some of his most distinguished Spanish friends who fell victims to the intolerance of the Spanish Inquisition, such as, Juan de Vergara, Alonso de Virués, and the brothers Valdés, filled him with constant fear and bitterness. The life of an intellectual in Spain was, according to his own words, "full of uncertainty and darkness." [41] Like Erasmus, he saw the academic community of Spain enslaved by an "angry herd of monks." In June, 1527, Vives wrote to Erasmus a letter with a bitter attack against the "tyranny" of the Spanish clergy:

The *Enchiridion* is spreading fast in Spain and, according to the reports I hear, the monks are going to lose no little amount of their grip ... many people begin to feel ashamed of that disgraceful slavery which, *even in our nation* [Spain] is burdensome and absolutely intolerable not only to born slaves but even to mules themselves.[42]

The result of the tyranny was that in Spain everything was "darkness and night" with "no intellectual climate at all." [43] With sad irony he listed the reasons for the weak opposition his own books met in Spain: "First because I live very far away [from Spain]; second because there are very few people who read my books; and finally, because there are even fewer who understand and hardly any who buy them: such is the cool indifference of our countrymen in the pursuit of their studies." [44] Writing to Vergara who seemed to be somewhat more optimistic about the intellectual level of Spain, Vives replied that he would never believe that there are in Spain many men of letters, "until I am told

[39] M, VII, 146; R, II, 1679 a. "... et Politianus, et Priscianus, atque etiam Isidorus, quam pauca, quam incerta, et obscura, nec raro etiam falsa reliquerunt, ut nihil esse plane dicas, si conferas cum Baudaicis *De asse*." (Vives' letter to Halewyn).
[40] See below, p. 42, note 54.
[41] *LC.*, 164, vv. 18-20. Letter from Vives to Cranevelt. "In Hispania omnia tam vel incerta, vel occulta, ut ex duobus tabellariis qui heri illinc venerunt, nihil omnino licuerit cognosci."
[42] *EE.*, VII, 1836, vv. 45-56. Letter from Vives to Erasmus.
[43] *LC.*, 56, vv. 18-21, 35-40. Letter from Vives to Cranevelt. "Distuli hactenus si qua spes affulsisset ex Hispania. Tenebrae omnia et nox non in rebus maior quam in animo ... nec res se peius in Hispania habebit, quam quod negant me litteratas consuetudines inventurum."
[44] M, VII, 222; R, II, 1733 a. Letter to Maldonado. "Nam invidos habere me non credo, in Hispania praesertim, multis de causis; primum, quod absum; deinde, quod opera mea legunt isthic pauci, pauciores intelligunt, paucissimi expendunt, aut curant, ut sunt frigida nostrorum hominum ad litteras studia."

that there are at least a dozen printing presses which publish and spread the works of classical antiquity." [45]

For many years Spanish historians have spoken of Vives in highly patriotic terms, frequently in a rhetorical and chauvinistic vein which totally misrepresents Vives' personal attitudes. The refreshing truth is, however, that Vives was never enticed by the senseless nationalism of his day. The Erasmus circle, to which he somehow belonged, was a promising group of cosmopolitan Europeans without the provincialism of the Florentine aristocrats and the growing nationalistic tide of Celtis or Ulrich von Hutten.[46] The victories of the Spanish soldiers never aroused the enthusiasm of Juan Luis Vives; on the contrary, he thought that they were brave but extremely brutal.[47] The glorious deeds of the American conquistadores left him totally unimpressed. The only time he spoke in rather epic terms about the American conquistadores his words were not addressed to the Spanish but to the Portuguese Monarch.[48] The conclusion should not be drawn, however, that Vives was a cynical outcast or a homeless wanderer without the warm associations of local friends, without the familiar sounds of his native tongue, coldly detached from his Spanish background. Wherever he went he searched and found Spanish friends. Young men from Valencia were his companions in Paris; in Bruges he lived with the Spanish Jewish community; he went to England to serve a Spanish Queen and returned to Bruges to marry the daughter of a Valencian Jewish merchant. He invariably went back to Bruges in times of moral depression or poor health, probably – as Namèche points out – because he never truly adapted himself to the customs of Flanders and because he preferred to eat something with Spanish flavor rather than the Flemish sausages which he hated. Vives had indeed the intimate kinship with geography and history and blood which centers the life of an individual in its proper local setting, together with the wide horizons and the free perspectives which are the privilege of a true cosmopolitan.

---

[45] R, II, 1796 a. This letter is missing in Mayans' collection.
[46] On the subject of Erasmian cosmopolitanism, see W. Ferguson, *The Renaissance in Historical Thought*, p. 30.
[47] M, VI, 463; R, II, 396. "Nominasti Hispanum militem? Sunt quidem milites omnes praefervidi, arrogantes, incompositissimi ... Hispani tum milites, nullis aliis cedunt improbitate, duritia cordis, atrocibus dictisque factis ..." (*De Europae dissidiis*).
[48] See the dedication of *De Disciplinis* to Juan III of Portugal (M, VI, 1-4; R, II, 337-340).

CHAPTER 3

THE STUDENT OF MONTAIGU (1509-1512)

In the fall of 1509 Juan Luis Vives arrived in Paris. He was at that time seventeen years old, probably one or two years older than most of his fellow freshmen in the University Arts course.[1] By contemporary standards, it is difficult to imagine the feelings and experiences of a Valencian young man traveling through the Kingdom of Louis XII. Throughout the Middle Ages students enjoyed in all the kingdoms of Christendom a special recognition ratified by legal privileges and exemptions. Because of their papal origin, most of those rights conferred to the students some kind of an international status.[2] On the other hand, Vives' journey to Paris coincided with the first ominous signs of the clash between French and Spanish nationalism.

France had reached its geographical and dynastic unity a few years before Spain. The political skill of Louis XI (1461-1483) had succeeded in halting the ambitions of the House of Burgundy, in keeping the English outside of France after the prolonged hostilities of the Hundred Years' War (1328-1453), and, finally, in laying the foundations for an absolute monarchy. Unfortunately, under Charles VIII (1483-1498) the transition from dynastic consolidation to dynastic imperialism was completed. The Italian dreams of the new House of Orleans collided head on with the similar endeavors of Ferdinand of Aragon. The status quo reached by the Treaty of Cambrai (1508) did not last long. In 1512 Julius II, Henry VIII, and King Ferdinand joined in a league to expel

---

[1] As a rule a boy would study grammar until the age of ten, rhetoric from twelve to fourteen; at fifteen, therefore, he was ready for the University. Ong, *Ramus,* pp. 137 and 140, points out that nominalistic logic cannot be fairly judged without taking into account the extreme youth of the pupils to whom it was adapted.

[2] Pope Alexander III (1159-1181) granted to students the privilege of exemption from local courts. Philip Augustus confirmed this immunity in 1200. Students were also exempt from taxation. Graduates of Paris, Bologna, and Oxford were entitled to teach everywhere (*jus ubique docendi*). The cosmopolitanism of the medieval university has, unfortunately, been partially lost in our Western tradition. See Lowrie J. Daly, *The Medieval University* (New York, 1961), pp. 163-169.

the French from Italy. The situation of the Spanish students in Paris became a little tense. In the same year Vives moved to the Low Countries.

In spite of Vives' short residence in Paris, and notwithstanding his disappointment with the performance of the University, he always kept a sincere affection for France. After the defeat of Francis I at Pavia, Vives wrote a touching letter to Henry VIII exhorting him and the Emperor to make a lenient use of their victory:

We earnestly hope that you will act moderately in this time of triumph and that you will not devastate this innocent nation (France), the most flourishing realm of Christendom; that you will not pluck one of the eyes of all Europe. Why should the people of France be punished if the decision to make war was only a blind whim of the King against all the members of his Council? ... Who will be able to describe the consternation of the French people when they heard that their King was in captivity? Everywhere silence and shock, bewilderment and fear.[3]

Vives' sharp criticism of the University of Paris cannot be fully evaluated without taking into account the enormous prestige of the institution in the religious life of Europe since the thirteenth century. Before the Council of Trent, Rome was only a distant court of final appeal; Paris was the intellectual headquarters of the Christian world. The theologians of Paris decided dogmatic questions, inspired the conciliaristic movement, condemned heretics, and, in some cases, they even arrogated themselves the privilege of infallibility. Marsilius of Padua and Gerson were both rectors of the Parisian University. Still during the years of Vives' residence in Paris, one of the most significant controversies of that age, the dispute between Reuchlin and Pfeffekorn was being investigated by the professors of La Sorbonne.[4] But this was to be one of the last testimonies of the ecclesiastical ascendancy of the University. Two of the greatest humanists of Northern Europe, Erasmus and Vives, were instrumental in giving a mortal blow to the prestige of the school. In the very year that Vives arrived in Paris, Erasmus made his last visit to the University and published the *Praise of Folly*. The University was not mentioned by name, but the faculty knew well that its foundations had

---

[3] M, VI, 450; R, II, 23 b -24 a. (*De Francisco capto*).

[4] John Pfefferkorn, a Jewish convert, obtained from Maximilian in August, 1509, a decree against all Jewish books, especially the Talmud and the Kabbalistic texts. The decree was fiercely opposed by John Reuchlin, one of the greatest Hebrew humanists of central Europe. In 1514 the trial was moved from Cologne to Paris where the conservative party succeeded in confirming the condemnation of Reuchlin. See Augustin Renaudet, *Préréforme et Humanisme a Paris pendant les premières Guerres d'Italie* (1494-1517), 2nd ed. (Paris, 1953), pp. 645-655, 661-663.

been badly shaken. A few years later Vives characterized the venerable institution as "an eighty-year-old lady, sick, decrepit, and in imminent danger of death." [5] As we shall see, there was ample justification for this severe diagnosis.

When Vives joined the University of Paris in 1509, the great institution was going through some of the roughest years of its long history. Basically the problem was the antagonism between its conservative clericalism on one side, and the new trends of religious reform, political nationalism, and humanistic revival on the other side. The crisis of the University presented a triple character: administrative, moral, and intellectual.

At the root of all administrative problems was the constant fight for the control of the University by the Pope, the King of France and the Bishop of Paris.[6] Torn between papal jurisdiction, the interference of the local ecclesiastical authorities, and the ambitions of the monarchy, the University had a hard time in preserving its liberties and independence. The history of Paris presents one more case of the old struggle between the regimentation imposed by the financial powers which support the University and the intellectual freedom which students and teachers strive to maintain alive. Born as a guild of masters under the leadership of the Chancellor of Nôtre Dame, the University became soon a powerful institution which both the Capetian Kings and the Papacy attempted to control. After the opening of the Faculty of Theology to the regular clergy in 1253, the ecclesiastical and papal influence reached its climax. Civil Law, Medicine, and even the Humanities began to decline in Paris. The professorate was made up of clergymen or unmarried laymen. Not until 1452 were married laymen allowed in the Faculty of Medicine; in the Faculty of Arts the permission was not granted until 1499.[7] In the fourteenth century, however, the University reacted sharply against Boniface VIII, and henceforth became the champion of Gallicanism and Conciliarism. Both Charles VII (1422-51) and Louis XI (1461-83) tried to take advantage of this new situation and to control the life of the University. The reform of 1452, which among other things established the textbooks Vives himself had to use, was carried out by a

---

[5] M, III, 65: R, 313 b. "Non tibi Parisiensis schola tamquam anus quaedam post octingentesimum suae aetatis annum . . . delirare videtur?" (Adv. ps-d.).

[6] Of special interest for the study of the relations between State, Church, and University is Maurice Crevier, Histoire de l'Université de Paris depuis son origine jusqu'à l'anné 1600, 2 vols. (Paris, 1761); also, Joseph Calmette, L' elaboration du monde moderne (Paris, 1942).

[7] Denifle H. and Chatelain E., Chartularium Universitatis Parisiensis, 4 vols. (Paris, 1889-97), II, n. 565.

papal legate and a royal inspector.[8] In 1473 Louis XI forbade the teaching of Nominalism in the University and confiscated all the books not professing an orthodox Realism.[9] The institution of the so-called College of France by Francis I, only thirty years after Vives' departure from Paris, put an end to the ecclesiastical management of the University. Symbolically enough, the first appointee to this college was a close friend of Vives, Guillaume Budé.

Vives never wrote a word about the administrative problems of the University of Paris. But it is absolutely clear that the academy of Vives' dreams was to be a completely secular institution, financed by each municipality, without any ecclesiastical interference.[10] Vives set forth in clear terms the doctrine that the education of youth ought to be in the hands of professional teachers, not in the hands of the clergy. The school itself must be a separate building without any connection with cathedral or monastery.[11] The Christian education of the youth was to be reduced to some common prayers and, primarily, to the good example of a carefully selected faculty.[12] A system of education like that of the Jesuits never crossed the mind of Juan Luis Vives.[13] The notion of secular and public education, which today we take for granted, owes a great deal to him. His influence on the powerful system of public education in Central European schools has been widely recognized.[14]

The second crisis of the University was a pervasive corruption of morals both among the clerical faculty and the student body. All the

---

[8] Ricardo G. Villoslada, *La Universidad de Paris durante los estudios de Francisco de Vitoria O.P. (1507-1522)* (Rome, 1938), p. 4, points out that the statutes of 1452 were nothing else than a proclamation of the rules given by the legates of Urban V in 1366. In some important details, however, the statutes were strongly revolutionary, as in the permission granted to the masters of Medicine to get married, a novelty which helped much the cause of an independent medical school.

[9] *Der Sentenzenkommentar Peters von Candia*, ed. F. Ehrle (Münster i. W., 1925), pp. 313-314. The document recommends Averroes, Albert the Great, Thomas Aquinas, Giles of Rome, Alexander of Hales, Scotus, and Bonaventure (in this order!).

[10] M, VI, 275; R, II, 553 a. (*DD.*, II, 2,1). According to H. Rashdall, *The Universities in the Middle Ages*, 5th ed. 3 vols., (London, 1958), II, 107, the University of Valencia was "peculiarly interesting as an indication of the zeal of Spanish municipalities in the cause of education." Actually, the city itself petitioned the King for a *studium generale* in 1374, and even proceeded on its own responsibility to hire a bachelor of Arts to begin teaching in Valencia. The Papal Bull of foundation was first obtained in 1500.

[11] M, VI, 273; R, II, 551 b. (*DD.*, II, 2,1).

[12] M, VI, 255-262; R, II, 533-536. (*DD.*, II, 1,4). Vives himself wrote a little prayer to be recited at the beginning of the school. (M, I, 131; R, I, 531 a., *Preces*).

[13] Lange, *Luis Vives*, pp. 153-155, makes a comparison between the pedagogy of the Jesuits and that of Vives. We will return to the subject in chapter 9.

[14] See below, p. 295.

associations evoked by the expression "Latin quarter" are historically related to such disreputable streets as those of Glaitigny or Cour Robert where the students of Paris were intensively dedicated to finding a nightly compensation for the daily routine of the scholastic *lectiones*. The pages of Rabelais, Ulrich of Hutten, Brantôme, or Marguerite of Navarre; [15] the severe sermons of Maillard against gamblers and prostitutes; [16] the crapulent songs of the goliards endlessly repeated in innumerable taverns and public baths, all give us a vivid picture of the merry life of the Parisian student.[17] The colleges were originally an attempt to provide the students with a supervised residence. In 1463 the *martinets* (students not allocated to any college) were denied registration at the University.[18] But the size of those colleges increased at such a rate that an efficient surveillance of the student body became more difficult every day.[19]

Paris was not an exception to the proved kinship of frivolity and violence. Today's examples of student agitation are only atavic reversions to a well-established tradition. The theologians, more conservative and mature, were in perpetual conflict with the artists, by far the younger and larger section of the student population. The decretists, or students of Canon Law, were disliked by all for their privileged position in the pursuit of ecclesiastical performents. Nations fought against Nations, faculty against faculty, college against college. The yearly elections of the rector were almost always marked by riots and violence.[20] The town-versus-gown fights were an important part of the University tradition; in fact, most of its privileges and exemptions were won on the streets of

[15] *Oeuvres de Francis Rabelais,* ed. A. Lafranc, 3 vols. (Paris, 1922), I, xiii-xxii, "Rabelais et la Sorbonne"; Ulrich von Hutten, *Opera Omnia,* ed. E. Bocking, 7 vols. (Osnabrück, 1966), VI, 8-10, 14-16, 31-33; Pierre de Bourdeille, Seigneur de Brantôme, *The Lives of the Gallant Ladies,* trans. A. Brown (London, 1961), *passim,* offer a good picture of the sexual manners in the France of Francis I.

[16] C. Schmidt, "Der Prediger O. Maillard; ein Bild aus dem Ende des XVten Jahrhunderts," *Zeitschrift für die historische Theologie,* XI (1856), 489-542.

[17] The drinking habits of the Parisian students were especially repulsive to Vives who hated all sorts of excess. See the realistic description of drunkenness in his dialogue *Ebrietas* (M, I, 360-366; R, II, 938-942, *ELL.,* XVII).

[18] C. E. Du Boulay, *Historia Universitatis Parisiensis,* 6 vols. (1665-1673), V, 658: "Quod nulli de cetero in ipsa Artium Facultate tempus acquirent . . . nisi per tempus sufficiens ad gradum obtinendum moram traxerint in collegio, paedagogio, aut domo suorum parentium."

[19] La Sorbonne started with sixteen theology students; Daly, *Medieval University,* p. 185. One of the largest colleges in Paris, Navarre, had only thirty art students in 1304. See Jean Launoy, *Regalis collegii Navarrae historia,* 2 vols. (Paris, 1677), I, chapter 1.

[20] In 1485 the *martinets* violently opposed the election of Standonck who had the reputation of being a severe reformer. See Du Boulay, *Historia,* V, p. 769. The revolts of 1452, 1473, 1476, 1491 are strong proofs of student unrest. Renaudet, *Préréforme et Humanisme,* pp. 45-50.

Paris.[21] In 1452 the riots reached such an intensity that the whole University had to be closed for nine months.

This state of affairs was slowly counteracted by a growing reforming crusade. It is extremely important to become fully aware of this black picture of moral corruption to understand the appeal of some Parisian reformers to a selected minority of young students. Like many other humanists of Northern Europe, Vives cannot be fully understood without reference to this zeal for the ethical improvement of the individual and the society. One of the most important centers of moral and religious reform was precisely the college where Vives resided while in Paris, the College of Montaigu.[22] This institution, which counts among its alumni people like Erasmus, Calvin, Ignatius of Loyola, and Rabelais, is famous in the history of European education because of its connection with the imposing figure of Jean Standonck, who brought to Paris the religious fervor of the Brethren of the Common Life.[23] In 1483 Standonck took charge of Montaigu, which was at that time almost in ruins. The discipline of the Montaigu students became soon thereafter a legend in the life of the University. The daily routine was almost monastic. Missionaries from Windesheim were constantly invited by Standonck to visit the institution. In 1495 Erasmus stayed at Montaigu for a few weeks; he never forgot the rigors of Standonck's asceticism.[24] After the exile of Standtonck from Paris, the College was directed by Jean Mair and Noel Béde. With Mair the intellectual life of Montaigu took a powerful turn toward scholasticism, a fact of extreme importance to understand the intellectual training of Vives. Béde's leadership, on the other hand, somehow relaxed the severe discipline of Montaigu. Nevertheless, about 1509 Montaigu was still a reformed institution permeated by the missionary zeal of Standonck and the moral rigorism of Windesheim. In Montaigu, Vives' religious education was not only completed but also powerfully slanted toward the Devotio Moderna. Furthermore, the experience of Montaigu, crowded as it was with disciples of the Brethren,

---

[21] One of the most formidable weapons of the University was the *cessatio*, or the right to strike, granted to the Institution by Pope Gregory IX in 1231. See the fascinating document in Lynn Thorndike, *University Records and Life in the Middle Ages* (New York, 1944), pp. 35-39. Louis XI, however, obtained from Pio II the abrogation of such privilege. See Villoslada, *Universidad de Paris*, p. 39, note 26.

[22] Ríos Sarmiento, *Juan Luis Vives*, p. 31; Renaudet, *Préréforme et Humanisme*, p. 467, note 4.

[23] On Standonck see A. Renaudet, "Jean Standonck, un reformateur catholique avant la Reforme," *Bulletin de la Societé de l'Histoire du Protestantisme Francais* (January, February, 1908), pp. 5-81.

[24] Erasmus draws a bitter picture of Montaigu in his dialogue "Icthyophagia" (*Opera omnia Erasmi*, ed. J. Clericus [Leiden, 1703-1706] I, 806 b-807 c; *ibid.*, 632 a; also *EE.*, I, introd. to letter 43, p. 146).

helps us to understand Vives' otherwise strange decision to move to the Netherlands after 1512. Finally, it is important to remember that the reform introduced by Standonck into the College had also a strong social overtone. According to the regulations of 1503 the College was open exclusively to needy students.[25] It is interesting to observe that Vives always showed a little contempt for the rich, lazy, and restless students of his time, a type he mercilessly ridiculed in his Dialogue *Princeps Puer*.[26] As for the education of the poor, it will be enough to say that an equal right to education guaranteed by public funds is one of the landmarks of Vives' pedagogy. The good seed planted by Standonck gave its fruits in the writings of Juan Luis Vives.

The last and most important crisis of the University of Paris, in the first decades of the sixteenth century, was evidently the intellectual mediocrity of its academic life. A clear indication thereof was a drastic reduction in the number of students. While in the thirteenth century Paris had more than ten thousand students, in Vives' time the student population was less than five thousand. Two decades later the University of Salamanca had almost eight thousand registered students.[27]

The organization of the University was still fully medieval. The first and most important structure was the division of teachers and students alike into four "Faculties": the Faculty of Arts (Philosophy), the Faculty of Theology, the Faculty of Law (also called Faculty of Decrets), and the Faculty of Medicine (for the "physicians"). Of these four Faculties, the first, or Faculty of Arts, was a necessary prerequisite to the study of Theology, and, partly at least, to that of Medicine and Law.[28] The normal procedure for the student was to complete the Arts course in three years, to obtain the master degree in one more year of graduate study combined with some tutorial teaching, and then, already as a member of the masters guild, to strive for a doctoral degree in either Theology, Medicine, or Law. This last stage could take between seven and ten years of study and teaching. Since Vives spent only three years

---

[25] Marcel Godet, *La Congregation de Montaigu* (1490-1580) (Paris, 1912), p. 144. The statutes of 1503 say: "Ut in ea dumtaxat domo admittantur et tollerentur veri pauperes et egeni, non divitum filii et potentum, prout passim inique fieri cernimus."

[26] M, I, 371-385; R, II, 946-951. (*ELL.,* XIX).

[27] Villoslada, *La Universidad,* p. 39.

[28] The "Nations" were not strictly geographical. Spanish students and teachers were mostly members of the French Nation, which included also all the Italians and Portuguese. As the *Chartularium Universitatis Parisiensis* shows, the "Nations" were, specially in the fourteenth century, an important part to the disputes and problems of the University. (*Chartularium,* III, 12-13, 38-39, 56-59, 203-205, 209-211, 232-233).

in Paris, his philosophical training was reduced to the Arts course. It is, however, impossible to evaluate this training without making a clear distinction between the Arts scholasticism of the professional teacher of philosophy and the philosophical undertakings of the theologians.[29] To understand how independent from each other were philosophers (or "artists") and theologians, it will be enough to remember that the members of religious orders were never allowed to teach philosophy in the Faculty of Arts, although they taught it in their own monasteries.[30]

The University of Paris was also divided into Colleges. Although they never became as important as in Oxford or Cambridge, in the first half of the sixteenth century the Parisian colleges were not only residential quarters but also centers of academic life. Thus, for instance, the College of La Sorbonne founded in 1274 for poor students of theology became progressively identified with the Faculty of Theology itself.[31] The students who were members of a religious order lived, of course, in their respective convents, some of which, like the convent of Saint Jacques and Les Cordeliers, were of extreme significance in the intellectual life of the University.

The third and last structural division of Paris was the organization of the Masters of Arts into four "Nations" or teachers corporations grouped according to their geographical and political background: the French Nation, the Norman Nation, the English Nation, and the German Nation. Interestingly enough, Spanish and Italian masters were mostly incorporated into the French Nation. The division in nations was very characteristic of Paris and reveals its cosmopolitanism.[32] Since Vives

---

[29] Medicine was more closely allied to Arts scholasticism than Law. To study Law the student was not required to have completed the Arts course. The *Chartularium* lists many Medicine students who were only bachelors of Arts, not masters. (*Ibid.*, VI, 120-121). Ong (*Ramus*, p. 133) observes that although the theologians were inclined to shorten the philosophy curriculum, the physicians emphasized the importance of the third year where the course on physics was heard.

[30] Ong, *Ramus*, p. 134, has emphasized this point of particular importance for the understanding of medieval thought. What we today call "Scholastic philosophers" were for the most part theologians who seldom taught philosophy. On the other hand, the medieval masters of Arts – such as Buridan and Albert of Saxony – were logicians with no interest in theology proper.

The content of Arts scholasticism will be discussed later. See below p. 41. Its importance can be guessed from the register of the professorate sent to Pope Urban V in 1362. It included 25 theologians, 11 professors of law, 27 professors of medicine, and 449 professors of arts. (*Chartularium*, III, 78-92. In 1387 there were 458 "artists" against 15 theologians. *Ibid.*, 446-463).

[31] Already in 1527 Erasmus calls Vitoria *"Theologus hispanicus Sorboniensis,"* although, as a member of the Dominican order, Vitoria lived and studied in the convent of Saint Jacques. (*EE.*, VII, 1909; also, Villoslada, *La Universidad* pp. 346-349). Today La Sorbonne is simply identified with the University of Paris.

[32] See below, p. 83 on the role of the Nations in Oxford.

never became a master in Paris, he did not have the opportunity to join any Nation.

The decadence of the University affected all four of its faculties. Even the Faculty of Theology, which was supposed to be the pride of Paris, was languid and old-fashioned. The textbooks prescribed by the statutes of 1452 were the Holy Scripture and the *Sententiae* of Peter Lombard, with the explicit recommendations to avoid any logical or philosophical scrutiny.[33] Text criticism of the Bible was impossible due to the general ignorance of Hebrew and Greek; Patristic exegesis was derived from Carolingian compilations like the *Glossa ordinaria* of Walafried Lelouche, a disciple of Rhabanus Maurus, or from even more questionable lexicons and dictionaries like the *Catholicon* or the *Mammotrectus.* The endless and sterile disputes about the Immaculate Conception almost completely succeeded in silencing the promising return to Saint Thomas advocated by Peter Crockaert in the convent of Saint Jacques (where Francisco de Vitoria was one of his brightest disciples). As Maldonado later complained, the theologians in Paris were totally unprepared for the Lutheran onslaught.[34] The useful suggestions of Erasmus or Lefèvre d'Etaples, which could have helped to prevent the disaster, fell on deaf ears.

For several reasons the Faculties of Law and Medicine never fared in Paris as well as they did in Bologna and Montpellier. Lawyers and physicians had always been the best paid professionals, and greed was an alluring temptation to students oriented to the services of the Church. The discovery of Justinian's *Pandects* in 1113 and the reinforced study of Civil Law were taken as a threat to Canonical studies. Consequently, Pope Honorius III prohibited the study of Civil Law at Paris, a prohibition which was not abrogated until 1679. Vives' inherited concern with the study of Civil Law, especially in its Roman version, could not find in Paris the least encouragement. The "Decretists" of the Law Faculty were almost exclusively absorbed in the study of Gracian. Medicine, of course, was always considered taboo for clerical students. Since its prohibition in 1131 by the Council of Rheims, medicine had taken refuge in the famous school of Montpellier.

---

[33] *Chartularium,* IV, 713-734; also, III, 143-144: "Quod legentes *Sententias* non tractent quaestiones aut materias logicas vel philosophicas, nisi quantum textus *Sententiarum* requirat."

[34] In the words of Maldonado, the theologians of Paris had nothing but long sticks to match the modern weaponry of the protestants: "Quo tempore adversum ingruentes ex Germania haereses oportebat scholae theologos optimis armis esse instructos, eo nulla prorsus haberent, nisi arundines longas, arma videlicet levia puerorum." Cited by Villoslada, *La Universidad,* p. 249, note 8.

Vives' personal experience in Paris was limited to the Faculty of Arts which, therefore, deserves more of our attention. Theoretically the educational program was supposed to be framed upon the scheme of the seven liberal arts of the *trivium* and *quadrivium*. Reality, however, was totally different. The first two arts of the trivium, Grammar and Rhetoric, also called the *artes sermocinales,* had always had a rough time in Paris. Their study was considered from the very beginning too elementary for University education.[35] The excessive influence of the regular orders in the thirteenth century did not foster the case of the grammarians.[36] Until 1499 the students of grammar were not allowed to register in the University, and, at the time Erasmus was in Paris, the teachers of grammar and rhetoric were still considered strangers to the rest of the Parisian masters.[37] Fully in line with this tradition, John Dullaert, one of Vives' teachers, constantly reminded his students that normally the best grammarians make the worst dialecticians.[38]

Since Vives had already taken Latin grammar and rhetoric in Valencia, his three years in Paris were exclusively dedicated to the study of "philosophy." Taught at the Faculty of Arts as an immediate preparation for theology or Canon Law, the contents of philosophy had been reduced to its very essentials. The real issues of natural philosophy were handled by the school of Medicine; in many cases even the treatises *De Anima* would become a summary of Galen's physiology and anatomy. The Faculty of Theology was very eager to discuss metaphysical questions like the existence of God or the immortality of the soul. Philosophy in the context of Arts scholasticism meant nothing else than a long course in logic and an abbreviated course in physics, together with some rudiments of moral philosophy and metaphysics.[39]

Although there was a certain uniformity in the educational program, imposed by the regulations of 1452, each college represented a different tradition. About 1509 the convent of Saint Jacques was trying to keep

---

[35] Compare with the tradition of Louvain's Pedagogies. See below, p. 58.

[36] Crévier, *Histoire,* insists upon this point throughout his first volume.

[37] Sixteenth century scholasticism had disintegrated the *trivium-quadrivium* scheme to the point that grammar and rhetoric were taken as a propaedeutic to the logic-physics real body of knowledge. Launoy, *Navarrae historia,* I, 399, leaves out all the "grammatici" from the list of the College. Vols. III and IV of the *Chartularium* do not even mention them.

[38] M, I, 26 (*Vivis Vita*).

[39] Ong, *Ramus,* p. 141, proves with significant data the low prestige of metaphysics in the Arts course. Pierre Tartaret, the author of very popular textbooks on scholastic philosophy, wrote a commentary on Aristotle in which six pages of metaphysics are lost in a book of three hundred pages. As for ethics, it will suffice to remember that according to the regulations of d'Estouteville six weeks were considered enough to study six of the ten books of *Ethica Nichomachea.*

alive the Thomistic school; the Bourgogne college had opened its gates
to the refreshing influence of Pico della Mirandola; the professors of
Les Cordeliers defended a stubborn Scotism.[40] However, the most active
school of those days was Montaigu. Under the guidance of Jean Mair a
powerful group of logicians was spreading all over Paris the endless
niceties of terministic dialectic.

From the books and the correspondence of our Humanist, from the
regulations of the University and the record of books printed in that
decade, and, finally, from the particular histories of the College of
Montaigu we can largely reconstruct Vives' intellectual experience in
Paris.[41]

His first impression was indeed a very unpleasant one. Vives' *Dialogues* are a first-hand report of the student life in Paris at that time.
He was disgusted with the conceit of the richer students;[42] with the
folly of academic honors and degrees;[43] with the excessive time dedicated to the classroom, at least nine hours every day.[44] The passionate
"disputationes" were, from the very beginning, completely repulsive to
his calm and modest, almost shy, character.[45] He disliked his teachers:
they were sloppy and dirty "like cooks or muleteers," vain and conceited
in their remote world of useless subtleties.[46] In one of his books Vives

[40] Renaudet, *Préréforme et Humanisme,* pp. 209-289.
[41] The books of Vives related to Paris are the following: *De Disciplinis,* especially
the chapters dedicated to the corruption of grammar (M, VI, 77-110; R, II, 399-
421) and logic (M, VI, 110-152; R, II, 438-453); *Exercitatio linguae Latinae,*
especially dialogues vi, xii, xix, xxiii, and xxiv (M, I, 283-404; R, II, 882-
971); *Veritas fucata* (M, II, 517-531; R, I, 277-279); and *Christi Jesu Triumphus*
(M, VII, 110-133; R, I, 259-269).
For a catalogue of the books printed in Paris at that time, see J. Brunet, *Répertoire
des livres francais parus de 1501 à 1530* (Paris, 1930); also Buisson, *Répertoire.*
Villoslada, *La Universidad de Paris,* pp. 49-53, presents a catalogue of the books
printed in Paris from 1470 to 1500.
On Montaigu, see Marcel Godet, *La Congregation de Montaigu* (Paris, 1912);
also, Renaudet, *Préréforme et Humanisme,* pp. 175-177, 463-467, 655-658.
[42] See the dialogues *Princeps Puer* (M, I, 371-378; R, II, 946-951) and *Regia*
(M, I, 366-371; R, II, 943-946). Although Montaigu had been founded for poor
students, in Vives' time the College included also self-supporting, richer young men
from all over Europe.
[43] See the dialogues *Schola* (M, I, 334-338; R, II, 920-923) and *Garrientes* (M,
I, 301-310; R, II, 897-903).
[44] See Godet, *Congregation de Montaigu,* pp. 143-70, and Villoslada, *La Universidad de Paris,* p. 44, for the schedule of the Parisian colleges. The first lecture
began before breakfast at 5 a.m. From 8 to 11 a.m., the hungry students were
subjected to three more classes. During lunch the students had to listen to the
reading of the Bible. From 3 to 5 p.m. more lectures; after one hour of *disputatio*
they had dinner at 6 p.m. followed by another hour of discussion. Before they went
to bed, around 9 p.m., they had one hour or two of religious services.
[45] M, I, 334-335, 337; R, II, 899, 901, 902. (*ELL.* VII)
[46] M, I, 335-336; R, II, 900-901. "*Nugo:* Quid ergo? Expectabas [causam]
philosopho dignam? Posce a novis illis Magistris Parisiensibus. *Gracculus:* Plerique

makes a description of the Parisian professors which deserves to be quoted in full:

When these people leave the nest of their schools to mix with normal and prudent folk, they act so stupidly that one gets the impression that they grew in the backwoods. You should see the expression on their faces when they are confronted with reality. They just behave as if they were coming from a different world, to such an extent they ignore real life and common sense. You could swear they were not human beings.[47]

Of all his professors in Paris he had only one nice word of praise, this for the amazing memory of Gaspar Lax.[48] The domestic life in Montaigu was hard and austere. Food was scarce, two eggs for dinner; the kitchen work was too long; and the time for sleep totally insufficient. The fleas and the dirt of Montaigu were proverbial. Erasmus and Rabelais use their most selected Latin vocabulary when it comes to describe the "merdae Gallicae" of the College.[49]

In order to be admitted into the University, Vives had to prove his acquaintance with the Latin grammar of Alexander Villedieu and the Greek manual of Evrard de Bethune.[50] In his charming essay *Sapientis Inquisitio*, Vives ridicules the content of the contemporary grammars in the following conversation between a professor of grammar and a student:

> *Grammarian*: Tell me, boy, in which month did Vergil die?
> *Student*: In September, my beloved Master.
> *Grammarian*: Where?
> *Student:* In Brindis.
> *Grammarian*: What day of the month?
> *Student*: The twenty-first.
> *Grammarian*: You idiot! Stop putting me to shame in front of these respectable gentlemen! Bring me the stick, hold your robe,

---

illorum vestibus sunt Philosophi, non cerebro. *Nugo:* Quid ita vestibus? Non coquos potius dixeris, aut muliones. Gracculus: Quia gestant eas crassas, detritas, laceras, lutulentas, immundas, pediculosas."

[47] M, III, 60, R, II, 309 b. (*Adv. ps-d.*)

[48] M, VII, 110; R, I, 260 b -261 a. (*C. J. Triumphus*). In his essay *Adversus pseudo-dialecticos* (M, III, 63; R, II, 312 a.) Vives introduces Gaspar Lax and Dullaert as converted to the new trends of the day. "Dullardum ego et Gasparem Laxem preceptores olim meos, quos honoris causa nomino, quaerentes saepe summo cum dolore audivi, se tam multos annos rei tam futili atque inani impendisse."

[49] See *EE.*, I, 103, v. 11, Letter from Erasmus to Andrelinus.

[50] Renaudet, *Préréforme et Humanisme*, p. 28. Although these books were written in the thirteenth century, the reform of Cardinal d'Estouteville in 1452 still prescribed them as textbooks for the University.

extend your hand! How do you dare to say the twenty-first instead
of the twentieth?

Let us see now. And you, gentlemen, pay attention to this ignorant and conceited young fellow! In the introduction to the *Co-
niuratio Catilinae* did Sallustius write *Omnes homines* or *omneis
homines?*
Student: According to most scholars he wrote *omneis,* but I think
that it should read *omnes . . .*

Grammarian: What was the name of Remus, and of which color
was his beard? . . .

Grammarian: How did Alexander the Great get up the first time
he fell down in Asia? . . .[51]

In the second book of his encyclopedic treatise *De Disciplinis,* Vives
deals with the causes of the corruption of grammar: an excessive formalism has neglected the use of the language itself by its classical masters.
The third chapter of the book seems inspired in Nebrija's *Apology.*
Vives defends the study of Greek and Latin against those who claimed
that it opened the way to dangerous heresies against the Bible.[52]

The first two years at the Faculty of Arts were dedicated to the study
of the *Organon,* according to the personal interpretation of each professor. In Montaigu, Vives was subjected to the terministic logic of the
disciples of Jean Mair who had been himself under the influence of
Geronimo Pardo and Thomas Bricot.[53] Mair was the rector of Montaigu
during the time Vives resided there. Mair had a legendary admiration
for Standonck, a fact of no minor importance to understand Vives'
personal development. Besides, Mair, like many of his colleagues, knew
how to make compatible his almost stubborn orthodoxy with a strong
Gallicanism and a radical Ockamistic criticism.

The whole professorate of Montaigu followed the line of the Rector.
"Unfortunately," Vives wrote, "most of them are Spanish":

Most intelligent people blame the Spaniards for these disorders, and they
are right. The Spaniards, men of indomitable character, apply all their

[51] M, IV, 23-24; R, I, 864 b.-865 a. (*Pr. in Sap.*).
[52] M, VI, 88-93; R, II, 408-412. (*DD.,* I, 2, 3).
[53] One year after the arrival of Vives in Paris, Mair published the commentaries
of Dorp on Buridan. In 1513 he published his own *Quaestiones in insolubilibus
disputatae* and in 1514 the *Medullae Dialecticae.* (Renaudet, *Préréforme et Humanisme,* pp. 590-591). Villoslada dedicates to Mair one full chapter (VI) of his
book *La Universidad de Paris,* pp. 127-165. See also Carl von Prantl, *Geschichte
der Logik im Abenlande,* 2nd ed., 4 vols. (Graz, 1955), III, 247 ff.

energies to the defense of this fortress of foolish ignorance; intelligent as they are, they have become the best in all the aberrations which has given Paris such a disreputable name the world over. In other universities you will find a mixture of insane and true knowledge; Paris alone is exclusively dedicated to finicky trifles.[54]

The best known names are: Antonio Coronel, Gaspar Lax, Juan Dolz, and Fernando Enzinas. In spite of Vives' sharp criticism, modern logicians seem greatly impressed by the achievements of the Montaigu group.[55] Its influence was indeed felt at that time in all the colleges of Paris. One of the disciples of Mair, John Dullaert, although teaching at Beauvais, attracted to his lectures many students from Montaigu. One of those sudents was Juan Luis Vives, a fact which has misled some of his biographers into believing that Vives attended the Beauvais College.[56]

After two years of logic, the student dedicated only one year to the rest of philosophy; physics, metaphysics, and ethics. Of these three, physics took by far the most time. As textbooks, the statutes of 1452 mentioned Aristotle's *Metaphysics* and a large section of the *Ethica Nichomachea*. For the teaching of physics the statutes did not recommend any book in particular. Actually, the books used for this purpose in Vives' days were the *Arithmetica* of Boethius and the treatises of Jean of Holywood and Pièrre d'Ailly about the *Sphaera*.[57]

Vives' reaction against the intellectual training received at Paris was violent and bitter, almost revolutionary for those times. He used to say that in Paris he had only learned "silly and empty sophismata." [58] He complained about the excessive time dedicated to dialectic and the "slight touch of philosophy" he received in the short and anarchic third year of the curriculum. His opinion about the textbooks used in Paris was not very complimentary.[59] In one of his *Dialogues*, Vives feigns the conversation of two students on the subject:

---

[54] M, III, 38; R, II, 293 b. (*Adv. ps-d.*). According to Erasmus, Vives himself, while in Paris, was one of the brightest sophists among the students. (*EE., IV*, 1107, vv. 11-13).
Vives also confesses that he became completely absorbed in the study of nominalistic logic. (M, III, 39; R, II, 294 b., *Adv. ps-d.*).
[55] See Prantl, *Geschichte*, IV, xxii Abschnitt: "Reiche Nachblüthe der Scholastik Logik," 173-293.
[56] See, e.g., Riber, introduction, I, 30; also Ríos Sarmiento, *Juan Luis Vives*, p. 31.
[57] *Chartularium*, IV, 725.
[58] M, III, 39; R, II, 294 a. (*Adv. ps-d.*).
[59] *LC.*, 13, vv. 1-2, Letter to Cranevelt: "I do not want to discuss any philosophical subject with you for the simple reason that I never had more than a slight touch of it." (*vix umbram vidi philosophiae*).

Tyrus: What are those books doing over there?
Spudaeus: They are just books for idiots and ignoramuses: the *Catholicon*, Alexander, Hugocius, Papias, *Sermonarii*, books of dialectic and sophistic physics . . .
Tyrus: It is good that anybody can take them away and liberate us from this burden.
Spudaeus: It amazes me that nobody has picked them up when there are so many asses around here . . .[60]

Vives' first sizable book, the *In Pseudo-Dialecticos* (1519), published only six years after his departure from Paris, was a tremendous and uncompromising attack against the venerable institution and the core of its philosophical training, terministic logic.[61] This book, considered as the epitome of Vives' critical attitudes toward the past, deserves a chapter of its own.[62] But it reveals also an intellectual posture which has nothing to do with the logicians of Montaigu, but rather with the heralds of the Northern Renaissance. There is no doubt that Vives had a clear awareness of the revival of letters which Northern Europe was experiencing at that time. With an almost prophetic tone Vives writes:

Everywhere, in every nation, I see men of great intelligence, daring, free, independent, tired of being slaves, ready to shake off the yoke of this mad and violent tyranny. These men will rescue our freedom as individuals and bring back to the republic of letters the sweetest of liberties . . ." [63]

Actually, Vives' first book, *Christi Jesu Triumphus* (1514) clearly proves that his decisive turn toward humanism took place precisely at Montaigu.[64] Although there are some indications that the book was implemented about 1519 in Louvain, most of it was evidently written in April, 1514, when Vives first returned to Paris for a short visit.[65] The book tells the story of a gathering of students with Gaspar Lax of Sariñena, one of their most respected teachers. It takes place on Easter, 1514. Vives and his two friends, Peter Iborra and John Fort, meet

---

[60] M, I, 336-337; R, II, 921 (*ELL*, dialogue *Schola*). For other textbooks, see Ong, *Ramus*, pp. 72-91.
[61] M, III, 65; R, II, 313 b. (*Adv. ps-d.*).
[62] See below, pp. 149-175.
[63] M, III, 62; R, II, 311 a. "Erigunt enim sese apud nationes omnes clara, excellentia, liberaque ingenia, impatientia servitutis, et jugum hoc stultissimae ac violentissimae tyrannidis ex cervicibux suis animose depellunt, civesque suos ad libertatem vocant, vindicabuntque totam prorsus literariam civitatem in libertatem longe suavissimam . . ." (*Adv. ps-d.*).
[64] M, VII, 108-131; R, I, 259-277. (*C. J. Triumphus*).
[65] See below, p. 55. This mention of Erasmus clearly indicates that the work was retouched after 1517, the year Vives and Erasmus met for the first time.

Gaspar Lax at the entrance of the Montaigu College where the latter was known as the "Prince of the Parisian sophists." In the poor *cubiculum* of the master, two more students, also from Valencia, Michel Santangel and Francis Cristobal, join the rest of the group which gets involved in a serious dialogue about the triumph of Christ on Resurrection day.[66] The content and the style of this conversation prove beyond any doubt Vives' familiarity with some of the favorite topics of Northern Humanism. In fact, the whole essay is an echo of the Erasmian attack against Caesarian heroism and war-glorification.[67]

Says Gaspar Lax:

> Christ, our Lord, waged five different wars: the first against the demons, the second against the world, the third against the flesh, the fourth against the Jews, the fifth and last against death.[68]

Santangel's description of the triumphal entrance of Christ in heaven after his resurrection from the dead is based on an accurate knowledge of ancient sources and history which Vives secured for himself while in Paris independently from the academic programs. However, the importance of this book lies in the fundamental fact that all of its basic assumptions coincide with the main trends of Northern Humanism. The study of classical antiquity is not an end in itself but a means of Christian reform. The admiration for the heroes or the poets of Greece and Rome is full of dangers and threats. In this sense the introduction to the book, which Vives wrote years later under the strange title of *Veritas fucata* (The Smeared Truth), contains a severe denunciation of wanton literature very much in the tradition of Gerson.[69]

> As Jerome says, the offspring of the poets is nothing else than the pasture of the demons; those poets who learned to lie to themselves and teach others to do the same; those poets who follow the leadership of that blind and insane and decrepit Homer, the lover of deceit, the maker of Ulysses.[70]

The second part of the *Christi Jesu Triumphus,* entitled *Virginis Dei Parentis Ovatio,* applies to the mother of Christ, the central message of the book: true heroism is only victory over sin and evil.[71]

[66] The dialogue started when one of the students showed to the group a devotional book enriched with the exquisite coloring of Flemish miniatures. Puigdollers suggests (*Filosofía española de L. Vives,* pp. 81-82) that Vives became a great admirer of this form of religious art in Bruges, the home of Memling and Claus Sluter.
[67] See Adams, *Better Part of Valor,* pp. 37, 69, 264, 189.
[68] M, VII, 111; R, I, 261 b. (*C. J. Triumphus*).
[69] M, VII, 101, 110; R, I, 278-285 (*Veritas fucata*). On Gerson, see Renaudet, *Préréforme et Humanisme,* pp. 74-79, 112-114, 254-256.
[70] M, VII, 106; R, I, 281 b. (*Veritas fucata*).
[71] M, VII, 122-131; R, I, 269-277. (*C. J. Triumphus*).

Altogether, these early productions of Vives present a fascinating document of the Northern Renaissance. The poor students who met in the room of Gaspar Lax stand in sharp contrast both to the wordly constituents of the Florentine Academy, and also to the old-fashioned dialecticians of the Parisian University.

It is rather surprising, however, that (except for Erasmus) Vives never mentions the names of those Parisian Humanists who were no doubt instrumental in his intellectual conversion. In any case, the picture of the University of Paris would be utterly incomplete without at least a short mention of the hidden but profound streams of humanism, mysticism, and reform which, for many years, coexisted with Scholastic philosophy in mutual distrust and contempt.[72]

In 1457 the first chair of Greek was introduced at Paris. In the third quarter of the fifteenth century Fichet brought to La Sorbonne his personal admiration for Bessarion. In charge of the first Parisian printing press, Fichet published Cicero, Salustius, and the *Elegentiae Latinae* of Laurentius Valla.[73] At the same time Robert Gaugin concentrated his attack on the manuals of nominalistic logic, while remaining basically Thomistic and orthodox. Vives never mentions Gaugin in his writings, but from men like him he learned the difficult but same compromise between stiff conservatism and plain heterodoxy.

In addition to these, there are three names closely related to our Humanist: Jacques Lefèvre d'Etaples, Budé and Erasmus. The relations between Vives and Erasmus will be examined later. Here it is important to notice that the most important books of Erasmus became known in Paris precisely in the first decade of the sixteenth century; the *Enchiridion Militis Christiani* appeared in 1504, the *Encomium Moirae* in 1511.

Guillaume Budé, who was born twenty-five years before Vives (1467) but died three months after him, was already a well-known Humanist when Vives joined the University of Paris. The incredible erudition of the French *savant* matched his serene zeal for the Reform of Christendom.[74] In 1508 Budé published his *Adnotationes* to the first twenty-four books of the *Pandects,* a painstaking philological research into the sources of Roman Law against the medieval *glossatores* and Bartolists; in 1514 Budé's masterpiece, *De Asse,* was printed in Paris.

[72] See Renaudet, *Préréforme et Humanisme, passim.*
[73] The *Elegantiae* of Valla were therefore one of the first books ever printed in Paris. In 1505 Erasmus published also Valla's *Annotationes in Novum Testamentum.* There is no doubt that Vives knew those books, for which he probably had great curiosity since his speech against Nebrija in the University of Valencia.
[74] Renaudet, *Préréforme et Humanisme,* pp. 667-682.

46 THE LIFE OF JUAN LUIS VIVES

Vives' acquaintance with Budé dates from his second return to Paris in June, 1519, as a preceptor of William of Croy, the Archbishop elect of Toledo.[75] At that time Vives was fortunate enough to meet twice the greatest hellenist of the French Renaissance. From Croy's letter to Erasmus and from Budé's own correspondence we know that both men were deeply impressed by each other and filled with mutual admiration.[76] Erasmus, who in those days had some differences with Budé, invoked the help of Vives to restore their long friendship. Nevertheless, Vives was so successful, and Budé was so enthusiastic about Vives, that Erasmus was filled with envy.[78]

The friendship between Vives and Budé lasted as long as they lived. It seems that in 1520 Vives made a third short visit to Paris, a city to which he was deeply attached in spite of the bitter memories of Montaigu.[79] After this visit he wrote a long praise of Budé to Erasmus, to which belong the following lines:

One of the greatest experiences of my trip to Paris was to meet your, and now our, common friend, Budé. For Christ's sake, what a man is he! Intelligent, erudite, honest, fortunate ... He has read everything and all of it with extreme seriousness and accuracy. What about his memory? His chest is not a human chest but a library! He speaks and writes Latin like a contemporary of Cicero; the Greeks confess that they could learn Greek from Budé. His work is so great that all the Hermolaos, the Picos, Politians, Gazas, Vallas, and the whole of Italy should feel ashamed ...[80]

To this letter the Dutch humanist answered in more friendly terms.[81] Vives also met Budé's wife, Roberte le Lieur, whom he praises as a

---

[75] See below, note 79.
[76] *EE.*, III, 958, v. 112. Letter from Croy to Erasmus. "Quid loquar de Gulielmo Budaeo, amoribus atque deliciis Musarum et Graecarum et Latinarum? Cuius laudandi numquam Vives meus finem facit."
EE., III, 987, vv. 1-5. Letter from Erasmus to Budé. "Ludovicus Vives, homo literarum bonarum feliciter studiosus ... mire nomini tuo meoque favere mihi visus est ... eius humanitas singularis et erudita glutinum, ut arbitor, tenacissimum esse poterit in postremum tuendae retinendaeque nostrae amicitiae." (Also *ibid.*, III, 992, vv. 1-2).
[77] *EE.*, III, 810, 896, 906; IV, 1004, v. 8. From Erasmus to Budé. The last letter is almost entirely written in Greek.
[78] *EE.*, IV, 1066, v. 52. Erasmus writes to Budé: "Quomodo tibi successerit expeditio ... partim ex tuis ad Ludovicum Vivem literis intellexi, nimirum adeo venustis, adeo doctis ... ut homo vix hostibus invidere solitus inviderim homini imprimis amico."
[79] There is some confusion about Vives' trips to Paris. It is no easy matter to decide whether there was only one trip in 1519 or 1520 or two different journeys, one in 1519 and another in 1520.
[80] *EE.*, IV, 1108, vv. 85-196.
[81] *EE.*, IV, 1104. Although this letter is printed by P. S. Allen before letter 1108, in my opinion it is a clear answer of Erasmus to Vives' previous letter (1108).

model of womanhood.[82] Unfortunately, the frequent correspondence between the two men has been partially lost, thus robbing us of one of the most fascinating sources for studying the relations of Vives to the French Renaissance.[83] Budé's name appears frequently in Vives' books.[84]

The relations between Vives and Lefèvre are still intriguing and mysterious. Our Humanist mentions Lefèvre's name without any special praise, and very seldom. The best explanation of Vives' apparent prejudice against Lefèvre lies in the fact that their trends of thought were highly incompatible. Against the subtle but profound currents of scepticism inherited from nominalistic criticism, Lefèvre appealed to a rather confused combination of Augustinian voluntarism, Cusanus' intuitionism, and Ruysbroeck's mysticism. Through his publications and lectures, the Hermetic books, the writings of Lully and Sabiunde, Dyonisius Areopagita and the Alexandrian exegetes, Catherine of Siena and Francis of Paula, Pythagoric, Kabbalistic, and astrologic speculations were introduced, not without scandal, into the classrooms of the old University. The following pages will, hopefully, make clear how distant Vives was from this intellectual approach. Erasmus himself never felt totally at ease in the company of Lefèvre. Nevertheless, Vives probably admired the righteous erudition and humanism of the French scholar and deeply regretted the attacks of Zúñiga against him as well as the manoeuvers of the Sorbonne divines in 1525.[85]

Those who believe in a revolutionary progress of nominalistic physics in the fifteenth century will certainly be surprised not to find a single reference to that movement in the books of Juan Luis Vives ,a man with a great interest in the pragmatic side of human knowledge. The omission is especially intriguing because Vives, as we shall see, did encourage the inductive observation of Nature as a remedy against the speculative physics of the School; and also, because one of his most respected

---

[82] M, IV, 209; R, I, 1101 a. (De IFC, II, 5). Knowing Vives' feelings about children, we are not surprised at his silence over the maternal qualities of Budé's wife, the mother of ten children.

[83] In his treatise De conscribendis epistolis, Vives himself mentions some letters to Budé which have not been found in any collection. (M, II, 294-295; R, 866 b. -867 a.).
On this correspondence, see L. Delaruelle, Répertoire analytique et chronologique de la correspondence de G. Budé (Toulouse, 1907), and Eulitz, Der Verkehr zwischen Vives und Budaeus (Paris, 1941).

[84] LC., introd. to letter 167. See also M, I, 277, 279; II, 314; VI, 90, 332, 336, 337, 344. R, II, 332 b, 334 b, 409 b (DD., I, 2, 3); II, 601 b, 604 b, 606 a, 611 a (DD., II, 3, 6, 7, 9).

[85] EE., V, 82-85. Letter from Vives to Erasmus.

teachers, John Dullaert, was a recognized authority on Buridanus.[86] However, if we keep in mind that the Parisian student had only one year for metaphysics, ethics, and physics, we will not find it strange that he completely ignored the very specialized questions elaborated by Albert of Saxony, Domingo de Soto, Buridan, and other nominalistic physicists. In any case, it remains unquestionable that the advance of nominalistic physics, at least up to 1512, were more professional works of specialization than an integral part of the general curriculum.[87]

In 1512 Vives left Paris with the depressing conviction that he had wasted several years of his life, a feeling which seemed to have spread even among some of his professors.

It is remarkable that all through his life Vives, one of the founders of modern Pedagogy, felt out of place in the great universities of his time. Paris, Louvain, and Oxford were to him disappointing and wasteful. One is tempted to agree with Hamilton that, at least in the sixteenth century, the European universities did not rise to the challenge of the time.[88] In Germany the Convent of Saint Agnes was more important than Heidelberg; Deventer in Holland had a greater impact on that generation than the University of Louvain; in England the household of Thomas More was the center of a new intellectual climate, rather than Oxford or Cambridge; and finally, in Italy it was the Court of the Medicis where humanism was born. Possibly the reason was that the university worked as a tool of the intellectual establishment rather than as a palestra for a new order. This was particularly true in the case of the University of Paris where the theologians had the upper hand in matters of doctrinal importance. Indeed, the revolution of the next century took place not in the Faculty of Arts, but mostly in the Schools of Medicine where the scientists could think and plan without being forced into the difficult compromise of the humanists.

---

[86] John Dullaert published the *Quaestiones* of Buridanus on the *Physics* of Aristotle in October, 1509. (Prantl, *Geschichte,* IV, 256-257).

[87] Garin, *La cultura filosofica,* pp. 388 ff., has convincingly tried to refute the "arbitraria construzione del Duhem" about the Parisian forerunners of Galileo. Vives' testimony seems to strengthen the position of Garin and of those Italian scholars who have belittled the influence of Paris upon the University of Padua in general and Galileo in particular. See, e.g., Garin, "Le fonti dei manoscritti di Leonardo da Vinci," *Giornale Storico della Litteratura Italiana,* Supplement X-XI (1908), 1-344.

[88] William Hamilton, *Discussions on Philosophy and Literature* (New York, 1856), pp. 204 ff.

CHAPTER 4

FROM BRUGES TO LOUVAIN (1512–1523)

It is difficult to say whether Vives himself was aware of the significant part which the Netherlands were to play in the cultural history of Europe when he decided to establish his residence in Bruges.[1] The Netherlands of 1512 roughly included the modern nations of Belgium, Holland, and Luxembourg, plus the northern part of the French regions of Artois and Picardy. They formed a triangle, crossed by the Rhine, which was already the vital artery of commercial Europe. From a political standpoint, the Netherlands were the heritage of the proud Burgundy Dukes; but the marriage of Lady Mary with Maximilian in 1473 placed them under the rule of the Hapsburgs. The rivalry between Charles V and Francis I, and the alliance between Charles V and Henry VIII, converted the Netherlands into the political headquarters of Europe.

In the seventeenth century, the Netherlands became the stage of the most brilliant baroque civilization, the age of Spinoza and Grotius, Rubens and Van Dyke. The Netherlands were also the only haven of free thought where people like Descartes, Locke, and Bayle found refuge and liberty. What really made the difference was a fresh spirit of respect for human dignity and of tolerant democracy born in the northern part of the country after the fight against Alba and the Inquisition. The

---

[1] For the history of the Netherlands in the sixteenth and seventeenth centuries, see *The Historians' History of the World*, ed. H. S. Williams, 25 vols. (London, 1907), XIII, part xvii, "The History of the Netherlands." Also, Myron P. Gilmore, *The World of Humanism, 1453-1517*, 2nd ed. (New York, 1962), pp. 78 ff, 120 ff.

Of particular interest for the study of Vives in the Netherlands are the following writings: Paul Kalkoff, "Die Anfänge der Gegenreformation in den Niederlanden," *Schriften des Vereins für Reformationsgeschichte*, LXXIX-LXXXI (1903-1904); A. Roersch, *L'Humanisme Belge à l'Epoque de la Renaissance* (Brussels, 1910); H. de Jongh, *L'Ancienne Faculté de Théologie de Louvain au Premier Siècle de son Existence, 1432-1450* (Louvain, 1910).

Besides the books already mentioned by Paquot, de Vocht, Namèche, Van den Bussche, Nève, and P. S. Allen, see Henry de Vocht, *History of the Foundation*, pp. 1-59.

glories of the Dutch Baroque cannot be fully understood without a thorough knowledge of Vives' century. Although the Spanish Humanist resided mostly in Flanders and Brabant, his name deserves to be more closely connected with the free, progressive, and liberal Rotterdam of Erasmus than with the inquisitorial and retrograde Louvain. After all, while Vives lived in Louvain his father was sacrificed by the same Inquisition against which the Northern Netherlands were to revolt.

Vives' life in the Netherlands before his first visit to England in 1523 can be divided into two periods. The first one is associated with the City of Bruges where he lived, almost without any interruption, from 1512 to 1517. The second, and by far the most important, is centered around Louvain where Vives spent most of his intellectual energies and time from 1517 to 1523. Of the two, Bruges was the preferred residence of Vives, the object of his particular affection. Even after his stay in Oxford during the spring of 1523, Vives felt that Bruges was his permanent address. Thus, in the dedication of his essay *De Subventione Pauperum* to the Senate of Bruges, Vives did not hesitate to claim that he had lived there from 1512 to 1526.

Bruges was not only the largest city of the Netherlands in 1512, but also a beautiful and prosperous metropolis with a fascinating past. Located in the northwestern part of Flanders, eight miles away from the harbor of Blankenberghen, Bruges was crossed by a multitude of canals and picturesque bridges ("bruggas") from which the name of the city was derived. Although, in comparison with Valencia, the weather was miserable and cold, Vives was very much impressed from the first moment by the cleanliness of the town, by the politeness of its inhabitants, by the social order of the thriving municipality, and by the local pride of its able magistrates. The contrast between Bruges and Paris was obvious and enlightening. If Paris was the symbol of monarchic power and centralized absolutism, Bruges, for many years the rich capital of the Hanseatic League, represented the municipal privilege, the local thrust, and the community pride which was the mark and the promise of the Italian signories and the Swiss cantons.

In 1526 Vives wrote to the magistrates of Bruges:

I love Bruges as much as I love my native Valencia. I call this town my home because I have lived here for fourteen years . . . I have always admired your administrative system, the courteous manners of your citizens, and the incredible harmony and peace of this community.[2]

---

[2] M, IV, 420; R, II, 1552-1556. (*De SP.,* Preface). In *De Concordia,* Vives describes the people of Bruges as being "populo mansuetissimo et civilissime educato" (M, V, 231; R, II, 112 b).

Three years later, in his book *De Pacificatione,* Vives wrote a beautiful page which brings forth the humanistic cosmopolitanism of his life:

What is more pleasant and enchanting than a peaceful and harmonious
community where everything and everybody invites and holds you with
kind smiles and obliging words? ... No wonder that many a man of talent
and wealth, after wandering through every corner of the world, forgets
fatherland and relatives and stays there where according to the traditions
of the past and the moderation of the present he can live in peace and
harmony; there is his country, there is his family; there are his possessions
where justice and order are constantly respected.[3]

Vives' enthusiasm for Bruges (not his affection) was, however, slowly
tempered with the passing of the years. The very social conditions which
De Subventione Pauperum was attempting to remedy in 1526, unem-
ployment and professional mendicity, were an unequivocal indication
of the city's economic decline. Rigid municipal regulations and old-
fashioned monopolies – which neither the Englisch nor the Dutch continued to observe – weakened Bruges' position in relation to Antwerp, a
much more liberal and convenient harbor. Vives' lack of sensibility for
the economic revolution of his age might have had something to do with
the conservatism of Bruges' financial establishment, an important section
of which was the large colony of Spanish Jews resident in Bruges since
the end of the fifteenth century.[4]

One of the best known and best situated Jewish families of Bruges
were the Valdauras, a distinguished branch of the Valencian Valdauras,
who in all probability were distant relatives of Vives himself.[5] The
mansion of the Valdauras was no doubt the first refuge of Vives in
Bruges. Bernard Valdaura and his wife Clara Cervent had three
children: Margaret (the future wife of Vives), Maria, and Nicholaus.
Bernard died before 1523 after a seven-year long sickness which Vives
describes in his works with revolting realism.[6] Vives' admiration for

[3] M, V, 248; R, II, 274 b – 275 a. (*De Pac.*)
[4] According to J. A. Goris, *Étude sur les Colonies des Marchandes Méridionales
à Anvers* (Louvain, 1925), pp. 37-59, the Portuguese Jews favored Antwerp over
Bruges. These colonies of Jews were very much exposed to the advances of Lutheranism and played an important part in the history of the Reformation in the
Netherlands. See Kalkoff, "Anfänge der Gegenreformation," LXXIX, 41-45; LXXXI,
9-12.
Bonilla, *Luis Vives,* III, 27-30, notes 40-45, offers abundant bibliography on the
subject.
[5] In his treatise *Adversus pseudo-dialecticos* Vives calls one of the Valdauras his
"relative" (*Nicholao Valdaurae consanguineo meo*) five years before his marriage
with Margaret Valdaura. The name Valdaura appears in the processes of the
Valencian Inquisition recently published by Pinta and Palacio.
[6] M, IV, 196, 198; R, I, 1090 b – 1901 b. (*De IFC.,* II, 4)

Clara Cervent claims quite a few pages in his *Opera Omnia,* in spite of the trimming ordered by Erasmus, who was absolutely irritated by this invasion of Vives' mother-in-law into the gardens of Academe.[7]

As a young preceptor to the children of a family well respected in the community, Vives had from the first day an opportunity to meet the most interesting people in town. As a cultural center, Bruges was second only to Louvain. In fact, the long rivalry between Flanders and Brabant had manifested itself in the academic competition of the two cities. Hardly had the University of Louvain been founded in the fifteenth century when Bruges attempted to start a university of its own. Furthermore, in the spring of 1439, only fourteen years after the foundation of the University, Bruges tried to have in removed from Louvain.[8] Nobody was surprised, then, when in January of 1520 the magistrates of Bruges made generous overtures to the executors of Busleyden's will to secure the establishment of the Trilingue College within the walls of the old capital of Flanders.[9] Although all these attempts ended in failure, about 1512 Bruges took special pride in a selected group of outstanding scholars, all of whom played an important part in the life of Juan Luis Vives. From the very beginning the young and brilliant preceptor from Valencia was admitted into the small circle of Mark Laurin, John de Fevyn, and Francis Cranevelt. Mark Laurin (1488-1540), the dean of Saint Donatian's Chapter, was an old friend of Erasmus and a great favorer of literature. On more intimate terms with Vives was John de Fevyn (1490-1555), the schoolmaster of Saint Donatian – the chapter school of Bruges – who, years later, would perform the rites of Vives' marriage with Margaret Valdaura.[10] If Laurin probably introduced Vives to Erasmus, Fevyn opened to him the gates of the Princenhof, the old palace of the Burgundy Dukes where he himself lived, and where the intellectual nobility of Bruges could be introduced to ambassadors, legates, and, occasionally, even to the Imperial Court.[11] Of the three

[7] In a letter to Cranevelt of October, 1527, Vives calls his mother-in-law an "illustrious woman, glory of her sex" (*LC.,* 248, v. 56). See also M, IV, 196; R, I, 1091 a (*De IFC.,* II, 4) where Vives extends himself in the eulogy of Clara Cervent, a page which was considerably abbreviated in the Basle edition of Vives' works.
[8] De Vocht, *History Foundation,* pp. 130-131.
[9] *Ibid.,* pp. 514-520. See also *LC.,* Introd., pp. xlvi-liii.
[10] The biographical details of Mark Laurin can be read in *LC.,* introd. to letter 6, pp. 13-14. Laurin studied with Erasmus in Louvain (about 1502) and Bologna (about 1507). Erasmus was the guest of Laurin in Louvain in 1517 (*EE.,* II, 651, v. 1), in 1519 (*EE.,* IV, 1010) and in 1521 (*EE.,* IV, 1223). Laurin was probably the first link between Vives and Erasmus.
[11] De Vocht in *LC.,* Introd., pp. xxxvi-xlii, sketches a well-documented biography of Fevyn from a family closely related to the Court of the Duke of Burgundy. In fact, John de Fevyn himself lived for a while in the Princenhof, the magnificent

men, however, Francis Cranevelt became, and remained for life, Vives'
most beloved friend. Born in 1485 at Nijmegen of noble and rich
parents, Francis received an intense education which culminated with
the degree of *Doctor Utriusque Iuris* by the University of Louvain in
October, 1510. In 1509 he married the daughter of a distinguished
Brabant family, a young woman of many charms to whom Thomas
More used to refer jokingly as "our common wife" and whom Vives, in
a more chaste and serious vein, called "my sister." [12] Probably the sharp
contrast between the forced celibacy of Erasmus and the natural, happy
family life of Cranevelt and Thomas More was of some importance to
the direction of Vives' future. After several years in Louvain, Cranevelt
was appointed city attorney of Bruges in 1515, and probably he was
immediately introduced to Vives by his own old fellow-student, John
de Fevyn. The correspondence of Cranevelt, published in 1928 by Henry
de Vocht, includes a large number of letters from and to Vives, John
de Fevyn, Martin Dorp, Gerard de Geldenhower, Pope Adrian VI, Thomas More, Adrian Barlandus, Peter de Corte, and many others. This
correspondence, which was not known to Bonilla – although it was
published one year before Bonilla's second edition – is absolutely indispensable for knowing the intimate character of Vives and for per-
ceiving the thrust of Flemish Humanism in the first decades of the
sixteenth century.

Laurin, Cranevelt, and Fevyn were indeed typical products of
Flemish education. All three were devout Christians, men of literary
taste, liberally minded, and fully aware of the challenges of their age.
Their training was connected in the past with the school of Deventer
and the *Devotio Moderna,* and in the future with the promises of Erasmus and the longings of their own pursuits and intellectual search. The
Humanistic trend of Deventer was a unique blend of the intense piety

palace arranged by Philip the Good where the Imperial Court used to stay while
in Bruges. (*LC.,* introd. to letter 21, p. 57) Wolsey, Thomas More, and Erasmus
resided there more than once. Erasmus was actually so enchanted with the place
that he asked permission to take permanent residence there, a request which was
politely ignored. (*EE.,* IV, 1012).

Fevyn introduced Vives to the world of politics. It was in the magnificent halls
of the palace where Vives met Juan de Lanuza, the ambassador of Ferdinand of
Aragon. (Bonilla, *Luis Vives,* III, 27, note 39). Lanuza's visit to the Netherlands
took place in October, 1512, only a few months after Vives' arrival in Bruges.

[12] More to Cranevelt: "In the meantime take good care of yourself, and of your
wife, who is yours during the night, mine during the day, and common to both of
us as our lady." The Latin text, which resists any acceptable English translation
says: "Interea vale cum uxore, diurna mea, nocturna tua, domina vero communi"
(*LC.,* 156, vv. 3-5). Apparently More was quite pleased with this type of remark
which he repeats in *LC.,* 177, v. 16, and again in *LC.,* 262, v. 13. For the more
serious approach of Vives, see introd. to letter 200 in *LC.*

of Gerhard Groot (1340-1384) and Florentius Radewyns (1350-1400) together with the classical revival of the Italian quatroccento. After all, for many years, Bruges was the port where the South met the North, and where large colonies of Genoese, Lombard, and Florentine merchants established their warehouses and their offices.[13] The three great protagonists of humanism in the Netherlands – Hegius, Rudolph Agricola, and Wessel Gansfoort – were themselves the product of Deventer; their influence totally permeates the history of Flemish education at that time.[14]

In the first two decades of the sixteenth century, the Christian Humanists of the Low Countries were exposed first to the Erasmian gospel of the *Philosophia Chritsi,* and then to the open rebellion of Lutheranism. The Erasmian exposure preceded, by several intense and confused years, the shock of Wittenberg. In the summer of 1514, two years after Vives' arrival in Bruges, Erasmus visited Liège, Antwerp, and Louvain on his way to Basle to prepare the edition of Saint Jerome.[15] His trip along the left bank of the Rhine was a triumphal journey.[16] His name was preceded by a tremendous reputation. The "permanent peace" signed July 10 of the same year by Henry VIII and Louis XII was widely attributed to the efforts of the English Humanists of whom Thomas More, John Colet, and Erasmus himself were the best known champions. Furthermore, the author of the *Enchiridion* (1501), the *Annotationes* to Valla (1505), the *Adagia* (1506), the *Praise of Folly* (1509), and the *Julius exclusus* (1513) was not only the best-selling author of Europe but also the herald of a new Christianity in which virtue was more praiseworthy than either dogma or sacrament, and biblical criticism counted more than scholastic theology or ecclesiastical definitions. The lay piety of Erasmus was much more radical than anything the *Devotio Moderna* ever produced.

The reaction of Flemish Humanism to the challenge of Erasmus varied from loyal enthusiasm to suspicion and open opposition. Vives' friends became, almost without exception, followers and admirers of Erasmus. The correspondence between Erasmus and Cranevelt, Fevyn,

---

[13] See, e.g., A. Duclos, *Bruges. Histoire et Souvenires* (Bruges, 1910), 47 ff., 74 ff., also L. Gilliodts, Van Severen, *Cartulaire de l'ancienne Étaple de Bruges* (Bruges, 1905), pp. 6-14, 270-273, 282-288.
[14] De Vocht, *History Foundation,* pp. 139-158, 161-163.
[15] From Erasmus' correspondence we can trace his journey through Louvain (*EE.,* II, 304), Liège, (*ibid.,* 299), Mainz (*ibid.,* 300), and Schletstadt (*ibid.,* 305).
[16] *EE.,* 301, v. 45: "Germany received me with so much honors that I almost felt ashamed." (*Germania tanto honore me excepit ut propemodum puderet*).

and Laurin is an eloquent testimony of such friendship.[17] Vives' trip to Paris in April, 1514, probably confirmed his opposition to medieval scholasticism and inclined him even more to the fresh approach of Erasmus. The small group at Bruges was nevertheless an exceptional case of unanimous acceptance. The theologians of the University of Louvain were a different matter. Martin Van Dorp, a professor of philosophy in the Lily College since 1510 and a student of theology until 1515, wrote a letter to Erasmus with a friendly but ominous warning. The theologians were displeased with the negative and sarcastic criticism in the *Praise of Folly*; more importantly, they were extremely alarmed by Erasmus' intention to revise the traditional Vulgate edition of the New Testament.[18] Erasmus' long answer did not prevent future persecutions by the Faculty of Theology, but it did help to persuade Dorp to change his mind to such an extent that years later he became an intimate partner of the Erasmian circle.[19] Perhaps the initial attacks against Erasmus in Louvain moved Vives to pay a few visits to the City. At least one of his private disciples in Bruges, James de la Potterie, introduced him to a well-known professor of humanities in the University, Adrian Baarland. We know for sure that as early as March, 1514, Baarland published a collection of sayings from Vergil at the recommendation of Vives, whom he praised as one of the leading Humanists of the Low Countries. Two years after his arrival at Bruges, Vives already had a reputation in the academic world of Louvain. Such a reputation was much more the result of his personal charm and thoughtful eloquence as a private preceptor than the outcome of his early publications. Neither the presumptuous mannerism of his *Triumphus Christi* (published in Paris, April, 1514), nor the edition of Hyginius' fables were likely to grant him the admiration of the Lovanienses.[20]

[17] *LC.* includes twelve letters from and to Erasmus, ninety-one from and to Fevyn, six from Laurin, and forty-seven from and to Vives. The references to these and other close friends of Vives are in the hundreds; altogether they present a vivid picture of the circle in which Vives moved.

[18] See *EE.*, II, 304, especially vv. 81-117.

[19] In January, 1524, Dorp wrote to Cranevelt a totally Erasmian letter (*LC.*, 85). Fevyn was informed of the change in attitude and wrote: "Dorpium laudo quod aliquando resipuit. Utinam ille numquam prior in Moiram." (*LC*, 91, vv. 17-18). One year later Vives mentions Dorp with great affection (*LC.*, 80, vv. 109-110; see also *LC.*, 157, vv. 25-34 with Vives' eulogy of Dorp after his death on May 31, 1525).

[20] P. S. Allen (*EE.*, III, introd. to letter 927, p. 508) mentions the edition of Hyginius of March 31, 1514. According to Riber, however, (I, 536) the edition of Hyginus was made by Lambert in Paris three years later and was followed by a letter of Vives to John Fort in which Vives wrote: "When I publicly read Hyginius in Paris I decided to have it printed for the sake of my students." (R, II,

The year 1515 does not provide us with any information concerning Vives' activities in Bruges. Politically the year was significant because of the coronation of Francis I (January 1, 1515), who, before the year was over, confirmed the French presence in Italy with the impressive victory at Marignano proving that the legendary Swiss mercenaries were entirely vulnerable. On the other hand, the Archduke Charles took over the government of Flanders, thus setting the stage for the unfortunate confrontation of French and Hapsburg power in the second decade of the century.

Probably in the summer of 1516 Vives and Erasmus met for the first time in Bruges.[21] Never before nor after did Erasmus' name mean so much to Christian Europe as in those years between the French-English peace of July, 1514, and the death of Maximilian in January, 1519. The year 1516 especially displayed the best glories of the Erasmian group. In March Erasmus dedicated to Leo X his *Annotationes* to the New Testament, printed by Froben in Basle; the *Institutio Principis Christiani* appeared in May and was dedicated to the Archduke Charles, whom he had counseled since the beginning of the year. The pacifistic efforts of the London Reformers were crowned in July with the peace of Noyon between Spain and France; finally, in December, Thomas More published the *Utopia*. The impact of Erasmus upon Vives' life after their first encounter in Bruges cannot be fairly appraised without taking into consideration the enormous prestige of the Erasmian movement one year before the rebellion of Luther. The extent of that influence will be the object of a whole chapter in the second part of this book.

In 1517 Vives' life took a decisive new dimension. Maybe on the recommendation of Erasmus, who was his intimate friend, William of

---

536 a-537b). The last intriguing remark might refer to some public lectures held by Vives in Paris during his trip of 1514, or to some tutorial teaching of his senior year at the University.

[21] Allen bases this guess on a letter from Erasmus to Thomas More (March 8, 1517) where Erasmus writes: "If Vives came to see you it will not be difficult for you to imagine what I had to go through in Brussels being daily greeted by a mob of Spaniards, French, and Italians." (*EE.*, III, introd. to letter 927, v. 508; II, 545, vv. 15-16). Erasmus stayed in Brussels in July, 1516 (*EE.*, II, introd. to letters 410 and 438, pp. 240 and 277-278). The mention of Vives' name, although backed by the authority of P. S. Allen and M. Bataillon (*Erasmo y España*, p. 77) has been rejected as a spurious interpolation by H. de Vocht, *Monumenta Historia Lovaniensia*, (Louvain, 1934), p. 1, note 2; it is also certain that More never heard Vives' name until 1519. It remains, then, highly probable that Vives was introduced to Erasmus by Laurin, in whose house Erasmus stayed for a while in July or August, 1517. (*EE.*, III, 651, v. 1).

Croy chose Vives as his private preceptor.[22] Outside the Royal Family, William was the most glamorous private student any teacher could have. Nephew to the Lord of Chièvres, the controversial preceptor of the future Charles V, William, nineteen years old in 1517, was already Bishop of Cambrai, Cardinal, and Archbishop-elect of Toledo in succession to Cardinal Cisneros. In the company of his pupil, Vives moved from Bruges to Louvain where he established his residence in Lent of 1517. His position there was from the very start a prestigious and influential one. The University and the intellectual elite of the city were trying to ingratiate themselves with Vives' pupil whose ecclesiastical career promised to take him to the highest positions of the Church. One of those erudites was James Latomus, the director of the Standonck College in Louvain from 1502 to 1505 and a doctor of theology, who in August, 1519, published a pamphlet against Erasmian Humanism dedicated to Croy.[23] Vives' surprising authority among the Lovanienses can be ascertained from several significant details. As early as April, 1518, Vives attended the high-level conversations between Erasmus and the leader of the Louvain theologians, John Briart.[24] In December, 1519, Vives and John Paludanus, one of the most influential members of the Faculty of Arts, tried, although in vain, to have Cranevelt appointed to the chair of Canon Law.[25] It is even possible that Vives' constant interest in legal processes, his good sense, and personal charm played an important part in the complicated negotiations which preceded the acceptance of the Trilingue College by the University.[26] At least Vives' assistance was decisive in the final arrangement which ended the three-year struggle between the University administration and the executors of Busleyden's will.[27] In fact, in recognition for his services, in March, 1520, Vives was granted the license to deliver public lectures, although

[22] See the correspondence between Erasmus and Croy (*EE.*, III, 917, 945, 951, 957, 958, 959).

[23] See the interesting biography of Latomus in *LC.*, introd. to letter 46; also, *EE.*, III, 934, note 3. Latomus is of some importance in Vives' life for two main reasons. First, because he served as the link between Vives and the future Pope, Adrian VI, a close friend of Latomus. Secondly, because of Latomus' work on Agricola's dialectical books which became known to Vives during his residence in Louvain. An indication of Latomus' eagerness to establish personal contact with the Cardinal is the fact that after the premature death of the latter, Latomus became the instructor of Croy's younger brother, Robert (*LC.*, introd. to letter 23, p. 59.)

[24] De Vocht, *History Foundation*, p. 329. On Briart, see below note 32.

[25] *LC.*, 1, vv. 1-16. The promotion went instead to Gabriel Van der Meeren.

[26] This seems to be the interpretation of Vives' words in the dedication of the *Meditationes in Psalmos Poenitentiales:* "Quum eo tempore (1518) inter oratores versarer frequenterque de rebus aliis profanis in genere judiciali declamarem..." (M, I, 163; R, I, 292 a.)

[27] De Vocht, *History Foundation*, pp. 526-30.

he was never matriculated as a master of the University of Louvain.[28]

Vives' life in Louvain was both enrichting and frustrating. Caught in the middle of all the tensions which immediately preceded and followed the outbreak of Lutheranism, Vives was significantly influenced by the liberal group of Flemish and Brabant humanists but also repelled by all the wasteful suspicions, the endless controversies, and personal rivalries which threatened the academic life of the institution.

The University of Louvain was actually opened in 1426, founded by the Duke of Brabant and, at least partially, modeled after the constitution of Paris. Like Paris, Louvain had four Nations (of lesser importance) and four faculties. Besides the regular colleges of private foundation, Louvain had four famous pedagogies or schools of grammar taken over by the Faculty of Arts. The most important colleges were the College of Saint Donatian (founded 1484), the Standonck College (founded 1499), and the College of Malines (founded 1500). The names of the four pedagogies were Castle (where Vives taught), Porc, Lily, and Falcon.[29] To these the Collegium Trilingue has to be added, founded by the Humanist Jerome Busleyden for the study of Greek, Latin, and Hebrew. The study programs and the level of education were very similar to those of Paris and Cologne, the two institutions with which Louvain was in close contact.

The professorate of Louvain was roughly divided into conservative theologians and more liberal-minded Humanists. The closer connection of the Faculty of Arts with the teaching of grammar and rhetoric in the pedagogies reinforced the position of the latter group, at least in comparison with other universities. The opening, however, of the Trilingue College in 1520 and Erasmus' association with the new institution led to a sharper polarization of both groups. Although Vives' sympathies were undoubtedly with the Humanists, he managed to remain aloof from personal rivalries and, in some cases at least, to moderate the opposition of the theologians.

The conservatism of the Louvain theologians became a favorite target of pamphleteers and reformers. In June, 1523, an anonymous pamphlet

---

[28] Vives was the first exception ever made by the University of Louvain. Erasmus himself was duly impressed by it, and, for a moment at least, he conceived the hope that Vives' exceptional treatment would help to relax the stiff regulations of the University. (*EE.*, IV, 1111, vv. 54-55; also, de Jongh, *L'ancienne Faculté,* p. 20.) De Vocht (*History Foundation,* p. 528, note 1) quotes part of the document: "Ludovicus Vives pluries supplicavit apud dominos rectores huius universitatis suos precessores pro licentia legendi certum opus, quam hucusque obtinere non valuit ..."

[29] See H. Rashdall, *The Universities of Europe,* II, 263-268. De Vocht (*History Foundation,* pp. 63-99) gives ample information on the Colleges and the Pedagogies of the Brabant University.

began to acquire some publicity in which the theologians were called pigs, donkeys, and camels. The Humanists were delighted with such a publication.[30] Ulrich von Hutten made John Briart the victim of his devastating sarcasm, while Vives himself at the end of 1519 bitterly remarked that the theologians were acting as if they were obliged under oath to destroy the University.[31] The leader of the group was John Briart, who after some initial opposition to Erasmus refrained from further attacks inspired maybe by the good sense of his close friend Adrian of Utrecht (the future Pope Adrian VI) and Vives himself.[32] Briart's partial conversion toward Erasmus was also felt by his best known disciple, Martin Dorp, a theologian with a brilliant humanistic training who – as we said before – finally joined the Erasmian movement.[33] Much more conservative and anti-Erasmian were James Latomus, who was the instigator of much persecution against Erasmus and whom Vives ridiculed in his letters; [34] Nicolas Beachem of Egmond, one of Erasmus' most decided antagonists among the friars; [35] Paschasius Berselius, the changeable Benedictine from Liège; [36] and, finally, Nicolas de Bureau, Bishop of Sarepta who criticized Erasmus and attacked Vives' *De Subventione Pauperum*.[37]

Facing such formidable opposition was a brilliant phalanx of Humanists, most of them associated in one way or another with the Trilingue College. We can find most of their names in a letter of Erasmus to a friend in which he praises the revival of studies under the "beautiful sky of Louvain." [38] Besides the close circle of Vives' friends, the following names deserve at least some mention: Adrian Baarland or Cornelissen, the first Latin professor of the Trilingue College; [39] John de Nève, the glory of the Lily Pedagogy and Bishop of Cambrai after Croy's death; [40] Jerome de Busleyden, the founder of the Trilingue College; [41] Rutger Rescius, the first professor of Greek at the Trillingue whom

[30] See the witty account of Fevyn (*LC.*, 58, vv. 15-17 and 61).

[31] *LC.*, 1, vv. 15-16: "Omnia sunt hoc anno talia, ut alia via non ingrederentur, si iurassent ταύτην' Ἀκαδημίαν eversuros . . ."

[32] John Briart was the Vice-chancellor in succession to Adrian of Utrecht. Erasmus was delighted with Briart's approval of his new edition of the New Testament (*EE.*, III, 670, introd. p. 93). See Briart's biography in *LC.*, 24 a.

[33] See note 19. Dorp's biography in *LC.*, 24 b.

[34] See below, pp. 130-132.

[35] See below, pp. 131-133.

[36] See his biography in *LC.*, 150, e.

[37] See his biography in *LC.*, 246, a, b. In the same letter (vv. 27 ff.) Vives calls the Bishop "homo latinissimus et callentissimus veterum religionis nostrae scriptorum."

[38] *EE.*, IV, 1237, vv. 10-47.

[39] *LC.*, 62, a-c.

[40] *Ibid.*, 26, a-f.

[41] *Ibid.*, General Introduction, i-lxxxvii.

Francis I tried to allure into the College de France; [42] Conrad Goclenius, who replaced Baarland in the Trilingue; [43] the Spanish Jew, Mathew Adrianus, one of the best Hebraists of his day; [44] Peter de Corte from a noble family of Bruges, an intimate friend of Vives and Laurin, professor of eloquence in the Lily, Rector of the University since 1530, and later one of the champions of the Counter-Reformation in the Low Countries; [45] and many others of lesser importance or more distantly related to Juan Luis Vives.

In the four years of Croy's preceptorship (1517-1521) Vives' own ideas began to take shape in response to the challenge of his own environment. We can classify the thirteen publications of Vives in those four years in three different categories: philosophical, religious, and literary works. The first group will be the object of a more careful study in the second part of this book.

The religious books of this period were four: *Meditationes in septem psalmos Penitentiales* (Louvain, 1518), *Genethliacon Jesu Christi* (Louvain, 1518), *De tempore quo natus est Christus* (Louvain, 1518), and finally *Clypei Christi Descriptio* (Louvain, 1518). The number and the religious fervor of these early writings of Vives betray beyond any doubt a very serious and sincere commitment to the same kind of piety his closest friends had imbibed from the pure sources of the Devotio Moderna and the writings of Erasmus.

The *Meditations to the Psalms* were written on two different occasions.[46] The first series was started in Cambrai where Vives was visiting in the company of his pupil, William of Croy. Vives started with the sixth Psalm, which was his favorite, probably because of its poignant recognition of human guilt. He later completed all seven Psalms at the request of William of Croy to whom he dedicated the pious book. The *Genethliacon Jesu Christi*, dedicated to John Briart – "the wisest of all theologians and the closest and most erudite of all my friends" – was written during the Christmas days of 1518.[47] Vives admits in the dedication that his first intention was to write a poem but that he was forced to give up such an idea because of his "clumsiness and poor style." The few verses which Vives did include at the end of this essay will certainly fail to carry his name into the sanctuary of poetry. This piece is, further-

[42] *Ibid.*, 150, e-i. Also, *EE.*, II, introd. to letter 546.
[43] *LC.*, 95, a-j. Also, *EE.*, IV, introd. to letter 1209.
[44] De Vocht, *History Foundation,* pp. 241-250.
[45] *LC.*, 83, a-h.
[46] M, I, 32-33. (*Vivis Vita*) The text of the meditations is in M, I, 162-255; R, I, 291-363.
[47] M, VII, 1-18; R, I, 366-379 (*Genethliacon Jesuchristi*).

more, a highly immature example of Christian Humanism. Pages of as-
sumedly tender devotion follow others of inflated and showy erudition;
Biblical prophecies alternate with classical anecdotes of pagan wisdom.
The message, however, is clear and orthodox: Christ's destinies are directed by the providence of God, not by the signs of the Zodiac. The
supernatural cannot be brought to the level of either nature or history.

In December, 1518, Vives also wrote two short religious essays which
he dedicated to a friend from Valencia's aristocracy. The first one, *De
Tempore quo, id est, de pace in qua natus est Christus,* reveals a truly
Augustinian conception of history as a harmonious synthesis of free
human decisions and God's providence.[48] In this particular meditation
Vives shows how Christ's birth coincided with the *pax romana* of the
Augustan empire. Besides this praise of peace which is characteristic of
the Erasmian circle, these pages prove Vives' extraordinary familiarity
with Roman history. In fact, this part claims so much of his attention
that it is hard to decide whether Vives succeeded in invalidating the
charge of which he was fully aware – that he was writing "more the
history of the Roman people than a Christian meditation." [49]

The second composition, *Christi Clypei descriptio,* is a summary of
Biblical history from Adam's fall to the evangelization of America. The
main events appear engraved as the heraldic bearings of Christ's coat of
arms.[50] Vives uses this artistic device of narrative description – clearly
inspired by the eighth book of the *Aeneid* – in an attempt to sublimate
the Humanistic obsession with heraldry.[51]

Compared with the *Christi Jesu Triumphus,* these four religious
writings of Vives point to a more mature and unvarnished style, and
bring to light some of the basic concerns of his future intellectual
endeavor, especially the central and unresolved case of Christian Humanism – namely, the balanced relationship of nature and grace, history
and revelation, human values and religious merit.

The literary works Vives wrote between 1517 and 1521 draw their
inspiration not only from his own teaching experience but also from his
increasing attention to the riddles and contrasts of human existence.
The most important is the *Fabula de Homine* (1518), dedicated to

[48] M, VII, 2032; R, I, 380-391. (*De tempore*)
[49] M, *ibid.,* 20; R, *ibid.,* 380 a. "Nec id altius repetam, ne historiam populi
Romani scribere videamur potius quam de Natali loqui Christiano." (*De tempore*)
[50] M, VII, 33-40; R, I, 285-291. (*Clypei Christi descriptio*)
[51] Adams, *Better Part of Valor,* pp. 237-238, 248, presents a few instances of the
humanistic attack on the arrogance of the Ferocities and Beasts which were constantly used in emblems and heraldic symbolism.

one of his disciples in Louvain.[52] The *Fabula* is perhaps the only composition of Vives obviously inspired by and related to Italian Humanism, in particular to Pico della Mirandola's *De Hominis Dignitate.* Instead of the celebrated speech of the Italian Humanist, Vives presents a mythological sketch. The goddess Juno gives a party for the other divinities; as entertainment Jupiter introduces his best creature, man, who is a copy of Jupiter himself.

Here is the description of man and his achievements:

They investigated one by one and examined the many hidden secrets of man and derived more pleasure from this than from the spectacle of all the plays. "Nor having seen him once are they content; they wish to linger on." There indeed was a mind full of wisdom, prudence, knowledge, reason, so fertile that by itself it brought forth extraordinary things. Its inventions are: towns and houses, the use of herbs, stones and metals, the designations and names of all things, which foremost among his other inventions have especially caused wise men to wonder. Next and no less important, with a few letters he was able to comprise the immense variety of the sounds of the human voice. With these letters so many doctrines were fixed in writing and transmitted, including religion itself and the knowledge and cult of Jupiter, the father, and of the other brother-gods. This one thing, which is found in no other animal but man, shows his relationship to the gods. Of little good would all these inventions have been if there had not been added, as the treasury of all things and for the safekeeping of these divine riches, a memory, the storehouse of all that we have enumerated. From religion and memory, foreknowledge is almost obtained, with the prophecy of the future, evidently a spark of that divine and immense science which perceives all future events as if they were present.[53]

The assembly of the gods and the goddesses is captivated by man's greatness; as a token of their admiration, the divinities allow man to take a seat among them and "to enjoy forever the eternal bliss of the banquet."

In a way it is unfortunate that the *Fabula* was chosen to represent Vives' thought and style in a well-known English translation of Renaissance compositions. The humanistic optimism of this writing is far from characteristic of Vives, but rather an exceptional tribute to one of the few Italian Humanists whose work seems to have been very influential in the circle of his early teachers and friends.[54] The consciousness of sin, the awareness of human misery and fallibility, the broken heart and the humble mood of the *Meditations on the Psalms* describe

---

[52] M, IV, 3-9; R, I, 538-543. (*Fabula de homine*)

much better Vives' attitude toward man. In the introduction to the book Vives sounds much more like himself:

The argument of this writing is as old as it is sober and earnest, in spite of its witticism and jest; it shows to the reader the wretchedness and emptiness of all the things for which we work with blind and mad dedication. Everything that life can offer – with the single exception of virtue – is a childish game, an ephemeral absurdity bound to vanish any moment.[55]

Perfectly in tune with these words is Vives' introduction to Cicero's *De Senectute,* a short and exquisite eassay entitled *Anima Senis* (1518).[56] Vives begins with an initial confession:

Many times in the past I wanted to peek into the soul of an elder person and to fancy what kind of a human being I would be if God granted me a long life.[57]

Vives' wish is now fulfilled: the soul of an elder man shows up and reveals to him all the secrets of senility. The description betokens Vives' unique power of introspection, the secret of much of his future writing. The old soul speaks:

I am sceptical by instinct; I do not grant my friendship to others right away. No human greatness gives me joy, no vain glory nor pride drags me into action. I seek only things of absolute necessity, and even those with extreme moderation. I do not sacrifice oxen but little birds, and I wish the gods would content themselves with mosquitoes or flies . . . By nature I am circumspect, suspicious, always ready to avoid the slightest occasion of danger . . . Fear and pusillanimity have made me unsociable, querulous and often demanding what is beyond my right.[58]

[53] Translated by Nancy Leskeith in *Renaissance Philosophy of Man,* ed., Cassierer et al., pp. 385-396.
[54] Vives' familiarity with Pico della Mirandola dates no doubt from his Parisian studies. Pico della Mirandola visited Paris in 1485-86 and left there a lasting impact. Three years later the University of Paris surprised everybody by refusing to confirm Rome's condemnation of some of the teachings of the Italian Humanist. Mirandola's love for the Kabbala and the mystics was transmitted to Lefèvre d'Etaples, who became the champion of the Florentine Humanist in the University of Paris. (Renaudet, *Préréforme et Humaisme,* pp. 126-129, 141-143, 388-392.)
On Thomas More and Pico, see R. W. Chambers, *Thomas More,* 2nd ed. (Ann Arbor, 1962).
On the strong influence of Pico della Mirandola on Flemish Humanism, see De Vocht, *History Foundation,* pp. 310-311.
[55] M, IV, 2; R, I, 537 b. "Omnia enim quae sunt in humana vita, prater virtutem, tamquam pueriles quidam lusus, ridicula sunt, ac subito utpote inania evanescunt. . ." (*Fabula de homine*)
[56] M, IV, 9-20; R, I, 553-563. (*Anima senis*)
[57] M, *ibid.,* 9; R, *ibid.,* 553 b.
[58] M, *ibid.,* 11; R, *ibid.* 555 b.

Such is Vives' picture of man's old age. It is difficult to avoid the impression that the pessimistic tone of his thoughts is anything but the result of his own premature disenchantment with life.

The third significant writing of Vives in this period, *Aedes Legum* (1520), is an eloquent testimony to Vives' constant concern with the philosophy of law.[59] His ideas on the subject of legal reform and his commitment to the ethical quality of jurisprudence stand forth with an exceptional maturity for a young man who never had professional training in law. Impressed by this performance, a few biographers of Vives have claimed for our Humanist the Doctorate of Law from the University of Oxford, a claim which has not been backed by reliable evidence.[60]

The main ideas of Vives' *Aedes Legum* are an integral part of his global conception of philosophy and a sketch of his future intellectual achievements. As such, they will be further discussed in the second part of this book. Here it will suffice to point out that the traditions of the Faculty of Law at Louvain, because of its close relations with Bologna and still under the impact of Agricola's and Hegius' teaching, might very well have influenced and increased the inborn interest of Vives.[61] Moreover, the intimate friendship of the young Spanish scholar with Cranevelt, the city attorney of a prosperous and complex metropolis, was probably based, among other things, on their common enthusiasm for the law.[62]

The rest of the literary work of Vives in this time can be classified into two categories: rhetorical pieces and prelections. Both are more academic exercises than truly creative essays; yet, for different reasons, they arc worth mentioning here.

The chronologically first "declamatio" is entitled *Pompeius fugiens* (1519) and is dedicated to the mentor of William of Croy.[63] After the defeat of Pharsalus, Pompei, "the last survivor of Republican freedom," bitterly complains about the inexorable shift of fate and the treason of

[59] M, V, 483-494; R, I, 681-691. (*Aedes legum*)
[60] The title of "LL.D. beyond the Seas" which some biographers attribute to Vives was never conferred to him; he certainly did not have such a degree when he arrived in Oxford and nowhere in his correspondence is there the least allusion to his having received it. On the contrary, frequently in his correspondence he professes himself as an apprentice in jurisprudence. (See, e.g., *LC.*, 23, v. 24; 193, v. 40.) It is also a mistake to say with Underhill that Vives was made "to expound civil law before the whole University" (cited by de Vocht, *Monumenta*, p. 7, note 4), a quotation which according to *LC.*, 144, v. 23, has to be referred to Peter Garcias de Laloo's promotion.
[61] M, V, 494-507; R, I, 691-703. (*Praelectio in leges Ciceronis*).
[62] De Vocht, *History Foundation*, pp. 150-151, 228, 451.
[63] M, II, 502-517; R, I, 581-595. (*Pompeius fugiens*)

his friends. The moral intention is clear: to learn "from the examples of great men in the past and from the precepts of the Christian religion" to despise human glory and to accept with equanimity the "erratic fluctuations of destiny." The *Declamationes Syllanae* (1520) are of special significance in the life of Vives because they were the first book he dedicated to a prince, the Archduke Ferdinand, and were preceded by an introduction by Erasmus himself.[64]

Erasmus writes:

> While others scream, Vives declaims with unique wisdom and serenity . . . Spain had before men of this type like Seneca and Quintilian, among many others. But they were in Rome, not in Valencia . . . Believe me, change titles and names and listening to Vives you will fancy yourself to be living again in the golden age of Cicero and Seneca . . . His ability to find arguments and evidence does not surprise me because I know well that he is solidly trained in every branch of philosophy . . . In fact, nobody was a better sophist than Vives when he was dedicated to those disciplines where eloquence is impossible and only argute logomachy counts . . . I hardly know anybody of our generation comparable to Vives . . . at least I do not know anybody whose stream of eloquence is equally matched by so much philosophical wisdom.[65]

The preface to the *Declamationes* includes for the first time an accurate description of the purpose and method of philosophy. Vives' line of thought, which will later be expounded in detail, is no doubt a testimony to the pervasive influence of Rudolph Agricola upon the intellectual youth of our Humanist. Actually, two of Vives' best friends were at that time engaged in publishing the work of Agricola. The first, Bartholomew Latomus, published his commentaries on Agricola in 1530; Martin Dorp had just completed (1515) the edition of the *De Inventione Dialectica* in cooperation with Alard of Amsterdam.[66]

The book includes five speeches. The first, by a friend of Sila, tries to persuade the dictator not to resign his extraordinary dictatorial powers, while the second tried to encourage him to do so. The third is Sila's speech of resignation; the fourth and fifth are bitter attacks against Sila attributed to Lepidus. The style of these speeches is completely Ciceronian; the content is a magnificent example of "dialectical invention." Evidence for and against is derived from every possible source and point

[64] M, II, 321-472; R, I, 703-829. (*Declamationes Syllanae*)
[65] *Ibid.,* 316; 704 a.
[66] *De Inventione Dialectica* was printed by Th. Martens in Louvain, on January 12, 1515. On the importance of Latomus' work on Africola, see Ong, *Ramus,* pp. 126-130. Also, *Ramus and the Talon Inventory* (Cambridge, 1958), p. 542.

of view; reasoning is conceived as a persuasive accumulation of convergent proofs directed to a specific and practical conclusion.

The prelections of this period (1517-21) are five. The first, *Prelectio in Georgica Virgilii* (1518), is probably the most interesting because it shows a radical change in Vives' literary taste.[67] The "insanus senex Homerus" of the *Triumphus Christi* (1514) has become now the poet par excellence. Once again the Brabant "alma mater" had a decisive influence upon Vives; the Greek teaching of Dorp, Goclenius, and Josse Vroeye changed Vives' attitudes toward the giant of Greek literature.[68] Nevertheless, Vives was never a Greek scholar in the full sense of the word, although he knew Greek well enough to use it in his private correspondence as a safety device for daring criticism or less orthodox comments. Vives' own preferences were undoubtedly with the golden days of the Roman Republic, the free community of law-givers and farmers abiding by the dictates of Nature, the "guide of life." Three years before his death Vives published his *Bucolicarum Virgilii interpretatio,* a much more mature work which proves his constant admiration for the author of the *Aeneid.*[69] Although we do not have any explicit testimony of a personal influence of Baarland upon Vives during these years, the editions of Vergil, published at that time by the Latin professor in the Trilingue, increased Vives' interest in Vergilian studies.

The second prelection, *Praefatio et Vigilia in Somnium Scipionis* (1520), will be studied together with the other philosophical works of this epoch. The others are of minor importance, except for their value in illustrating Vives' teaching in those years. They are three: *Praelectio in Convivia Francisci Philelphi* (1521), and two more already in 1522, *Praelectio in quartum Rhetoricorum ad Herennium* and *In Suetonium quaedam.*[70]

---

[67] M, II, 71-83; R, I, 543-53. (*In Georgica Vergilii*)

[68] The interest in refined Literature, both Latin and Greek, was a proud tradition of the Louvain Pedagogies, which since 1478 were endowed with a lecture of Poetica by the Archduke Maximilian. Martin van Dorp opened new ways by concentrating his attention on the explanation of literary models, selected sometimes with a rather liberal spirit. Thus, e.g., in February 1514, he produced with his students the *Aulularia* of Plautus, and in September of that year his pupils acted in the Porc the *Hecuba* of Euripides in Erasmus' translation. See De Vocht, *History Foundation,* p. 217.

In *EE.,* IV, 1192, vv. 8-83, Erasmus rejoices at the progress of a disciple of Goclenius who was now ready to read Homer in Greek. Josse Vroeye was a specialist in the syntaxis of Homer's language. See De Vocht, *History Foundation,* p. 223.

[69] Although Baarland began with Plautus, soon his more severe taste inclined him to Terence, Aesopus and Pliny, whose letters he edited in April, 1516. In Baarland's lectures Virgil claimed a very special position (De Vocht, *History Foundation,* p. 268).

[70] M, II, 83-87, 87-89; R, I, 855-859, 859-863. (*Praelectio in convivio Philelphi, In quattuor Rhetoricorum ad Herennium*)

It is no easy matter to reconstruct Vives' teaching experience in the Netherlands. The first five years in Bruges (1512-17) were probably dedicated to private lessons and to more advanced studies, very much as today's graduate students alternate teaching and seminars. Besides the Valdaura children, history has kept the names of two illustrious pupils of Vives in Bruges. The first was J. Martinez Poblacion, the future physician to the court of Francis I, whose books on mathematics are highly praised by Vives.[71] The second was the son of a distinguished Bruges family, James de la Potterie, who in 1514 moved to the University of Louvain.[72] It was through him that Vives obtained the latest publications of Baarland and heard first-hand reports about the academic life of the Brabant University.

The first months in Louvain (1517) were probably exclusively dedicated to William of Croy. Vives' reputation as a preceptor spread so fast that in March, 1519, Erasmus suggested Vives' name instead of his own to supervise the studies of Prince Ferdinand. After the customary eulogy of his protegé, Erasmus writes:

> To all these talents add that, as a native Spaniard, Vives speaks perfect Spanish and, because of his long stay in Paris, beautiful French too. He understands our language better than he can speak it. I do not know, however, whether Cardinal Croy will agree to give up such a man; I know he loves him with the great affection he deserves; nor do I know whether Vives himself is willing to detach himself from so great a patron . . .[73]

Apparently Erasmus' fears were well justified. In spite of Erasmus' pressure on Croy, the plan never worked out.[74] It is true that Ferdinand wished to have no other than Erasmus himself and that he was slightly irritated by Erasmus' refusal to undertake a job which, according to people of great influence, was worth considering.[75] In an interpolation to the *Christi Jesu Trimphus,* Vives himself expressed the wish that Erasmus would accept the job.[76]

---

[71] M, V, 405; R, II, 256 b. (*De Pac,* dedication). Also, M, VI, 372; R, II, 634 a. (DD., IV, 5). See also, *EE.,* IV, 1108, vv. 28-30, and note 28, p. 271.

[72] *LC.,* introd. to 2333; De Vocht, *History Foundation,* p. 228.

[73] *EE.,* III, 917, vv. 35-45. "Ad huius dotes et illud accedit, quod et Hispanice callet, utpote natus Hispanus, et Gallice perbelle, ut qui Lutetiae sit diutule versatus. Nostrum sermonem magis intelligit quam sonat. Verum haud scio, primum an Card. Croius, cui praeceptor est, passurus sit hominem a se divelli – diligit enim eum, ita ut meretur, effussissime; postremo nondum habeo compertum an Vives ipse sustineat avelli a tanto patrono . . ."

[74] *EE.,* III, 927.

[75] *Ibid.,* III, 952, vv. 61-62; 943; 940.

[76] M, VII, 130; R, I, 275 b. "Utinam frater eius Ferdinandus Erasmum Roterodamum amicum meum probatissimum et eruditissimum virum nacisceretur . . ." (*C. J. Triumphus*)

Another clear proof of Vives' success in the intellectual education of Croy is the fact that, after his death, the younger brother Robert, also Bishop of Cambrai, asked Vives to give him at least some private lessons, a job which Vives had to share with Latomus.[77]

Besides his duties as a preceptor, Vives seems to have found some time in Louvain for private lectures in Latin poetry and rhetoric. He was particularly popular among Spanish and English students. Until 1559, when Philip II forbade Spanish youth to attend foreign universities, the number of Spanish students abroad was truly impressive. Mayans gives the names of three of those students: Honoratio Juan, Diego Gracian de Alderete, and Peter Maluenda.[78] The presence in Louvain of a considerable number of English students proved to be a meaningful fact in the life of our Humanist.[79] Of the local students, two deserve special mention: Antonius Berges, to whom Vives dedicated the *Fabula de Homine*, and Jerome Ruffald, an excellent friend of Erasmus whom Vives praised on different occasions.[80]

From the beginning of his stay in Louvain Vives tried hard to obtain from the University permission to give public lectures. In spite of his close association with Cardinal Croy, such permission was not obtained until March, 1520, as a very special reward for the role Vives played in the negotiations leading to the acceptance of the Trilingue College.[81] The reasons for the long delay were numerous and complicated. Academic appointments in Brabant were attached to ecclesiastical endowments which civil magistrates were eager to keep in the hands of local people; regulations excluded from the *licentia docendi* anyone who was not matriculated into the University. The theologians were inclined to veto the official recognition of the foreign Humanists who, attracted by the dubious reputation of Erasmus, were flocking into Louvain in excessive numbers. To make things worse, probably Vives was not author-

---

[77] *LC.*, 33, vv. 1-3; introd. to 46.

[78] M., I, 33 (*Vivis Vita*).

[79] Louvain enjoyed a great prestige in England throughout the fifteenth century and the first decades of the sixteenth century. Erasmus' close association with Cambridge brought the two institutions close together. English and Flemish Humanists formed a very intimate circle of friends. In the fall of 1508 Thomas More visited Louvain to study its programs and methods: "Dedi operam quae in utraque [Paris and Louvain Universities] tradantur quisque sit utrobique tractandus modus, ut scirem." Cited by Germain March' Hadour, *L'Univers de Thomas More* (Paris, 1963), p. 157.

[80] M, VI, 438; R, II, 530. (*DD.*, II, 1, 2)

[81] According to De Vocht (*LC.*, introd. to letter 2, p. 5) Vives never followed a regular training in order to obtain a degree. His name is totally missing from the *Liber III Institutorum 1485-1527*. The *Chartularium* does not mention the name of Vives. Furthermore, the early editions of Vives' books do not add to his name any title or degree.

ized to teach by any academic degree.[82] In the preface to the *Declamationes Syllanae,* Vives bitterly complains against the stiff bureaucracy and the narrow-minded traditions of the Brabant University.

Vives' first experience as a member of the professorate was rather humorous. In a letter to Cranevelt, Vives tells the story:

> I asked permission to lecture on the *Somnium Scipionis.* When the rector of the University and the other officials heard the word *somnium* (sleep, dream), they burst into laughter. I am sure they were delighted with the mention of "sleep," an occupation to which they are enthusiastically dedicated. With a little irony they asked me to which faculty did the *Somnium* belong . . .[83]

The incident, however, was also seriously disappointing since the *Somnium,* as we shall see in chapter seven, was one of Vives' favorite books for which he had written a prelection clearly intended for the Louvain students. The public lectures in Paris during his visit of 1520 (see chapter seven) was little compensation for the fiasco of Louvain.

In spite of this irksome incident, Vives became more and more absorbed into the life of the University. In October, 1521, Erasmus mentions Vives' name among the teachers of the Castle Pedagogy, although he adds that, in his own opinion, Vives "seems to hate this place." [84] This last remark reflects not only Vives' difficulties in adapting to a full-time academic job, but also Erasmus' own irration against the malevolence he himself was experiencing at that time. In January, 1522, Vives reported to Cranevelt that he was teaching mornings in the University Halls, the subject being probably the *Epistolae Plinii*; and, in the afternoon, he was giving private lessons on the *Georgics* of Vergil. Other subjects taught by Vives either publicly or privately were Suetonius, the *Chorographia* of Pomponius Mela, Cicero's *De Senectute* and *De Lege,* his own *Christi Jesu Triumphus,* and probably Hyginius, Herenius, and Filelfo.[85] Vives' private teaching took place in a building which he

---

[82] M, II, 322; R, I, 708. (*Declamationes Syllanae*)

[83] *LC.,* 2, vv. 1-11. Vives' encounter with the conservative administration was characteristic of the institution. In March, 1519, the same officials had forbidden Alard of Amsterdam to lecture on a book of Erasmus (*LC.,* introd. to 2; also, De Jongh, *L'Ancienne Faculté,* p. 12). In November of the same year William Nesen was ordered to interrupt his lessons on Pomponius Mela (*EE.,* IV, 1046, 1057), an incident in which, according to Erasmus (*EE.,* IV, 1111, v. 54) Vives himself became somehow involved. As late as March, 1526, the University of Louvain forbade Rescius to read the *Institutiones Imperiales* of Justinian.

[84] *EE.,* IV, 590, v. 87. In this letter Erasmus calls Vives "vir undequaque doctissimus."

[85] The selection of Pomponius Mela might very well have been recommended to Vives by Erasmus, who was extremely irritated by the incident of Nesen. *Letters and*

describes in some detail in the dialogue *Deambulatio Matutina*.[86] The
number and the eager dedication of his students were to him a constant
source of joy, even in the middle of the disgraces which began to accumulate after the accidental death of Cardinal Croy in January,
1521.[87]

The last two years in Louvain (1521-23) were critical in the life of the
Spanish Humanist. Two important aspects of this crisis will be considered
elsewhere. The first was the progress of the anti-Erasmian movement in
Louvain and the beginning of the Counter-Reformation in the Netherlands (see chapter seven). The second was Vives' hectic attempt to establish solid contact with the Court of Henry VIII as a possible alterna-
tive for his future (see chapter five).

The intensification of Vives own problems went hand in hand with an
alarming deterioration of the political and religious conditions of Europe.
Although, for a while at least, the concurrence of both his personal and
the international calamities threatened to shatter Vives' moral and intellectual stamina, the final solution to the crisis proved the generous
and noble features of his character. "Who can be so selfish" he wrote to
Cranevelt "as to remember his own personal problems in the face of
such public disasters?" [88] And to Erasmus:

> When I was young I used to run after fame and reputation. Now, how-
> ever, I understand that all is vanity and emptiness and that those who
> reach it are foolish themselves. The only thing I value at the present is to
> be able to do something for my fellow men.[89]

The important result of such an attitude was a shift in Vives' intellectual
concern and interest. Literary and pious works, of the kind we have
considered so far, clearly yielded the palm to essays on educational and
political matters, a tendency which Vives' future contact with English
Humanism strongly reinforced.

The first trouble of Vives after the shocking news of Croy's death was
a long sickness which forced him to seek the help of his countrymen in
Bruges from February to June, 1521. Still, in July Vives wrote to
Erasmus:

Papers of Henry VIII, ed., J. S. Brewer (London, 1862), III, 2052, contains a letter
from one of Vives' auditors in the lecture on Pomponius Mela.
    [86] M, I, 323-330; R, II, 912-17. (*Isocrates*)
    [87] Croy died from a horse fall while hunting. He was twenty-three years old.
In a letter to Budé, Erasmus sadly commented: "periit velut flosculus tener in ipso
exortu succissus" (*EE.,* IV, 1184, v. 4).
    [88] *LC.* 48, vv. 44-45.
    [89] *EE.,* V, 1362, vv. 48-51.

Seeing that I would never recover my health in Antwerp, I decided to go to Bruges for one week or two; in fact I spent there more than six weeks, such was the stubbornness of this disease. Now I feel better although not yet entirely normal.[90]

By this time Vives was already intensively working on the commentaries to Augustine's *Civitas Dei*, a book which, as we shall see, demanded an exhaustive effort and seriously threatened his friendly relations with Erasmus. On the international scene the year was an ominous one. In April the Diet of Worms failed to achieve the reconciliation of Luther; in August Belgrad fell to the Turks; in November France was invaded by English troops as the result of the alliance between Henry VIII and Charles V; Pope Leo X died in December.

Financial difficulties began now to haunt Vives. Although in July, 1521 – thanks to Thomas More's personal intervention – Vives was endowed by Queen Catherine with a small pension, his correspondence with Cranevelt and Erasmus betrays a serious concern with the material support of his life.[91] In August, 1522, Fadrique de Toledo, the second Duke of Alba and a very important official in the court of the Emperor, planned to trust to Vives the education of his two grandsons, Bernardino and Fernando, the future scourge of the Netherlands under Philip II. Unfortunately, the Dominican friar who was supposed to bring to Vives Alba's letter decided to keep the message for himself. Alba, probably offended with Vives' inculpable silence and lack of response, appointed another friar to the handsomely-paid job. Vives wrote to Erasmus:

See what we have to suffer from our Brethren! What can we expect from strangers? These friars are not satisfied with assaulting our ideas; now they also covet our money. Only God can punish them as they deserve . . .[92]

Vives' correspondence with Cranevelt and Erasmus becomes day by day more bitter and desperate. The war, his own health conditions, the tense relations with Erasmus, the senseless and endless altercations of the Louvain academicians, everything concurred to torture his soul.

---

[90] *EE.*, IV, 1222, v. 13.

[91] Vives reports to Erasmus that he is being supported by the generosity of the Queen. See *EE.*, IV, 1222, v. 17: "Pecunia Reginae [Catherine] me huc usque alui et alo." According to Vives himself (M, II, 484; R, I, 839 a, *Declamatio pro noverca*), the favor was due to Thomas More's mediation with the Queen. See also M, I, 40 (*Vivis Vita*).

[92] *EE.*, V, 1271, vv. 129-160. The Dominicans were also attacking Vives' Commentaries on Saint Augustine's *De Civitate Dei*. (See below, p. 131). On Fadrique and the Albas, see Brewer, *Letters and Papers*, IV, 3151; also *EE.*, V, 1256, note 32.

I have not been able to sleep for three days . . . I am afraid that if this goes on something much worse is going to happen . . .[93]

I wish God granted mankind to wage war in such a way that all sides involved could only experience material losses, no loss of blood, life, honesty, religion, and justice.[94]

Everything here in Louvain remains the same, dirty, stupid, and intolerable. There is something about this city that I simply hate and always did. Nowhere in the whole world do I feel more miserable than here.[95]

My health is now worse than ever. My whole body is about to collapse. The uncleanliness and the misery of this place is going to kill me.

I am totally benumbed by these crazy wars. Let all these soldiers go mad: someday they themselves will get fed up with it. Where is the gospel of Christ? Where are the theologians now? Where are the priests? . . .[96]

To Erasmus:

My nerves are about to break down. I feel as if three huge towers were leaning against my head. Are these the rewards of my honest efforts?

The school bores me to death. I shall do anything rather than go back to those dirty kids.[97]

Three months later, however, Vives admits to Cranevelt that he is pleased with the number and quality of his students.[98] The fluctuation of Vives' comments is a clear indication of his emotional crisis. The last weeks of 1522 brought to a climax Vives' predicament and the European emergency. In December, Rhodes fell to the Turks; in January of 1523 the news reached Louvain spreading panic all over. Vives himself was stunned by the report.[99] In spite of the appeals of the new Pope, Adrian VI, the nervous reaction of the Christian princes failed to materialize into a defensive coalition. The medieval concept of a united Christendom was inoperative and dead. A new order of things was in the making.

In the last gloomy weeks of December, 1522, Vives was struck by the rumor first, and then by the tragic news of his father's trial with the Spanish Inquisition. In a letter to Cranevelt dated December, 1522,

---

[93] *LC.*, 6, vv. 42-44.
[94] *LC.*, 6, vv. 30-36.
[95] *LC.*, 8, vv. 31-35. "Peregrinatio mea non tam mihi molesta fuit quam Lovaniensis mansio ubi semper omnia mihi videntur sui similia, id est, sordida, insania, et prorsus inamabalia; indubie genus huius urbis genio meo est inimicissimus; nusquam sum illibentius; nescio qui fit ut numquam mihi arriserit."
[96] *LC.*, 13, vv. 54-56, 73-80. Most of the last part of this letter is in Greek.
[97] *EE.*, V, 1306, vv. 8-11, 42-46. ". . . quam ad has redire sordes et inter pueros versari."
[98] *LC.*, 23, v. 5. "Delector tanta frequentia auditorum et tanta alacritate."
[99] On the reaction of Louvain to the news of Rhodes, see *LC.*, 37, v. 12. On Vives' own response, *LC.*, 45, vv. 13-17, and especially note 17. See also Brewer, *Letters and Papers.*

Vives uses for the first time the Latin word *Fortuna* to signify with certain caution the inexorable power of the Holy Tribunal: "It is true that when *Fortuna* hurts us it always begins with our most dear ones." [100] The correspondence of the following months repeats the tragic word with painful insistence. In January, 1523, Vives wrote to Cranevelt:

I am terribly sorry I missed you in Bruges; your company and conversation could have been of such help to me.

Last week I heard that my younger brother died; but this news was not the worst. My father seems to be involved in a most hateful trial which threatens all our family possessions . . . I still have three sisters, now orphans and destitute. Why should I always complain? Why can I never send to you some good news about me? I am more and more concerned with such news; there is nothing I can decide about my future since all my life hangs from what happens in Spain. I do not know whether it is prudent to go or to stay here. Do they need me? *Fortuna* could have never made anybody unhappier than me. This is what we deserve for our philosophical endeavors: *Fortuna*, cruel and pitiless, directs all its power against us . . .[101]

At the end of January, 1523, Vives left Louvain for Antwerp; perhaps his intention was to get some information of a possible passage to Spain by ship, a trip which the buccaneers of Francis I could make rather risky for a vessel of Castile. He returned to Louvain where he stayed ten days. From there he went to Bruges in the second week of February. He needed the comfort of his intimate friends, the familiar sound of the Valdaura family, Jews and Valencians like himself. He was bewildered and confused. In a rather mysterious turn of phrase Vives writes to Cranevelt:

I found my friends in Bruges in good health and without any problem, a needed compensation for my horrible journey [from Louvain to Bruges]. They are so peaceful and tranquil! I am going to try to do the same. I would like to make peace with *Fortuna* at any price as long as I do not act against virtue because I see that without either one, or with both rather, it is impossible in our times to reach the smile of Democritus. Oh! The power of *Fortuna* upon us, baptized Christians, no matter how hard Christ tried to free us from it! But speak and they will call you a heretic . . .[102]

---

[100] *LC.*, 30, vv. 7-8. "Plane verum est Fortunam laedendo nostra charissima quaeque impetere prima."

[101] *LC.*, 32, vv. 13-18, 24-29.

[102] *LC.*, 45, vv. 5-16. "Amicos offendimus incolumes et laetos, quod nobis superiorem itineris molestiam compensavit. O felices quietos! Mihi certum est dare operam ut quiescam! Cum Fortuna vellem in gratiam redire quibuscumque condicionibus, modo ne contra Aretem, quandoquidem video sine utraque illarum, seu ambabus potius (ut nunc sunt mores et tempora) ἀδύνατον συμβῆναι τὴν εὐθυμίαν

Vives had three choices: to stay in the relative safety of the Nether-lands, to go back to Spain, or to seek refuge in the court of Henry VIII. Although he felt an extreme reluctance to return to Valencia, the ex-treme need of his sisters imposed upon him a tremendous responsibility he could not ignore. Ironically enough, while his father was being tried by the Inquisition of Aragon, the University of Alcalá in Castile was extending an invitation to Vives to accept the chair of Humanities left open by the death of Nebrija.[103] Alcalá's offer – extremely flattering to anybody else in other circumstances – only increased Vives' moral torture.

In March, 1523, he wrote to Cranevelt:

I do not know yet what I shall do. I hate to go back home, but to stay here is not possible. Now they are calling me; recently I had another letter [from my sisters]. The expenses of the journey are intolerable; the danger terrifies me.[104]

Two days later, 17th of March, 1523, Vives wrote to Cranevelt the gloomiest page which ever came from his pen:

When I wrote about my friends that "they are so peaceful and tranquil," of course I wanted to include you among them ... You have such a beauti-ful occupation as a lawyer with something new and interesting day after day ... You have also time for your wife, your children, your household, to take care of them and to be taken care of by them ... We on the contrary, weary and sick, caught in the middle of a summer storm, overcome by nausea and terror, wander from here to there trying desperately to stick to something, still unwilling to accept the fact that yesterday's safety and stability are gone forever...[105]

The 10th of May, 1523, Vives wrote two letters; one to Cranevelt, the other to Erasmus. In both he announced his projected trip to Spain via

ἐκείνην τὴν τοῦ Δημοκρίτου. O magnum Fortunae in nos regnum (pudet dicere) homines sacris Christi initiatos, quum nihil magis curarit Christus, quam ut nobis esset cum illa negocii quam minimum! Ἀλλα μένψαι καὶ, κληθήσει ἐρετικος."
[103] Bonilla, Luis Vives, I, 167. The text of Vergara's letter can be read in Revue Hispanique, VIII (1901), 247, 260.
[104] LC., 47, vv. 3-6. "Incertus quid mihi faciendum. Redire in patriam non libet; manere hic non licet. Nam illuc revocor: nuper denuo per litteras. Attamen me retrahunt sumptus; deterret periculum!"
[105] LC., 48, vv. 4-26. "Quod exclamavi 'O felices quietos' horsum spectat ad beatos istos; ad te quoque non parum ... Alit vos exercitatio forensis pulcherrima, vel potius varietas illa spectaculi quottidie aliquid objiciens novum et admirandum ... licet officia uxori, liberis et familiae dare et ab iis illa exigere ... Nos vero interdum altissimo veterno marcidi languentes, quasi in aestiva tranquillitate tempestate coorta, incauti et improvidi deprehensi, coepimus evomere, nauseare, haerere ad singula, concursare hac et illa, multum queri, nimium affligi ..."

England. In both he made absolutely clear that he had arrived at that decision with enormous reluctance, after a prolonged delay, and only because the journey was his inexorable duty. Two days later Vives landed in England in a miserable state of mind: "everything is just darkness and night around me. I intend to retire into an innocent silence," he wrote to Erasmus on the eve of his journey.[106]

Fortunately, the future was full of surprises. The Spanish trip never took place, and England offered to Juan Luis Vives the unique opportunity of his life.

[106] *LC.,* 56, vv. 14-16; *EE.,* V, 1362, v. 103.

CHAPTER 5

VIVES IN ENGLAND (1523–1528)

On November 11, 1523, six months after his departure from Bruges, Vives wrote Cranevelt an enthusiastic letter about his promotion to one of the readerships at Oxford University.[1] The long document does not contain a single reference to Vives' projected trip to Valencia, nor any expression of concern about his father's destiny in the hands of the Spanish Inquisitors. The sharp contrast between the spirited animation of this letter and the bitter pessimism of Vives' correspondence before his arrival in England clearly indicates that in those six months the life of Vives had taken entirely new perspectives. What had happened was that Vives' most cherished aspiration had finally been fulfilled: now he was able to live and work in the kingdom of Henry VIII and Catherine of Aragon. Overwhelmed by the joy of this event Vives found it easy to drop his planned visit to Spain, a visit he terribly feared. Probably a well-intentioned but vague promise of mediation with the Spanish authorities by Catherine or Wolsey helped Vives to get rid of any scruples. Besides, the traditionally long trials of the Spanish Tribunal – Luis Vives' case took more than two years! – allowed Vives a few months of uncertain hope which he probably tried to keep alive to excuse himself from squarely facing the cruel reality. There was no doubt some weakness in the final decision, a weakness, however, which is difficult to condemn. Vives was intelligent enough to know the endless capacity of the Spanish Inquisition to swallow potential heroes into barren anonymity. And he preferred to live. England was there.

Vives' admiration for England was, first of all, the result of its close association with Flanders and Brabant. Geographically speaking, Flanders is the continent's balcony to the English channel; Bruges is only ten

---

[1] *LC.*, 80, vv. 28-30. "Itaque ex gratulatione tua, mi Craneveldi, nihil equidem legi libentius, licet omnia libentissime, quam Regis et Reginae laudes." This letter is evidently Vives' reply to the congratulation of Cranevelt for the happy turn of events in England.

miles from Ostende and fifty miles away from Calais, the continental
counterpart to Dover. Politically, the Netherlands and England, Charles
V and Henry VIII, were at that time close allies against the French
monarchy. In 1523, once again, from West Flanders and the Artois one
could almost see the banners of Suffolk's army marching south toward
Boulogne en route to the French capital.[2] Economic and trade relations
between the Netherlands and England were probably the most intense in
Europe. In fact, Thomas More was commissioned several times by
Henry VIII to mediate in the disputes between English traders and the
officials of the Hanseatic staple in Bruges.[3]

More significant to us was the exceptional partnership of English and
Flemish scholars, a partnership which could boast the boundless erudition of Erasmus of Rotterdam and the personal charm of the future
Chancellor of England, Thomas More. We shall have to emphasize the
extent of the Erasmian influence upon Tudor Humanism and the Henrician establishment in the second part of this book. Here it must be
remembered that Erasmus' love for England outlived all his terrible disappointments. Probably Vives heard from Erasmus himself the warm
praise of such people as Thomas More, John Fisher, Cuthbert Tunstall,
and Lord Mountjoy, all of whom eventually became his own personal
friends. One of the concrete results of this cultural alliance was the invasion of the University of Louvain by English students. History has
kept the names of some of Vives' English pupils in Louvain. Among
them were Giles Wallop who became a priest and whose brother John
was an attendant to Queen Catherine;[4] Nicolas Wotton, whom Vives
mentions in the essay *Veritas Fucata*;[5] Maurice Birchinshaw, an Oxford
teacher of grammar;[6] William Thale, a companion to Richard Pace's

---

[2] Adams, *Better Part of Valor*, pp. 218-219.

[3] Thomas More had the ideal qualities of an arbitrator. Already as an under-
sheriff of the City of London in 1510, he was a frequent royal appointee to mediation teams. (Marc-Hadour, *L'Univers de Thomas More*, pp. 171, 197, 199).
More visited Bruges in 1515 as a member of a royal commercial mission to which
also Tunstall belonged. In the summer of 1517, More was in Flanders once again
for the same purpose.

[4] In all the details of Vives' relations with England I am greatly indebted to
De Vocht's "Vives and his Visits to England."
    In January, 1524, Vives met Giles' brother, John, in the Court of Henry VIII.
At John's request, Vives wrote a long letter to his former student, who, at that
time was considering the priestly vocation. (M, VII, 208-210; R, 1724 b-1727 a).

[5] M, II, 530-531; R, II, 893 a. (*ELL.*, VI). Nicolas Wotton became afterwards
one of Tunstall's officials, dean of Canterbury and York, Secretary of State, and
finally, ambassador of Mary to Hungary's Court.

[6] His name appears frequently in Erasmus' letters to Vives. (*EE.*, V, 1526, v.
90, v. 121; 1303, vv. 48-50).

mission to Italy;[7] Richard Warham, a relative to the famous Archbishop of Canterbury;[8] Nicolas Daryngton who back in Cambridge became an enthusiastic propagandist of Vives;[9] and finally, the well-
known physician John Clement who stayed several months with Vives in
Louvain.[10] Vives' early publications and the enthusiastic endorsement of
Erasmus made him known in England long before he began planning
to settle there. In March, 1520, Erasmus' introduction to Vives' *Declamationes Syllanae* encouraged Thomas More to read the books of Vives
brought to him by Baarland from Louvain. In May of the same year
More wrote to Erasmus:

Although I enjoyed all of his writings, nevertheless his treatise *In Pseudo-
dialecticos* gives me an especial pleasure. Not only because of Vives' skill in
making a mockery of such absurd fallacies and in confuting the sophists
with devastating reasoning, but particularly because he deals with those
questions in exactly the same fashion I had in mind to do myself long
before I ever read the book of Vives.... Considering Vives' youth, style,
fertility, and depth of thought, I feel ashamed of myself trying so hard to sell
one or two silly booklets of my own ... It is indeed quite an achievement to
master either Latin or Greek; Vives is good in both of them ... Who teaches
better, more efficiently, or more charmingly than Vives?

There is only one thing, my dear Erasmus, I would tell Vives if I knew
that he was ready to take some advice from a stranger. You better tell him
that some passages of the *Aedes legum* and the *Somnium Scipionis* are
rather unintelligible, except to a small group of scholars. Maybe a little
explanation or a footnote here and there will make these books easier to a
larger number of readers ...[11]

Erasmus replied right away:

I am delighted to see that your opinion of Vives coincides with mine.
Vives is one of those who in time will overshadow Erasmus' name. I do not
feel the same toward other people. I even love you more just because you
like him too. Vives is a powerful philosophical mind ...[12]

[7] Thale was an elder student at Louvain where he matriculated following Erasmus'
recommendation. (*EE.*, IV, 1224, v. 11; see also, *EE.*, V, 1526, v. 90; 1303, v. 51).
Thale and Erasmus studied together in Ferrara.
[8] Warham was also encouraged by Erasmus to take the classes of Vives. (*EE.*, V,
1256, vv. 90-91).
[9] Brewer, *Letters and Papers*, III, 2052.
[10] *EE.*, V, 1256, v. 122; 1271, v. 115. See also *LC.*, introd. to letter 154, c.
[11] *EE.*, IV, 1106, vv. 20-108. History has decidedly shown More's modesty in
this letter. Among his "silly booklets" (*uno aut altero libellulo, eoque fere inepto*)
was the *Utopia*, a book which has obviously overshadowed any of Vives' books.
[12] *EE.*, IV, 1107, vv. 6-13. "De Ludovici Vives ingenio gaudeo meum calculum
cum tuo consentire. Is unus est de numero eorum qui nomen Erasmi sint obscuraturi."

About this time, the spring of 1520, More became involved in an unpleasant quarrel with the French Humanist Brixius. In the middle of that storm, "the beginning of sorrows," (Chambers) More found comfort in repeating the names of all the great European scholars with whom he felt in complete accord. Among them were Juan Luis Vives and, surprisingly enough, Ulrich von Hutten.[13]

In the summer of the same year, French and English nobility, Church dignitaries, and Royal courtiers surrounded Henry VIII and Francis I at their historical meeting near Calais, at the Field of the Cloth of Gold. The medieval pageantry of that hypocritical display of chivalry hardly concealed the games of Wolsey. The meeting of the English and the French Monarchs was preceded and followed by the intrigues and the secret alliance of Henry VIII and Charles V directed against France. Hardly had the meeting of the English and the French concluded when English, Spanish, and Flemish officials began to fraternize in Calais, Bruges, and Louvain. Thomas More, already a member of the King's Council, remained in Flanders a few weeks to lead the conversations with the merchants of the Hanse. Erasmus arrived in Bruges with the train of the Emperor. From Spain came Juan de Vergara and Fernando de Valdés to hold preliminary conversations with William of Croy, the patron of Vives and Archbishop-elect of Toledo.[14] Charles V was in Bruges from July 25 to 29. It was then, or immediately after, that Erasmus introduced to Thomas More a selected group of his Flemish friends, among them Goclenius, Cranevelt, and Juan Luis Vives.[15] The eulogy of Thomas More in Vives' commentaries on Saint Augustine's *Civitas Dei* speaks loudly for the instant friendship and admiration between both Christian Humanists. As More wrote about his friendship for Vives, it was as if "a common star would link our souls with a secret power." [16]

More's loyalty to Vives was tested much sooner than expected. After Croy's death in January, 1521, Vives, pressed by financial difficulties, called upon More's help to obtain a royal pension from Queen Cathe-

---

Nec aliis tamen aeque faveo, et te hoc nomine magis amo, quod huic tam candide faves. Est animo mire philosophico."

[13] See the details of the Brixius' dispute in Chambers, *Thomas More,* pp. 190-191. More mentions Vives (and Hutten) among his supporters in a letter to Erasmus. (*EE.,* IV, 1087, vv. 354-355).

[14] Bataillon, *Erasmo y España,* pp. 101-102.

[15] Cranevelt thanked Erasmus for having been introduced to Thomas More. (*EE.,* IV, 1145, vv. 5-7). It is almost certain that Vives was also there, because from this date on both Erasmus and Vives wrote about each other or to each other in very personal terms.

[16] *EE.,* IV, 1129; also, *ibid.,* introd. to letter 1130.

rine. In May, More was appointed Under-Treasurer of the Kingdom; in July, Vives reported to Erasmus that he had been taken under the protection of the Queen.[17] In the same year Vives wrote in the introduction to the *Declamatio pro noverca*: "I have received so much from his [More's] generosity that I am afraid people will say I am a better mercenary than a friend." And he goes on to praise More as a man "who was born to respect and cultivate friendship and to help his friends in trouble." [18]

The generosity of Catherine and the powerful friendship of Thomas More were no doubt the immediate reasons for Vives' initial desire to settle down in England. From his English patrons Vives expected no less than a secure and constant income which would allow him a life totally dedicated to study. In July, 1521, he candidly confessed to Erasmus that such was the favor he was expecting to obtain from More's planned visit to Bruges in August.[19] This time, however, Vives was bitterly disappointed.[20] He decided then to try a different strategy. On July 7, 1522, he dedicated to Henry VIII his commentaries on Saint Augustine's *Civitas Dei*. After More's visit to Bruges he even planned to take the book personally to the King and to stay in England for two or three months.[21] He asked Erasmus for a letter of recommendation to Bishop Fisher, a letter which unfortunately did not reach Belgium until the middle of September. Vives' book was not out in print until the end of that month. His plans were ruined and the trip to England was canceled.[22] But he never gave up his hopes. In April, 1523, he resolved to appeal to the kindness of his own countrywoman, Queen Catherine, and he dedicated to her his important treatise *De Institutione Feminae Christianae*.[23] After that, events ran out of control: the terrible news from Spain, the projected trip to Valencia, the confusion and desperation of the last weeks in Louvain, and finally, the crossing of the channel on

---

[17] *EE.*, IV, 1222, v. 17: "Pecunia Reginae me hucusque alui et alo."

[18] M, II, 484; R, I, 839 a: "Is tantus amicus, cuius ego benevolentiae tot fructus percepi ut metuam ne cui credar amicitiam colere mercenariam."

[19] *EE.*, IV, 1222, v. 17: "Moro scripsi me prolixe collocuturm cum eo cum venerit. Suspicari potest quid velim, sed non aperte quicquam, quum nollem te inconsulto ..."

[20] It seems that the only result of that interview was Vives' promise to More to write Quintilian's answer to *Paries Palmatus*, a rhetorical exercise which More seemed to have particularly enjoyed. (M, II, 472-500; R, I, 839-855).

[21] *EE.*, V, 1306, vv. 37-44. Letter from Vives to Erasmus. "Proximo mense cogito in Britanniam transmittere."

[22] Some biographers, however, still believe that Vives visited England for the first time in September, 1522. See *EE.*, III, introd. to letter 927; *ibid.*, V, introd. to letter 1362. Also Sandys, *A History of Classical Scholarship*, II, 214. De Vocht, "Visits to England," pp. 3-4, convincingly refutes such an opinion.

[23] M. IV, 65-70; R, II, 985-989. (See also *EE.*, VII, 1847, vv. 20-25).

the 12th of May, 1523. Although that was not exactly the way he had planned it, at last Vives was in England.

The first impression of London was not very encouraging. England was at war with France, and the people of the realm were finding it increasingly expensive to pay for Wolsey's follies. The Parliament was summoned, Wolsey presiding for the last time. It was indeed an historical occasion. Wolsey was in the twilight of his power. Thomas More, the speaker of the House and a prisoner of his conscience, had to support taxation for a war he could not approve, while Cromwell raised for the first time his strong voice in the name of political expediency.

In the middle of such storm, Vives felt neglected and forgotten; he was, anyhow, in a terribly pessimistic mood. Through his letter to Christopher Miranda we can reconstruct in detail his early weeks in London. He was utterly bored "doing nothing all day long." The room was an "undersized den, without any desk and hardly a chair," besieged by the terrible noise of the inn and the city. The living quarters provided no space for something Vives considered essential for his health, a short walk after dinner. He was convinced that should he fall sick again he would be "thrown into a dungyard like a dirty and vicious dog." [24]

Soon, however, help came from where it was least expected. This time it was Wolsey, the Chancellor of England, who needed a teacher of Latin, Greek, and rhetoric to take Lupset's chair in his own foundation, the Cardinal College. It is true that Wolsey's first choice for the job was nobody less than Erasmus. In the summer of 1523, however, Vives' appointment to the readership appeared to Wolsey as indeed a wise political move. Charles V was Henry's ally against the French, and a Spanish Queen, Catherine of Aragon, was, for the time being, England's only hope for a male heir to the Tudor Crown. It is not impossible either that Lupset suggested Vives' name to take his place; at least he had a long conversation with Vives in Bruges on his way to Italy, shortly before Vives' departure from the Netherlands.[25] In July, Livinus Algoet brought from London to Bruges the rumor that Vives' condition in England had

[24] M, VII, 201, 202; R, II, 1721, 1722: "Habeo pro cubiculo gurgustiolum angustissimum in quo mensa est nulla, vis septem, septum utrinque aliis cubiculis, et frequentia strepentium, clamantiumque ... Ibi si coenatus sum, non deambulo in his angustiis, quis enim possem? ... Serviendum est valetudini, praesertim hic ubi si aegrotem, in stercorarium aliquod abjiciar; nec erit qui magis me respiciat, quam vilem aliquam et morbidam canem."
[25] EE., V, 1362, vv. 44-46. Letter from Vives to Erasmus. Thomas Lupset, an English Divine, (1498-1530) was a close friend of Erasmus and Linacre. After leaving England in 1523 he proceeded to Padua where he was Reginald Pole's tutor until 1525.

greatly improved.[26] In August, Vives had already been appointed to Wolsey's readership and was teaching in Richard Fox's institution, the Corpus Christi College, while the College of the Cardinal was being built.[27] At first Vives was delighted with an appointment which simply made possible his life in England and distracted his mind from the nightmares of the last weeks. Soon, however, the old mood of discontent and moaning took possession of him again. He was disgusted with the food and the climate of Oxford:

> The sky is full of clouds and storms, sad as it is gray; the food is just repulsive; the air full of diseases, some of them beyond any cure; the digestion here is slow, heavy, and painful . . . Just before I wrote this letter I had a terrible stomach ache . . .[28]

Again, the memory of his Flemish and Brabant friends filled him with a biting nostalgia: "How can I forget," he wrote to one of them, "the fatherland of my choice? Flanders and Brabant cling to the innermost recesses of my heart, and I live only with the hope of going back . . ." [29] Behind all these lamentations there was a more serious ground for dissatisfaction. The truth of the matter was that Vives' final ambition was to secure for himself a Royal pension rather than a teaching assignment. As Fevyn wrote to Cranevelt, "Vives was constantly expecting to be recalled to the Court by the King." [30] Grateful as he was to Wolsey, he took the first opportunity to make clear to the Cardinal how busy he was with his classes. In December, 1523, Vives dedicated to Wolsey a translation from Isocrates:

> Accept, please, these pages as a proof of sincere affection for all the favors I have received from you and will never forget. Take it also as a token for a future and more original work of mine. For the time being, distracted as I am with all the many duties of this public teaching at Oxford that you have imposed upon me, I was not able to create something of my own.[31]

Finally, in comparison with Louvain, Vives was rather disappointed with the academic life at Oxford. Fevyn reports Vives as saying that "there is

[26] *LC.*, 63, v. 23. Letter from Fevyn to Cranevelt.
[27] *LC.*, 71, vv. 25-31. Letter from Fevyn to Cranevelt. See also, Sandys, *History Classical Scholarship*, II, 214; P. S. Allen, "Vives at Corpus," *Pelican Record* (1902), 156 ff; *The Early Corpus Readerships* (Oxford, 1905), pp. 3-5.
[28] *LC.*, 80, vv. 10-21. Letter from Vives to Cranevelt.
[29] *Ibid.*, vv. 53-56.
[30] *LC.*, 71, vv. 25-30. Letter from Fevyn to Cranevelt. "De famulicio regio nihil, cum in hoc aspiraret hortari delectari Oxoniae cum musis; tamen non esse certum quanto tempore illuc detineri; sperare illinc a Rege avocari . . ."
[31] M, V, 2-3; R, I, 896 a. (*Isocrates,* introduction).

not much enthusiasm for study here." [32] To Giles Wallop Vives recommended staying in Louvain, "where you can learn much more than in England"; [33] and finally in a letter to Cranevelt Vives wrote that the climate of Oxford makes people "the laziest kind I have ever seen." [34] Was Vives' judgment fair and objective, or was it the result of his own pessimism?

In many respects Oxford was very similar to Paris and Louvain; the curriculum, the degrees, the textbooks, the faculties, and the basic orientation to an ecclesiastical career were common to all great medieval institutions. Oxford, however, from its very start had been more independent from ecclesiastical administration than either Paris or Louvain.[35] The initial guild of the Oxford masters was not the continuation of a monastic or cathedral school. The chancellor of the University was indeed an official of the Bishop of Lincoln, but the chancellorship was kept as a ceremonial and honorary position. Besides, Lincoln was a hundred and twenty miles away, too many for the Bishop to ride back and forth. In fact, the practical exemption of the University from episcopal control dangerously favored the expansion of Wyclifism in the first decades of the fifteenth century. Oxford was in many respects more English than Paris was French; the nations were abolished in the thirteenth century as a symbol of national unity. On the other hand, the predominance of the Faculty of Arts was stronger than in Paris or Louvain.

The most important characteristic of Oxford University in the century of Vives was no doubt the extent of collegiate teaching made possible by the endowment of professorships on the part of rich and influential patrons. It is highly significant that most of these endowments were made by men with humanistic preferences. It was an old tradition which started with Humphrey, Duke of Gloucester (1391-1447), after the visit to England of Poggio, Aeneas Sylvio Piccolomini, and Manuel Chrysoloras. In the last decade of the fifteenth century the generosity of Lady Margaret – the patroness of Fisher and Caxton and the foundress of Christ's College in Cambridge – made possible a large number of such endowments. About this time Grocyn, Latimer, and Linacre returned to England after their visit to Politian and Hermolao Barbaro in Italy. Clergy reformation and humanistic education converged in the great

[32] LC., 71, v. 31. Letter from Fevyn to Cranevelt. "Illic frigere nonnihil studia."
[33] M, VII, 210; R, II, 1326 b. (De VF., preface)
[34] LC., 90, vv. 124-125: "Tanta est socordia! Est desidiossissimum genus hominum! Quod non tam illis imputo quam genio loci."
[35] On the history of Oxford, see Rashdall, Medieval Universities, III, 1-123.

foundations of this century. Sir Richard Sutton and Bishop Smith founded the Brasenose College in Oxford (1509). Two years later John Fisher lay the foundation of Saint John's College in Cambridge; his action was paralleled in 1516 by Richard Fox in Oxford with the foundation of Corpus Christi College, where Vives was teaching until the completion of Cardinal College, founded by Wolsey in 1521. With these new centers of learning, Renaissance education was definitively secured in England.

We are especially interested in Corpus Christi College because of Vives' association with it.[36] Richard Fox (1448-1528) was Lord Privy Seal from 1485 to 1516.[37] His foundation was an Erasmian adaptation to England of the University of Alcalá. The curriculum was "the most radical departure from traditional studies yet seen in England" (McConica). In the humanities the textbooks were without exception favorites of Erasmus: the *Elegantiae* of Valla, Lucian, Isocrates, the *Noctes Atticae* of Aulo Gellio, Politian, and Thucydides. In theology, medieval authorities were replaced with Patristic sources: Jerome, Augustine, Origen, and Chrisostom. Cardinal College only imitated and enlarged the ideas and initiatives of Richard Fox's institution. We can therefore say without exaggeration that in the summer of 1523, Vives was teaching in one of the most Erasmian, progressive, and promising institutions of Renaissance England. Nevertheless, his lack of enthusiasm was well justified. By the time Vives arrived in England all the great humanists of the century had removed permanently from the university (either Oxford or Cambridge) to the city of London. Already in 1499, Grocyn, Latimer, and Linacre were in London where they met Erasmus.[38] Colet also made the break with Oxford in 1504 and rejoined the circle as Dean of Saint Paul's. Thomas More spent only two years in Oxford; the rest of his training was received in the Inns of Court of the city of London "where a young man of birth and ambition might at this date best be brought up" (Chambers). The three most revolutionary institutions of the century were founded in London by three friends of the Erasmian circle, the Doctors Common by Grocyn (among others) in 1509, the Saint Paul's School by Colet in 1510, and the College of Physicians by Linacre in 1518. Small wonder that Vives' dream was to become in time a scholar of Henry VIII's Court.

---

[36] On the significance of Corpus College, see McConica, *English Humanists*, pp. 80-83.

[37] See a short biography of Richard Foxe in *EE.*, I, introd. to letter 187, p. 146.

[38] The best illustration of Erasmus' first visit to England in 1499 is his own correspondence from Greenwich, Oxford, and London. (*EE.*, I, 104-118).

Vives' first series of lectures in Oxford lasted from August, 1523, to April, 1524. In spite of his initial unwillingness, his teaching was a complete success. The reception of the University was friendly and cordial. The president of the College, John Claymond, became and remained always a loyal and helpful friend.[39] Among his students were the most promising graduates of that generation: Nicolas Udall, Reginald Pole, Edward Wotton, Richard Pate, and John Heliares. Two of them, Richard Pate and Antony Barker, became so attached to Vives that they followed him to Bruges when Vives returned there in April of 1524.[40] Some of them, like John Heliares, constantly begged him to resume his lectures in Oxford in December, 1524.[41] In the middle of September the University wrote to Wolsey about Vives' excellent performance.[42] In October the King and the Queen broke a long tradition of the English Crown and entered the city of Oxford to pay a visit to Vives.[43] The historians of the day report the event with a charming feeling of admiration and disbelief: "protected by his good conscience, (Henry) dared to enter Oxford without suffering any evil, surrounded by the joy of his peoples." [44] Soon the legend was born that the Monarchs, a crowd of Courtiers, and the whole University converged into Vives' classroom to hear his lessons.[45] It is true, however, that not only Vives but the University itself felt extremely gratified by the Royal visit. The Corpus

---

[39] Vives mentions Claymond as one of his early friends in England in his first letter to Cranevelt from London (LC., 80, v. 5). After Vives' exile from Henry VIII's kingdom in 1528, Claymond was a helpful and loyal friend assisting the Spanish Humanist with regular financial help. (M, VII, 142, 204, 214; R, II, 1675 b, 1722 a, 1728 b). At that time Vives was so bitter that he even questioned the loyalty of Thomas More. (M, VII, 142; R, II, 1675 b, Letter to Pate).

[40] Richard Pate became ambassador to Spain in 1533 and bishop of Worcester in July, 1541. At Elizabeth's accession he was deprived of his dignities and sent into exile where he died in 1559. Vives mentions him as a good friend on several occasions. (M, II, 287, 303; VII, 141; R, II, 860 b; 1675 a; 873 a).

On Antony Baker, a friend of Pate, see De Vocht, "Visits," p. 11, note 3. In July, 1524, Vives sent to the Bishop of Lincoln, the uncle of Pate, a report on the academic performance of both friends. (M, V, 461-464. Riber omits these lines for no apparent reason).

[41] The letter was first published by De Vocht in "Visits," pp. 14-16 .

[42] Erasmus mentions this report in a letter to Goclenius. (EE., V, 1388, note 4).

[43] LC., 90, vv. 6-25 .Vives describes the royal visit to Cranevelt: "Quum hac fecisset iter Regina, venissetque una Rex ipse, ausus contemnere veterem superstitionem qua oppidum hoc reges vetabantur ingredi." What Vives here calls a "superstition" was an old legend about one of the Saxon reguli who was struck blind at the gates of the city when he was about to rape one of the local girls. (Polyodorus Vergilius, Anglicae Historiae libri XXVII, 2nd ed. [Basle, 1556], p. 90).

[44] Quoted from Vergilius by De Vocht, "Visits," p. 9, note 7. Vergilius was a close friend of Erasmus who, already in 1515, had serious problems with Wolsey. (EE., IV, introd. to letter 1175, p. 426).

[45] De Vocht, "Visits," p. 9, note 8. The legend was recorded by Brian Twyne in Antiquitatis Oxoniensis Apologia (Oxford, 1608), III, p. 328.

Christi College alone spent 28 shillings on gloves for the ladies and enter-tainment for the whole Royal cortege.[46] More relevant to Vives' future was the Royal invitation to spend the impending Christmas holidays at Court in the Windsor Palace. This was no doubt one of the happiest moments in the life of the scholar of Valencia. Vives was deeply con-vinced that he belonged in the Court rather than in the classroom. Not only because, as he candidly confessed, he enjoyed intensively the compa-ny of the powerful and the rich, but especially because of his sincere belief that the education of the Christian Princes was the first step to bring a better life to the people.[47] Precisely in those days he had finished writing his first pedagogical treatise *De Ratione studii*, a plan of studies for the seven-year-old Princess Mary which he personally offered and dedicated to Queen Catherine during her visit to Oxford.[48] Furthermore, Vives believed in the close association of intellectuals and politicians, the thinkers and the decision-makers. At the request of the imperial ambassador to England, Louis of Flanders, Lord of Praet, Vives com-posed in Oxford an important political treatise on diplomacy and ne-gotiations, *De Consultatione*.[49] Evidently, in spite of the academic obli-gations imposed upon him by Wolsey, Vives found in Oxford some free time for creative writing. The two books are characteristic of Vives' English period and will be studied later in more detail.

Vives' Christmas holidays with Henry VIII and Catherine of Aragon were indeed a memorable occasion. Like most humanists of that time, Vives felt a sincere admiration for Henry, an admiration which outlasted the King's favors and protection. In the eyes of Vives, Henry was not only the *Defensor Fidei* and the close ally of the Emperor, but he was also the enlightened and well educated patron of the arts. In 1523 Henry VIII was undoubtedly loved and respected by the Erasmian circle of English Humanists. Thomas More dedicated to him three of his Latin Epigrams; Linacre's translation of Galen was preceded by a word of recognition to the Crown; Erasmus dedicated to the King some of his Lucian's translations; and Vives himself offered to the Monarch the painstaking effort of his commentaries on the *Civitas* Dei. All these dedi-

---

[46] De Vocht, "Visits," p. 10, note 1.
[47] *LC.*, 80, vv. 35-40, v. 51. Vives writes about himself to Cranevelt: "Quando speras me Principibus charissimum et gratiossissimum fore factus es voti compos; votum tantum equidem quantum si vel optassem, fuissem impudens, vel si ex-plicarem, jactator . . . nam si quid Vivi credis, incredibilis mihi precii esset loco ab eiusmodi diligi etiam privatissimis."
[48] M, I, 257-283; R, II, 317-327. (*De RSP.*).
[49] M, II, 238-262; R, II, 807-819. (*De consultatione*).

cations were more than simple favor-seeking or pure flattery, they were sincere testimonies of unfeigned respect and devotion.

The Spanish Queen found in Vives a prudent adviser, a brilliant teacher, a personal friend, and the ideal partner in long, nostalgic, confidential, and spirited conversations in their native language. One of those conversations impressed Vives in some particular, mysterious way. From Oxford, on January 25, 1524, Vives wrote to Cranevelt:

> At times I was able to have some philosophical talks with the Queen, one of the purest and most Christian souls I have ever seen. Thus, a couple of days ago, on our way by barge to a certain monastery of nuns, we came to talk about adversity and prosperity in this life. The Queen said: "If I could chose between the two, I would prefer an equal share of both, neither complete adversity nor total success. And if I had to choose between extreme sorrow and extreme well-being, I think I would prefer the former to the latter, for people in disgrace need only some consolation while those who are too successful frequently lose their minds." [50]

What Vives and Catherine could not foresee in January, 1524, was the extent to which the sober desires of the Queen would be fulfilled by the tragic events of 1528. The rest of those holidays were spent in noisy merrymaking. After describing the games, the masquerades, the clowns, the banquets and the musicians, "the jumping camels and the wild bulls" of the circus, Vives adds with serious irony: "Who in the world could find there a short break to read or to write?" [51]

The monastery visited by Vives in the company of the Queen was the famous convent of Saint Saviour and Saints Mary and Bridget, better known as the House of Syon at Isleworth, not far from London. Together with the Carthusian House of Shene and the Franciscan Convent at Greenwich, Syon was one of the religious centers taken under the patronage of Lady Margaret at the turn of the century. Catherine's close association with the Brigettine House of Syon is an eloquent testimony to the continuous influence of the Queen in the intellectual life of sixteenth century England. Syon was not only a religious center but also a focal point of humanistic education for women. In fact, the pietistic literature, both in Latin and the vernacular, of the three first decades of the century in England sprang from, or was closely related to, Catherine's favorite refuge. Through her association with Syon and Shene, through her personal friendship with the circle and the daughters of Thomas More, and finally through her patronage of Vives, Linacre, and

[50] *LC.*, 90, vv. 26-39.
[51] *Ibid.*, vv. 20-25.

Pace, Catherine exercised a powerful influence upon the intellectual life of England.[52] Carefully educated by the Italian scholars in the Court of the Catholic Kings, her parents, and sincerely admired by Erasmus as a "Royal woman of high learning," Catherine of Aragon rightly deserves a name among other great women of the Renaissance such as Vittoria Colonna, the Duchess Rene of Ferrara, and Marguerite of Navarre. Foster Watson, the enthusiastic English scholar, has called this period of English history "the age of Catherine." [53] The expression might be exaggerated, first because Catherine's influence lasted only until Anne Boleyne charmed the King with her graces; second because Catherine's patronage of the arts was only one among many equally powerful. What nobody will deny is that if the scholarly community of Ascham, Cheke, and Coverdale in the reign of Edward VI was greatly influenced by Catherine Parr, the Erasmian circle, before the divorce of Henry VIII, cannot forget the name of Catherine of Aragon. By the same token, Vives' revolutionary ideas on the education of women are nothing else than a portrait of Henry's first wife. Vives himself proclaims this fact in the dedication to Catherine of his tract *De Institutione Feminae Christianae*:

I dedicate to you this book, Noble Queen, like a painter who designed your portrait; in the canvas you would find an image of your body, in my book you will encounter a likeness of your soul. As a young girl, an espouse, a widow, and now a wife – for many years to come, as I hope and pray! – you have left to all women in every way of life a magnificent example.

I know you would prefer to have feminine virtue praised, rather than yourself. Difficult as it is, I will try to obey you in this respect and avoid mentioning your name in every page. Let is be known however that everything I praise in this book is an eulogy of my Queen.[54]

Like almost everything in Vives' life, the noble friendship with Catherine would in time be also severely tested.

[52] McConica (*English Humanists*, pp. 53 ff.) describes the "patterns of patronage" of that century. Catherine's favours were a constant source of inspiration and help to many scholars.

[53] Watson (*Luis Vives, el gran Valenciano*, pp. 23-30) stretches Catherine's influence until Elizabeth's reign: "We may designate the period as the age of Catherine, and ascribe to it the origins of the educational development, brilliant as it appears in William Harrison's account, of the Court of Elizabeth."

[54] M, IV, 69; R, I, 988 b-989 a. "Hoc opus non Tibi secus offero, Regina inclyta, quam si pictor faciem tuam artificiosissime expressam daret; siquidem ut in illa imaginem Tui corporis depictam cerneres, sic in his libris imaginem videbis animi; quippe quae sic in his omnibus vitae generibus cursibusque Te gessisti ut exemplum reliquis . . .

Sed Tu mavis virtutes laudari quam Te . . . parendum erit Tibi, modo scias, sub excellentibus et egregiis virtutibus alias . . . Te semper (etsi tacite) praedicari . . ." (*De IFC*, dedication).

On January 10, 1524, Vives returned to Oxford to resume his academic obligations. The winter was hard, and once again his health suffered a setback.[55] After the school year was over, Vives returned to Bruges where he arrived "safe and sound" on April 24, 1524. His first visit was to Fevyn, to whom he reported with enthusiasm that:

... there is nothing the King and the Queen [of England] seek more earnestly than a stable peace; that the King is, physically and intellectually, an extremely talented person a loving patron of men of learning, with special consideration and esteem for Latin Humanists like More and Erasmus; that the Queen's piety is more than anybody can expect; that the English nobility is extraordinarily benevolent toward all kinds of scholars; and, finally, that he, Vives, was honoured so much by the King, the Queen, and the Cardinal [Wolsey] that there is nothing in the world he would not do for them.[56]

Such was the encomiastic impression of England after almost one year of rich experiences on the Island. Never before nor afterwards was ever a Spanish scholar treated that well west of the Channel.

Vives visited Fevyn in Bruges to ask him to perform the priestly functions of his impending wedding. Fevyn was more than willing, but he was so surprised that he even forgot to ask the name of the bride. Fevyn wrote to Cranevelt right away: "Our friend came here to get married, with whom I do not know. I know, however, that by Royal order he is supposed to be back in England in October."[57] The news was no surprise to Cranevelt because Vives had frequently spoken to him about his marriage projects.[58] But Cranevelt himself had to be informed by Vives on the important subject of the bride's identity:

I plan to marry the daughter of Bernard Valdaura, not because of her wealth or her beauty but only because of the clean and refined education she has received from her holy mother and grandmother, and also because of the integrity of her father I have come to know so well in the last twelve years of my life.[59]

On May 26, 1524, the feast of the Corpus Christi, Juan Luis Vives of Valencia, thirty-two years old, and Margaret Valdaura of Bruges, nineteen years old, became husband and wife in a simple ceremony presided

[55] *LC.*, 90, v. 40. Letter from Vives to Cranevelt: "Redditus sum libris et studiis, ac vereor ne etiam morbis."
[56] *LC.*, 100, vv. 4-15. Letter from Fevyn to Cranevelt. This letter was written the same day Vives arrived in Bruges after one year of absence.
[57] *Ibid.*, vv. 19-20.
[58] *LC.*, 102, vv. 10-16. Vives to Cranevelt: "Puto me crebro dixissse tibi habere in animo uxorem ducere."
[59] *Ibid.*, vv. 6-14.

by their friend John Fevyn. As a testimony of gratitude, Fevyn was presented with a copy of *De Institutione Feminae Christianae,* the book wherein Vives describes the ideal model of the perfect wife as he himself had come to contemplate it in the daily life of the exemplary Valdaura women. The large circle of Vives' and Margaret's friends was delighted with the "ideal match." At least this was the impression Vives reported to Erasmus:

On the festivity of the Blessed Sacrament I surrendered myself to the marriage-yoke, so far a pleasant one. At least I do not have the slightest desire to throw it off. God will take care of the rest. I think I did the right thing and all our friends here were delighted with it. They say they have never seen a wedding like ours.[60]

As far as we know, Erasmus never answered this letter.

The new couple decided to stay with Margaret's mother, Clara Cervent, who needed constant medical care. By his marriage with Margaret, Vives had three brothers-in-law. They were Nicholaus, his favorite, a well-established physician in Bruges, Bernard who moved to Naples in 1558, and Gabriel who probably entered the service of the Church.[61] Vives' letters of the following months reflect unmistakably the happiness and contentment which the young wife brought into the existence of the serious scholar. By a happy coincidence, on the same day of Vives' wedding, Cranevelt's wife had her seventh child, a girl who was called Margaret, probably as a token of affection for the young bride of our Humanist. On June 7, 1524, Vives wrote to Cranevelt the following letter:

This time I have a good excuse for not having answered your letters. The excuse is so good that our Lord uses it in the Gospel as one of the best in

---

⁶⁰ *EE.,* V, 1455, vv. 6-11. "Feriis Eucharistiae subieci cervicem iugo muliebri, nondum mihi quidem gravi et quod cupiam adhuc excutere: sed euntum Deus viderit. Hactenus nec mihi factum displicet, et iis omnibus qui nos norunt, mirifice placet; ut aiunt, nihil hic esse multis annis actum tanta omnium approbatione."

Vives' wedding provoked some sympathetic jokes among his friends. Cranevelt wrote to Fevyn that whatever Vives had written about dreams and wives, (*In Somnium Scipionis* and *De Institutione feminae Christianae*) was now a reality for him. (*LC.* 107, vv. 7-11). Fevyn commented on the letter to Vives, who laughed heartily at it. (*risit affatim, ibid.,* v. 10). On the other hand, Thomas More, who was well informed on matrimonial life and choice of wives (he married his second wife one month after the death of his first wife!), wrote to Cranevelt in a little more cynical way: "It is impossible to live comfortably with a woman, even with the best." (*ut ne cum optima quidem sine incommodo vivi posse putem*) (*LC.* 115, v. 17). Cranevelt agreed with More. He was at that time the father of seven children.

⁶¹ See *LC.,* introd. to letter 102 b.

the world. Now, however, lacking any real excuse, I feel forced to write to you.

You congratulate me for my wedding; I congratulate you for your new child. You compliment me for the leaves of spring; I compliment you for the fruits of the fall. I truly enjoyed your ethymology of the word "connubium"; might Christ our Lord keep it that way more and more every day. I hope so. The education and the family background of my wife, my motivation and attitude of mind in this matter are indeed a good start . . .[62]

Margaret's devotion and courage played an important part in the life of Vives. His poor health, his natural pessimism and bitterness, the terrible storms and disappointments of the days ahead were no doubt a hard test for the young woman. Vives never took her with him on his future visits to England. In spite of the warm welcome by the Court, Vives was afraid of Wolsey's influence and Henry VIII's moods. The assassination of the Duke of Buckingham in 1521 was only the beginning of a long series of "judicial murders" which proved Vives' fears well justified. Vives' correspondence or writings do not betray much tenderness of affection toward Margaret. Unfortunately, if Vives ever exchanged some letters with his wife – as we can presume he did – that correspondence has entirely disappeared. After several years of marriage all he had to write about her to his friend Vergara was that she had never spoiled one minute of his private study.[63] Vives' ideas on marriage were so severe that even Erasmus had to write to him: "You seem so harsh on the role of the wife in marriage that all I can say is that I sincerely hope you will be a little more soft toward your own wife." [64] In spite of Erasmus' warning, I am afraid that Vives' marriage was far from being exciting and healthy. Of course, there was no erotic romance in its preparation because Vives thought that instead of flirting, young women were supposed to be in Church praying that God would inspire their parents the right choice of a bridegroom.[65] His sexual life as a married man might have been dictated by his own condemnation of sex as a brutalizing experience.[66] As for children, there was not the slightest longing for them: life was too disappointing and too bitter to be per-

[62] *LC.*, 106, vv. 1-12. The evangelical excuse refers to Luke XIV, 2: "Uxorem duxi et ideo non possum venire." Cranevelt replied that the biblical quotation was a good excuse for not having visited him in Mechlin, but not for not having written.

[63] The letter of Vives to Vergara was first published by Bonilla in *Revue Hispanique*, VIII (1901), 263. The Spanish translation is included in R, II, 1733 b-1736 b.

[64] *EE.*, VII, 1830, vv. 14-16: "In matrimonio durior videbaris in uxores; opinor in tuam te magis comem esse."

[65] See below, p. 210.

[66] See below, p. 211.

petuated in his own flesh. Margaret died childless. In fact she was never
pregnant, as far as we know.

In spite of all these limitations Vives' marriage was a significant break
with the medieval tradition of the priestly scholar consecrated to Wisdom
in the temple of Philosophy. In fact, Vives was the first lay scholar of
modern Spain and one of the first in modern Europe. The examples of
More, Cranevelt, and Budé might have powerfully influenced his decision. Remember that even the secular professors of the medieval universities were forbidden to get married until late in the fifteenth century.
Even Thomas More himself was puzzled by the fact that a married
man like Budé had been able to acquire such portentous erudition.
When, a few years later, the great French pedagogue Baduel, a close
friend of Vives, decided to marry, he still felt obliged to write a little
essay to justify himself and to emphasize the advantages of married life
for a Christian intellectual.[68] Vives might very well have thought exactly
in the same manner.

Between his wedding and his second visit to England (October, 1524),
Vives found time to write a precious collection of moral axioms and
advices, very much in the style of the Syon devotional books, which he
dedicated to the future Queen of England, the Princess Mary. This
book, called *Satellitium sive Symbola*, made a deep impression on the
young Princess.[69] Actually, her first decree as a Queen was to have a
coin struck with the legend *Veritas, temporis filia*, taken from Vives'
collection.[70]

On October 2, 1524, only five months after his wedding, Vives left
Bruges without his wife for his second visit to England.[71] In Calais,
waiting for a favorable wind to cross the Channel, Vives once more was
overcome by a strong feeling of boredom and nostalgia: "I am writing
to you from Calais expecting any moment to cross over to England with
Christ's help to take up again the burdensome tasks of this wearisome
and boring life, full of longing for my newly discovered love," he wrote
to Cranevelt.[72] In London he was informed that a stubborn pest had

[67] M, IV, 254; R, I, 1137 b (*De IFC.*, II, 5).

[68] See M. J. Gaufrés, *Claude Baduel et la Réforme des études au XVI siecle*
(Paris, 1880), pp. 121-123. Baduel's close friend, Bigot, followed again the same
example and got married one year later. Baduel's treatise was entitled *De ratione
vitae studiosae ac litteratae in matrimonio collocandae ac degendae* (Lyon, 1544).

[69] M, IV, 33-65; R, I, 1177-1204. (*Satellitium*).

[70] See more details on this matter in De Vocht, "Visits," p. 12, note 5.

[71] *LC.*, 100, v. 20. Letter from Vives to Cranevelt. Also, *EE.*, 1455, v. 2, letter
from Vives to Erasmus.

[72] *LC.*, 119, vv. 1-5: "Caliciis ad te scribo, traiecturus in Britanniam, Christo

forced the closing of Oxford University for the Michaelmas term; [73] accordingly, he remained in the City sharing a room with his friend and countryman, the merchant Alvaro de Castro, whom he loved as a brother.[74] Probably at Castro's suggestion Vives solicited from his powerful friends in the Court a special trade monopoly privilege which, under the management of his in-laws in Bruges, could make him financially self-supporting and free from any teaching obligation. Such Royal favors were no exception at that time, and no less a man than Thomas More followed the example of Vives by securing for himself on June 13, 1526, the privilege to export woolen clothes.[75] While waiting for the Royal decision, Vives began to work on his new moral treatise *De Officio mariti*, which was not published until 1528. In the meantime Oxford was reopened, and in January, 1525, Vives returned to his chair of Humanities where he was eagerly expected by both the students and the faculty.

This second and last visit of Vives to Oxford (January, 1525-May, 1525) was not a very happy one. He missed the attentions of his wife; he waited impatiently for the Royal decision on the trade grant; the climate of Oxford, "the marsh with the damp air," ruined his health again; [76] the news from Spain were "tristissimae": in fact the execution of his father probably took place in early January, 1525. The international situation was worse than ever; in Germany the Peasants revolt had just left behind 60,000 victims. On February 24, 1525, the Imperial army broke the French power in Pavia to celebrate the birthday of Charles V. The rapidly growing power of the Emperor suggested to Wolsey a shift in the balance of international alliances. The humanistic

---

propitio, ad continuandos labores aerumnosae vitae huius, maximo taedio vitae, maiore desiderio novorum amorum."

[73] *LC.*, 128, letter from Vives to Cranevelt. Also, *ibid.*, 130, v. 10, from Fevyn to Cranevelt. A few days later Vives announced to Erasmus the death of their common friend, Linacre. (*EE.*, V, 1513, vv. 4-16. Erasmus' answer to Vives; *EE.*, V, 1531, v. 23). In a letter to Cranevelt, Vives calls Linacre "litteratorum numen nemini secundum." (*LC.*, 122, v. 13).

[74] On Alvaro de Castro's relation to Vives, see De Vocht, "Visits," p. 13, note 5.

[75] Brewer, *Letters and Papers*, IV, 2248.

[76] M, VII, 207; R, 1274 b, letter from Vives to Hector Decamius: "In causa est coelum nimis humidum et hic Oxoniae, nempe loco palustri, crassum." Erasmus, in sharp contrast with Vives' feelings, calls the weather of England "coelum tum amoenissimum tum saluberrimum." (*EE.*, I, 118, vv. 17-18, Letter to Robert Fisher).

Probably at this time a swarm of bees settled between the ceiling and the eaves near the cloister chamber where Vives lived. The complaints of the Spanish professor became well known to the rest of the University family. In fact those bees, which survived there until 1648, were jokingly called "Vives his bees," as Wood says, "to perpetuate the memory of this mellifluous Doctor [Vives], as the University styled him in a letter to Card. Wolsey." (Quoted by Thomas Fowler, *The History of Corpus Christi* College [Oxford, 1893], p. 71, note 1).

dreams of peace were shattered into pieces. A cloud of desolate pessimism
darkened the correspondence of Vives' friends. Fevyn wrote to Cranevelt: "I fear the insolence of the Emperor." [77] More wrote to Crancvclt:
"The madness of war prevails everywhere." [78] In this critical point of
European history Vives' voice was the most serene and the most powerful. Erasmus was in Basle, too far removed from the scene. More was a
prisoner of his own dignities and office: in October, 1525, he had been
made Lord Chancellor of Lancaster; in November he was elected High
Steward of Cambridge. Still in London, at the end of 1524, Vives
published his letter to Adrian VI entitled *De Bello et Luthero*; [79] in
March of the following year he sent to Henry VIII his letter *De Francisco Galliae Rege a Caesare capto*. [80] Both letters epitomize the best
English Humanism ever produced: "the assertion of the implicit rights
of the common people" (Adams), and the practical advice to seek peace
not in one-sided treaties but in the balance of self-interest at the international level.

On April 28, 1525, Vives and his family were granted the license to
import every year 300 tons of Gascon wine and Toulouse wool, and to
export corn to the continent. [81] With this prospect and the Royal pension
he was still receiving Vives could hope to leave Oxford as soon as the
academic year was over. At the beginning of May, Vives left Oxford
never to come back.

Shortly before receiving the good news from the Court, on March 15
Vives wrote a long letter to Wolsey with a handful of suggestions concerning the ways in which the University should be reformed. Vives
recommended the abandonment of the useless scholastic abstractions and
the strengthening of the study of grammar, rhetoric and poetry. [82] Vives'
teaching and programs were no doubt of great influence in the reform
of English universities; nevertheless, his impact upon English Humanism
was in no way limited to the academic world. His writings became, and
remained, highly popular among the leading classes of the nation for
two or three generations. Richard Hyrde, the tutor of More's children,
translated into English Vives' *De Institutione Christianae Feminae*, a

---

[77] *LC.*, 130, vv. 9-28.
[78] *LC.*, 115, v. 27. "Belli furor ad hunc modum ubique ardescit."
[79] M, V, 164-175; R, II, 9-19. The letter is also known as *De Europae Statu ac
tumultibus*. It was written in October, 1522, from Louvain, but was not made public
until 1524.
[80] See above, p. 30.
[81] De Vocht, "Visits," p. 19, notes 2 and 3.
[82] *Ibid.*, p. 17, note 7. The document can be found in Brewer, *Letters and Papers*,
IV, 1187.

book which More himself had planned to translate.[83] Sir Richard Morison made an English version of the *Introductio ad Sapientiam*; [84] and finally, one of his disciples in Oxford, Thomas Paynell, translated *De Officio mariti* in 1550.[85] Vives' *Linguae Latinae Exercitatio,* published in 1538, was used as a textbook in English schools for many years.[86] Surprisingly enough, Vives' devotional books became a part of English religious life by being translated and included in Edward's and Elizabeth's prayer books.[87] The repertoire of English editions and translations of Vives' works gives an impressive dimension to Vives' impact upon British culture, the true extent of which has not yet been carefully investigated.[88]

From Oxford Vives moved to London where he spent one week or two in the company of Thomas More. Then rather unexpectedly on May 10, 1525, he hurried back to Bruges where Margaret was afflicted by a dangerous eye infection which she was making worse "crying day and night." [89] As Vives put it, he arrived in Bruges *"desideratus et desiderans."* Margaret's eye healed shortly thereafter. During the first year of their marriage Vives had been absent for seven long months. This time, however, he remained in Bruges longer than he himself had planned. The grave illness of Clara Cervent, his mother-in-law, prevented

---

[83] The translation had the title *The Instruction of a Christian Woman.* It was published by Th. Berthelet, London, 1540. On the history of the translation and More's intention to translate the same book, see Watson, *Vives and the Renascence Education of Women,* pp. 14 ff.

[84] *An Introduction to Wysedome,* published in London, 1540, both by John Daye and Th. Berthelet.

[85] *The Office and the Dutie of an Husband,* published by J. Cawood, London, 1550.

[86] The book was licensed to Th. Gubbin in 1589.

[87] The editor of the Protestant primer of 1545 drew heavily on Vives' prayers and books of devotion. *The General Prayer Books* written by Bradford in 1578 are mostly a translation of Vives' *Preces et Meditationes Diurnae.* For a general view of Vives' impact upon Protestant English devotional literature of the Tudor period, see Helen C. White, *The Tudor Books of Private Devotion* (Wisconsin, 1951), pp. 128-129, 183-185, 242-245. John G. Underhill, *Spanish Literature in the England of the Tudors* (New York, 1809), maintains that Vives was also responsible for making Spanish literature better known among English writers (pp. 82, 92-95, 99-100).

[88] In "Visits," p. 18, note 8, De Vocht announced that Fernand Kunsch was preparing a detailed study of Vives' influence on England in the sixteenth century. The book has not yet been published.

[89] *LC.,* 153, vv. 1-8: "Redditus sum Brugis meis et uxori desideratus et desiderans . . .; ipsa [uxor] alioqui morbum metu augebat; noctes et dies flebat, verita ne ex eo morbo remaneret unocula." Vives' departure from London was so unforeseen that Cranevelt kept on sending his letters to Vives to More's address. (*LC.,* 151, v. 6. Letter from More to Cranevelt).

him from going back to England in October and he stayed at home
until February of the following year (1526).[90]

At the request of Louis de Praet, Imperial Ambassador to England,
Vives began to work on his social tract *De Subventione Pauperum* which
was dedicated to the magistrates of Bruges and published in 1526.[91]
Vives was well aware of the importance and novelty of his book. In fact
he even tried to keep secret the subject he was dealing with for fear of
looking too daring or presumptuous.[92] The final product was an investigation into the causes of social injustice and a manual of public welfare
and education of the poor and the handicapped. Vives' treatise is comparable to the first book of More's *Utopia* by which it has been unjustly
overshadowed. If Vives' book never reaches the platonic idealization of
More's masterpiece, it surpasses the *Utopia* in the prophetic pragmatism
of its programs. The serene and thoughtful style of the book reflects
Vives' passionate concern with the social turbulence of his days: the
peasants' revolt in Germany; the insurrection of the Communes and the
Germanias in Spain; the uprising of the common people in England
against Wolsey's war taxation, "the most violent financial exaction in
English history" (Adams); the pest and the hunger in the desolated fields
of France and Southern Spain; and finally, the distress of Bruges gradually yielding to the competition of Antwerp and the tricky maneuvering
of English merchants.

The book furthermore conveys the deep-rooted persuasion that human
miseries are only the result of human mistakes and vices. In particular
Vives insists on the close alliance of poverty and the unbelievable foolishness of war. Vives' correspondence in those months reveals a strong
obsession with the chances and hope of a European settlement after the
Imperial victory of Pavia. The one-sided negotiations of Francis I with
Henry VIII and later with Charles V were an ominous sign of a new
alignment of powers instead of the equilibrium which was Vives' dream.
His fears and foresight prompted him to write once again to Henry VIII
on October 8, 1525, begging the King to foster the reconciliation of *all*

---

[90] *LC.*, 171, vv. 5-12. Vives gives all kinds of details about Clara's disease in this
letter to Cranevelt. It was this type of medical description which Erasmus disliked
most in Vives' writings. On a similar occasion Erasmus wrote to Vives this frank
remark: "De scabie nimis multa." (*EE.*, VII, 1830, v. 16).

[91] M, IV, 421-492; R, I, 1356-1409. (*De SP.*).

[92] *LC.*, 157, vv. 42-46. Even Cranevelt was only given a hint about the book: "I
have started a book of such importance that for the moment I do not dare to tell
you about it lest you think that I am crazy. In fact I myself feel somehow ashamed
of my own boldness." (See also *LC.*, 160, v. 22; 163, vv. 1-12).

Christian Princes.[93] This noble message marked the beginning of Vives' miseries in England. In the new game of Wolsey's alliance with France against the Emperor, Juan Luis Vives, the Spanish confident of a Spanish Queen, was, to say the least, an unwelcomed guest.

As soon as Vives arrived in England for his third visit in February, 1526, he felt that things were not the same: he was "sailing against the stream," repudiated by many former friends.[94] At the Court circumstances were also highly unpleasant. Henry VIII spent most of his time away from Catherine absorbed in wild hunting parties with his illegitimate son, Henry Filzroy. Wolsey was doing his best to keep the Queen in isolation and Henry far removed from his pro-Spanish courtiers. Already in February of the same year (1526) the Cardinal made sure that Vives could not regain his professorship at Oxford. In feverish hurry he tried to have him replaced by Erasmus who rejected the offer because the England of 1526 was not the shelter of peace he was seeking. Goclenius, the professor of Latin at the Trilingue College and a good friend of Vives, also received a personal embassy from the Cardinal with an identical offer. The prudent professor rejected the plan.[95] Although Wolsey's efforts failed for the time being, Vives was intelligent enough to see into the Cardinal's intentions. On the other hand, nobody was more reluctant to go back to Oxford than the victim of Wolsey's machinations. "The memory, however, of the excellent lectures delivered by the son of Valencia in Oxford" – wrote De Vocht – "did not end with Wolsey's favour; in 1534 the University Council expressed a wish for professors 'from beyond the sea, as was Mr. Vives.' " [96] In this time of distress Vives found a loyal supporter in "the man for all seasons" (Erasmus), Thomas More. Having already described Vives' contribution to English life, it is only fair to pause for a moment to emphasize how much Vives did receive from English Humanism in general and from

[93] M, V, 175-181; R, II, 27-39. The letter bears the title *De Pace inter Caesarem et Franciscum Gallorum regem deque optimo regni statu.*

[94] *LC.,* 185, v. 22. Vives to Cranevelt: "In rebus meis navigo hic nonnihil adverso flumine." Also, *LC.,* 182, vv. 18-22 (Fevyn to Cranevelt). "I know that Vives has lost several powerful friends (in England). I wish he would lose more so that we could enjoy his presence here!"

[95] Wolsey sent Charles Harst as his confidential messenger to Erasmus (*LC.,* 172). At this time Erasmus was being invited not only by Wolsey but also by the Pope, by Francis I, by the Emperor, by Prince Ferdinand, and even by the clergy of Poland. The old Humanist enumerates these invitations with obvious delight in his answer to Wolsey. (*EE.,* VI, 1697, vv. 94-112). Erasmus' reluctance to settle in England after his departure from Louvain in 1523 has something intriguing about it.
As for Goclenius' refusal to the invitation personally presented to him by no less a person than the English ambassador to the Court of Margaret, see *L.C.,* introd. to letter 95. Also Brewer, *Letters and Papers,* IV, 2161, 2177.

[96] De Vocht, "Visits to England," p. 11.

the More circle in particular. This is, moreover, our last chance to do so before we engulf ourselves in the tragic events which followed Anne Boleyn's control of Henry's heart and Wolsey's final madness.

Vives' literary production in England stands in sharp contrast with his early books of the Bruges and Louvain period. Gone are the purely academic *prelectiones* and *declamationes*; gone also the intensively religious meditations which he dedicated to Croy, Archbishop of Toledo. The English era opens with a treatise on women dedicated to a Spanish Queen and closes with a moral tract on the duties of husbands dedicated to a Spanish Duke. During his sojourn in England Vives wrote a letter to the Pope, one letter to the Bishop of Lincoln, a dialogue, and two letters to Henry VIII, dealing in each one of these writings with the concrete problems of the European political situation. To the same period belong a revolutionary social treatise and two collections of moral axioms more stoic in character than purely Christian. Like Erasmus himself, Vives learned from the London reformers how to apply his humanistic ideals to the practical end of educational, social, and political reform. The means and the goals of such a reform are not religious but purely natural. Like More's *Utopia*, Vives' vision encompasses a well-educated layman assuming the leading role in a community of individuals and nations socially and politically regimented by the universal precepts of the Law of Nature. In only two respects Vives proved himself totally impervious to the genius of the More circle: the historical criticism of the Bible (Colet) and the use of Lucianesque satire as a social weapon (More and Erasmus).

When we speak of British Humanism and its impact upon Vives, we think above all of Thomas More. The future victim of Henry VIII was to Vives a delightful, likable, and loyal friend. "Has nature ever moulded, anything gentler, pleasanter, or happier than the mind of Thomas More?" wrote Erasmus in the name of all the Northern Humanists.[97] In Thomas More Vives saw the ideal figure of the new age: a layman of deep Christian faith, the respected head of a happy family, the loyal servant to his King, and the well-educated scholar. There was only one great difference between the two men. The utopian writer was much more a practical politician and a skillful negotiator than the author of the first modern program of public welfare. It is even possible that Vives somehow resented More's brilliant political career. There was no jealousy on the part of Vives, only the feeling that More's dignities were irreconcilable with More's ideals. More's silence after the

[97] *EE.*, I, 118, vv. 23-24. Erasmus to Robert Fisher.

assassination of Buckingham, More's robust speech in favor of Wolsey's war money, More's signature of a treacherous treaty with France against the Emperor were, in the mind of Vives, far from utopian ideals of righteousness. Vives' reaction to More's promotions was never enthusiastic. When More was appointed Chancellor of the Duchy of Lancaster, Vives' only comment was to give a detailed account of his new salary.[98] When he heard that More was the Chancellor of England, he commented with certain sarcasm: "Now we have More as a Chancellor. Will he think now of his poor friends?" [99] Vives did not have the temper of a martyr; he was prudent and shrewd enough to avoid the situations in which either minor concessions or tragic sacrifices could be demanded from him. Henry's divorce led More to the guillotine; Vives had left England in time. Of course, Vives' memory has vanished from the popular mind while More's death has erased from history the less heroic details of his life.

In the house of Thomas More Vives became familiar not only with the learned daughters and sons-in-law of the English Humanist but with the elite of London intelligentsia.[100] In his first letter to Cranevelt from England Vives mentions first of all Thomas Linacre, the translator of Galen and founder of the College of Physicians in 1518, with whom Vives was to share the preceptorship of Princess Mary in his fourth visit to England.[101] There was also William Blount, fourth Lord of Mountjoy, the English patron of Erasmus to whom the Dutch Humanist dedicated the first edition of his *Adagiorum collectanea* in 1500, and to whose son Vives dedicated the second part of his *De Ratione studii puerilis*.[102] In

---

[98] *LC.*, 167, vv. 11-14. Vives writes to Cranevelt: "More has been made the Chancellor of Lancaster; this is a job of prestige and endowed with a huge salary ... He will receive more than fifteen hundred ducats ..."

[99] M, VII, 142; R, II, 1675 b. Vives to Pate: "Morum habemus Cancellarium; nescio an meminerit tenuium amicorum." Fevyn, commenting on More's participation in Wolsey's mission to Francis I in 1527, wrote: "This Cardinal has been sent to France to procure the peace between England and France; they say he is carrying so much gold that he could support a whole army of a hundred thousand soldiers for a whole year. More is with him: a good man for such cause! (*bonus ad eam rem auctor*)." (LC., 243, vv. 40-43).

[100] *LC.*, 185, v. 34. In this letter to Cranevelt Vives calls the daughters of More "filiabus facundissimis et fecundissimis." More had two daughters; Margaret, married to the famous William Roper, and Elisabeth, married to Giles Heron. Margaret was the favorite of Vives, who loved her as a sister. (M, II, 308; R, II, 874 b., *Salutandi formulae*, I).

[101] *LC.*, 80, v. 5. Vives to Cranevelt. Only one letter from Vives to Linacre has been preserved. In it Vives confesses with tender words his filial affection for Linacre. (M, VII, 207-208; R, II, 1724). After Linacre's death, Vives wrote a short eulogy calling Linacre "Litteratorum lumen nemini secundum." (*LC.*, 122, vv. 12-19. Also *EE.*, V, 1513, v. 31; 1531, v. 23).

[102] On the importance of Mountjoy's patronage in the history of Tudor Humanism,

Thomas More's house Vives also met John Fisher, the head of the episcopal party which included Warham, Cuthbert Tunstall, Richard Fox, and John Longland, all of them close friends of Vives. "It is impossible to describe the ineffable mixture of erudition, kindness, and moral nobility of these great men," Vives wrote to Cranevelt.[103]

However, the peaceful days of intimate conversations with More did not last very long. In May, 1526, Vives was back in Bruges writing his dialogue *De Europae dissidiis et Bello Turcico*, an almost cynical and despairing proof of Vives' concern with the expansion of Soliman's power.[104] The death of Louis of Hungary in August and the conquest of Budapest by Soliman's troops in September of that year fully confirmed the apprehensions of Vives.

Vives stayed in Bruges for almost a whole year, from May, 1526, to April, 1527. After the cool reception of his third visit to England, excuses piled up to remain at home with his wife and his friends.[105] Finally at the end of April he sailed off from Calais. This time he was received better than he ever expected. Wolsey's machinations had been powerfully curtailed by the opposition of the rival parties.[106] The personal relations of Henry and Catherine had reached the last stage of apparent peaceful coexistence which usually precedes the final outbreak of emotions. Once again, however, the worsening condition of Clara Cervent and the anxiety of Margaret forced Vives to return to Bruges in a hurry.[107] Vives left London on June 27, 1527, amidst two highly disturbing rumors: the first was that finally the King had spoken to Catherine in clear terms about the impending divorce; the second was that the troops of the Emperor had sacked the Holy City of Rome. The Queen, lonely and helpless as she was, begged Vives to return in October to begin the teaching of Latin to Princess Mary during the winter.[108] Henry VIII also had two errands for the Spanish scholar: to

see McConica, *English Humanists*, pp. 6-8. Vives dedicated to Mountjoy's son, Charles, his second letter *De ratione studii puerilis*.

[103] *LC.*, 80, vv. 9-10. Vives to Cranevelt.

[104] Vives refers to the composition of this "opusculum" in his correspondence with Cranevelt. (*LC.*, 217, v. 9; 227, v. 3). The work is found in M, VI, 452-481; R, II, 39-63.

[105] In February Vives announced to Cranevelt his impending departure for England by the end of the month and his intention to remain there "or to come back according to the way things shape up there." (*LC.*, 227, v. 26). In April, however, Vives was still in Calais "waiting for a favorable wind." (*LC.*, 232, v. 14. See also *LC.*, 229, v. 21 and *EE.*, VI, 1792, v. 29).

[106] At least this was the situation as described by Fevyn to Cranevelt. (*LC.*, 235, v. 20).

[107] *LC.*, 237, vv. 21-25; 241, vv. 9-20.

[108] According to *EE.*, VII, 1836, v. 35, Vives agreed to the request of the Queen and promised to be back.

send him from London an Epitome of Erasmus' *Adagia,* and to write a reply against Luther's letter of September, 1525, in which Henry was presented as a victim of the Roman episcopate in England.[109] On July 13, 1527, from Bruges, Vives wrote to the English monarch:

> I am sending to Your Majesty a copy of Erasmus' *Adagia* which I bought here because in London it was sold out . . . I have also prepared my opusculum with the reply to Luther's letter; it can be printed as soon as I receive your remarks, unless Your Majesty prefers to have it printed in London.
>
> I heard that the Cardinal (Wolsey) is on a journey to France. I hope he will be able to reach a European settlement worthy of Your Majesty, the most kind, the most learned, and the most pious of all Princes; a settlement worthy also of the Cardinal, a bishop of the Church, a legate of the Vicar of Christ, the Master of Peace, a Cardinal whose purple robes should be to him a constant reminder of the Evangelical charity and the love for all men which seeks to reconcile *all* the children of God in mutual friendship . . .[110]

Unfortunately, Vives' libellus against Luther, which was never published, has not yet been found.[111] Thus we have been deprived of the one controversial writing of Juan Luis Vives. It must be added, however, that Vives wrote this document against Luther only to please Henry VIII and that his serene style was in no way adapted to this kind of invective and name-calling in which even the kind Thomas More was such a skillful master.

Vives' letter to Henry is a historical document and a masterpiece of delicate understatement. Vives' sincere affection for the Monarch prompted him to excuse all the wrongs and misdeeds of Henry as long as there was any hope. In October, 1527, Vives was still reluctant to admit all the rumors about Henry's plans for Catherine although on July 4 Wolsey had already tried to persuade John Fisher that a declaration of invalidity was very feasible.[112] On July 26 Cranevelt informed Erasmus about the threat to the royal marriage;[113] about the same time Fevyn was telling Cranevelt in clear terms that "the insane Cardinal" was pushing the King into a repudiation of his wife.[114]

---

[109] De Vocht, "Visits," p. 23, note 3.

[110] This letter has been first published by De Vocht, "Visits," pp. 23-26.

[111] According to Jerome Emser the answer of Henry to Luther was printed in London on December, 2, 1526. But, in all probability, the final composition had nothing to do with Vives' manuscript. (See *EE.,* VI, 1773, vv. 16-21; 1736, v. 40).

[112] Vives writes to Cranevelt: "I only know the rumors; but I am sure that things are completely different from what we heard." (*LC.,* 248, vv. 35-36).

[113] *EE.,* VII, 1850, vv. 8-10: "Absit et illud, ut coniugium regale nunc demum fiat irritum, cum tot annis legitime coheserit . . ."

[114] *LC.,* 243, vv. 55-60: "Ab hoc insano Cardinale dementatur . . . Rursus hoc impulsore repudiat uxorem . . ."

Vives' emphatic insistence upon a "worthy" success of Wolsey's embassy to France manifests his own misgivings about the Cardinal's intentions. As a matter of fact, the treaty of Amiens (August 4, 1527) which followed such embassy, and which unfortunately carried the signature of Thomas More, brought about the doom of Catherine and the beginnings of Vives' miseries in England. Vives' private correspondence reveals that he and his friends were fully aware of Wolsey's game.[115] To Vergara, in Spain, Vives wrote very realistically that he was standing on a slippery path without hope or safety from one day to the next.[116]

Nevertheless, in the first days of October, according to the promise he had made to Catherine, he returned to Greenwich to teach Latin to the Princess.[117] The Spanish Queen was so comforted with the presence of Vives in the Court that she tried to persuade Margaret (now alone in Bruges after the death of her mother) to join her husband in England with the promise that she would always stand by her side.[118] Vives never allowed the journey of his wife. He knew too well that not before long Catherine herself would need much more help than she could give. According to Vives' fear, the events then took a quick pace. In January Vives wrote to Cranevelt that he was being closely watched.[119] Fevyn reported a few days later that Vives' life was being threatened.[120] In the first weeks of February Wolsey dared to cross-examine Vives about his

---

[115] The Royal divorce was viewed by Vives, Fevyn, and Cranevelt as a maneuver to separate Henry VIII from the Emperor and bring about the alliance with France. See, e.g., the letter of Cranevelt to Erasmus: "I heard that More arrived in Calais with Wolsey on their way to France. May God Omnipotent make this mission an honorable one to More himself and advantageous to our regions. There are people who think that this is only a stratagem against us and that Flanders is to be attacked from both sides (England and France). I just cannot believe such a thing from a King so close to the Emperor . . ." (EE., VII, 1850, vv. 3-9). And Vives to Cranevelt: "They say that the Cardinal of England is going to France. I hope God will help him to cut this knot, much more twisted than the Gordian one! These are the knots which Popes and Cardinals have to cut instead of closing alliances in which they themselves get trapped like birds." (LC., 241, vv. 24-28). Fevyn, as always, was much more radical in his comments: "This English Idol (Wolsey) terrifies me, pompously walking around Calais and threatening the Emperor. Everybody is here in a state of shock with this stinky legation . . ." (LC., 243, vv. 1-15).
[116] R, II, 1734, b. This letter was unknown to Mayans.
[117] LC., 248, vv. 18-20; 251, v. 4. Letters from Vives to Cranevelt.
[118] LC., 252, vv. 11-15. Fevyn reported to Cranevelt that Margaret had received a little gift from the Queen with a very affectionate letter "in which the Queen tries to allure her, or shall I say 'exhort her,' to join her husband in England."
[119] LC., 251, vv. 4-6: "Do not be surprised that it took me so long to write. Be rather surprised at the fact that I was able to write this letter at all."
[120] LC., 252, vv. 15-18: "Vives himself tells me – but please keep this absolutely secret and confidential – . . . that some people are threatening his life, and the swords are ready for action."

private conversations with Catherine; [121] he even demanded from Vives a written declaration explaining his part in the plan to inform the Pope about the Queen's situation through the Spanish ambassador Iñigo de Mendoza. Vives complied immediately. In noble and dignified style the Spanish scholar complained that his human rights were violated in being forced to break the secret of his conversations with the Queen; but since there was nothing he should be ashamed of, he was ready to obey the Cardinal's order. It was true that the Queen had found in him, "her countryman," a person to whom she could confide all her problems. According to Vives the Queen only complained about loosing Henry, " a man she loved more than herself"; and he added: "Who can blame me for listening to a sad and unfortunate woman? for talking to her with sympathy? for consoling a Queen of such noble ancestry whose parents were once my own natural Princes?" Finally Vives admitted that, at the request of the Queen, "sanctissima matrona," he himself asked the Spanish Ambassador to write to Charles V and the Pope about Her Majesty's case.[122] Vives' confession moved Wolsey to have him placed in strict confinement in the house of a councillor together with the Spanish Ambassador.[123] What Vives used to call, with a little exaggeration "custodia mea Britannica," lasted for 38 days, from February 25 to April 1, 1528. Henry VIII, informed of the "libera custodia" of Vives, was pleased with the "gentle" way the Spanish scholar had been treated although the King did not especially like Vives' complaint about the violation of his "humanum ius." [124] Still, for fear of the Emperor's reprisals, Vives was released on condition of not putting foot again in the Royal Palace. The noble Queen sent a secret messenger to Vives recommending that he leave England.[125] Vives was delighted to oblige: "id quod feci, hoc praesertim tempore, non invitus." [126] Nevertheless, he was at that time convinced that he had "done his best" for the cause of

---

[121] See the report of Fevyn to Cranevelt, *LC.*, 254.

[122] The document can be found, written entirely by Vives' hand, in Brewer, *Letters and Papers*, IV, 4912-5107. It has been published by De Vocht, "Visits," pp. 29-32.

Scarisbrick, *Henry VIII*, p. 166, writes: "There was Vives, the author of a long-winded but competent book on Catherine's behalf." In the footnote, the author gives as title of the book *Apologia sive Contutatio*, etc ... (sic). The authenticity of this document (it is not a "long-winded book") is more critically discussed by Henry de Vocht, "Visits," pp. 37-42.

[123] *LC.*, 254. Letter from Fevyn to Cranevelt.

[124] Asked by the King, J. Russell, one of the Royal agents, informed Henry about Vives' behavior and the way he had been treated. (Brewer, *Leters and Papers*, IV, 3943).

[125] M, VII, 148-149; R, II, 1681 b. Letter from Vives to Vergara.

[126] *LC.*, 261, v. 29. Letter from Vives to Cranevelt.

the Queen.[127] Back in Bruges on April 7, 1528, Vives was surprised to be informed by the Treasurer of Henry VIII that the Royal pension should be continued.[128] Nevertheless Vives was still shocked by the "stupidity and the mad love affair" of the King.[129] In May he wrote a letter to Erasmus begging him to attempt something for Catherine's sake. But the prudent Dutchman reacted with a tasteless remark: "Far from me to get involved in this affair between Jupiter and Juno; besides I would prefer to give to one Jupiter two Junos than to take one away from him." [130]

In November, 1528, Henry VIII granted Catherine the help of two advocates from Flanders and one of her own choice to assist her in the examination of her marriage by Clement VII's special legate, Cardinal Campeggio. Catherine appointed Vives, the only Spaniard Henry VIII had not explicitly excluded. On November 17, 1528, once again Vives crossed the English channel in the company of the two Flemish advocates of Catherine, the Vicar of Liégé diocese and a member of Mechlin Parliament. The last act in the tragedy of Vives' relationship with the desperate Spanish Queen was very sad. Vives' cool judgment in that moment was to advise the Queen to desist from any defense which he considered a total waste of time and a part of Henry's sinister game. The Queen was first terribly disappointed, then hysterically mad at Vives' attitude which she interpreted as surrender and cowardice. To Juan Vergara, Vives wrote: "The Queen was furious at me because I would not comply with her wishes right away. But I will obey my reason which takes for me the place of all kings and queens." A few days later Juan Luis Vives left England forever "as an enemy of the King, as a coward to the Queen, and deprived of any Royal pension." [131] When Vives arrived in Bruges a few days later he was a lonely, disappointed, and bitter man.

---

[127] To Cranevelt he wrote that he had helped the Queen "as much as it was in my power" (*pro virili mea: LC.*, 261, v. 28). To Vergara Vives wrote: "I joined the cause of the Queen because I thought it was the just one, and I did all I could with my words and my writings." (M, VII, 148; R, II, 1681 b).

[128] *LC.*, 260, vv. 14-21. Letter from Fevyn to Cranevelt.

[129] *Ibid.* The expression is Fevyn's, but, once again, it probably reflects his intimate conversations with Vives.

[130] *EE.*, VII, 2040, vv. 41-49: "Negocio Jovis et Junonis absit ut me admisceam, praesertim incognito. Citius tribuerem uni duas Junones quam unam adimerem."

[131] M, VII, 149; R, II, 1681 b.

CHAPTER 6

ISOLATION, MATURITY, AND DEATH (1528–1540)

The last twelve years of Vives' life, exceptionally creative as they were, are also the least known to us. The rich correspondence of Cranevelt closes on October 27, 1528, except for an appendix of twenty-three letters including only one from Juan Luis Vives.[1] The exchange between Vives and Erasmus also became increasingly more rare and less informative after 1528. From November of that year, until the death of the Dutch Humanist in July, 1536, the collection of Erasmus' letters includes only two from Vives to Erasmus and none from Erasmus to Vives. The Mayans' edition of *Vivis Opera Omnia* has only fifteen letters which can be assigned to this period.

The first weeks of Vives after his return to Bruges were no doubt reserved to the intimacy of his wife, his relatives, and a few, close friends. The tragedy of Catherine, the madness of Henry, the insolence of Anne Boleyn, the dangerous situation of Fisher and Thomas More in the hands of an ambitious Wolsey, had all left the tender-hearted scholar in a veritable state of shock. With the obvious exception of Anne, all the human beings involved in the sad events of the previous months had been, at one time or another, Vives' patrons and personal friends. The Spanish Humanist was not a man of changeable loyalties; reserved as he was in choosing his friends, once his affection had been offered the friendship was there to stay: "It is not a trivial thing for me to make a friend," he wrote in his private correspondence.[2] With gallant effort and noble compassion Vives tried to excuse the King for his love affair and Queen Catherine for the irritation of the last moment. Human weak-

---

[1] In the General Introduction to *LC.*, pp. lxxxv-lxxxvi, De Vocht gives the dramatic history of the two bundles of Cranevelt's correspondence which he himself managed to save from the German invasion in the First World War.

[2] M, VII, 206-207; R, II, 1724 b. Letter from Vives to Eccius. "Neque enim sic amicitias soleo demittere in pectus meum, ut intervallum aliquod consuetudinis aut officiorum intermissio, possit mihi eas eripere."

nesses and miseries only intensified the devotion to his friends: "In matters of friendship" – he wrote to Pate – "I do not follow prosperity or good luck; on the contrary, the more miserable my friend is the more I love him; compassion increases charity." [3]

To this generous, forgiving attitude, Wolsey might very well have been the only important exception. At least Fevyn's aggressive expressions when it came to the Cardinal seemed to echo the tone of his own conversations with Vives. The letter of Vives to Vergara, written in all probability during the first weeks in Bruges after the exile from England, betrays an enormous reluctance to detach himself completely from the country where, in a desperate moment of his life, he had found warm friends and a new inspiration to live. Throughout the letter one also feels Vives' relentless attempt to justify his own behavior with respect to Catherine. In January of 1529, the publication of his treatise *De officio mariti* gave him another opportunity to pay a warm tribute to the virtues of the lonely Spanish Queen:

"In our times Christ Our Lord gave us the example of Catherine, the Spanish Queen of England, the wife of Henry VIII . . . Everytime I think of such a woman I feel ashamed of myself. Among all the examples of fortitude in adversity which history has kept for us no one can be compared with the truly manly strength of Catherine amidst the most adverse and bitter circumstances. If Catherine had lived in an age where virtue was honored, people would have adored her in a temple as an oracle from above . . ." [4]

From Bruges, however, Vives could not do much for her. "In these rough and cruel times," he wrote to the loyal Claymond, "my voice has been almost reduced to silence." [5] It was, however, impossible to forget for a moment the tragedy which was unfolding on the other side of the English channel. Day after day the news from England kept Vives' pain constantly alive. In May, 1529, the trial of Henry's marriage with Catherine began in the presence of Campeggio, Wolsey, and a great number of English bishops. In June, Catherine dignified the farce with her beautiful presence. Kneeling in front of Henry, Catherine proclaimed

[3] Fevyn calls the Cardinal "the idol of England" (*LC.*, 252, v. 15) and "the insane Cardinal" (*Ibid.*, 243, v. 56). See also *LC.*, 254, v. 10.

[4] M, IV, 322; R, I, 1276. "Nec aetati nostrae voluit Christus deesse exemplum, multum etiam ad posteros manaturum, quod praebet Catharina Hispana Britanniae Regina, Henrici Octavi uxor . . . pudet memetipsius . . . quum feminam illam conspicio tanta inter res adversissimas ac tristissimas tamque robusta virilitate pectoris . . . ; si tam incredibilis virtus in illa incidisset tempora, quum honos erat propositus magnis virtutibus, iam olim haec et heroinarum splendorem obscurasset, et in templis tamquam Numen coelitus demissum adoraretur . . ." (*De O. M.*, 1)

[5] M, VII, 214; R, II, 1728.

aloud her unflinching love for her husband and begged him not to go
away. After that, Vives' advice finally prevailed, and the Queen completely withdrew into the privacy of her own suffering. Like most of the
King's victims, she loved Henry until the last day of her life.

Catherine's loneliness was made even more bitter by the apparent
complicity of some of her and Vives' closest friends. The appointment
of Thomas Boleyn, the father of Henry's mistress, as Earl of Wiltshire
and Ormonde was preceded by the appointment of Thomas More as
Chancellor of England. Erasmus also seemed completely blind to Henry's
injustice. In February, 1530, the Dutch Humanist dedicated to the same
Thomas Boleyn a meditation to Psalm 22; three years later, two months
after Henry's secret wedding with his pregnant cocotte, Erasmus dedicated to him another of his writings. Only John Fisher can share with
Juan Luis Vives the glory of an unwavering loyalty to the cause of
Catherine of Aragon.

In spite of such a loyalty to the Queen, Vives' attitude toward Henry
remained always noble and forgiving. On January 13, 1531, for the
last time in his life, Vives wrote a valiant message to the King. His words
were kind and frank, neither condoning the evil deed nor condemning
the individual conscience of Henry. Vives could not forget the favors of
the King nor betray the rights of the Queen. He was too humble to
allow himself an arrogant judgment, and too faithful to indulge in
hypocritical flattery. He was too aware of his own weakness to take
pleasure in presumptuous self-righteousness but he also knew the clear
limits of tolerant magnanimity.

For several years, the generosity of Your Majesty made financially possible for me a life of study. This is the third year I have not received anything
from Your Majesty, nor from the Queen, whom I very much want to see
happily going through the rest of her life in Your company . . .

Your Majesty asked me about the opinion of the universities on the words
of the Leviticus: "The brother shall not marry the wife of his brother." I
do not know what the professors will answer, but I know well what they
should answer. I myself wrote a little opusculum on the subject at the
request of Cardinal Wolsey. I will send it now to Your Majesty because I
am not sure Your Majesty ever read it.

Please think for a moment about what You are planning to do. Your
Majesty has a most prosperous kingdom. You are young, healthy, beloved
by all . . . What is the purpose of this war? To find a wife? But You have
a wife much more beautiful, illustrious, and noble than the one You seem
to lust for. Why men seek to get married? Certainly not for an obscene and

short pleasure. "I need children," You say, "heirs to my Crown." But You have a daughter of sweet disposition; You will be able to choose Your own son-in-law in a way You could never choose Your own son.

Who can guarantee to Your Majesty that You will have a child from this woman [Anne], a male who will live long enough to take the Kingdom from Your hands? . . . Finally, think seriously how great an occasion of civil disorder you will give to Your England in the future by complicating matters of legitimate succession with a new wedding!

I was moved to write all this, first, because of my obligations toward Your Majesty which are many and unforgetable; second, because of my love for England, which once before was to me the most benign hostess; and third, because of my concern and anxiety about the peace of the Christian world . . . Christ, the judge of all human intentions, is my witness. Please read this letter as written by the most faithful and loving of your friends. May the King of Kings help Your Majesty to do in everything whatever brings happiness to You and to Your Kingdom.[6]

Vives' letter did not change Henry's plans. In fact, it only helped to have Vives' name definitively removed from the list of those to whom a pension was due in the Account of the Treasurer.[7] From the letter to Henry we know that since 1528 Vives had been deprived of any regular income. The practical concern with the daily needs of his family tormented him throughout the last twelve years of his life. In a letter to

---

[6] M, VII, 134-136; R, II, 1670 a – 1671 b. "Inclyte Rex, aluit annos aliquot benignitas Tua otium meorum studiorum.: jam hic tertius est annus, ex quo nihil abs te accipio . . . Nec a Regina jampridem quicquam accipio, sed et Te et illam videre cupio concordissime, ac laetissime quod restat ex hac aevi brevitate, transigentes.

. . . Sciscitaris Academiarum sententiam de loco illo Levitici: "Frater non ducet uxorem fratris." Quid respondeant eruditi, nescio; quid responderi oporteat scio . . . Rogo te . . . fac consideres etiam atque etiam, an cogites quid in re tanta statuas, quid agas, quo progrediare. Habes regnum florentissimum, Tu optima ac virenti aetate carissimus tuis . . . At quid tandem queretur hoc bello? Uxor? At habes cui haec, quam concupiscis, nec bonitate, nec genere, nec forma, nec pietate Tui comparari possit; sed quid per uxorem quaeritur? Non credo voluptas brevis aliqua et obscoena; Liberi, inquis, heredes regni; at habes, Christi gratia, puellam mirae indolis; deliges arbitratu tuo generum, qualem non poteris eligere filium . . . Postremo reputa tecum, quantum in posterum belli civilis materiam relinqueres Tuae Britanniae, de legitima successione dissidenti, quam successionem novo hoc conjugio dubiam faceres . . .

Me ad hoc scribendum permoverunt Tui observantia . . . tum caritas erga Britanniam quae mihi aliquando fuit hospita benignissima . . . Christum invoco judicem cordium humanarum, me non alia mente aut gratia scripsisse . . . Faxit idem Rex regum semper statuas, quae Tibi, et regno Tuo sint felicia futura."

Scarisbick, *Henry VIII*, p. 508, writes: "It is also arguable that, though the need for a son was obvious, as things turned out, Henry placed England in at least as great political jeopardy by repudiating his first marriage as he would have if he had accepted his lot . . ."

[7] The omission was expressly recorded with these words: "Ludovicus Vives and R. T. are omitted." (Brewer, *Letters and Papers*, V, 325)

Vergara he confessed that "poverty terrifies me." And he added: "so far I have lived from the generosity of the Princes: what they give has no obligation attached to it." [8] He was convinced that the free and creative work of a scholar deserved the full support of the Royal Treasury because of its orientation to the common good. Now, except for some insignificant help from Claymond, he felt abandoned to his own resources.[9] Unfortunately, the wise Humanist was not a resourceful provider. Teaching, which was his natural solution, did not appeal to him. We know that the University of Louvain was interested in his services.[10] However, judging by the scanty information we have, it is almost certain that he never accepted a full-time position in its roster. On the other hand, there are indications that he occasionally lectured both at Louvain and at the University of Paris.[11] His in-laws tried to interest him in an active life of business. Indeed, for a short time at least, the pressing need of his family forced him into the public market.[12] But he was not born to be a merchant. His trade was elsewhere.

Following his own natural inclinations he searched, once again, for powerful patrons. In tune with the historical trend of the moment he decided to make the best of the Imperial benevolence toward the Erasmian circle after the conference of Valladolid (1527). In July, 1529, he dedicated his magnificent treatise *De Concordia et Discordia Generis Humani* to the Emperor, Charles V, from "Brugis tuis." [13] A few weeks later he offered a similar essay, *De Pacificatione,* to Alfonso Manrique, Archbishop of Seville and General Inquisitor of Spain.[14] In spite of

---

[8] R, II, 1734 b. Vives confesses to Vergara in the same letter that, as a young man, he thought of an ecclesiastical career as a solution to his financial problems.

[9] M, VII, 142; R, II, 1676 a. Letter from Vives to Pate: "Scito Claymundum senem optimum, scripsisse ad me litteras plenissimas humanitatis illius solutae adversus me, et misisse viginti solidos: quod munus fuit mihi longe gratissimum, non quod juvare me possit in tantis meis quotidianis sumtibus, sed quod ab animo benevolentissimo profectum."

[10] Bonilla, *Luis Vives,* I, 252-253, quotes the opinion of Aubert Lemire, according to whom Vives taught rhetoric in the University of Louvain in 1530. Vives' treatise *De ratione dicendi* (Bruges, 1532) is presented as a summary of such lessons. In the correspondence of Vives there is no trace of this teaching.

[11] According to Mayans, *Vivis Vita* (I, 141), the second edition of Hyginius' fables was published by Vives in Paris in 1536 after a course of public lectures on the subject. However, Vives' letter to Fort, printed at the beginning of this work, had been written in 1518; the words "cum essem Parisiis, publico professurus auditorio" have, therefore, to be dated back to 1518. The *Exercitatio Linguae Latinae,* however, written by Vives in 1538, has many and vivid descriptions of the academic life in Paris, and suggests that Vives was writing about recent events.

[12] See Namèche, "Memoire," pp. 136 ff.

[13] M, V, 187-404; R, II, 75-255. (*De Concordia*) Eight months later, in February, 1530, Charles V was crowned "Dominus totius mundi" by Clement VII in Bologna.

[14] M, V, 405-447; R, II, 256-293. (*De Pac.*) On Manrique's role at the conference of Valladolid see Bataillon, *Erasmo y España,* pp. 236-247, 252-253, 270-271.

Manrique's pro-Erasmian attitude in Valladolid, Vives could not waste this opportunity to vent his indignation about the methods of the Holy Tribunal:

To be an inquisitor is such a dangerous and momentous job that if you ignore its true purpose and finality you will gravely sin, particularly when the bodies, the possessions, the reputations, and the lives of so many people are involved. It is truly amazing that so much authority was ever granted to a judge who is not deprived of human passions or to the prosecutor who often enough is nothing but a cynic and hateful calumniator . . .[15]

In November of the same year (1529) Vives dedicated some devotional writings to Margaret of Austria, the aunt of Charles V and one of the leading figures at Cambrai.[16] The presence of the Imperial Court in Bruxelles since December, 1530, facilitated Vives' design. In August, 1532, he could finally report to Vergara that the Emperor was regularly sending him one hundred fifty ducats, "which," he added, "cover more or less half of my expenses provided I receive this money as safely and regularly as I used to receive the Royal pension from England." [17] To pay the other half, Vives was even ready to accept some ecclesiastical benefice through the mediation of Vergara, an ideal solution from the financial point of view which, unfortunately, never became a reality. The economic situation of Vives, however, improved much with the Imperial ducats. Probably at the end of this year (1531) Vives was able to invite his younger sister, Beatriz, to come from Valencia to Bruges.[18] The outcome of the Inquisitorial process against her parents had left her completely indigent.

The names of the people to whom Vives dedicated some of his books in this period suggest other sources of patronage. Among them we find the King and the Treasurer of Portugal, the Dukes of Gandía and Béjar, the Rector of the University of Salamanca, the Secretary to Charles V, and the future Philip II.[19] In the last years of his life Vives was taken

---

[15] M, V, 405; R, II, 256. "Accedit . . . munus inquisitionis haereticorum, quod quum tantum sit, tamque periculosum, nisi sciat quis quo pertineat, eo peccabit gravius quo de plurium salute, fortunis, fama, et vita agitur; mira dictu res, tantum esse permissum vel judici, qui non caret humanis affectionibus, vel accusatori, qui nonumquam ad calumniam, odium vel spes, vel prava aliqua impellit animi cupiditas." (De Pac., dedication)

[16] M, VII, 41-100; R, I, 391-441. (Sacrum diurnum)

[17] R, II, 1736 a. This letter, taken from Bonilla's "Clarorum virorum epistuale ineditae," published in Revue Hispanique, VIII (1901), was not known to Mayans.

[18] M, VII, 139-141; R, II, 1673 b – 1674 a. Vives wrote to Honoratus: "Sororem meam ad me accersam, nam hic, ut spero, commodius vel nubet vel vivet coelebs."

[19] De conscribendis Epistulis, was dedicated to the secretary of Charles V; De officio mariti went to the Duke of Gandía, father of Saint Francis Borgia, the second General of the Jesuits; De ratione dicendi has a dedication to the Rector

under the auspices of the Lord of Comines and Doña Mencía de Mendoza, the Duchess of Nassau. We know that in 1532 he spent a few weeks in the Chateau of Comines in the company of George of Halewyn, Viscount of Nieuport and Lord of Comines, cousin to the famous historian Philip of Comines, a great patron of Erasmian scholars, and a friend of Vives himself, at least since 1523.[20]

Dona Mencía de Mendoza was the daughter and heiress of Rodrigo, Marquis of Cañete. In 1524 she married the Duke of Nassau who was in Spain as a confidant and captain of Charles V.[21] Their marriage perfectly symbolized the political unity of Flanders-Brabant and Spain. After 1537, Vives divided his time between Bruges and the Nassau Palace at Breda where he supervised the humanistic education of Doña Mencía. After the death of the Duke in September, 1538, the well-educated lady intensified, even more, her private studies under the direction of Vives. Probably at her request Vives published his commentaries on the *Bucolica* of Vergil, in Breda (1537), the last and most mature work of this kind which he ever wrote.[22] Also in Breda, Vives published his *Censura de Aristotelis Operibus*, an intriguing book which will be discussed later and which, most likely, bears witness to the philosophical curiosity of Doña Mencía.[23] To this time also belongs the last letter of Vives included in the collection of Mayans. From Breda, on December 16, 1538, Vives wrote to Juan Maldonado, "the first historian of the Erasmian revolution in Spain'" (Bataillon), and a great admirer of Vives' books. The letter was sad and bitter. Maldonado's

of the University of Salamanca; Vives dedicated the *Exercitatio Linguae Latinae* to the future Philip II; *De Anima* was offered to the Duke of Béjar, the same Duke who years later would be honored by Cervantes with the dedication of *Don Quijote*.

The Portuguese Crown was also distinguished by Vives' dedications. Vives dedicated to the Treasurer of the Portuguese Kingdom his *Exercitationes animi in Deum*, while John III of Portugal was chosen by Vives to receive the dedication of his monumental work *De Disciplinis*. Damian de Goas, a powerful courtier of John III, was a good friend of Vives. (M, VII, 198; R, 1718. Letter from Vives to Damian).

[20] In April, 1523, Vives visited the castle for the first time, as Fevyn reports to Cranevelt (*LC.*, 53, v. 46). Vives describes George of Halewyn in the following terms: "Est quidem Haloinus amari dignus, sive quia litteratus princeps, sive quia vir humanissimus, sive quia me et ipse redamat" (*LC.*, 56, vv. 49-51. Letter from Vives to Cranevelt). From the correspondence between Vives and Halewyn only two letters have survived (M, VII, 146-147; R, II, 1678 b – 1680 a). Both are impersonal letters dealing with Budé's recently published *De Asse*.

For a comprehensive biography of Halewyn, see *LC.*, introd. to letter 56, d.

[21] For a short biography of the Lord of Breda, see *LC.*, 114, note 80. The biographical data of Doña Mencía can be found in Bonilla, *Luis Vives*, I, 269.

[22] M, II, 1-68; R, I, 921-972. (*Interpretatio allegorica in Bucolica Vergilii*)

[23] See below, pp. 170-171.

[24] M, VII, 221-222; R, II, 1732 b – 1733 b.

enthusiasm for Vives' work did not impress the Humanist. As for Spain, Vives knew well that he had no enemies there because no one understood or read his books.[24]

After 1528, the normal residence of Vives was Bruges, with some occasional journeys to Louvain where he still had close and powerful friends, and to Ghent and Bruxelles, the Court of Charles V.[25] From September to November of 1529, Vives and his wife had to leave Bruges because of the pest, and take refuge in the city of Lille. From a letter of Vives to a friend in Paris we know that Margaret returned to Bruges long before her husband, because "she had no apprehension whatsoever concerning the plague." Vives refused to join her "until there was no trace of danger." [26]

Life in Bruges was probably dull and uneventful. Only the presence of the Imperial Court occasionally brought some merry festivities to the cities of Flanders.[27] Apparently in 1536 Vives made a short visit to Paris where he lectured on Hyginius, one of his favorite poets.[28] Some biographers have suggested that in those years Vives cooperated with Erasmus in the edition of Seneca's works, but the correspondence between the two great Humanists does not seem to corroborate this opinion.[29] Others, for several reasons, have dramatized a possible visit by Ignatius of Loyola to Vives in August, 1530. It is true that Ignatius was at that time a student at Montaigu in Paris and that perhaps he visited Flanders on several occasions to beg for financial help for his own support from the rich Spanish merchants.[30] However, if he ever met Juan Luis Vives in Bruges, their conversation was likely casual and without special significance. At least neither man has left the slightest proof of a relevant exchange. A married man in his forties, as Vives was, did not exactly fit with Loyola's ideal of a future apostolic team. In fact, the group which

[25] In January, 1533, Vives wrote to Budé: "Dies est jam decimus mensis; sum Gandavi proficiscens Bruxellam." Quoted by Vives himself in De Conscribendis epistulis (M, II, 295; R, II, 867 a).
[26] M, VII, 220; R, II, 1731 b – 1732 a. Letter from Vives to Antonio Barquero.
[27] Vives mentions some of those "ludi celeberrimi" in a letter to Erasmus (EE., IX, 2502, vv. 8-10).
[28] See above, note 11.
[29] See EE., VII, 2040, 2056, vv. 1-11; 206, v. 1.
[30] Bonilla quotes Francisco Sacchini, Historia del instituto de San Ignacio, in favor of this interview. (Luis Vives, I, 201) According to Sacchini, Vives was deeply impressed by Loyola and even said to his friends: "This man is a Saint, and undoubtedly he will found a new religious order" (Ibid., p. 201). Actually the prophecy was written after the Order had been approved by Paul III. Although Mayans (I, 85, Vivis Vita) brings also this anecdote, his only source was the testimony of Sacchini whose book has all the defects of hagiographical literature Vives himself criticized in his treatise De Disciplinis. (M, VI, 107-108; R, II, 423 a-b)

assembled around the founder of the Jesuits at Montmartre in August, 1534, was a youthful, uncommitted and still manageable troupe.

Of much more significance than any certain or uncertain event of this time was the intellectual and spiritual transformation of Juan Luis Vives in the years which followed his return from England.

The books he wrote in the last period of his life are by far the most creative and original. Up to 1528 Vives had been indeed a significant member of the Erasmian circle, a historical character of relative importance for the understanding of Flemish and English Humanism. However, in the last twelve years of his life, Vives became one of the most important reformers of European education and a philosopher of universal relevance to the history of sixteenth-century thought. Such a change was the result of a long series of heart-breaking tribulations. Suffering forced him into a square confrontation with the mystery of man himself. Man's passions had deprived him, little by little, of everything he used to love and to value. Racial and religious prejudice had sent his father to the fire, and his mother and sisters into poverty and humiliation. Fear had kept him away from his native town, which he now missed with touching nostalgia. Vives wrote to a friend who had been in Valencia, in May, 1531: "I received your letter from our common fatherland; if I loved you less I would envy you." [31] The threat of the Inquisition had forced him into places and together with peoples who remained always foreign and strange to him. The lust of a king had robbed him from two of the best friends he ever had: Catherine of Aragon and the unique Thomas More. He saw at close quarters the trickery and deceit of an ambitious Cardinal and after only one year lost the only Pope he sincerely admired. He loved peace and harmony and had to live amidst a storm of religious hatred, nationalistic wars, and the threats of the Turks. He was alienated from the classroom by all the petty intrigues of the professorial cliques, and lost the affection of Erasmus because his books were not selling well in the fair of Frankfurt. Furthermore, he was poor and ill. Life had reduced him to that silent loneliness where the mediocre man sinks into resignation and shallow routine while the genius arises to creative meditation. It was precisely at this conjuncture when his Jewish talent for meeting outside persecution with the hope and the wealth of internal reflection led him to the climax of his intellectual career. Vives' private correspondence echoes with singular eloquence the incidents of the struggle. A pervasive disappoint-

---

[31] M, VII, 139; R, II, 1673. "Epistulas tuas accepi duas ... alteram ex communi patria, cuius aspectum equidem inviderem tibi si minus te amarem."

ment with life and a growing longing for death was already clearly expressed in October, 1527, a few weeks after Clara Cervent's decease:
"I cannot see how life can be sweet or desirable to anybody in this world
of ours." [32] In the same letter (vv. 10-15) Vives wrote a rather cynical
remark about his own diseases: "Only one thing makes me happy; to
think that if these pains last long enough they will bring the end of all
my suffering." In January, 1528, he wrote to Cranevelt: "O, if the Lord
wished to free His creature from this mortal corruption . . . ! If everything continues as it is now, my dear Cranevelt, we must rejoice at already being above thirty-five years of age." [33] Cranevelt was forty-three
and Vives, thirty-six. Five months later he asked himself: "In the storms
of this world how can death be anything but a gift? So far as I am
concerned, life is not very pleasant and I am glad that most of it, I
think, has already been thrown away." [34]

The first positive result of this overpowering sadness and loneliness
was a radical sincerity *vis-à-vis* the problems of man's existence. Human
glory and human applause ceased to be perceptible from his poor house
of Bruges. In August, 1529, Vives wrote to Erasmus:

"I am glad you mentioned my name in the introduction to Saint Augustine,
only because it was you who did it as a sign of our mutual friendship.
Otherwise I do not care much about being mentioned or being admired;
not even bile is more bitter than human glory. Even if the whole world
applauded me as in a theater I would not feel one inch better or happier;
on the contrary, more miserable and a worse human being. The noise of
the applause pulls me out of myself; I cannot keep my eyes or my reflection
concentrated upon myself, busy as they are with the audience outside of
me . . . Please do not talk so much to me of the incitement of reputation
and fame; keep in mind that I do not care the least about it . . ." [35]

The "world outside" provided Vives with enough examples of the vanity
of human glory. In October, 1529, Wolsey fell and was deprived of all

[32] *LC.*, 248, vv. 67-68. "Nec video cui magnopere possit esse dulcis vita aut
expetenda, hoc orbis totius statu."
[33] *LC.*, 251, vv. 14-15. "Quod se res pergant ut coeperunt, gaudere utique
debemus, mi Craneveldi, nos esse iam quintum et tricessimum annum praeter-
gressos."
[34] *LC.*, 261, vv. 13-15. "Cui enim his mundi tumultibus non magni cuiusdam
beneficii loco sit mors? Mihi certe vita non est admodum jucunda, et gaudeo mihi
τὸν τοῦ βίου πλεῖον sicut credo, ἐκτετοξεῦσθαι.
See also *LC.*, 251, vv. 21-24. "Finita fabula, nihil opus est cultu scenico; at in
fabula, quid habent aliud histriones primarum partium, quam laborem et periculum,
dum vanam populi voluptatem captant?"
[35] *EE.*, VIII, 2208, vv. 18-32. "Etiamsi orbis totus tamquam in theatro me
admiretur, mihi applaudat, non sentio me pilo meliorem factum aut feliciorem,
miseriorem saepe ac peiorem."

the possessions carefully accumulated in long years of struggle; More was appointed Chancellor, but in May, 1532, his own conscience forced him to resign; in June, 1533, Catherine was humiliated with the crowning of Anne Boleyn; a few months later, Princess Mary, the pupil of Vives, was declared a bastard and excluded from the Crown; almost at the same time Henry VIII, the Defensor Fidei, was excommunicated by the Pope; in May, 1534, Vives reported to Erasmus that More, Fisher, Vergara, and Tovar were in jail; in July, 1535, the head of Fisher was replaced on the London Bridge by the head of the former Chancellor of the Kingdom, Thomas More; in January, 1536, the former Queen of England, Catherine of Aragon, died in poverty, completely alone; in May of the same year, Anne Boleyn was decapitated; three days later the King was engaged to Jane Seymour, who died the following year; in July, 1536, Erasmus died in Basle, and his disciples were then persecuted in every corner of Europe by the Spanish Inquisition; in October of the same year, Tyndale was burned in a somber "auto de fé" in Bruxelles, the Court of Charles V.

In addition to a detachment from any human consideration and respect, the last period of Vives' life brought forth a clear revival of religious fervor. The spiritual life of Vives is faithfully portrayed in the writings of this time. The very first occupation of Vives after his departure from England was to write, at the request of the provost of Saint Donatian, a liturgical prayer to the bloody sweat of Christ in Gethsemani.[36] The occasion was the plague known as *Sudor anglicus* or sweating sickness which infested Bruges in 1529.[37] Vives added a sermon to this composition on the same subject and a meditation on the passion of Christ.[38] Of the same character, is a collection of prayers written by Vives in 1535 under the general title, *Excitationes animi in Deum*.[39] All these writings are totally lacking in any dogmatic slant, but they express with enormous sincerity the longing of Vives' soul for a closer union with God and an affectionate admiration for Christ, the Symbol of all human suffering and the Carrier of all human guilt.

However, the most important aspect of Vives' inner transformation in those years can be described as an intense compassion for all the miseries of the individual and the human community together with an

[36] The Latin title was *Sacrum Diurnum de sudore Domini Nostri Jesu Christi.* (M, VII, 42-59; R, I, 391-407)

[37] Bonilla, *Luis Vives,* III, note 17 to chapter 9.

[38] M, VII, 59-100; R, I, 408-441.

[39] M, I, 49-162; R, I, 441-531. This collection of devout writings includes rules for meditation, daily prayers, prayers for every occasion, and a commentary on the Dominican prayer.

equally firm conviction that the improvement of the first would lead to the reform of the latter. This sympathetic concern with the destiny and the suffering of man inspired each page written by Vives in the years of his intellectual maturity. "My friend, Valdaura," he wrote to Budé in November, 1529, "will present you with a copy of my book, *De Concordia,* written last summer out of the compassion I feel for our times. ·Weak as I am to remedy all the evil around me, at least to write about them gives me some consolation and peace of mind." [40] And shortly before that, in August of the same year, Vives wrote to Erasmus: "The only thing I consider solid and permanent is to be of some help to the public good." [41] The fascinating novelty of Vives' late work springs from this tormented, hopeful, concentrated meditation on the miseries and resources of man. Taking himself as a point of departure Vives made man the center of his reflective observation, rather than the recipient of a pompous eulogy framed on philosophical abstractions or theological schemes. Like Pascal, a hundred years later, Vives described man both as a potential monster and a potential saint. Although he called man "a difficult animal," Vives' late work on peace and education was derived from the premise that the only hope of a miserable man is an enlightened man, and that vice, the source of all suffering, is nothing else than a stupid miscalculation and an erroneous value judgment.

The first tract of Vives in this time, the magnificent *De Concordia et Discordia Generis Humani* (1529), is not anymore a historical judgment on a concrete event of the day, but a superb meditation on the relationship between international disasters and the disorder of human passions.[42] Adams writes of this book: "In this essay [Vives] brought to a climactic summary the constructive idealism and criticism developed by the early Tudor group centered around Colet, More, and Erasmus ... In a word, Vives' effort was to arouse the Emperor to rise and meet the challenge of leadership which makes Machiavelli's advice to his prince on how to be a locally successful Italian tyrant seem petty and provincial ..." [43]

The second masterwork written by Vives in this period is his encyclopedic *De Disciplinis* (1531).[44] According to Brucker and Comenius this

[40] M, VII, 218; R, II, 1730. "Accipies a Valdaura meo librum *De concordia* scriptum a me proxima aestate, dum me horum temporum miseret; et quando remedium tot malis adferre nequeo propter imbecillitatem virium, chartis saltem animum meum testor, in quo uno me consolor, ac utcumque quiesco."
[41] *EE.,* VIII, 2208, vv. 29-30. "Si qua hominum moribus prodesse queam, id demum solidum esse arbitror et permansurum."
[42] M, V, 193-403; R, II, 80-254.
[43] *Better Part of Valor,* p. 287.
[44] M, VI, 5-438; R, II, 337-689. The treatise is divided in two parts (*De causis corruptarum artium, De tradendis disciplinis*), books, and chapters.

book could have made Vives "the greatest philosopher of his century" if the author had given more time to some constructive suggestions for the future.[45] Some scholars, however, have gone far beyond this evaluation. According to R. Simon the book is more valuable to the history of philosophy than all the writings of Erasmus put together;[46] the Dutch scholar Andres Schott finds *De Disciplinis* more significant than the *Novum Organon* of Bacon.[47] Wychgram more prudently wrote that the history of philosophy in the sixteenth century cannot be grasped without it.[48] But, as Ortega y Gasset has rightly pointed out, *De Disciplinis* is more than just a revolutionary program of education.[49] It is an ambitious meditation on the purpose and the limits, the corruption and the reform of all human culture. In its approach *De Disciplinis* was in its century an absolutely original work destined to be in the future "more frequently plundered than loyally quoted" (Lange). The book is divided into two parts. The first deals with the causes of the corruption of studies in general and each discipline in particular: Grammar, History, Rhetoric, Natural Philosophy, Mathematics, Medicine, Ethics, and Civil Law. The second part is subtitled *De Tradendis Disciplinis*. Besides its purely pedagogical value, this part is historically informative because Vives gives a very detailed account and personal criticism of all the textbooks and works of reference available to both the students and the teachers of those days.

The third great tract of Vives was printed only two years before his death. The title of the book is somehow misleading, *De Anima et Vita*.[50] In spite of its conservative title and occasional traditional technicism, this book of Vives inaugurated in European thought the study of man based on reflection and observation without any metaphysical scheme. Lange calls Vives "the father of modern psychology," Schauman describes Vives as an "anthropologist," and Dilthey, who dedicates to Vives a great deal of attention in his brilliant essay on *Die Funktion der Anthropologie in der Kultur des 16. und 17. Jahrhunderts,* sees in him

---

[45] Brücker, *Historia,* IV, 88; Kayser, *Luis Vives,* p. 341, gives Comenius' quotation.
[46] Richard Simon, *Bibliothéque choisie,* II, 137.
[47] Quoted by Namèche, "Mémoire," p. 51.
[48] Quoted by Kayser, *Luis Vives,* p. 341.
[49] José Ortega y Gasset, *Vives-Goethe,* p. 63. The Spanish scholar, somehow exaggeratedly writes: "Vives was the first man of that century who stopped for a while the wild course of the Renaissance and asked himself about its meaning ... Vives' work is the first reflection of the western man upon his own culture, and his book should properly be called 'A Treatise on Human Culture.' "
[50] M, III, 300-520; R, II, 1147-1323. (*De Anima*)

an immediate forerunner of Telesio and Spinoza.[51] Because of its extra-ordinary importance, Vives' treatise will be widely discussed in this book.

In the last two years of his life (1538-1540) Vives was intensively dedi-cated to writing a comprehensive apologetical book which he intended to offer to the Pope. The work was never finished. However, after Vives' death, and at the request of his widow, Margaret, his loyal friend, Cranevelt, published the book in January, 1543, and dedicated it to Paul III.[52] With Vives' books of prayers and the Commentaries on Saint Augustine, this treatise, De Veritae Fidei Christianae, is the most im-portant document left to us for appreciating the religious life of the Jewish convert when the end of his earthly existence was well in sight. With this long book the literary production of Vives was completed. Altogether it includes fifty-two titles. Among the books of lesser im-portance written by Vives during his last years in Bruges, the Linguae Latinae Exercitatio (1538), a brilliant collection of dialogues written as a textbook of basic Latin vocabulary and grammar, deserves special mention.[53] In many ways these dialogues are better suited for their pur-pose than the Erasmian counterpart which in its social criticism was frequently too sharp and crude for use by children in the classroom. Erasmus was fully aware of the competition, and his judgment of Vives' dialogues was unjustly severe. The amazing popularity of Vives' book is abundantly proved by the number of its editions.[54] Other writings include: De communione rerum ad germanos inferiores (1535), a book which we have already mentioned; De Conscribendis epistolis, an inter-esting and autobiographical essay on epistolar style; [55] a short rhetorical essay, De Ratione dicendi (1532), and finally a prelection on the poet Hyginius.[56]

Since his return to Bruges, from England, Vives' health began to present alarming symptoms. All his life he had been plagued by frequent headaches and what probably can best be described as an ulcer of the

---

[51] Lange, Luis Vives, pp. 17 ff; the complete title of G. Schaumann's dissertation was "De J. L. Vives, Valentino philosopho, praesertim anthropologo, ex libris eius De Anima et Vita," published as Appendix VIII by Bonilla (Luis Vives, III, 149-160). This interesting document, first published in 1831, might very well be one of the first examples of the modern usage of the word "Anthropology." For Dilthey, see below p. 289, note 44.

[52] This book, with the dedication of Cranevelt to Paul III, is printed in vol. VIII of Mayans; R, II, 1323-1669.

[53] M, I, 283-409; R, II, 881-979.

[54] See below, Appendix I, pp. 300-306.

[55] M, II, 263-315; R, II, 841-881. (De conscribendis epistulis)

[56] M, II, 93-238; R, II, 689-807. (De ratione dicendi)

stomach.[57] The change in food and in climate always affected him very badly. The excess of work brought him more than once to a nervous collapse. From 1530 on, Vives' concern with his health became almost obsessive, or at least this is the impression we get from his private correspondence. Since early in his forties he had been tormented by a bad case of arthritis which almost crippled him. "This damned gout," he wrote to the Lord of Praets, "is causing me a terrible suffering; it crept up through the knees and reached my arms, my hands, and my shoulders." [58] To Erasmus in May, 1534: "Last summer I was seriously sick with a vicious colic. My arthritis has become by now familiar to me. I guess I got it because of the bad weather." [59] In the *Linguae Latinae Exercitatio* Vives wrote the following dialogue:

> Teacher – Tell me, what is Vives doing now?
>
> Nepotulus – He is acting like an athlete, but not very sportly.
>
> Teacher – What do you mean?
>
> Nepotulus – He is constantly wrestling, but not with great bravery.
>
> Teacher – Wrestling with whom?
>
> Nepotulus – With his podagra.
>
> Teacher – That is a treacherous fighter who always begins by grasping the feet.
>
> Nepotulus – Rather it is a cruel butcher who tortures the whole body.[60]

To his real diseases, Vives added the imaginary ones. He could not even see cherries without feeling nauseated, because as a child they had given him bad indigestion.[61] Without medical prescription he tried all kinds of medicines imported into Europe from the American Indians – strange behavior for a man who was constantly proclaiming his detachment from the vanities of human existence and longing for the eternal reward.[62]

On May 6, 1540, Juan Luis Vives died in Bruges, probably of a

---

[57] For the study of Vives' health, see Gregorio Marañon, *Españoles fuera de España*, 5th ed. (Madrid, 1961), pp. 20, 46-49.

[58] M, VII, 136; R, II, 1571. "Me podagra mea gravissime divexat, serpsit ad genua, ad manus, ad brachia usque ad humeros."

[59] *EE.*, X, 2932, vv. 5-7. "Podagra mea facta est mihi adeo familiaris ut iam minus sit ex assuefactione gravis. Eam puto me contraxisse e frigore potius quam ulla alia de causa. Aestate superiore graviter et periculose aegrotavi e colica."

[60] M, I, 299; R, II, 895 a (*ELL.*, VI).

[61] M, III, 350; R, II, 1189 a-b. "Puer quum Valentiae febri laborarem, et depravato gusto cerassa edissem, multis post annis quoties id pomum gustabam, toties non solum de febri memineram, sed habere mihi illam videbar." (*De Anima*, II, 2)

[62] This story is quoted by Puigdollers, *Filosofía española*, p. 310.

biliary calculus.[63] His life had been intense, but ridden by sadness. At twenty-seven Vives was not sure whether he could live ten years more.[64] At thirty-six he felt and spoke like a decrepit patriarch. The joy of the Renaissance, the age of "the rediscovery of the world and of man," was not meant for him. He was buried under the altar of Saint Joseph in the Church of Saint Donatian which today does not exist. His brother-in-law, Nicholaus, placed a gravestone with Vives' name there. His childless wife joined him twelve years later.

Jan Van Berghe's drawing of Vives portrays him as a well-built man of middle height, wide shoulders, and dignified countenance.[65] The forehead was ample and serene; the eyebrows, thin and unobtrusive; his eyes, slightly close-set, large and penetrating, saddened but kind; the nose, large and straight; the mouth, small and firmly closed with a slight touch of seriousness and tenacity due to a strongly protruding underlip; the small chin in sharp contrast with a robust neck. Juan Luis died without enemies or disciples. He was peaceful, serene, and nonaggressive. He never founded a sect because he never created a mistake of his own. Instead of raising a new flag he thought deeply and modestly about all the human achievements of the past and all the partial errors of his predecessors. He was both affectionate and reserved. He was deeply and easily hurt by other people, but he never hurt anyone. He was neither brilliant nor humorous but rather judicious and calm. In spite of all the disasters he had to witness he died with the firm persuasion that man could do, and would in the future do, much better than before. Vives was a remarkable man.

---

[63] The calculus is mentioned by Cranevelt in the dedication of the treatise *De Veritate fidei Christianae* to Paul III (M, VIII, ii; R, II, 1324).

[64] M, III, 57; R, II, 307 a. "Si decem annos valetudine non prorsus adversa vixero, e mentibus illorum . . ." (*Adv.* ps-d)

[65] For Vives' iconography, see Jesus Gil y Calpe, "Iconografía de Luis Vives," *Cultura Valenciana,* II (1927), 125-130.

VIVES' THOUGHT

CHAPTER 7

IN THE STEPS OF ERASMUS AND BEYOND

"Homo homini par"
From *Satellitium animi*.

The second half of this book deals with the thought of Juan Luis Vives. Our task is not an easy one, partly because of the encyclopedic wealth of Vives' ideas, and partly because they are unsystematic, complex, and sometimes even nebulous and contradictory. Another major difficulty in grasping the originality and individuality of Vives' thought is the fact that both his name and his work have been unduly overshadowed by the still glamorous figure of Erasmus of Rotterdam. Scholars with a mediocre knowledge of Vives' intellectual life have not hesitated to characterize Vives simply as a disciple of Erasmus, if not as a full member of the Erasmian movement in Spain, at least as a loyal representative of the Erasmian circle in the Netherlands and England. My contention is that such characterization is unfair to Vives. Therefore, in this chapter I shall review the personal relations between the two men as the best means to qualify the extent and the limitations of Erasmus' influence upon Vives' thought. This chapter will also be a convenient link between the narrative of Vives' life and the description of his intellectual achievements.

There is no doubt whatsoever that Erasmianism was Vives' point of departure after his break with the languid and stiff routine of medieval scholasticism. In fact Vives' rejection of Parisian conservatism was greatly influenced by Erasmus' early and revolutionary writings. When Vives arrived in Paris in the fall of 1509, Erasmus was forty years old. Although his reputation at that time could not be compared to that of Lefèvre or Gaugin, Erasmus' name was already well-known in Paris. In a way Erasmus was unique in his intellectual cosmopolitanism. By birth and education he was associated with Deventer and Agricola; as a former student of Montaigu, he was a close friend of Gaugin and

Andrelini. In England he had learned Greek from Linacre, worked with
Thomas More in the translation of Lucian, and planned with Colet a
new orientation in Biblical studies. In 1500 he had become a Doctor of
Theology, and his books were an amazing success. Also in 1500 Erasmus
had published the *Adagia*, in 1503 the *Enchiridion*, in 1505, the commentaries to the *Annotations* of Valla, and in 1506, the translation of
Lucian's Dialogues. When Vives was in Paris, Erasmus published the
Praise of Folly (1511), a book which shook the self-complacency of the
university professors. In these writings Vives saw the ideal synthesis of
Windesheim and Florence, devotion and letters, which he was fundamentally seeking. Perhaps the general trend of Erasmus' thought reminded him of Nebrija's ideals and the movement started by Valla in
Bologna. In any case he received the definite impression that something
excitingly new was brewing beyond the narrow borders of the University
of Paris. Actually, the lavish praise of Erasmus in Vives' first book,
Christi Jesu Triumphus, seems to indicate that one of the strongest
reasons behind Vives' decision to settle in the Netherlands was the
proximity of the Master.[1] Vives' encounter with Erasmus in 1516 was
a decisive event in the life of the young scholar. Under the patronage of
Erasmus, Vives' name and early writings were introduced to the great
circle of Flemish and English Humanists.[2] The first epistolar exchange
between the two men, in the summer of 1520, reveals Vives' juvenile
enthusiasm for Erasmus and the surprising intimacy of their relations
(Erasmus was twenty years older). The occasion was Vives' first visit to
Paris as a tutor of Cardinal Croy. Vives wrote Erasmus a long and vivid
report of the unexpectedly friendly reception he had enjoyed in Paris:

I thought that a visit [to Paris] at that time would be rather unpleasant
to me having just written the *Adversus Pseudo-Dialecticos*, explicitly
against the Parisian sophists ... But what happened was entirely different ...
As soon as I notified them of my arrival they came to see me and greeted
me with welcoming and polite words.[3]

[1] M, VII, 130; R, I, 273 b. "Habet quidem suum Adrianum noster Princeps;
utinam frater eius Ferdinandus Erasmum Roterodamum amicum meum probatissimum
et eruditissimum virum nancisceretur ..." (*C. J. Triumphus*).
[2] Erasmus wrote the introduction to Vives' *Declamationes Syllanae* (M, II, 315-
317; R, I, 703-704) and urged Thomas More to read Vives' *Adversus pseudo-
dialecticos* (*EE.*, IV, v. 1082). As we know, he also recommended Vives as a possible
preceptor to Prince Ferdinand (*EE.*, II, 917, v. 2045: "hoc saeculo vix alium norim
quem ausim cum eo committere.").
[3] *EE.*, IV, 1108, vv. 5-15. "Illud perincommode rebar accidisse, quod eo tempore
adversum pseudo-dialecticos scripsissem, eosque nominatim Parrhisienses ... Verum
re ipsa longe aliud sum expertus ... Venio Parrhisios ... et amicis per famulum
significo me adesse. Convolant ad me frequentes, salutant officiose, gratulantur
adventui."

The reason for this amazing friendliness was, according to Vives, a complete change in the attitude of the Parisian professors. The former victims of Erasmus' sarcasm were now his devout disciples.

Many times during and after the meals we talked about you. O my Erasmus! I wished you would permit me to praise you as they did ... According to them you have brought Saint Jerome back to life, your notes on the New Testament have done more for the Christian religion than a thousand years of scholastic discussions. They even enjoy your *Praise of Folly*. Finally, whether you like to hear it or not, these people think that you are supreme, admirable, and perfect ... There is certainly nothing they would not do for you; they want you to know that their homes and everything therein, their families and friends, are entirely at your disposal ...[4]

Of course, Erasmus knew well that the picture was highly exaggerated. "Although I have experienced the good disposition of the French people," he wrote back to Vives, "I am afraid that your last letter was only the expression of your own feelings toward me." Jokingly Erasmus expressed his satisfaction with Vives' pleasant visit to Paris: "I thought that by going to Paris, the capital and fortress of sophistry, you were risking being stoned to death or pierced by the horns of those blockheads." On the other hand, Erasmus' response was equally flattering to his young friend, to whom he gave the delicate mission of mediating his dispute with Budé. The letter ended: "Take good care of yourself, my most learned Luis. We want you back as soon as possible, happy and smiling." [5]

As we might expect from observing such a close relationship, Vives' writings were decidedly Erasmian in character. The most remarkable is

---

[4] *Ibid.*, vv. 50-69. "Ad mensam tertio verbo sermo statim de te varius, multus etiam sublatis mensis. O mi Erasme, dicerem omnia si patereris te in epistola ad te laudari ... Tacendum itaque erit invito quid illi dicant de Hieronymo tua opera sibi ipsi restituto, quid de Novo Testamento suae integritati reddito, labore longe Christianae pietati utiliore quam quae sunt intra mille annos in scholis clamata ... ut Moria sit omnibus in deliciis ... Illud nunc feres velis nolis, nulla te illos ex parte spectare, unde non occurras summus, admirabilis, absolutus ... nihil se tua causa non facturos, suas esse tibi apertas domos, si illuc iveris, paratas facultates, familias, opes, amicos."

[5] *EE.*, IV, 1111, vv. 70-73. "Porro quod scribis istic plerosque tam magnifice sentire de lucubrationibus meis, equidem ut agnosco candorem gentis Galliae erga me, ita vereor ne hic sane nonnihil de tuo in me studio sis admensus." And, toward the beginning of the letter: "... praesertim Lutetiae, ubi quod huius disciplinae veluti regnum et arx quaedam esse videbatur, periculum erat ne lapidareris aut crabronum aculeis confodereris." (vv. 6-9). Finally at the end of the same letter: "Bene vale, Ludovice doctissime, et cura ut te quam primum hic hilarem ac lubentem videamus." (vv. 92-93).

the lengthy meditation on the Penitential Psalms dedicated to Cardinal
Croy. Vives was well aware of the lack of originality in the choice of his
subject. The intense spirit of compunction and self-reproach which characterizes these prayers of David provoked a stream of pious literature in
the sixteenth century. Saint John Fisher dedicated one of his early publications to these Psalms, and Luther, the very first of his writings.[6]
Lefèvre d'Etaples had published his own commentaries on the Penitential Psalms in March, 1509, and Erasmus worked for many years on
the edition of Arnobius' book on the same subject.[7] John Longlond, the
Lenten preacher at the Court of Henry VIII, made these Psalms the
unique matter of his sermons in 1518, the same year in which Vives
published the *Meditations*.[8] Perhaps on account of this abundant literature Vives was very eager to make clear that he had not imitated any
one: "Actually," he wrote, "I did not even consult any of these writers,
since I was taking a totally different approach."[9] The truth of the
matter is that Vives' book, far from presenting any "new approach,"
merely stresses some of the basic principles of Erasmus' *Philosophia
Christi*. As Erasmus recommended, Vives sought to enliven his religious
life through personal contact with the Scripture: "Very frequently" –
he wrote in the dedication of this book to Croy – "I read the Penitential
Psalms, especially the fifth."[10] The reading of the Bible, as Erasmus recommended it, was not only a pious exercise but a serious, scholarly
endeavor. Such was Vives' enthusiasm for it that at that moment of his
life he was contemplating a total dedication to Biblical exegesis. With
almost juvenile affectation Vives lets the reader know that in writing his
meditations, the author has used all the critical apparatus available: the
Latin translation of Saint Jerome, the Greek version of the Septuaginta,
and even the Hebrew original and the Chaldean paraphrase. The last
part of the claim, however, sounds rather unbelievable since Vives confesses on the same page that "I do not know a word of Hebrew or
Chaldean."[11]

[6] The full title of Fishers' book was *The Exposition of the Seven Psalms,* edited
in London (1508) by W. Worde. Luther wrote "Die erste Psalmenvorlesung." See
Luther's Werke, ed. O. Clemen, 7 vols., 5th ed. (Berlin, 1959), V, 38-221.
[7] On Erasmus' work on Arnobius, see *EE.,* 1304, introd., pp. 99-100. On Lefèvre's
edition and commentary on the Psalms, see Renaudet, *Préréforme et Humanisme,*
pp. 512-514.
[8] See Marc Hadour, *L'Univers de Thomas More,* p. 213.
[9] M, I, 217; R, I, 336 a. "Neque vero sum aliquem eorum qui de hac ipsa re
scripserunt aemulatus, quippe qui nullum viderim, et forsitan longe ab illis diversum
sectatus sum iter." (*Meditationes*).
[10] M, 217; R, 335 a. "Septem paenitentiae psalmos recitabam frequenter, et
delectabar in primis ipso quinto." (*Meditationes*).
[11] M, I, 163; R, I, 292-293. In the introduction to the second series of meditations

Other traits of the Erasmian Gospel are equally conspicuous in this youthful work by our Humanist. Erasmus' distrust of speculation manifests itself in Vives' constant words of disdain for all human knowledge:

Blessed are the little ones who have reached the Wisdom of God rather than the foolishness of this world; those who ignore everything but Christ crucified ... What else can they know, those who already know it all? Is it not true that whoever knows God, the Creator of the Universe, knows whatever can be known?

Mad, abortive pieces of clay and dust are those men who proudly imagine themselves to be Your [God's] confidants and secretaries, and dare to make bold statements about any imaginable thing. The mysteries of God should rather be worshipped in silence than tarnished with human words.[12]

Erasmus' emphasis on the Pauline dualism of a spiritual soul and a sinful flesh finds a vigorous expression in Vives' harsh condemnation of the body:

Such is the virulence of sin that through the body it penetrates and infects the soul.

Our souls carry the heavy burden of the bodies with great misery and pain; because of the bodies, the souls are confined to the narrow limits of this earth where all the filth and smut seems to converge.[13]

Erasmus' attack on ceremonial acts of devotion as a betrayal of true piety and religion was eloquently carried on by his young admirer:

I know well that the bloody sacrifice of innocent beasts is of no avail as long as the sinner retains the crime he himself committed. Therefore, o God, I offer myself as a host in expiation for my sin.[14]

The unresolved conflict of human and supernatural values, which is the

---

Vives writes: "Satis mihi fuit capita quaedam praecidere, et periclitari stylum in eo scribendi genere, cui nos aliquando totos sumus tradituri."

[12] M, I, 175; R, I, 301 b. "O quanto sunt feliciores illi parvuli, illi stulti, qui sine prudentia mundi adepti sunt divinam sapientiam ... qui aliud nihil sapiunt nisi Christum et eum crucifixum ... Sed quid dixi? Aliud nil sapiunt? Quid aliud saperent qui omnia sapiunt? An non universa sapiunt qui Deum universorum sapit?" (*Meditationes*).

Ibid., 206; 327 a. "Heu dementiam eorum qui homuli ex argilla et luto ficti, de te tuisque rebus, admirande Deus, tamquam secretarii tui, nihil se nescire putant, nihil non audent temerarii affirmare."

[13] M, I, 169; R, I, 297 b. "Simul ac infusum in corpus est, summo cum dolore uno temporis puncto hominem leto affligat amaro.

Ibid., 231; 346 a. "Sarcina corporis mens nostra obruitur et premitur, agit hic in terra, in quam fertur velut in sentinam quicquid est foetens, quicquid immundum, quicquid sordidum in toto mundo."

[14] *Ibid.*, 214; 333 a. "Ceterum novi parum ad rem facere cruorem et corpora caesa pecorum, quae nihil commerita sunt, quam is qui commeritus est, spectet ridens atque securus. Quare meipsum offero hostiam pro peccato meo."

distinguishing mark of Erasmianism, finds an easy solution in this immature work of Vives. According to him, Christian revelation is nothing more than a solemn proclamation of the natural law: "That very law which God impressed in our hearts was proclaimed with resounding and clear voice to all mankind." [15] Even such a concrete aspect of the doctrine as the existence of Purgatory "was revealed by the Holy Spirit to the Jews, to the philosophers, and to the poets." [16] A quotation of Vergil is brought here to prove the point; a few pages later "the divine poet Homer" is quoted in favor of the dogmatic truth of the Angel's fall, "a truth which Homer borrowed from the Scripture." [17] This is the way Vives understood Erasmus in 1518.

Vives' uncritical and enthusiastic Erasmianism (1514 to 1518) was soon tested and progressively tempered by events which disrupted one of the happiest and most creative periods in the life of the Dutch Humanist. After an unpleasant encounter with Martin Dorp, which was amicably resolved in 1516 through the mediation of Thomas More, Erasmus had enjoyed a period of relative calm in Louvain.[18] As a professor of theology, and in keeping with the program of reform set forth by himself in his essay, *Ratio verae Theologiae* (1518), Erasmus began to correct and complete the popular *Paraphrases* of the New Testament which he had started in 1517. In January, 1519, he concluded the Epistle to the Corinthians, and in May of the same year, the Epistle to the Galatians.[19] His prestige was enhanced by the foundation of the Trilingue College, including a group of humanists basically loyal to his own ideas. Vives, the tutor of Cardinal Croy, was a powerful ally. In Erasmus' eyes Vives was the ideal layman of a new Christianity; he could write devout meditations in classical Latin and reject scholastic speculations with devastating criticism.

This period of promising calm was shattered by the rebellion of Luther in 1517. The zealots of the theological faculties in Cologne and Louvain, who had always worried about Erasmus' detachment from

[15] *Ibid.*, I, 232; R, I, 346 b. "Quam legem ipse in cordibus nostris scripserat, eandem voce exerta claraque apud totum mundum pronuntiavit."
[16] *Ibid.*, 233; 347 b. "Haec quidem tradita a Spiritu Sancto Israeliticae familiae, philosophi et poetae, ut etiam alia permulta, acceperunt."
[17] *Ibid.*, 244; 355 b. "Haec prava mens quae nostrum genus perpetuo insectatur ... est Ata illa, quam ex sacris litteris, ut alia pleraque, Homerus mutuatus est."
[18] *EE.*, II, 304. The first letter of Dorp to Erasmus, who answered to him in a long of May, 1515 (*ibid.* 337). The second letter of Dorp was much more positive and friendly (*ibid.*, 347). On More's intervention see, *ibid.*, introd. to letter 388.
[19] On the history of the *Ratio Verae Theologicae,* see *EE.*, III, introd. to letter 745, pp. 175-176. *Ibid.*, letter 710, with the dedication of the *Ad Romanos Epistolae Paraphrasis* to Cardinal Grimani.

scholastic theology and sacraments, were soon able to discover appalling similarities between him and Luther. The slogan, "Erasmus laid the egg and Luther hatched the chicken," became dangerously popular among potential inquisitors. Erasmus made things worse by refusing to break clearly with either Luther or Melanchthon. In 1519, a few months after Louvain censured the doctrine of Luther, Erasmus was still addressed by the rebel of Wittenberg as "our glory and our hope." [20] After the excommunication of Luther in 1520, Erasmus' position in Louvain began to worsen day-by-day. The correspondence of that year portrays a man "sick and sad," trapped in the middle of "inseverable embroglios," whose life had been "made impossible by the cruel tyranny of the guardians of orthodoxy." [21] In June, 1520, an extraordinary papal legate arrived in the Netherlands with full inquisitorial powers.[22] Unfortunately, the legate was an old rival of Erasmus, the Cardinal Jerome Aleander, whose future ecclesiastical career depended on his ability to stop the spread of Lutheranism in the Low Countries. Aleander went to work immediately against the Augustinians, the Portuguese Jews in Antwerp, and against the Erasmians in Flanders and Brabant. Erasmus' close relations with the printers of Antwerp and the imprduent zeal of some of his disciples helped only to precipitate the inevitable end. After a tense meeting with Aleander in July, 1521, Erasmus decided to flee from Louvain to Basle.[23]

All this time Vives remained a close witness to the ugly persecution. Although he had friends and patrons on both sides, his loyalty to Erasmus was unshaken. The sudden departure of the master left him very depressed. In 1522 his correspondence with Erasmus became extremely frequent, long, affectionate. The letters were full of flattering remarks: "the youth is all yours"; "Christ has prepared for you a generous and large reward"; "most people want you back very badly."

[20] *EE.*, III, 933, v. 2. "Salutem. Toties ego tecum fabulor et tu mecum, Erasme, decus nostrum et spes nostra, necdum mutuo nos cognoscimus."
Two months before this letter from Luther to Erasmus, Melanchthon wrote also a friendly letter to Erasmus in which he called him "my brother and my master." (*EE.*, III, 910, v. 20). In the same letter Melanchthon writes: "Martin Luther, who is one of your greatest admirers (*studiossissimus nominis tui*) wants very badly to have your approval." In his answer Erasmus wrote that he had not yet read anything written by Luther. (*EE.*, 947, v. 33: *"ipse libros illius nondum legi"*).
[21] For those expressions, see *EE.*, IV, 1111, vv. 1, 77; 1104, vv. 3, 28.
On Erasmus' endless controversies with the ambitious Lee and the quarrelsome Latomus, see *EE.*, III, 365; 934, vv. 2-8.
[22] For the study of Aleander's activities in the Netherlands I have closely followed Paul Kalkoff, *Die Anfänge der Gegenreformation in den Niederlanden*.
[23] See *EE.*, IV, introd. to letter 1242, pp. 598-600, with the details of Erasmus' departure from Louvain and his journey to Basle.

The adversaries of Erasmus were characterized with almost bigoted disdain, an exception in the otherwise restrained style of Vives: "It is true that some people call you a Lutheran; but you know what kind of people they are, full of hatred and envy"; "they are not many, but they make a lot of noise"; "these old men are like beasts, they bite harder when they are about to die." [24] Under the safety device of Greek vocabulary Vives did not even hesitate to call these people by the nicknames apparently used in the circle of Erasmus' intimate friends. Latomus was called "the Lame" (ὁ χωλὸς) and "the Rocky" (in Latin, *Saxicida*); Nicholas of Egmont, "the Camel" (ὁ κάμηλος); and, finally, the friendly papal legate who was ready in his own words "to burn a dozen Lutherans," was ironically labeled "the Roman Angel" (ὁ ἄγγελος Ρωμαιὸς).[25]

In spite of these and other testimonies of Vives' devotion to Erasmus in the years of the persecution (1520-1522), a closer analysis of Vives' behavior and attitudes reveals a complex and slow process of detachment from Erasmian positions. Vives was not only neutral in the dogmatic disputes which caused the turmoil, he was simply not interested. For his own peace Vives would not have hesitated to make a formal pronouncement against Luther. In fact, a few years later (1524), when the rumor spread that Erasmus was planning to return to England, Vives bluntly urged him to take some dramatic step against Luther, not because of the merits of the case, but simply and purely in order to avoid complications with the Court of Henry VIII. "Otherwise," he wrote to Erasmus, "you will corrugate the foreheads of those whose good disposition toward you interests you most." [26] Shortly after Erasmus' departure from Louvain, Vives was still confident that a nice little word of praise for Aleander could make "the Roman Angel totally yours" [Erasmus'].[27]

Besides his lack of interest in the dogmatic issues at stake, the disgusting behavior of all concerned in the dispute forced him to think of those problems on a totally different level. Although he felt no sympathy

[24] In 1522 Vives wrote to Erasmus five letters (*EE.*, V, 1256, 1271, 1281, 1303, 1306).

[25] Vives accumulates all these nicknames in *EE.*, V, 1256, vv. 24, 30, 73.

[26] *EE.*, V, 1455, vv. 29-34. "Alii te in Britanniam venturam affirmabant... Venisses gratus optatusque Regi, Cardinali, et toti nobilitati. Sed si id statuis, incipe simul aliquid κατ' ἐκεῖνον μελετᾷν : aliter nonnullis corrugabis frontes, quorum imprimis convenit tibi esse exporrectas." The truth was that Erasmus was very reluctant to live in England: "In Anglia non libet vivere." (*EE.*, V, 1386, v. 15). On the other hand the Lutherans in Basle were threatening him with a martyrdom which, as he ironically said, "did no yet deserve." (*ibid.*, v. 17).

[27] *EE.*, V, 1256, vv. 67-68. The words "totally yours" were written in Greek, probably because Vives did not underestimate the "Roman angel's" ability to intercept the mail going from Louvain to Basle.

for Luther, the actions of the Roman inquisitors reminded him too much of the "most hateful process" his own parents were going through in Valencia. The cruelty of Aleander, the vanity of Lee, the extravagances of Latomus, the fanaticism of Egmont, did not represent exactly the human virtues he admired most. It was perhaps not too clear to Vives which side was right in the interpretation of the Epistle to the Romans; it was evident to him, however, that the theologians involved in the dispute were themselves not exemplary Christians. In his treatise *De Concordia* (1529), Vives wrote:

I know well that the bloody sacrifice of innocent beasts is of no avail so long as the sinner retains the crime he himself committed. Therefore, O God, I offer myself as a host in expiation for my own sin.[14]

The world has never before seen such a lack of piety; never before was there more calumny and defamation. The reproach of impiety is mutual: individuals blame individuals, nations accuse nations of poor Christian spirit ... Unfortunately, their reproach is well-founded; their only mistake is that each one excludes himself from it. All are equally impious; having lost even the shadow of Christianity they dare to inquire into the life of other people, to condemn and to punish with the loss of fame, possessions, and even life ... How can they dare to judge about something they never saw, not even in dreams? [28]

With his master, Erasmus, Vives could say: "Both sides press me badly; in either side I see evils which I cannot tolerate." [29]

That he was much more successful than Erasmus in remaining aloof and safe can be clearly seen from his relations with the papal legate. Aleander, who was indeed an efficient and zealous investigator of other people's minds, made a special trip to Bruges to check on the Erasmian group there: Cranevelt, Fevyn, Laurin, and probably Vives himself. After long conversations with Cranevelt, he was pleased to report to Rome that the Bruges' Erasmians were "not dangerous." [30] After that visit, Aleander dealt very warmly with Vives, with whom he had long discussions about Erasmus' case. It is even probable that Erasmus, now

---

[28] M, V, 210; R, II, 94 b – 95 a. "Numquam fuit minus in orbe Christianae pietatis, numquam magnificentius quisque de se sentit et peius de socio; homines hominibus, nationes nationibus impietatem objiciunt, quod parum sint Christiani; quasi qui exprobrat, extra eiusmodi esset probrum; quid causae est? in objiciendo non falluntur, omnes aeque sunt impii ... et quum Christianitatis nomen ac propre umbram amiserimus, tamen alii de aliorum Christianitate testificantur, inquirunt, accusant, pronuntiant, addita capitis, famae, et fortunarum poena; quomodo judicant de re quam numquam, ne per somnium quidem viderunt?" (*De Concordia,* 7).

[29] *EE.,* V, 1531, vv. 5-7. "Urgeor utrinque, dici vix potest quam odiose, sed in utraque parte video futuros intolerabiles, si vincant."

[30] See Kalkoff, *Anfänge,* pp. 120 ff.

in exile in Basle, became a little irritated with Vives' invulnerability. Erasmus' letters to Vives from Basle in 1522 (all of which have, unfortunately, been lost), were so formal and cool that Vives felt obliged to write back:

> You really hurt me with the expression "I shall not molest you hereafter with my frequent requests..." ...And the same with the head of your letter "To my respected friend." If from now on you allow your amanuenses to write to me in this style I will have to throw away your letters.[31]

In only one instance did Vives share with Erasmus the *odium theologicum* of the most conservative elements of Louvain. In the spring of 1520 Vives agreed to help Erasmus in a projected critical edition of the ever, did not last much longer than his youthful admiration for the old a philosophical commentary to the *Civitas Dei*.

The Dominicans of Louvain criticized Erasmus and Vives for their bold attempt. In a Church sermon Erasmus was accused of attempting "to correct the books of Saint Augustine without any sufficient knowledge." [32] Vives was told several times that he was wasting his time, since, after the work of the Dominican commentators, there was nothing to revise in the "plain and lucid edition of *Civitas Dei*." [33] Vives made things worse by ridiculing those commentators. "Long before you told me," he wrote to Erasmus in April, 1522, "I had in mind to show in the introduction of my book what kind of scholars wrote on Saint Augustine before me, and to make them the object of public ridicule. In the book itself I will spread here and there a few quotations from their commentaries and from the notes of Passavantius as precious little flowers destined to entertain my readers." [34] After a few years of close contact with Erasmus, even the kind and reserved Spanish Humanist was able to brandish his own kind of sarcasm. This type of partisan fervor, how-

---

[31] *EE.*, V, 1256, vv. 100-115. "Verberasti animum meum illo tuo verbo, 'Non ero tibi toties flagitando molestus'... Tale est illud in superscriptione, 'Amico meo observando'... Si posthac ad hunc modum permiseris istum sive Ioannem sive Livinum scribere, rejiciam litteras." The two people mentioned by name were Erasmus' amanuenses.

[32] *EE.*, V, 1342, vv. 120-123. Erasmus himself attended the religious services that day. The preacher was a Dominican friar, Laurentius, who was more eager in his attacks against Erasmus than Aleander himself.

[33] *EE.*, V, 1271, notes 33, 35, 38. Vives writes to Erasmus about his problems with the friars of Louvain.

[34] *EE.*, V, 1271, vv. 34-40. "Et alioqui in praefatione, etiamsi non monuisses, erat animus ostendere cuiusmodi homines in Augustinum scripsissent; idque faciam et propinabo illos lectori bellissime ridendos. Tum in opere ipso interspergo velut flosculos ex eorum commentariis et Passavantii additionibus, quorum lector suavi odore reficiatur minusque sentiat vitae molestiam."

ever, did not last much longer than his youthful admiration for the old master.

Vives' cooperation with Erasmus in the monumental work was in itself more a testimony to that admiration than the result of his own inclinations. Vives' detachment from Saint Augustine in religious matters can perhaps be explained by the pessimism of the Saint's response to Pelagius; in any case, Vives does not seem to have read much of Saint Augustine's work besides *Civitas Dei,* the only book he recommended, with certain reservations, as a model of classical Latin.[35] Erasmus himself, after having asked Vives to undertake this formidable work, became distracted with other projects and partially lost his interest in Saint Augustine's Biblical exegesis. Augustine's works were not published until 1528, due to these and other difficulties.[36] The cooperation between the two men became more a test to their friendship than an occasion of mutual enrichment. First of all, Vives' work proved much more difficult than he had imagined. The impatience of Erasmus did not help under the circumstances. Vives complained to Cranevelt: "If you could only see the letters Erasmus writes to me! Just today I received one so sharp, so demanding, so irritating!" [37] As a matter of fact, Vives' work was quite an accomplishment. He began in January, 1521; by July he had finished six books. In January of 1522 he dispatched to Basle seven books ready for print. In April of the same year he sent ten more, and the rest in July.[38] The last weeks of the hard work brought, first, a prolonged insomnia, and then a total breakdown in Vives' health. In June, 1522, Vives wrote to Cranevelt that he had not been able to sleep for three days; [39] four weeks later he was afraid that "in building the eternal city"

---

[35] M, VI, 340; R, II, 608 b. "Augustinus multum habet Africitatis in contexto dictionis, non perinde in verbis, praesertim in libris *De civitate Dei* ... (*DD.* II, 3, 8).
  Ibid., II, 312; II, 877 b. "Augustinus, item Afer, mollior, sed minus tersus et comptus." (*De conscribendis epistolis,* 4).
  Furthermore, in *De Disciplinis* (M, VI, 124; R, II, 435) Vives quotes the name of St. Augustine among those who "corrupted the dialectic of Aristotle." (*dialecticam suam depravarunt*).
  Vives' tendency to present Saint Augustine as a model of classical education and style was entirely in tune with the Humanistic culture of the day. See Kristeller, "Augustine and the early Renaissance," *Review of Religion,* VIII (1944), 345-347. See also Watson, "J. L. Vives and St. Augustine"s *Civitas Dei,*" *Church Quarterly Review,* LXXXVI (1913), 143-145.
[36] *EE.,* III, 844. In this letter to John Eck, Erasmus explains his preference for Saint Jerome.
[37] *LC.,* 8, vv. 11-12. "Si videres quas epistolas accipio ab Erasmo! vel hodie unam quam acrem! quam expostulatoriam! quam fulmineam!"
[38] See *EE.,* IV, 1222; V, 1256, 1271, 1303.
[39] *LC.,* 6, v. 44. "... tertia nocte iam insomnio ducta."

he was going to "ruin the dwelling of the body"; in August, finally, the burden became too much for Vives' sickly nature.[40] Still the end product failed to please Erasmus. Exhausted as he was, Vives allowed Erasmus to make all the changes he, Erasmus, thought were needed.[41] Erasmus' criticism was also spurred by Froben's disappointment with the poor sale of the book: "Froben complains that he has not been able to sell a single copy of your book in the fair of Frankfurt"; "the book," Erasmus wrote, "is too long and carelessly done." [42] Modestly, Vives pointed to the mistakes of the amanuensis and to his own limitations.[43] It was the first and the last time they worked together. Erasmus' insinuations about a possible cooperation with Vives in preparing an edition of Seneca, in 1529, found a cool response on the part of the humble but prudent Humanist from Valencia.[44]

In spite of Erasmus' criticism, the publication of Vives' Commentaries to Saint Augustine on the eve of the Reformation was a fact of extraordinary importance. Vives' edition was not the only one, however; the *editio princeps* had been issued as early as 1467 at the Monastery of Subiaco and reprinted in Rome one year later. The *Civitas Dei* had been printed as a part of the comprehensive work of John Amorbach in Basle in 1489. Nevertheless, Vives' edition was the first one to procure a more accurate text by choosing between the variants of at least three different manuscripts.[45] Together with the other work of Saint Augustine, printed by Erasmus in 1528, Vives' text remained standard until it was replaced in 1576 by the text of the Lovanienses. In *Essays,* Montaigne quotes the *Civitas Dei* from Vives' edition. Vives' notes and commentaries were translated into English and French, and repeatedly printed in different parts of Europe.[46]

The commentaries are by far the most compromising work Vives ever wrote – at least from a Catholic point of view. Opinions of a clear

---

[40] *LC.,* 8, vv. 8-9. "... cui *Civitati Dei* sic sum noctes et dies intentus, ut misere timeam ne, dum Civitatem construo, corpus destruam."
[41] *EE.,* V, 1303, vv. 9-11. "Ea tu leges prius quam imprimantur, et censura tua omnia temperabis; addes et mutabis quae videbuntur..."
[42] See *EE.,* V, 1351, v. 36; V, 1271; VII, 1831, v. 13.
[43] *EE.,* V, 1362, vv. 5-7. "Nemo magis est, si qua est fides, imperitiae meae conscius meo ipso, nec minus dissimulator." It is hard to find similar expressions of sincere modesty in the correspondence of Erasmus.
[44] *EE.,* VII, 2061, vv. 4-5. "Malo autorem illum (Senecam), legi et cognosci multo dignissimum ex tua castigatione in studiorum manus venire quam ex mea."
[45] For a comparison of the editions of Saint Augustine printed during the Renaissance, see B. Dombart, *Zur Textgeschichte der Civitatis Dei,* (Leipzig, 1908), pp. 43 ff. Watson, "Vives and St. Augustine," 133-134, gives interesting details about the manuscripts used by Vives.
[46] See below, Appendix I, pp. 300-306.

Erasmian character are presented without the slightest reticence. As a device to protect the religious orthodoxy of their own countryman, a few Spanish scholars have maintained the theory that the least Catholic views expressed in the commentaries were not a part of the original text, but Erasmus' own corrections and additions.[47] Such an opinion, however, stands in direct opposition to Erasmus' expressed statement in the introduction to the book.[48] This youthful work of Vives was forbidden by the Jesuits, condemned by the theologians of Louvain in 1546 and by Pope Paul IV in 1559, included in the *Index* of forbidden books impressed in 1584 by order of the General Inquisitor of Spain, Gaspar Quiroga, and, finally, added to the Roman Index of Pope Gregory XVI as late as 1862.[49]

Most of the opinions banned by the Ecclesiastical authorities were unmistakably Erasmian. The most significant can be listed as follows:

1 – That scholastic theologians contradict the Fathers to the point that, "'if Augustine lived nowadays, he would be held a pedant, or a petty orator, and Paul a madman, or a heretic." [50]

2 – That the popes ought to set an example of humility and should "not imitate the example of Essau," and that priests should not waste their money with "their sonnes if [they] have them, and have them [they] will, unlesse [they] be eunuchs." [51]

3 – That the baptism of infants was not practiced in the Apostolic Church, a fact to be considered if we want "to explaine the meaning of Augustine more fullie." [52]

4 – That the mendicant orders of the Church should return to their primitive poverty instead of being "rich beggars fed with partridge and capons."[53]

5 – That theological speculations are not useful to a Christian life since "words add little to religion," that the discussions about the Immaculate Conception are only "discussions of old wives," and that the disputes about the predestination are mere "goose-traps." [54]

---

[47] In fact the Commentaries on St. Augustine's *Civitas Dei* are not included in the Mayans edition of 1782, nor in the Spanish translation of Riber. For this reason I have been compelled to use the English translation of John Healey, in its second edition (London, 1620), which bears the title *Of the Citie of God: with the learned Comments of Jo. Ludovicus Vives* (Hereafter cited as Healey, book, chapter, page).

[48] Quoted in the original Latin by Bonilla, *Luis Vives*, III, 42, note 5: "nihil est nostrae industriae."

[49] For a typical Spanish approach to the problem of Vives' orthodoxy, see M. Puigdollers, *Filosofía española*, pp. 128-134. The conclusion of the author could not be more unequivocal: "Afortunadamente no hay motivo para sospechar ni un ápice de la ortodoxia de Vives."

[50] Healey, XIII, 24, p. 295.

[51] *Ibid.*, XVII, 5, p. 630.

[52] *Ibid.*, II, 26, p. 34.

[53] *Ibid.*, VII, 26, p. 281.

[54] *Ibid.*, XI, 10, p. 417; XX, 26, p. 828; V, 10, p. 212.

6 – That Saint Paul was not "curious in the choosing of his words," and even Saint Augustine was misled by the Greek translation of the Septuaginta.[55]

7 – That all war is impious, even the battles of Israel.[56]

8 – That some theological formulations are questionable, such as "the Son is the Wisdom of the Father" or "Christ assumed a human nature." [57]

9 – That the history of Susanna is apochryphal, and that "the Latin Church held the Epistle to the Hebrews not to be canonical." [58]

All these pronouncements, together with the destructive sarcasm against the "smattering fellows" who commented on Saint Augustine through the middle ages, was simply too much for the Holy Office. It would be false, however, to assume that Vives' book is primarily a theological treatise. The bulk of Vives' remarks deals rather with the cultural background of Saint Augustine's thought. What is truly amazing in this book is its evidence of a superb knowledge of Roman history and law, of mythology and classical literature. This is true in spite of the occasional lack of accuracy which later scholars objected to in Vives.[59] Vives himself described the book as a philosophical treatise "with slight touches of theology here and there." [60] Although such theological remarks were enough to provoke the anger of the zealots, Erasmus and his friends were probably disappointed with them. The interest of the Erasmian circle in Saint Augustine – initiated by Colet and Thomas More – followed essentially the pattern of Petrarch's Augustinism. Saint Augustine was viewed as the perfect synthesis of a highly personal form of religious life with a solid education in classical antiquity.[61] In the eyes of Erasmus, the latter was subordinated to the former. In spite of

[55] Ibid., II, 21, p. 91; XVIII, 43, p. 733.
[56] Ibid., II, 20, p. 34.
[57] Ibid., XI, 21, p. 428; IX, 17, p. 353.
[58] Ibid., XVIII, 31, p. 718; XVI, 6, p. 597.
[59] Bonilla, Luis Vives, III, 47, note 63, gives the following quotation of Julius Caesar Scaliger: "Vives fuit doctus; quae scripsit in Augustinum sunt optima, si spectemus illud saecculum; sed si nostrum, nihil est. Fuerunt aliqui Lusitani docti, pauci Hispani."
Erasmus himself wrote to Vives: "Alard complains that your text was written carelessly; but I know him well. It is true, however, that in a few details, very few, you went to sleep while writing. You remember the case of 'Typho,' among others." (EE., VII, 1889, vv. 19-21.) Vives explained the Greek word τύρω, which means "pride," as the proper name of a mythological giant: "Typho fuit gigas terrae filius immanissimus."
[60] M, VI, 340; R, II, 608 b. "Id enim (opus) bona ex parte in media philologia versatur." In the Commentaries, Vives wrote about the Augustinian doctrine on the original sin (one of the most important theological parts of the book): "What light Augustine gives I will take, and as my power and duty is, explaine; the rest, I will not meddle with." (Healey, XIII, 5, p. 315).
[61] Kristeller, "Augustine and early Renaissance," pp. 348-352.

his ill-fated utterances of strong Erasmian philosophy, Vives seemed constantly much more interested in the history of Roman jurisprudence than in Saint Augustine's interpretation of Genesis, more concerned with Cicero and Quintilian than with Saint Paul or Saint Jerome. Furthermore, Vives' book contains some important views, not typically Erasmian, which were also condemned. Such is, for instance, the belief that pagans "may attain the glory of a Christian by keeping the two abstracts of all the Law and the Prophets, perfect love of God and his neighbour," and, that "the nations which have no law but nature are a law to themselves." [62] Of the same naturalistic character is the interpretation of the rule that the perfection of all laws is love: "Love thou Him who is above, as well as thou canst, and Who is next thee like thyself; which doing thou keepest all the laws, and hast them perfect . . . Thou shalt, then, be greater than Plato or Pythagoras, with all their travels and numbers; than Aristotle with all his quirks and syllogisms." [63] The perfection of love, however, presupposes a true knowledge: "The excellent perfection of virtue," Vives writes, "is proper to the witty alone." [64] These statements are not incompatible with Erasmus' views, but the emphasis is certainly different. The uniqueness of "Christ's philosophy" is nowhere evident.

Froben's failure to sell the commentaries and Erasmus' criticism coincided with the tragedy of Vives' parents in Valencia and with the nervous breakdown which followed his final effort in writing the book. It was at that time that Vives made up his mind to leave the Netherlands and to seek a Royal Scholarship in England. Both decisions were important and intimately related. The idea of a secluded life, totally dedicated to study and research, was probably suggested to him by Erasmus himself in a moment of frustration as a professor of theology in Louvain. In July, 1521, Vives reported to Erasmus that he had in mind requesting from Thomas More some financial help to settle in England:

I have decided to wait here for the King [Charles V] and for Thomas More to discuss with them possible ways of supporting myself in the immediate future. I wrote to More that I wanted to have a long talk with him. Probably he guesses what my intentions are, but I did not want to give him further details without having had a chance to hear your advice on the matter. One thing I know for sure you will recommend: to miss no opportunity to secure myself a quiet life of private study.[65]

[62] Healey, XVIII, 47, p. 739.
[63] Ibid., XI, 12, p. 419.
[64] Ibid., IV, 21, p. 287.
[65] EE., IV, 1222, vv. 15-21. ". . . manebo hic Regem et Morum, ut videam quo

There were many reasons – we have considered them before – why Vives selected England as the most suitable place for his plans. One of those reasons, directly related to Erasmus, deserves some special attention. At the risk of oversimplification, it can be said that Vives chose England because, at least in 1523, the Kingdom of Henry VIII embodied what Vives considered the most constructive and valuable aspects of Erasmianism. Not only was England geographically distant from the Lutheran storm, but Vives hoped that London would be one of the few European cities where it would still be possible to sell a few copies of his *Somnium Scipionis,* a book which was "neither for nor against Luther." [66] Moreover, Vives was under the impression that, after Colet's death, the London reformers were much more interested in the moral reform of the individual and the society than in Biblical criticism, a field he himself had long abandoned. Was not the *Utopia* a program of social action in spite of its mythical reveries? Were not Erasmian Humanists like Fisher and More, Mountjoy and Fox, the champions of international understanding and political moderation? Was not Linacre one of the leading European reformers in the field of scientific education?

Modern research has proved that Vives' judgment was sound. The history of the Henrician period and the Elizabethan settlement, of the English Renaissance and the University Reform, are inseparable from the pervasive impact of Erasmian attitudes upon English life and institutions.[67] There is no doubt that Vives' best credentials in England were his association with Erasmus, and Erasmus' letters of recommendation to Fisher. Vives' high expectations were not frustrated in the first years of his residence in England. His tracts on education and social ethics – the subject of chapters nine and ten – were an integral part of English Erasmianism. It has to be emphasized, however, that the concern of the London reformers with education and the political balance of power in Europe was more a secular interpretation than a servile repetition of Erasmus' gospel.

The bitter end of Erasmus' life in England and his booming influence

pacto sit mihi vivendum posthac. Pecunia Reginae me huc usque alui, et alo. Moro scripsi me prolixe collocuturm cum eo cum venerit. Suspicari potest quid velim, sed non aperte quicquam, quum nollem te inconsulto; tametsi consilium tuum propemodum novi, ut parem ocium ad vitam studiosam undecumque queam."

[66] *EE.,* V, 1513, v. 47. Vives complains that the only books which sold well in those times were "pro Luthero vel in Lutherum." Notwithstanding, he sold quite a few copies of his *Somnium* in England. (*EE.,* V, 1362 vv. 45-46).

[67] The best study of Erasmian influence upon English life is McConica, *English Humanism and Reformation Politics,* especially chapters 2 and 3, "Erasmianism," "Erasmians and Policy: the Crisis from 1529 to 1534."

in Spain in those years (1527-1529) brought about a radical change in Vives' attitude toward the chances of an Erasmian reform in the domains of the Emperor.[68] Vives' relations with the Erasmian group in Spain had been, up to that time, friendly but inconsequential. The only significant event had taken place in the summer om 1520 when, for the first time, Vives met in Bruges one of the future champions of Spanish Erasmianism, the theologian from Alcalá, Juan de Vergara.[69] For many years, Vergara was the only close friend Vives had in Spain and his exclusive source of information concerning the progress of the Spanish disciples of Erasmus. It was Vergara's idea to offer Vives the chair of rhetoric in Alcalá, left vacant by the death of Nebrija. In spite of Vives' youthful enthusiasm for Erasmus, the idea of campaigning at home for his master was never appealing to him. Erasmus himself, at least in the first decade of the century, could hardly conceal his heartfelt dislike for Spain. When in 1516 Cardinal Cisneros begged him to join the team of scholars working on the *Biblia Polyglota,* Erasmus refused without hesitation. The reason was very simple: "The Cardinal of Toledo," he wrote to Thomas More, "invited me to Alcalá; but I do not like Spain." [70] And to Beatus Rhenanus: "The Cardinal urges me, but I am just not planning right now to 'go Spanish.' " [71]

One year later Erasmus was again confronted with a similar situation. Only this time the refusal to visit Spain was much more embarrassing. Since January, 1516, Erasmus had been drawing a substantial Royal pension of 200 florins as a councillor to the future emperor, Prince Charles of Ghent.[72] When the Court of the Prince moved to Spain in the summer of 1517, many of Charles' high courtiers urged Erasmus to join them in the journey.[73] The occasion was unique, and Erasmus hesi-

[68] For the progress of Erasmianism in Spain in those years the classical source of information is Bataillon, *Erasmo y España,* chapters 4, 5, and 6.

[69] Juan de Vergara was one of the first students in Alcalá; he worked on the Latin version of the Biblia Complutensis; he went to the Netherlands with Alfonso de Valdés to inform Croy about the diocese of Toledo. On that occasion he met Vives and Erasmus; later he became chaplain to Charles' Court, professor in Alcalá, and, finally, in 1524, secretary to Fonseca, the Archbishop of Toledo. He was accused of Lutheranism and condemned to imprisonment in the last years of his life. Juan de Vergara should not be confused with Francisco de Vergara, a professor of Greek in Alcalá. (*EE.,* V, introd. to letter 1277, vv. 51-52).

[70] *EE.,* III, 597, vv. 47-51. "Non placet Hispania; nam huc rursus vocat Cardinalis Toletanus."

[71] *Ibid.,* III, 628, v. 53. "Cardinalis Toletanus nos invitat; sed non est animus hispanizein."

[72] *Ibid.,* II, 370, note 18. This is the first mention of Erasmus' appointment.

[73] *Ibid.,* V, 1431, vv. 33-35. In March, 1524, Erasmus regretted his decision to move to Basle instead of having accepted another opportunity to go to Spain. However, Erasmus adds: "I found here [in Basle] so many calamities, that if I had known it beforehand, I would have even chosen to live among the Turks!"

tated for awhile. Nevertheless, he preferred to stay in Louvain, a decision he was to regret in the not-too-distant future. The wandering scholar of the Northern Renaissance never visited the country where years later his cause found not only enthusiastic disciples but also an impressive number of martyrs. Erasmus' objections to Spain were various. The emotional exuberance of the southern people irritated him at times.[74] Probably, Cisneros' reform appeared to him too clerical and narrow-minded. He could not share Alcalá's respect for the Vulgate nor the Cardinal's faith in Scotism.[75] His lack of Hebrew placed him in an inferior position with respect to linguists such as Pablo Coronel, López de Zúñiga, and Demetrio Ducas. Nebrija's troubles with the Inquisition were not a promising sign. Further his deep-rooted anti-Semitism predisposed him against a nation where – in his own words – "there were more Jews than Christians." [76]

The first two years (1520-1521) of Spanish Erasmianism confirmed the fears and reservations of both Vives and Erasmus. As expected, Spain came up with a strong orthodox reaction against the initial progress of the Erasmian movement. The first to raise a voice of warning against Erasmus was a respected teacher from Alcalá, Diego López de Zúñiga. In 1519 Zúñiga published some critical observations on Erasmus' *Novum Instrumentum* (1516), and in 1520 a merciless attack against the Erasmian New Testament. Erasmus' *Apologia* helped as little as any apology he was forced to write in his life. In March, 1522, Sancho Carranza de Miranda, a Spanish theologian in Rome, assailed Erasmus in similar terms, although with more moderation.[77] On both occasions it was not Vives but Vergara who jumped into the arena to protect the good name of Erasmus.[78] Vives, obviously irritated with the

---

[74] In March, 1517, Erasmus wrote to Thomas More: "If Vives has visited you already, imagine what I had to go through in Bruxelles with such a crowd of Spanish visitors..." Although Bataillon, uncritically, takes here for granted that this is an authentic mention of our Vives (*Erasmo y Espana*, p. 77), De Vocht has convincingly proved that it is an interpolation. See above note 21 to chapter 4.
On the same subject of Spanish exhuberance, see *EE.*, III, 873, vv. 8-9. "... reieci Hispanos quosdam odiose, pertinaciter colloquium meum expetentes; quos scio ob hoc infensos fore, ut est gentis ingenium."

[75] Cisneros' enthusiasm for the philosophy of Scotus (Bataillon, *Erasmo y Espana,* pp. 16-19) contrasts sharply with the well-known anti-Scotistic diatribes of Erasmus.

[76] On Erasmus' anti-Semitism, see Bataillon, *Erasmo y España,* p. 78. In March, 1518, Erasmus wrote to his friend Capito that he would prefer to see Christianity poisoned by Scotus rather than by the Talmud and the Kabbala. (*EE.*, III, 798, vv. 2-22).

[77] On the controversies with Zúñiga and Carranza, see Bataillon, *Erasmo y España,* pp. 91-96, 115-133.

[78] The letters from Vergara to Zúñiga and vice versa make the Appendix XV of the *EE* collection, IV, pp. 620-631.

dull obstinacy of his countrymen, refused to get involved in the theological debate. But there was absolutely no doubt where his sympathies
lay. In June, 1524, Vives wrote to Erasmus:

> One of the best pieces of news I have received for a long time is that
> your books begin to be enjoyed by "our Spaniards." I truly hope that, once
> they get used to your ideas, they will sober up a little and will abandon
> some barbaric conceptions of life which they hand down to one another,
> not because they lack intelligence, but simply because they do not know
> what it is to be human.[79]

Vives' hopes were fulfilled in surprising measure. The translation of
the *Enchiridion* in 1524 opened a new era in the history of Spanish
Erasmianism. The intense piety of the book was easily assimilated by the
powerful streams of mysticism and illuminism which underlay the
Spanish religious life of that time. Erasmus' detachment from dogma
and institution strongly appealed to the more liberal section of Spanish
theologians, especially to those of Jewish ancestry. The most articulate
and sophisticated men of that generation became enthusiastic followers
of the *Philosophia Christi* – men like Miguel de Eguía, Juan Maldonado, Alonso de Virués, Juan and Alfonso de Valdés, and Juan and
Francisco de Vergara. Even the General Inquisitor, Alfonso Manrique,
was a sincere admirer of Erasmus. The influence of such people was so
powerful in the Court of the Emperor – Alfonso de Valdés was Charles'
Secretary – that soon religion and politics merged together in a fantastic
dream of religious unity, moral reform, and Spanish hegemony. Part of
their creed was that Charles had been chosen by God's providence to
impose upon Europe a political solution guaranteed by Imperial power,
and to solve the religious schism with a general council where dogmatic
differences of detail could be absorbed by an Erasmian formula of conciliation. The victory of Pavia was the best proof of the messianic calling
of the Emperor. Even the sack of Rome (1527) was interpreted by Valdés
as a "judgment of God" against papal abuses. The theological conference of Valladolid in 1527 marked the official proclamation of this
Erasmian imperialism.[80]

---

[79] *EE.*, V, 1455, vv. 21-26. "Nihil audivi multis diebus gratius quam opera tua
nostris quoque Hispanis esse cordi. Spero fore ut illis et similibus assuefacti
mansuescant, exuantque barbaricas aliquot de vita opiniones, quibus acuta quidem
ingenia, sed ignoratione humanitatis, sunt imbuta: quas alii aliis velut per manus
tradunt."

[80] See Bataillon, *Erasmo y España,* Chapter 5, "El año del saco de Roma. La
conferencia de Valladolid (1517)," and chapter 8, "El Erasmismo al servicio de
la política imperial. Los *Diálogos* de Alfonso de Valdés."

These events coincided with the rapidly worsening situation of Vives in the Court of Henry VIII. In Vives' correspondence one begins to feel a change of attitude toward the Emperor, a growing interest in the advances of Erasmianism in Spain, and even a warmer feeling toward Erasmus himself. Vives came to see in Charles V the instrument of God's providence. In June, 1526, Vives wrote to Cranevelt:

> They say that many people are conspiring against Charles. But this is Charles' destiny that he cannot win unless he defeats a large number of enemies, to make his victory a more glorious one. This is the hand of God, Who wants to prove to all men how weak they are against His power.[81]

In December, Vives accused the Pope of planning "to take away from *us*" the Kingdom of Naples;[82] shortly before that, in August of the same year, Vives wrote an affectionate letter to Erasmus begging him to have all his works printed in a collected edition.[83] In 1527, the correspondence between Vives and Erasmus reached again the intensity of 1522. In March, Vives wrote to Erasmus:

> Your *Enchiridion* has begun to speak my native tongue in Spain. The same people who used to be under the tyranny of the Brothers, now enjoy your book . . . I wish, my master, you would write me your opinion about some of the books I have published in your absence. Moreover, if there is anything you want to criticize, do it as my master and my father . . .[84]

In June Vives recommended to Erasmus that he get in immediate contact with the Emperor and the Primate of Spain, a recommendation Erasmus followed without the least hesitation.[85] In the same letter Vives reported that he was in close contact with Virués and Maldonado; he also gave Erasmus personal information about some of the new Spanish Erasmists, Luis Coronel, Francisco Vitoria, and others. Vives added:

> All these men make me hope that your cause — which is the cause of true culture and religion — will finally prevail . . . The rest of the crowd cannot

---

[81] *LC.*, 193, vv. 28-30. Letter to Cranevelt. "Dicunt coniurare multos adversum Carolum: at hoc est Caroli fatum, ut vincere non possit nisi multos, quo clarius vincat. Dei potius sunt haec ut ostendat hominibus quam imbecilles sunt nostrae vires adversum suam potentiam."

[82] *LC.*, 217, v. 13. Letter from Vives to Cranevelt. "Aiunt Pontificem velle nobis Neapolim adimere."

[83] *EE.*, VI, 1732.

[84] *Ibid.*, VI, 1792, vv. 15-18. "In Hispania *Enchiridion* tuum coepit loqui nostrati lingua, et quidem secundo populo, qui solebat esse in potestate τῶν ἀδελφῶν . . . Amabo mi praeceptor, si quid vidisti eorum operum quae te absente edidi, perscribe ad me sententiam tuam, imo vero magistri et patris reprehensoriam adminitionem."

[85] Vives' letter to Erasmus, *EE.*, VII, 1836, vv. 66-70. Vives' letter was dated June 13, 1527. Two months later, in August 26, Erasmus wrote to Manrique, the Primate of Spain (*ibid.*, 1864), and in September 2, to the Emperor (*ibid.*, 1873).

be compared with men like these ... In fact, many people are already ashamed of the slavery in which they used to live, which slavery, if everywhere horrible, in our country is intolerable even to mules ... Of course, the Brothers did not like the idea that one book [the *Enchiridion*] could threaten their dignity, their riches, and their good fortune ... [86]

The most compromising paragraph of the letter was written in Greek:

Christ has given us a fantastic opportunity with the victories of the Emperor and the imprisonment of the Pope. I wished you would write to the Archbishop of Seville about your personal problems and to the Emperor about the political issues of common concern.[87]

One month later, in July, Vives wrote Erasmus a long report of the conference of Valladolid. The letter concluded: "Take good care of yourself, my father and my master." [88] In his correspondence with Cranevelt, Vives condemned the violence of the sack of Rome, but he hurried to remark that, had they won, the Pope's soldiers would have behaved much worse.[89] In July, 1529, Vives himself wrote a long letter to the Emperor urging him to call an ecumenical council.[90] In August Vives wrote to Erasmus the last testimony of his faith in the destiny of Charles V:

Probably you have heard the Emperor left Barcelone with a powerful armada of fifty triremes, seventy cargo ships, and ten frigates. With him are not only the Imperial courtiers, but also the flower of the Spanish young aristocrary and ten thousand sailors carefully selected from all corners of Spain. They write from Marseille that they saw this fleet sailing along the French coast, the fifth of August. Some people say that they have already landed in Genoa ... May Our Lord Jesus grant him the power and the will to reform the Christian world ... [91]

---

[86] *Ibid.*, vv. 40-43, vv. 47-56. "Qui mihi optimam spem praebent futuram tuam causam, hoc est literarum et pietatis, superiorem ... nam reliqua turba quid erit ad eos? ... Et fortassis iam coeptum est fieri, videlicet excitatis ea lectione multorum animis ad cognitionem magnarum et pulcherrimarum rerum, quae tandiu fuerant occultatae; tum etiam quod coepit permultos pigere indignissimae servitutis, qua quidem hactenus presserunt miseram plebem. Quae servitus quum ubique ... gravissima est, tum vero in nostra natione ne servis quidem aut asinis tolerabilis ..."
[87] *Ibid.*, 1836, vv. 66-70.
[88] *Ibid.*, 1847, v. 141. "Vale plurimum, mi praeceptor et pater."
[89] *LC.*, 246, vv. 17-18. "... peiora designasset Sanctum illud Foedus, si vicisset."
[90] M, V, 187-193; R, II, 75-80. The letter is also the dedication to the Emperor of Vives' tract *De concordia et discordia in humano genere*.
[91] *EE.*, VIII, vv. 40-50. "Credo audivisse te Caesarem solvisse Barcinonae cum classe instructissima, in qua sint triremes quadraginta, naves onerariae septuaginta, celoces decem: his vehi, praeter comitatum aulicum et florem nobilis juventutis Hispaniae, socios navales ad decem millia totius Hispaniae lectissimos. Massilia scribunt visam eam classem legentem oram Galllici maris quinto die mensis Augusti: sunt qui addant ad septimum diem eiusdem mensis tenuisse Genuam ... D. Jesus

The touching and sad nostalgia of this letter, written one year after Vives' exile from England, presaged ominously the events to come. The campaigns of the Emperor in Italy, the persecution of the Spanish Erasmists since 1530, the failure of the Diet of Augsburg, and more importantly, the intellectual change of Vives himself, led to a radical abandonment of any Erasmian scheme for the future. A few scholars have even suggested that the relations between Vives and Erasmus became extremely tense around 1530. It cannot be denied that, after the selfish attitude of Erasmus in blaming Vives for the financial failure of the Commentaries to Saint Augustine, the correspondence between the two men does not exhibit nearly the warmth of Vives' letters to Cranevelt or Erasmus' to Amorbach and Pirckheimer. Moreover, after 1524, Vives' letters reveal here and there a certain bitterness and independence of mind. His open criticism of Froben in November, 1524, irritated Erasmus, who badly needed Froben's services.[92] In August, 1526, Vives did not hesitate to criticize Erasmus' dialogue about the religious vows as "totally out of place." [93] Erasmus wrote back: "It amazes me that a man like you should be incapable of finding some justifying reasons, even if my cause had been the worst in the world." [94] In the same letter Erasmus criticized Vives' severity with women. The answer of Vives was terse and frank: "How can *you* say that, being responsible as you are for the edition of Saint Jerome?" [95] One year later Erasmus failed to mention Vives' name among the masters of Latinity in his book, *Ciceronianus*. The only excuse he found for this incident was his own weak memory, although in a previous letter to Velius (July, 1528), he had written that he would not mention Vives' name unless requested by Vives himself.[96] From Goclenius we know that Erasmus had advised some people to avoid any close contact with Vives.[97] The last letter of

servet eum, atque eam largiatur illi et facultatem et voluntatem, ut res Christiani orbis in meliorem statum reponat."

[92] See *EE.,* V, 1531, v. 36. Erasmus complains about the financial failure of the book at the fair of Frankfurt.

[93] *Ibid.,* VI, 1732. Vives writes to Erasmus about the dialogue de Voto: "alienissima videtur mihi et loco et personis illa dissertio."

[94] *Ibid.,* VII, 1830. *"De Colloquiis* demiror tanto patrono vel in pessima causa desse rationes."

[95] *Ibid.,* 1847, vv. 37-39. "Foeminas ais a me durius tractatas: hoc tu dicis, homo qui nobis Hieronymum restitueris?"

[96] *Ibid.,* VII, 2040, v. 20. Erasmus writes to Vives: "Velius expostulat quod in Ciceronianus te praeterierim, quamquam id prorsus oblivione factum est." Nevertheless, in a letter to Velius himself Erasmus admits: "Sunt quos nolim attingere nisi volentibus ipsis. In hoc numero propemodum pono Vivetem." (*EE.,* VII, 2008, vv. 19-21).

[97] *Ibid.,* 2026, vv. 5-6. Goclenius wrote to Erasmus: "Egoque tuum consilium secutus cum Vive praeter civilem amicitiam nihil habui commune."

Erasmus to Vives (September, 1528) was unnecessarily cruel and harsh.[98] To make things worse, this was the letter in which Erasmus dismissed Vives' request for help in the case of Catherine with an insolent remark, although the old man knew well that the fate of his friend, Thomas More, was involved in the affair. In 1529 Erasmus published a second edition of the *Civitas Dei*, but left out completely Vives' Commentaries. In 1531 a French printer, Chevallon, published the same book, including Vives' notes but omitting the lavish praise of Erasmus which Vives had written in his youth.[99] In 1533, the final incident took place. Vives failed to attack Carvajal, one of the last critics of Erasmus, with the loyalty and enthusiasm of years past.[100] In 1534, Vives wrote the last letter to Erasmus with a sad account of the persecution of Vergara, Tovar, More, and Fisher. The letter ended with a cynical remark: "These are times when to keep silence is as dangerous as to speak out." [101] Two years later Erasmus died in Basle.

From this account of the personal relations between Erasmus and Vives, it is obvious that, in spite of a sincere admiration, at least since his residence in England, Vives never felt nor acted as a servile pupil. Vives was too strong-minded and critical to become the disciple of any-body (as he was, on the other hand, too humble to proselytize for his own cause). Besides, there were profound differences between the two men. Vives was nostalgically attached to the memories of his childhood, to the ideal parents he could not forget in his writings. Erasmus had no country nor family to speak of. As a Jew, Vives was an heir to a glorious tradition and loyal to a well-defined social and racial group; Erasmus was a man without a past. Vives was a married man, Erasmus a dis-appointed and baffled monk. As a humanist, Erasmus became an inter-nationally known figure; Vives had only a few friends, and most of them, like Cranevelt, were not the leading protagonists of the day, but simply warm and loyal human beings. Erasmus was conceited, over-confident, and constantly anxious about his own reputation. Vives was modest, self-effacing, and totally detached from posterity's opinion. Erasmus' brilliant style tended sometimes to mask the shallowness of his

[98] *Ibid.*, VII, 2040. See especially vv. 35-40, where Erasmus recommends to Vives to write something practical, like Bayf's treatises on kitchen utensils (*EE.*, VII, 1962).
[99] For the history of St. Augustine's editions, see *EE.*, V, introd. to letter 1309, pp. 117-118.
[100] *EE.*, X, 2932, vv. 22-25. Vives tries to excuse himself in a sad letter to Erasmus where he speaks about "amicitiam et familiaritatem *aliquando* nostram . . ."
[101] *Ibid.*, vv. 28-29. "Tempora habemus difficilia in quibus nec loqui nec tacere possumus sine periculo."

thought. Vives was a man of ideas rather than of words, and although he was capable of writing beautiful Latin, his style could be at times clumsy and repetitious. Erasmus loved Lucian, Vives forbade reading his books. Erasmus was witty, imaginative, sarcastic, sometimes even obscene, coarse, and bawdy; Vives had no spark of humor, was serious, reserved, dry, always dignified and proper. By nature Vives was a judicious thinker, and Erasmus a gifted propagandist. All these differences reflect somehow a more radical distinction in their mental attitudes. Erasmus was much more a religious reformer than a philosopher, while Vives was exactly the opposite. As Erasmus himself wrote to Vives, his contest was with the theologians, Vives' struggle was against the sophists.[102] Erasmus' ambition was to become a doctor in theology, a degree he obtained from the rather modest University of Turin. Vives never studied theology, and he was totally aware of his shortcomings in this field. Erasmus owes his reputation to Biblical studies and religious writings, Vives to his pedagogical and philosophical works. It is true, however, that Erasmus' religious attitudes were based on certain philosophical views of extreme importance in the intellectual history of pre-Reformation Europe. Behind Erasmus' rejection of scholastic theology and philosophy there is a subtle form of scepticism which cannot be ignored. In opposition to Luther, Erasmus developed also an optimistic humanism of dubious Pelagian flavor. Both trends, the sceptic and the naturalistic, are essential to the understanding of Vives' philosophy.

To conclude, we can summarize Erasmus' influence upon Vives' thought in the following way. It is true that the intellectual youth of Vives was totally Erasmian. To this period belong the first devotional books and, most of all, the Commentaries to Saint Augustine. The educational and political works of Vives in England, however, represent a partial but significant departure from an evangelical Erasmianism, in that they overemphasize its more secular applications. Between 1527 and 1529, Vives, who had been rather detached from the Erasmian movement in Spain, became briefly but intensely involved in the Erasmian messianism of Charles V's Court. The letter to the Emperor is the most typical document of this time. Finally, from 1530 to the year of his death, Vives was personally, geographically, and intellectually independent from Erasmus. It was precisely in those years when the philosophical thought of Juan Luis Vives reached its maturity and creative originality. In the history of philosophy, Erasmus deserves a place only

---

[102] EE., 1104, vv. 5-15.

because the philosophical assumptions of the *Philosophia Christi* were highly symptomatic of the intellectual crisis out of which the modern mind was born. Vives belongs to the history of European philosophy because he was, on his own merit, a pioneer of new trends of thought. I shall attempt to back this contention in the remainder of this book.

CHAPTER 8

THE ECLECTIC CRITICISM OF VIVES

"Veritas, temporis filia"
From *Satellitium animi.*

Vives' journey from Paris to the Netherlands in 1512 was a crucial event of marked symbolism. Left behind were the sterile routine of the *schola* and the wasteful speeches against Nebrija. In spite of all the frustrations which Vives experienced in Paris, it was there where he began to feel, like many a Spaniard has, the spell of the North: the refreshing individualism of the *Devotio Moderna,* the enlightened social criticism of Erasmus, the restlessness of the German reformers, and the concerns of the English Humanists. "My dear Fort," he wrote to a fellow student, ". . . I thank God every day for the blessed moment I left the Cimmerian darkness of Paris and went out into the light." [1] Had he remained there or returned to Spain, we would find his name today among the editors of the *Biblia Polyglota Complutensis,* the logicians of Montaigu, or even among the victims of the Spanish Inquisition. Vives was an exceptional man in his generation because he had a clear vision of the possibilities which the present could offer to the future, if men were able to learn from the past. Vives knew well that human culture was at one of its decisive crossroads, and that the men of his day had the unique opportunity to clean up "the gangrenous pest which had poisoned the human mind for five hundred years." [2] When he left the old university, at the age of twenty, he wrote with juvenile enthusiasm: "If God gives me ten years of good health, I shall erase from their minds

---

[1] M, III, 63; R, II, 311 b. ". . . ego quidem mi Fortis, gratias ago et habeo, et ago permagnas Deo, quod aliquando e Parisiis quasi ex Cimmeriis tenebris in lucem egressus sum . . ." (*Adv. Ps-d*).

[2] *Ibid.,* 61; 310 a. "Has animorum gangrenas et pestes . . . adduci non possum ut credam diu duraturas; iam satis super quingentos fere per annos multa mala mentibus hominum invexerunt . . ."

all those stupid errors." [3] He had chosen sides; his plight was with those "bright, excellent, and free-minded men of the literary Renaissance" who made his century a glorious time to be alive.[4] His vocation was to channel all the energies of the moment in the right direction and to warn the men of his time against all possible blunders. His program was clear: to embody in a new system of education all the lessons learned from a critical survey of human history.

Logically, then, there is no better introduction to the study of Vives' thought than a summary of his critical views. The present chapter offers such a summary in three different parts: the first is dedicated to Vives' philosophy of history; the second describes some of the guiding principles underlying Vives' critical evaluations; and the third part includes a sketch of Vives' concrete historical views. Although occasionally I will refer to other books of Vives, the main sources of this study are the following books: *In pseudo-dialecticos,* written only seven years after Vives' departure from Paris; *De Initiis, sectis, et laudibus philosophiae* (1518), one of the first modern sketches of a critical history of philosophy; the first part of the encyclopedic treatise *De Disciplinis* (1531), in which Vives deals with the causes of the corruption of medieval culture; and, finally, the historical remarks in the Commentaries to St. Augustine's *Civitas Dei.*

a. Philosophy of History

Vives' philosophy of history is closely related to his general conception of the purpose and the range of human knowledge. Although we intend to dedicate a whole chapter to the subject, some of his views need to be briefly anticipated now.

Inferior as man is to the beasts in bodily energies, he has been endowed by God with the instrument of knowledge. This instrument is reliable insofar as it is used for the right purpose. Knowledge was granted to man first to give him power over nature, second to enlighten him in the moral ordination of his life, and third to lead him to the final goal of human existence, God Himself. Moreover, since man is a social being, knowledge is also a social instrument, not only because through lan-

---

[3] *Ibid.,* 57; 307 a. "... quem errorem ego, si decem annos valetudine non prorsus adversa Dei beneficio vixero, e mentibus illorum non argumentis, sed ipsa re delebo."

[4] In the introduction to *Adversus pseudo-dialecticos* Vives contrasts the "barbaries" of the Parisian University with the historical event of "renascentium litterarum" which made the most enlightened men of his days "ut gratulemur saeculo nostro." (*Ibid.,* 37; 293 a). Vives shared with Erasmus the persuasion that the Lutheran controversy was a threat to the literary revival of his days.

guage it *can* be communicated, but also because social and historical communication is the only way to transcend the limitations of an individual man and a concrete generation. The last remark leads us immediately into the core of Vives' conception of history. As a Christian, Vives believed that human nature is basically good but finite. This very finitude of man makes a process of melioration ontologically possible. Man can always be better because ... he is never as good as he could become. God does not change, the infinite has no history. The order of nature, on the other hand, has made possible the growth of the individual in society and in history. Man is enriched by the performance, and even by the mistakes, of other men. This temporal process of mutual supplementation is called history. It is an unbroken, continuous, and social process, from a modest start toward a goal which is never reached, but always envisioned and sought. Human perfection is never final, culture never "arrives," the task is never finished – there is always something left for others. "Truth is accessible to everybody and has not been confiscated by a few. A great portion of it is left to future generations." [5] Vives expresses the same principle in a colorful metaphor:

Shall I condemn those who have made a few initial mistakes? No, I shall not incriminate them any more than I would blame a person who, after much work, finds ... a mine of rich metals, but does not have time to polish them. It is impossible to find something and to finish it off at the same time ... The life of an individual is not long enough for it, nor the power of a single mind, limited and weak as we all are ...[6]

And again,

No art nor discipline was ever conceived at the beginning in such unblemished condition that did not have a mixture of useless and perishable waste. The powers of human nature never produce something perfect and complete; there is always something missing to the peak of possible perfection.[7]

---

[5] M, VI, 7; R, II, 342 a. "Patet omnibus veritas, nondum est occupata; multum ex illa etiam futuris relictum est." (*DD.,* preface).

[6] M, VI, 35-36; R, II, 365 b. "Damnem ego illos quod aliquoties lapsi fuerint? Equidem non, non magis, quam si quis maximo labore ... metalla multa eruerit, non tamen repurgarit; non possunt multa simul proferri et expoliri; non potest unum aliquod diu quaesitum ab eodem inveniri et excoli; non sufficit tot rebus vita, non humani ingenii vis brevis et infirma ... (*DD.,* I, 1, 5).

[7] *Ibid.,* 16; 350 b. "Numquam ergo vel perfectae fuerunt artes vel purae, ne in sua quidem origine ... non quod ars ulla vel ad absolutionem aliquam sit perducta, vel ita extersa ac expolita, ut nihil haberet admixtum inutile ac rejiciendum ... nihilque ita perfectum ac absolutum, cui non desint plurima ad cumulum perfectionis ..."

This relativistic conception of knowledge as a temporal process of increasing accuracy and reliability is applied by Vives even to the growth of each individual. "Is it not true that Aristotle knew more when he was old than when he was young?" [8] One of the most remarkable traits of Vives' thought is the contrast between the gloomy bitterness of his personal experience and character on one side, and his optimistic faith in the perfectibility of human nature on the other. The first sign of this faith was his persuasion that "Nature was the same," still full of surprises and possibilities. "It would be erroneous," he wrote, "to think that Nature is exhausted and that it will never produce again anything similar to the geniuses of ancient times." [9] But Vives' optimism did not stop there. Following an opinion well spread in his day, Vives believed that the passing of time inexorably corrects the mistakes of each generation.[10] There is a positive evolution of human thought because individual errors cannot survive the erosion of constant criticism. Only what is in accordance with Nature passes the test of history. "We have only one hope left," he wrote to Cranevelt, "that time will erase the wrong opinions and will confirm the solid judgments of Nature." [11] And even more explicitly: "It is absolutely impossible that men shall err for ever; little by little the minds of people will open to the truth, and after rejecting all trifles and bagatelles, will embrace the authentic disciplines." [12]

Nevertheless, Vives' optimistic belief in the necessity of an ascending evolutionary process did not exclude the possibility of long periods of cultural regression. Vives accepted this as factually evident without making the slightest attempt to systematize the cyclical rhythm of history into an aprioristic scheme. As a whole, however, history was taken as a progressive movement. Consequently, ancient culture appeared to him as the product of a youthful and immature world. Like Bacon, one

[8] *Ibid.,* 186; 481 a. "Ipse Aristoteles an non plura assecutus est senex quam juvenis?" (*DD.,* I, 5, 2).

[9] M, VI, 6; R, 341 b. "Neque enim effoeta est iam vel exhausta natura, ut nihil prioribus annis simile pariat; eadem est semper sui similis..." (*DD.,* preface).

[10] This topic became very popular in the second half of the sixteenth century and throughout the seventeenth. See, e.g., George Hakewill, *An Apology or Declamation of the Power and Providence of God in the Government of the World* (Oxford, 1630); Joseph Glanvill, *Plus Ultra or the Progress and Advancement of Knowledge since the Days of Aristotle* (London, 1668); Louis Le Roy, *Des Vicissitudes ou la Verité des choses* (Paris, 1579).

[11] *LC.,* 175, vv. 25-26. "Una restat spes, quod opinionum commenta delet dies, naturae iudicia vere et solida confirmat."

[12] M, III, 61; R, II, 310 b. "Neque enim fieri potest ut caeci semper mortales errent; aperientur sensim ingenia, et humanae mentes ex tenebris in lucem profectae, rejectis tam pravis perniciosisque nugis suas amplexabuntur veras disciplinas." (*Adv. ps-d*).

hundred years later, Vives considered Greek and Roman civilizations as the first steps of a primitive world: "ancient history is the childhood of man." [13] The fact that this view does not seem to fit well with the commonly accepted picture of the Renaissance, as a period fascinated by the superb achievements of classical antiquity, proves only the originality of Vives' thought and the complexity of his times.

I believe that Vives' commitment to the evolution of human thought is a further indication of his pervasive naturalism. For the medieval man, history was a part of the religious drama of the world. The climax of the drama was the coming of Christ. Whatever preceded the Revelation was seen as a providential preparation; whatever followed it was nothing but a *traditio* of the revealed message. Greek philosophy, Aristotle especially, was included in this scheme because its rationalistic accuracy made possible the expression of the content of the Christian dogma in sharp formulations. Vives' conception of history is a challenge to all these views. The fact of the Revelation loses its unique and central position in the organic process of growth. Vives explained the privileged position of modern man, not in terms of the Christian Revelation, but in terms of the "accumulated experience" available to him in the records of history.

There is no doubt that it is much better to apply our criticism to the writings of great authors of the past, than to rely only on their authority . . . The discoveries of the past and the long experience of other men open the gates to new learning . . . Nature is always the same; the only difference is that now, confirmed and strengthened by the energies accumulated through many centuries, it seems more robust and active . . . I even think that, if we apply our minds to it, we will be able to know more about nature and life than Plato, Aristotle, or any ancient philosopher. We are far ahead of them because men have accumulated through history a long and patient observation of nature, which observation was for the ancients more a source of admiration than a beginning of knowledge.[14]

[13] Charles Rémusat, Bacon. *Sa vie, son temps, sa philosophie,* 3rd ed. (Paris, 1877), pp. 183-184, comments on Bacon's dictum *antiquitas saeculi juventus mundi.*
In his book *De Veritate Fidei,* Vives presents the idea that the history of the world has hardly started: "pueri sumus, plane nunc incipimus." (M, VIII, 76; R, II, 1385 a).
[14] M, VI, 6-7; R, II, 341 a - 342 a. "Porro de scriptis maiorum auctorum existimare multo est litteris conducibilius, quam auctoritate sola acquiescere . . . Quantum enim ad disciplinas percipiendas omnes aditum nobis inventa superiorum saeculorum aperiunt, ex experientia tam diuturna? . . . Natura eadem est semper sui similis, nec raro, tamquam collectis viribus pollentior ac potentior, qualem nunc esse credi par est robore adjutam et confirmatam, quod sensim per tot saecula accrevit . . . ut appareat posse nos, si modo applicaremus eodem animum, melius in universum pronuntiare de rebus vitae ac naturae, quam Aristotelem, Platonem, aut

The first benefit to be gained from the past experience of man was, according to Vives, a solid knowledge of history. Vives dedicates to this subject – of enormous importance in his pedagogy – three chapters of his treatise, *De Disciplinis*.[15] In the first, he deals with the causes of the corruption of historical studies: the lack of truth, the fantasies and the tropes of the poets, the adulteration of chronological dates, the chauvinism of the historians, and the exaggerations of the eulogists. The second chapter describes the common abuses to be found in the books of history: excessive attention to imaginative details (even in stories of love-affairs!), glorification of wars, unfair comparisons, ignorance of social and even geographical background, and finally, plain falsity. Ecclesiastical historians were no exception; they also appealed to man's morbid inclination toward the mythical and the fantastic and thus, "they prostituted the bride of Religion into the harlot of superstition." [16] In the third and final chapter, Vives suggests ways of reform for the writing of history. He recommends striving toward an organic, synthetic view of history based on exact chronology, and emphasizes the importance of making a clear distinction between different historical periods and their factual liaison. Finally he makes clear that history is not only a source of positive knowledge, but an instrument of moral education which should underscore the bad consequences of evil and the rewards of virtue.

In conclusion we can say that Vives considered history as the memory of mankind, the collected reason of ages, involved in a temporal and social process of improvement and correction. From this conception of history Vives derives a far-reaching eclecticism. The individual transcends his own limitations by becoming an active member of the historical process, that is to say, by selecting the best from the past after a critical survey of its achievements. This critical scrutiny is, consequently, the first step toward a personal and positive contribution to the stock of knowledge history has massed together. As such it is a responsible operation which demands the highest ethical standards and the most enlightened frame of mind.

---

quemquam antiquorum, videlicet, post tam longam maximarum et abditarum rerum observationem, quae novae illis ac recentes admirationem magis pariebant sui, quam cognitionem adferebant." (*DD.*, preface).

[15] M, VI, 93-110, 392-401; R, II, 417-424, 651-658. (*DD.*, I, 2, 5-6; II, 5, 2).
[16] *Ibid.*, 103; 414.
[17] See below, pp. 288-289.

b. Principles of Critical Evaluation

It is only proper that we start our study of Vives' norms of criticism with his strong emphasis on the ethos of the scholar; after all, Vives' humanistic epistemology was based on the premise that wisdom without virtue is totally impossible.[17] The very first ethical condition of the would-be scholar is modesty. Serious pride or vain conceit incapacitates him from assimilating the lessons of the past.

The man who longs for knowledge has to be ready to learn from anybody who can teach him. Why should a human being be ashamed of learning from another human being, when mankind itself has learnt even from the beasts? Pride makes progress impossible, because proud men refuse to learn from other men . . .[18]

On the other hand an excessive admiration for the authority of others might imperil the accomplishments of the individual and undermine his own energies:

There is a gigantic number of writers; an infinite number of books. We do not even know what to read or where to start . . . Consequently, we choose our favorites, and we give them such a loyalty that we consider it a crime to deviate an inch from them. Perhaps this is because we think too little of ourselves; perhaps, we are too lazy to investigate the case. In the process we forget that they were infallible men like ourselves, and that what we received from them was only a rough product to be retouched and beautified . . . We thought that we were less than men, and that they were heroes or half-gods. Plainly false and silly is that saying, which most people readily accept, that "we are like dwarfs on the shoulders of giants." Not at all! Neither are we dwarfs nor were they giants. We can only see further afar thanks to them, provided we have the qualities they possessed: zeal, dedication, concentration of the mind, and love of Truth. Without them we are not even dwarfs, nor are we on the shoulders of any giants, but little men thrown down to the ground.[19]

[18] M, VI, 416; R, II, 670 b. ". . . non erubescet homo sciendi cupidus a quo-cumque discere qui docere quid possit; cur hominem ab homine pudeat discere, quum humanum genus multa a belluis discere non puduerit?" (*DD.*, II, after book 5).

[19] *Ibid.*, 38; 368 a-b. "Infinita est scribentium turba; ingens, inmensus librorum numerus; nescio cui me applicem . . . nos tamen ita illorum vestigiis adhaerere atque insistere decrevimus, ut nefas existimemus ab illis vel pilum unum deflectere, damnatione nostrorum ingeniorum, sive odio quaerendi; quum et illi fuerint homines ut nos, quorum est proprium falli et fallere; primique illi inventores, velut rudes modo quasdam massas, atque informes, sicut dicebam, tradiderint posteris suis expurgandas et formandas . . . Falsa enim est atque inepta illa quorundam similitudo, quam multi tamquam acutissimam atque apositissimam excipiunt: 'Nos ad priores

With a refined sense of humor, not too frequent in his writings, Vives ridicules the humanist's obsession with the glare of antiquity:

There are people inclined to think that the older an author is the more credit he deserves. How is that? Did not Aristotle live after Anaxagoras, Cicero after Cato, Demosthenes after Pericles, and Vergil after Ennius? Why, then, do these "lovers of antiquity" prefer in each of these cases the younger to the older? ... The truth is that such people are so sold on the good, ancient days, that they reject as bold novelty whatever they think to be new, even if it actually is very old, and worship everything they esteem to be old, even if in reality it is very new.

I have seen with men own eyes people taking off their hats in sign of respect for a poet of our own times because they found his verses covered with dust in some ancient library ... And I know of an individual who indignantly rejected a letter written by Cicero, calling it "a transalpine barbarism!" because it had a heading written in French.[20]

To this difficult balance between modesty and self-confidence, respect for others and uncritical admiration, Vives adds a more important quality: that of open-mindedness and ecumenical fairness. "No book is so good that it does not need correction, nor so bad that it does not include some truth." [21] Nothing is more opposed to Vives' frame of mind than a bigoted sectarianism. According to Vives the one-sided sectarian magnifies one partial mistake at the expense of all the correcting devices left out of his field of vision and paralyzes the historical process by taking permanent residence in one narrow and transient stage. He chokes the spontaneous energy of nature by denying recognition to its manifold channels of self-expression. This stultifying attitude is itself the product of passional disorders and short-comings of the mind. One of the worst kinds was indeed the exaggerated nationalism of his age. Vives had only disdain for those who accepted this or that thinker only

collatos esse, ut nanos in humeris gigantum': non est ita, neque nos sumus nani, nec illi homines gigantes, sed omnes ejusdem staturae, et quidem nos altius evecti illorum beneficio, maneat modo in nobis, quod in illis, studium, attentio animi, vigilantia, et amor veri; quae si absint, jam non nani sumus, nec in gigantum humeris sedemus sed homines justae magnitudinis humi prostrati." (DD., I, 1, 1).

[20] M, VI, 41-42; R, II, 370 b − 371 a. "Quemadmodum ille dicit, ut quanto sit quisque vetustior, hoc apud te sit nominis ac fidei potioris? Quid? an non Aristotles Anaxagora posterior, et Cicero M. Catone, et Demosthenes Pericle, et Vergilius Ennio? At posteriores istos antiquarii homines prioribus illis longe anteponunt ... ut quidquid non putent vetus esse, continuo damnent inauditum, incognitum, etiamsi maxime sit vetus, modo recens credant ... Vidi qui versiculos hominis viventis quod in pervetere bibliotheca reperti essent pulvere obsiti ... aperto capite veneratus sit tamquam Vergilianos ...; et alius Ciceronis epistolam, cui consulto praepositum nomen erat Gallicum, magno fastidio aspernatus est, addito etiam convicio barbariei transalpinae." (DD., I, 1, 5).

[21] Ibid., 38; 368 a. "Neque enim est ullus tam malus liber, qui alicui non placeat."

because "he is or is not from such a country." These people, he wrote, "deal with the acumen of the intellect as with a fruit or wine which is classified according to their place of origin." [22]

In most cases, Vives remarks, the hardening of the mind into a stiff bigotry begins in the early stages of the educational process:

The boy goes to school, and in no time he gets indoctrinated into the tenets of a particular sect: he listens, and long before he acquires the ability to judge, he gives his assent. Day after day, the teacher inssits on the same views with indomitable obstinacy and a ferocious expression on his face. His fellow students swallow everything the teachers throw at them with foolish gullibility and a stupid, wide-open mouth... Most of these blind people never recover the energies to shake off what they accepted that early in their lives.[23]

Once long use has confirmed a belief, it becomes like a fortress: "Whatever has been accepted for a long time, seems, just because of that, solid and inexpugnable." [24] In other cases bigotry is a subtle form of intellectual laziness. Some people find it easier to serve a master than to make up their own beliefs after a strenuous comparative study. This temptation was particularly strong in the days of the Renaissance when Greek and Roman thinkers in unprecedented large numbers began to address themselves to the European intelligentsia from the feverishly active printing presses of the day. "Most of those thinkers," Vives complained, "invite us to follow them exclusively, and to avoid the others." [25]

---

[22] *Ibid.*, VI, 44; II, 372 b. "Et affectus in re tantopere dominantur, ut etiam gentes ac nationes spectent: 'Non probo hunc, quia non huius aut illius regionis': quasi ingenia poma sint, aut vina, quae solo et regionibus censeri solent." (*DD.*, I, 1, 5).

[23] *Ibid.*, 40; 369 a. "Deducitur ad scholam filius ab indocto patre... imbuitur statim sectae placitis; recipit, assentitur, afficitur priusquam possit judicare; audit dici omnia constantissime a praeceptore ingenti asseveratione vultus, supercilii, sententiae; videt recipi omnia magno consensu atque admiratione a condiscipulis, credit esse mera oracula... multi eorum ne possunt quidem a receptis semel discedere..."

[24] *Ibid.*, 37; 366 b. "Quae usu semel sunt recepta et confirmata, ita fiunt sacra et fixa, ut nefas existimetur ab eis discedere..."

[25] *Ibid.*, 38; 367 b. "Ad haec, tot esse nobis obtulerunt duces, tot sunt nos ut sequeremur se unos adhortati, et alios ut omnes vitaremus tamquam in perniciem ducturos..."

[26] *Ibid.*, VI, 362; II, 626 a. "Si inveniri posset aliquis, qui unus haberet omnia optima... is esset sane imitandus solus, sed nullus est qui ab omni parte tam felix... est, Quintiliani sententia, qui, non qui maxime imitandus, eum solum imitandum censet." (*DD.*, II, 4, 4).

Ibid., 48; 276 a. "Ibi sudor et anhelitus in redigendis ad concordiam discordissimis. Dementes! non intelligunt eum qui tam multos et tam diversos sequatur, nullum sequi?" (*DD.*, I, 1, 6).

If it is foolish to give our undivided loyalty to one at the expense of all the rest, it is also wrong to attempt an unnatural symbiosis of all. Vives was opposed not only to those who believed in the *imitatio* of a well-chosen model, but also to those who, for instance, were trying a compromise of Platonic and Peripatetic philosophies. Vives' critical eclecticism was not based on covering up differences, but in learning from a vivid contrast. Eclecticism, as Vives understood it, does not proceed by agglutination, but organically and creatively.

If I could find a man with every imaginable virtue, that man should be the only example to follow ... But, unfortunately, there is no such man ... Moreover, I agree with Quintilian that nobody should imitate the best possible model to the exclusion of others ... To be the best does not make the others bad or despicable ...

How much effort and work is wasted in trying to reconcile what is irreconcilable! Do they not realize that by attempting to follow many and different leaders, actually they do not follow anybody? [26]

Other sources of critical misrepresentation and false judgment were, according to Vives, more intellectual in character. For instance, ignoring the historical background of a writer can lead to a terrible confusion. "There are people who seem to think that all the writers of the world lived at the same time; others totally misconstruct their chronological order. I have read that Boethius lived before Saint Jerome, and Saint Jerome before Aristotle ..." [27] It is also unwise to confer on all the writings of one single author the same degree of authority. Some difference has to be made between "the statements Cicero made in the *forum*, forced by the circumstances of the moment, and the views he expressed in his book, *De Officiis,* exclusively following the dictates of his reason." [28] A more dangerous mistake is "to judge the whole by a trivial detail," or to reject the content because of a defective expression.[29] Equally wrong would be to understand literally what was figuratively

---

Kristellers' description of Humanistic eclecticism as a search for "crumbles of knowledge wherever it could find them" (*Renaissance Thought,* p. 19) would be an unfair characterization of Vives' thought. Vives himself criticized the superficial and versatile eclecticism of Cicero. (M, VI, 362-363; R, II, 626).

[27] *Ibid.,* 47; 375 a. "Scriptores omnes vel aequales censent, vel etiam posteriores fecerunt priores, ut Boethium Hieronymo, Hieronymum Aristotle ..."

[28] *Ibid.,* "Eiusdem momenti sunt istis quae Cicero in foro dicit, tempori serviens ac causae, et quae in *Officiis,* ubi veritas ... ad exactum rationis judicium elimatur ..."

[29] *Ibid.,* 48; 376 b. "Si in re levissima scriptor fuerit negligentior, totum protinus opus rejiciunt ..."

meant, or to confuse history with epic, events with myths, poetic tributes with moral judgments.[30]

As was becoming to a man of the Renaissance, Vives launched a formidable attack against the medieval lack of respect for language. Much more than any other humanist, Vives' concern with language was a pragmatic prerequisite of his attempt to comprehend the thought of the past. "The effort to master all the languages of the world is a pure waste of time unless it is done with a practical purpose." [31] To him the knowledge of languages was nothing more than "the opening of the gates to all the beauties and all the marvels those languages keep locked inside." [32] This last metaphor, however, was not meant to open a breach between the formal linguistic expression and its material content. "In every speech," Vives wrote, "there are words and ideas, body and soul. The idea is the soul and the life of the word: without it, words die and vanish. The words, however, are the dwelling of the ideas, the lights which brighten the darkness of our spirits." [33] Vives proclaimed in equally clear terms that language, "the indispensable instrument of human coexistence and the shrine of erudition springs directly from human reason." [34] Precisely because language is the verbal expression of a given culture at a given time, Vives wanted the morphological and syntactical study of language to be inseparable from a simultaneous immersion into the cultural background of that age. Vives described the pseudo-scholars of the middle ages in the following terms:

They use names of plants for rocks, names of towns to signify rivers, proper names of people as names of ships; they forget the relevance of phraseology and idiomatic expressions, and neglect history, folklore, and ancient traditions. They confess not to care wether Hannibal or Scipio was

[30] Vives insists on these ideas in De Disciplinis, part 1, book 2, chapters 4, 5, 6. (M, VI, 93-110; R, II, 412-424).
[31] M, VI, 345; R, II, 612 a. "... nec linguas omnes labore illo propter se ipsas dignas esse, hoc est, si aliud nihil quaeratur, ut ad ea penetremus quae linguis illis includuntur velut thesauris quibusdam pulchra atque admiranda..." (DD., II, 4, 1).
[32] Ibid., "Meminerint homines studiosi, si nihil adjecerint linguis, ad fores tantum pervenisse artium, et ante illas, aut certe in vestibulo, versari..."
[33] What Vives was really attacking was a self-sufficient study of philology for its own sake. Philology, like logic itself, was only an instrumental art. "Aditus sunt quidem linguae ad artes omnes, quoniam illis sunt traditae, sed aditus, tantum, non item artes; ostia, non aedes." (M, VI, 30; R, II, 361 a).
[34] The title of chapter 1, book 3, second part of De Disciplinis, is "Animi index, lingua." In the same chapter Vives writes: "Prima in homine peritia est loquendi, quae statim ex ratione ac mente, tamquam ex fonte profluit... est etiam sermo societatis humanae instrumentum.... sacrarium eruditonis est lingua..." (M, VI, 298; R, 573 a).

the leader of the Carthaginians, whether Caesar defeated Pompei or vice versa, whether Babylon was in Assyria or in Mesopotamia . . .

If they make some poor historical remarks in their writings on philosophy, law, theology, or medicine, they excuse themselves by saying that history is not their business. If they make a big blunder in cosmography they say that cosmography is not their business. If they make ignorant statements about trees or flowers, they also say that natural science is not their field. What then is their proper business? Not to know anything? [35]

Vives' main accusation against medieval scholars was precisely their appalling misrepresentation of ancient culture. The first requirement of textual criticism is to establish the authenticity of a book.

In ancient times the grammarians used to make a solid and diligent critical scrutiny of books, to decide whether in fact such a book could be attributed to an individual writer. Now, the darkness of night seems to have swallowed those good old grammarians and the professors of arts in our days have expelled grammar from their classrooms . . . Consequently, the most ridiculous and obscene books are attributed to the most improbable geniuses of the past. Aristotle, Plato, Origenes, Cyprian, Augustine, Jerome, Boethius, Cicero, and Seneca, are blamed for monstrosities they never dreamed in their worst nightmares; atrocities unworthy not only of such men, but even of their Bulgarian or Chinese slaves, if they ever had them.[36]

In other cases, Vives adds, "the titles of the books were mutilated, changed, or simply invented." [37] The selection of the codices was random and careless. Medieval copyists used manuscripts "plagued by mistakes," "rotted by moth, humidity and dust," "perforated with pun-

[35] M, VI, 62; R, II, 387. "Herbas pro saxis, urbes pro fluviis, homines pro navibus usurpant: interciderunt, quod proximum est, phrases, et loquendi formulae, tum historia, mores populorum ac gentium, et tota cognitio vetustatis: negabant suae interesse, fuerit ne Hannibal Poenorum dux, an Scipio; vicerit Caesar Pompeium, an contra, Caesarem Pompeius; sit in Assyria Babylon, an in Mesopotamia . . . . . . Admiscet historiam ineptissime narratam et falso: 'Negat hoc esse suum institutum'; attingit aliquid de Cosmographia inscite: 'Negat hoc esse suum institutum'; loquitur de vi verbi imperite: 'Negat hoc esse suum institutum'; de arbore, de animante indocte: 'Negat hoc esse suum institutum'. Quod ergo est tandem tuum institutum? nihil statuisse recte dicere?" (DD., I, 1, 8).
[36] Ibid., VI, 44-45; 373. "Olim enim grammatici magna, et late patenti eruditione, per omnia scriptorum genera diligenter versati, non dicta solum, verum etiam integros libros . . . censebant, essentne, cuius inscriberentur, auctoris; . . . nunc vero, quia et grammatici se in tenebras quasdam pristini abdiderunt, et grammaticam professores majorum artium contubernio suo expulerunt . . . idcirco non modo dicta, et sensa, inepta ac stulta, sed sordidissima quoque, et abjectissima opera genti ac familiae clarissimorum auctorum supponuntur: adscripta sunt Aristoteli, Platoni, Origeni, Cypriano, Hieronymo, Augustino, Boethio, Ciceroni, Senecae, quae ipsis numquam, ne per quietem quidem, in mentem venerunt, indigna quidem non solum tantis ingeniis, atque illa eruditione, sed etiam eorum servis, si quos habuerunt Scythas aut Seres . . ." (DD., I, 1, 6).
[37] Ibid., 45; 373 b.

cheons," and totally illegible.[38] The chirographers themselves were almost without exception "poor ignoramuses, sometimes even women and nuns," who did not know how to read and made changes and substitutions according to their wild ignorance and imagination.[39]

Unfortunately,

... once the mistake was made, it was sinful to attempt its correction. There are cases where an Ecumenical Council was summoned by the Church to correct a silly mistake made by an ignorant lay brother, even if the lapsus was obvious even to children ... The only manuscripts which remained pure and reliable were those which were not found by the "culture" of that age and were protected by heavy layers of dust ...[40]

With the same uncritical naivete, the medieval commentators and interpreters made use of those faulty texts to build up their fantastic misconstructions. Aristotle was one of their favorite victims. "His Latin translators failed to make him speak in Latin, and left the original Greek text totally deteriorated." His interpreters, unable to make any sense out of such a mess, "invented their own elucidations to cover up their personal ignorance." The abuse was such that people began to think that "Aristotle's nose was made of wax, and anybody could shape it according to his own whim." [41]

The last fatal consequence of all this confusion was that the medieval man gave up any hope of obtaining an organic view of the historical process. Instead, he was satisfied with endless collections of unrelated aphorisms, quotations without context or historical background, superficial summaries of practical skills, or pure streams of verbosity, totally irrelevant to life. Hence the medieval passion for lexicons, manuals, encyclopedias, abecedariums, vademecums, dictionaries, "thesauri," "catenae," "florilegia," and their like.

---

[38] *Ibid.,* 45-56; 373 b – 374 a.

[39] *Ibid.,* 45; 373 b. "Interdum qui scribebant nesciebant legere, confudebantur omnia, ut compositio esset litterarum, et verborum contextus conjecturis investigandus ..."

[40] *Ibid..* "Quae vero semel mendae irrepserunt, religio erat attingere ac demutare; velut in mysticis libris inductus fuerat a librario illiteratissimo error, ad eum corrigendum putabant opus esse consilio totius ecclesiae, quantumlibet lapsus esset lucidus, et vel pueris perspicuus.

... Puriores sunt atque integriores, qui in vetustis bibliothecis situ ac pulvere latuerunt obsessi ... quam ubi viguerunt studia ..."

[41] M, VI, 70; R, II, 393 b. "... ut iam etiam vulgo inter eos, non omnino, ut solent, inscite, Aristoteles dicatur habere nasum cereum, quem quilibet, quo velit, flectat pro libito." (*DD.,* I, 1, 10). All the short quotations of this paragraph are taken from the same chapter 10 entitled: "Vitio interpretum artium forma et tamquam facies amissa, tum utilitas et honor."

Today Saint Jerome, Saint Augustine, Saint John Chrisostomus and the other Fathers of the primitive Church are known not through their own works, but through the *Liber Sententiarum* of Peter Lombard, the *Catena Aurea* of Saint Thomas, and similar collections. The physicians have their own *Florilegia* taken from the books of Galen, Hippocrates, and Avicenna. Tribonianus gleaned here and there for the jurists. Aristotle was decapitated in Paris, and arrived to us in two separate pieces. Moreover, the readers of today find even these anthologies too hard to read, and satisfy themselves with a short glance at the index of contents.

How is it possible to understand the meaning of the author without the support of the context? [42]

Vives' standards of historical criticism, both ethical and intellectual, were clearly shared by most humanists. His genius was not to invent, but to give an eloquent and judicious expression to the concerns and the goals of his generation and to embody them in a practical program of general education. However, in two points we have mentioned Vives' thoughts were more mature and original than the general trend of his age. The first was his own personal form of eclecticism as a modest and all-embracing, open-mindedness for the past achievements of men leading to a creative and organic cultural growth. The second was his enormous interest in history as the temporal dimension of man's society wherein the individual finds a chance to transcend his own limitations.

c. Concrete Historical Interpretations

It was Vives' firm persuasion that medieval decadence had reached its lowest point, and that according to the inevitability of progress in the historical process as a whole, the immediate future had to be better than the recent past.

I have always learnt from my parents and teachers what experience has confirmed in many different ways, namely, that bad habits cannot easily be cured unless they have reached an intolerable degree of depravation... "The better order" – says the proverb – "is born from the corrupted one, and the worst is always followed by the better"...

[42] *Ibid.*, 61; 386 b. "Ita nunc Hieronymus, August. Chrysost. et prisci illi ac primi religionis nostrae scriptores, non ex suis ipsorum monimentis cognoscuntur, sed ex collectaneis sententiarum Petri Lombardi, ex *Catena aurea* Divi Thomae, et aliis rhapsodiis eius notae: nacti sunt et medici suos decerptores flosculorum ex libris Galeni, Hippocratis, Avicennae: consuit centones jurisconsultorum Tribonianus: detruncatus est Lutetiae Aristoteles et traditus vix dimidiatus. Ne sic quidem breviaria haec lectores inveniunt, longum existimatur ea percurrere, sit satis indices aut rubricas inspexisse... Qui possunt auctorum sensus percipi, deserti et destituti suis velut fulcimentis, nempe iis quae antecedunt, quaeque subsequuntur?" (*DD*, I, 1, 8).

I do not believe that a change is far away anymore; darkness cannot grow any thicker than now; men have endured long enough all this foolish nonsense; our spirit, naturally inclined toward the better things, has reached the end of its tolerance . . .[43]

Vives believed that the literary Renaissance was the first step in the right direction, because he thought that a new encounter with ancient literature had to lead to a fresh confrontation with serious intellectual questions. If the generation of Petrarch, Salutati, Poggio, Bruni, and Filelfo was poor in speculative substance, that of Cusanus, Ficino, and Pico della Mirandola, combined a more or less thoroughgoing humanistic background with solid philosophical achievements. Born one generation before Peter Ramus, Telesio, Montaigne, Giordano Bruno, Cardano, and Zabarella, Vives and his two great contemporaries, Machiavelli and Pomponazzi, represent the definitive priority of thought over form which marked the rest of the century. I hope that a summary of Vives' historical views will give a concrete example of the catalytic effect of ancient culture upon Renaissance philosophy.

Vives thought that the historical process was carried by two different agents: the chain of external events and the internal development of man's spirit. Vives never attempted a theory of their mutual relationship, but occasionally in concrete cases, he pointed to their mutual bearing. Greece learned Oriental and Biblical myths because of its geographical position, the journeys of its merchants, and the struggle against the Persian armies. Rome became the heiress to Greek culture because of the expansion of the Empire.[44] The invasion of the Goths violently disrupted the historical process.[45] Islam, "the plague of mankind," conveyed to medieval Europe a misrepresentation of Greek thought.[46] The centrifugal forces of feudalism resisted cultural progress.

[43] *Ibid.*, III, 62; II, 310 b – 311 a. "Ego sane sic a parentibus, sic a prudentissimis viris accepi, sic rerum usu ac experientiis didici compluribus, pravas consuetudines non facile in melius viribus cujusquam commutari, nisi cum ipsa in tantam pravitatem pervenerint, ut omnibus fiant intolerabiles . . . unde est illud vulgare hominum sermone proverbium: 'Nasci optimum ordinem ex perversissimo, bonasque leges ex malis moribus procreari' . . . Neque id procul abesse crediderim, quum jam eo magnitudinis hae umbrae, caligines, insaniaeque venerint, ut mole laborent sua, sintque et aliis et sibi ipsae intolerabiles . . ." (*Adv. Ps-d.*).
[44] Vives presents these ideas in the first part of his *De initiis, sectis, et laudibus Philosophiae.* (M, III, 2-20; R, II, 293-300).
[45] *De disciplinis,* part I, book 1, chapter 4. "De bellis cum Septentrionalibus" (M, VI, 27-35; R, II, 358-364). See also the short essay *Quinam fueriut Gothi.* (R, I, 875-882).
[46] M, VII, 38; R, I, 288 b. ". . . ac Mahometaeo acerba peste generis humani." (*Clypei Christi descriptio*). Vives' antagonism to the Moslem religion was a medieval trait of his intellectual trappings and led him to a preposterous and exaggerated attitude against the Turkish Empire and to an unfair evaluation of the Islam

Although Renaissance scholarship considerably extended the knowledge of Greek classical sources, Vives' interest in Greece remained always
slanted and incomplete. The Greeks were to him "ostentatious and vainglorious," an accusation he repeats with suspicious insistence.[47] Greek
history was "a drove of fabulous fictions before the Olympiads, and not
totally free from falsehood thereafter." [48] In spite of Sophocles' popularity among many humanists, Vives practically ignored Greek tragedy;
and he had a scant knowledge of Greek legal monuments. Greek architecture and sculpture were no part of his otherwise mediocre artistic
taste.

Vives divided the history of Greek philosophy into two different
periods: before and after Socrates. The "pre-Socratic period" was described by Vives as "an investigation of nature"; it included the Ionian
and the Italian schools. The first was founded by "Thales, the master of
Anaximander, who was the master of Anaximenes, who was the master
of Anaxagoras, who was the master of Archelaus, who taught Socrates."
The Italian School was founded by "Telage (sic), the master of Xeno-
phanes, who was the master of Parmenides, who was the master of
Leucippus, who was the master of Democritus, who was the master of
Nausiphanes (sic), who taught Epicurus, in whom this sect died." [49]
According to Vives the concern with the study of natural things began
with a spirited study of astronomy and music, a clear proof of man's
longing for an extra-mundane reality. Rather bombastically Vives asks
himself:

Have we stopped to consider what kind of men were those – or shall I call
them immortal gods? – who rose up far beyond and above our modest roofs
and the reach of our bodies, and set foot in the very abode of the skies, where
not even the fabulous giants were ever allowed? [50]

philosophers. See, e.g., *De disciplinis,* I, 5, 3: "Irruit in Abenroem ... et atris
coloribus pingit metaphysicam Avicennae." (M, VI, 191-196; R, II, 485-490).

[47] Vives accuses the Greek of having being plagued by "an uncontrollable
yearning for originality" which led to a total falsification of the history of thought.
(M, VI, 19; R, II, 352 b, DD., I, 1, 3). More in concrete Vives attacked Plutarch
for his proud attempt to establish a comparison of Greece with Rome. Most Hellenic
writers following the example of Plutarch "inflated their words when their deeds
began to shrink, lest be overpowered by the gigantic bastions of Rome." (M, VI,
106; R, II, 422 a).

[48] M, VI, 394; R, II, 652 a. "Graeca historia fabulosissima est usque ad Olym-
piades, nec quisquam vera a falsis discreverit; sed neque quae deinceps sequitur
mendaciis caret, licet paulo verecundior." (*DD.,* II, 5, 2).

[49] These two genealogies of the pre-Socratic schools are expounded in Vives' *De
initiis, sectis, et laudibus philosophiae.* (M, III, 15; R, I, 572 b).

[50] M, III, 4; R, I, 565 b. "Quales homines illos, quos rectius immortales
dixerimus deos, qui supra tecta nostra, immo vero supra corporis sui elementa

Later philosophers turned their attention from the skies to the study of this earth: "rains, clouds, snow, lightning, the meteorites, the alternatives of light and darkness, cold and heat; the storms, the tides..."; from there to the study of plants, animals, metals, and finally, to the study of medicine, "the invention of the gods." [51]

If the first stage of philosophy was the investigation of things (*de rebus*), the second, inaugurated by Socrates, was the study of morals (*de moribus*). Socrates, "a truly divine master," "the sacred and sublime fountain-head" of Greek thought,

... was the first who applied philosophy to the service of people and cities, and brought back to life the intellectual effort being wasted in the curious investigation of the skies and their elements... And, being as he was the wisest of all mortals, he did not hesitate to proclaim his ignorance of the things of nature; he preferred to encourage men to give up the study of those mysteries and to apply the same energies to the reformation of their moral life.[52]

Socrates' impact upon the intellectual history of Greece was – according to Vives – extensive and long-lasting. Both the dogmatic and the sceptic branches of the Academy, as well as the Stoics, ought to recognize their Socratic ancestry.[53]

As for Plato, Vives' attitude was to a certain degree vague and fluctuating. His first personal encounter with Platonic philosophy – at least in a serious manner – probably took place during the preparation of his Commentaries on Saint Augustine's *Civitas Dei*. Vives was duly impressed by the preponderant part which Platonic and Neoplatonic thought played in the theological gestation of the Patristic age. His first natural reaction was to draw a comparison with the excessive influence of Aristotle upon sixteenth century scholastic thought. In 1523, Vives wrote to Erasmus:

I have tried to be concise, according to your wishes. In certain passages, however, I had to extend myself a little, because I was dealing with matters our theologians do not seem to know well, like history, literature, and phi-

sese extulerant, et quod gigantes immani corporis robore assequi nequiverunt, hi viribus suorum ingeniorum nixi, coelos ipsos penetrarunt?" (*De initiis*).
  [51] *Ibid.*, III, 9; I, 568 b.
  [52] *Ibid.*, III, 15; I, 572 b. "*Socrates* primus philosophiam, in coelis elementisque versantem et divagantem, ad civitatem atque hominum singulorum usus, vitamque devocavit... et quum esset unus omnium consensu et approbatione rerum eiusmodi scientissimus, affirmavit tamen, se illorum omnium ignarum esse, ut ceteri desperata ... tanta arcanorum scientia, illis relictis, ad morum compositionem totos se coverterent." (*De initiis*).
  [53] *Ibid.*, III, 15-16; I, 573-574.

losophy, especially Platonic philosophy. Consequently, books eight and ten became longer than I myself expected; I do not think that our theologians should ignore Plato. On the contrary, they should recognize that Plato does not have to envy Aristotle anything and become familiar with other authors besides Aristotle.[54]

In those years of Erasmian enthusiasm (1520-23), Vives' admiration for Plato, "the holy philosopher," was mainly religious. The spiritual loftiness and the eschatological bent of "the Athenian Moses" were naturally congenial to his intense devotion and religious thinking. However, the finest product of this early enthusiasm for Plato was – typically enough – an introduction and commentary, not to a Platonic dialogue, but to a highly eclectic synthesis of Stoic and Neoplatonic ingredients, Cicero's *Somnium Scipionis*, the first book he tried to "read" in the University of Louvain. Cicero's beautiful essay was not a discovery of the Renaissance. In fact Vives' familiarity with the commentary of Macrobius – rather than Chalcidius – indicates that he was well aware of the amazing popularity of the *Somnium* among medieval thinkers. Like the Humanists of Chartres, Vives profoundly admired the books' categorical assertion of the supremacy of the spiritual above the material, its belief in the organic unity of cosmic order and moral values, and, finally, its admiration for man as the microcosmic converging point of matter and spirit – the master of Nature and the image of God. For many years Vives was delighted with this harmonic synthesis of natural and moral philosophy, in which he saw the ideal combination of Pre-Socratic naturalism and Socratic moralism. In fact, he did not even hesitate to write that the *Somnium Scipionis* was second only to the Bible.[55] Nevertheless, I have the definite impression that even this Neoplatonic philosophy lost much of its appeal for Vives in later years. Vives grew progressively suspicious of Plato's use of the myth, at least as an educational device. Reluctantly he admitted that the poetical style and nebulous mysticism of Plato were ill-adapted to the conciseness and order of the class-room. Two years before his death, Vives wrote: "Plato

---

[54] *EE.*, V, 1271, vv. 10-17. "Ego enim in hoc opere brevitati, quantum potui, studui placere. Incurrerunt quidem loci in quibus id praestari non potuit, ut quum erant res non admodum theologis nostris cognitae, sicut philosophica, praecipue Platonica. Ideo in octavo et decimo libris longior fui forsan quam oportebat; tum ut recondita illis aperirem et proferrem, tum ut Platonica prorsus non ignorarent, viderentque haec nihil Aristotelicis cedere, et inciperent alios quoque magnos auctores velle cognoscere."

[55] M, V, 106; R, I, 633 b. "Nulla umquam hominum memoria scriptum esse librum (sacros nostrae religionis semper excipio) in quo plus rerum, plus artis, plus eloquentiae, sit comprehensum atque infarctum." (*SS.*, preface).

was the first philosopher in ancient times who wrote in a beautiful style; nevertheless, he does not fit well into the process of learning." [56] Besides, Vives lost more and more his interest in metaphysical speculation. Nature ceased to be part of a grandiose scheme; it became simply the source of materials for man's bodily needs. It was much more important to use it well than to attempt its conceptual elucidation. In only one important respect Vives remained basically Socratic and Platonic: in the firm persuasion that vice follows from a wrong judgment about the values of things, and that wisdom requires the total subordination of the inferior passions to the leadership of reason. Vives' unshakable faith in moral and intellectual education was his lasting tribute to the author of the *Republic*.

Vives' attitude toward Aristotle was also complex. There is no doubt that, in spite of some open criticism, he felt an endless admiration for the founder of the Peripatetic school. In 1518, Vives wrote: "My philosophers, however, are the Peripatetics, whose leader, Aristotle, is undoubtedly the wisest of all thinkers." [57] One year later, in the introduction to the *Somnium Scipionis*, Vives explained: "Far from me to belittle Aristotle, whom I place, without exception, before any other philosopher." [58] Finally, in one of his last writings, Vives censures Pliny for having praised Homer as the greatest genius of history: "I am sure that there has never been a man of Aristotle's stature." [59]

Vives had several reasons for such a preference. First of all, he saw in Aristotle the genius who brought to a constructive synthesis all the previous accomplishments of the Greek tradition. "Aristotle . . . gathered what was scattered and dispersed, structured what was just piled up together, arranged the chaos, elucidated what was dark and confused, and organized whatever he wrote about." [60] In this respect Peripatetic philosophy was for Vives a perfect example of constructive eclecticism. Furthermore, as a Pedagogue, Vives respected the straightforwardness,

---

[56] M, III, 25; R, I, 973 a. "Scripserunt veteri philosophi ante Aristotelem pauca, atque ea confuse; primus omnium Plato eleganter sane multa, et docte, sed ad docendum discendumque parum accomodate." (*Censura*).

[57] *Ibid.*, III, 18; I, 574 b. "At vero nostrates philosophi, quorum princeps idem, philosophorum omnium facile sapientissimus, Aristoteles Stagyrites fuit." (*De initiis*).

[58] *Ibid.*, V, 107; I, 634 a. "Nemo me suggillare Aristotelem credat, quem ego universis philosophis, nemine excepto, antepono . . ." (*SS.*, preface).

[59] See the introduction to *De Aristotelis operibus censura* (M, III, 25; R, I, 973 a).

[60] M, VI, 31; R, II, 361 b. "Aristoteles sparsa enim collegit, congesta digessit, confusa distinxit, obscuris attulit lumen, omnia ita reddidit concinna et apta ut percipi facile ac teneri queant . . ." (*DD.*, I, 1, 4).

the rigorous reasoning, the concise and sober style of Aristotle's definitions, precepts, and distinctions.

All the books of Aristotle have a perfect pedagogical order and structure. Nobody has ever had such skill in teaching. Aristotle's rules are concise and clear; memory finds it easy to retain them, and to apply them at the right opportunity. There is no other Greek writer with such a mastery of the language; his words seem spontaneously generated from the subject matter; he does not seek a flowery embellishment, nor does he attempt to entertain his reader with some niceties of expression which titillate his ear but leave him with empty hands . . .[61]

Vives believed also that Aristotle opened a new era in the history of philosophy by reducing to an art the study of human language in its triple aspect of grammar, rhetoric, and dialectic. If the Milesians were concerned with things (*de rebus*) and Socrates with the moral life of men (*de moribus*), the author of the Organon founded the art of the human word (*de verbis*).

Although Plato's books contain numerous seeds of every art and discipline and his dialogues in particular are excellent examples of dialectical reasoning, with the exception of some passages of the *Eutydemus,* there is no expressed formulation of dialectical precepts; the same is even more true in the case of Zeno and Parmenides, to whom the invention of dialectic has sometimes been attributed. The truth is that Aristotle was the first to systematize it, as he did with rhetoric.[62]

Vives' admiration for Aristotle was in one important respect totally different from that of medieval scholasticism. Like most Renaissance philosophers, Vives believed in a return to an original, authentic, and unadulterated Aristotle. "Our laziness and ignorance prompt us to believe that certain passages of Aristotle are a little obscure. The original Greek text is always more lucid and plain than the Latin translation of

[61] M, III, 25-26; R, 1973. "Aristotelis omnia ordinem et formam habent institutionis ac disciplinae, nec fuit dexteritas in aliquo ad artes tradendas par, omnia vero sunt illi certis praeceptis et formulis conscripta, ea brevitate ac gravitate verborum et sententiarum ut facile accipi et retineri possint, et ad usum, quum res postulat, accomodari; verba autem nullus Graecorum habet aeque apposita, ita ut ex rebus videantur nasci, quas tractat; non persequitur rerum flosculos et orationis deliciolas, quibus inani oblectamento delinitum lectorem tenat, postea remittat vacuum . . ." (*Censura*).

[62] M, VI, 114; R, II, 427. ". . . Nam Platonis, etsi magna sunt in illius operibus artium omnium ac disciplinarum sparsa semina, et dialecticae tota ratio ac exercitatio in eius dialogis eluceat, praeceptum tamen nullum fere disertis extat verbis, praeter litigiosa quaedam in *Eutydemo,* multo minis Zenonis, Eleatis et Parmenidis, ad quos refertur artis inventio; sed indubie Aristoteles eam in artis faciem reduxit, ut et rhetoricam." (*DD.,* I, 3, 2).

any interpreter." [63] In his rejection of commentators and interpreters Vives was much more consistent and uncompromising than many philosophers of his days, lost in a sectarian Averroism or Alexandrism. Vives was simply convinced that Aristotle's original text was more meaningful and enriching than any secondary source, including the Greek commentators like Alexander of Aphrodisias or Themistius, and the Latin interpreters like Boethius, Capella, or Saint Augustine.

The Greek commentators of Aristotle, such as Alexander, Themistius, Psellus, Simplicius, and Philoponus use more words than the master, but they have fewer meaningful sentences. Our ancient Latin interpreters, Apuleius, Capella, Saint Augustine, and Boethius, corrupted Aristotle's dialectic and desecrated the language of Rome.

... As for Averroes, although he became known as "The Commentator," all he tried to do was to explain his own ideas ... What were his qualifications to write a commentary on Aristotle? He certainly had no knowledge of ancient history; he had no idea of the ancient schools of philosophy which Aristotle mentions on every page. Ignorant as he was of Latin and Greek, his blunders were utterly ridiculous. He wrote Ptolomaeus instead of Prolus, Pythagoras instead of Protagoras, Democritus instead of Cratylus; he invented preposterous titles for Plato's books, and wrote about them in such a way that even a blind man can see he never read a word of them.[64]

However, Vives' demand for an authentic return to the original text of Aristotle did not spring from a blind submission to his authority. Such a rigorous standard of textual criticism was rather the necessary condition for an intelligent and realistic judgment on the value of Peripatetic philosophy. In fact, I dare to say without fear of exaggeration that Vives was the most outspoken, knowledgeable, judicious, independent, and

[63] M, II, 19; R, II, 575 b. "Torpor vero et negligentia nostra efficit ut nonnullae tenebrae in Aristotele esse videantur, qui superioribus collatus, ipse quoque meridie clarior est." (*De initiis*).

[64] M, VI, 124-125; R, II, 435. "Aristotelis enarratores Graeci Alexander, Themistius, Simplicius, Psellus, Philoponus, et alii, multum habent verborum, sententiarum non aliud quam ipse Aristoteles; Latini nostri prisci illi Apulejus, Capella, Augustinus, Boethius, dialecticam suam depravarunt, et vim attulerunt Romano sermoni..." (*DD.*, I, 3, 4).
Ibid., 192; 485. "Nomen est Commentatoris nactus, homo qui in Aristotele enarrando nihil minus explicat, quam eum ipsum, quem sucepit declarandum... Quid tandem afferebat, quo in Aristotele enarrando posset esse probe instructus? non cognitionem veteris memoriae, non scientiam placitorum priscae disciplinae, et intelligentiam sectarum, quibus Aristoteles passim scatet. Itaque videas eum pessime philosophos omnes antiquos citare, ut qui nullum unquam legerit ignarus Graecitatis ac Latinitatis, pro Prolo Ptolomaeum ponit, pro Prothagora Pythagoram, pro Cratylo Democritum, libros Platonis titulis ridiculis inscribit, et ita de iis loquitur, ut vel caeco perspicuum sit litteram eum in illis legisse nullam." (*DD*, I, 5, 3).

constructive critic of Aristotle among all the scholars of the sixteenth century.

Naturally, Vives' criticism only reached maturity after long years of study and reflection. The two philosophical works of Vives' youth, *De Initiis* and *In Pseudo-Dialecticos*, are more unsophisticated in their enthusiasm for Aristotle. The first, written in 1518, still describes Peripatetic philosophy as the most comprehensive and profound system of thought:

If you are concerned with the most abstruse mysteries of nature, read Aristotle's books on physics; if you are trying to find the most subtle rules of dialectic or be warned against the cunning trickery of the Sophists, you have ten books on logic, an art which had its beginning and its perfection in Aristotle. Twenty books on ethics may help you in ruling your moral life by the norms of practical wisdom. Those who have to govern a family or a republic may make use of the eight books of *The Republic* or the two books on domestic economy written for that purpose.[65]

Even Aristotle's style is praised by Vives as "lucid, transparent, and opulent." [66] The second book, *In Pseudo-Dialecticos* (1520), maintains the thesis that terministic logic is nothing but a corruption of Aristotelian logic introduced in the thirteenth century by Petrus Hispanus.[67]

The two sources of Vives' later criticism of Aristotle are *De Disciplinis* (1531), and the short essay, *Censura de Aristotelis operibus* (1538). Of the two, *De Disciplinis* is by far the more explicit and aggressive, although both coincide in the substance of their censures. *De Disciplinis* charges Aristotle with two main moral defects: a lack of honesty in describing the thought of his antecessors, and a proud fear of criticism. The first resulted in a conscious misrepresentation of Greece's intellectual history:

---

[65] M, III, 18-19; R, II, 575 a-b. "Si enim desiderantur naturae arcana et secretissimae rerum notiones, praesto sunt tam multi, tamquam varii Aristotelis de rebus physicis libri: sin vero dialectices subtilissimae rationes ac formulae, et callidi sophistae astuta cavilla, adsunt logica eius volumina, quae ars ab eodem et incepta et perfecta est ... si quis autem mores sibi poscit componendos, parata sunt ei moralium rerum volumina viginti; at gubernanda est sive respublica, sive res familiaris, conscripti sunt ad ipsum institutum libri de republica octo, de re vero familiari duo ..." (*De initiis*).

[66] *Ibid.*, "Omnia copiose, omnia dilucide, perspicueque."

[67] See the second part of the book (M, 49-68; R, II, 303-315). Although Petrus Hispanus is the main target of Vives' criticism, Vives suggests that it was probably in England or Ireland where such aberrations originated: "I would like to ask Petrus Hispanus, my own countryman, or whoever started this elegant form of dialectic – some scholars think that it all started in England or Ireland ..." (*Ibid.*, 52; 303 b).

On different occasions Aristotle mentions the opinions of other philosophers to point to their mistakes; occasionally, however, his quotations are
defamatory and hypocritical ... This attitude, among other things, deprived
us of a true knowledge of ancient philosophy ...[68]

For fear of being criticized by others the same way he himself had
treated his predecessors, Aristotle tried to conceal his true thought under
ambiguous and ambivalent expressions, "thus leaving always open a way
of escape." [69]

More important than any criticism of style or moral intention was
Vives' disagreement with Aristotle's doctrinal positions. For obvious
reasons we need to present here only a short summary of those dis-
crepancies. Vives' very personal conception of metaphysical knowledge
and his own theory of science – as explained in other chapters of this
book – were fundamental deviations from Peripatetic thought. Here it
will be enough to say that, according to Vives, Aristotle's metaphysical
books "contain a treasure of erudition, but also much obscurity." [70]
Furthermore, "those Aristotelian subtleties and spider-webs excruciate
our weak acumen and give some people the excuse to inquire into non-
existing realities." In Censura de Aristotelis, Vives does not hesitate to
write that the books on metaphysics are hard to understand simply
because Aristotle, himself "a pagan," ignored most such matters.[72] Unfortunately, the subtle scepticism which permeates these remarks of
Vives on Aristotelian metaphysics has been either ignored or exaggerated
by most of his biographers. It is also our contention that the collapse of
Aristotelian physics, which normally is attributed to the generation of
Galileo and Gassendi, had already begun in late humanistic thinking.
At least Vives' criticism of Aristotelian physics was frank and uncompromising. The first fundamental deviation in Aristotelian physics
was to attempt an explanation of nature instead of a guidance for its use.

[The ancient philosophers] ... scrutinized mysteries exceeding by far the
resources of a human mind and, ignorant of themselves, speculated about the
heavens, the elements, the essences, and faculties, with the categorical self-

---

[68] M, VI, 34; R, II, 364 a-b. "Aristoteles, ad eorum sententiam in alienissimam
opinionem detorquendam, vulgari est abusus significatione, ut eos consensu populi
premeret; ... ea res non solum veras antiquorum sententias nobis ademit ..." (DD.,
I, 1, 4).
[69] Ibid., "Ita cavit sibi semper via, qua elabi deprehensus posset ..."
[70] Ibid., 32-33; 361.
[71] M, VI, 352; R, II, 617 b. "Illae Aristotelicae subtilitates, atque adeo non raro
quoque pretenues minutiae frangunt ingenii aciem ac retundunt; praebuit etiam
nonnullis ansam ut quae numquam essent inquirerent ..." (DD., II, 4, 2).
[72] M, III, 32; R, I, 978 b. "Libri sunt plerisque in locis obscuri, difficiles, non
tam tractatione ipsa quam ignorantia earum rerum, quae tractantur ..." (Censura).

confidence of a man who has touched those things with his own hands. Plato and Aristotle especially dictate about the Author of the universe, matter, the constitution of the cosmos, the immortality of the soul, ... For these reasons, ignorance and pride, philosophers introduced into the knowledge of nature opinions and doctrines which even old matrons or little children turn into ridicule. Things of this type you will find by the hundreds in the works of Aristotle and Plutarch ...[73]

Vives was convinced that the fundamental concepts of Aristotelian physical theory badly needed revision. "Where is the intellectual supremacy of Aristotle? ... Does Aristotle possess unsurpassable truths? Much of what he says is true; but this applies to many other philosophers and even to many ignorant people ... There is no doubt that if Aristotle were alive today, and even if he were a monster of pride, he would scoff at the simplicity and stupidity of all these admirers more Aristotelian than Aristotle himself." [74]

As for Aristotle's scientific practice, Vives was extremely critical of what Bacon was to call "hasty generalizations."

In the first book, On Animals, Aristotle states as firmly established that the corpulence and size of belly and face, legs and arms, go always hand in hand. Nevertheless, there are many instances against this generalization. For instance, here in Flanders many people have extremely skinny thighs and muscular and plump arms. The same is reported about many princes, and today we have one example in Francis I of France ...[75]

In moral philosophy Vives rejected Aristotle's authority in energetic terms. The sixth book of De Disciplinis is a massive attack against Peripatetic ethics. In typically Erasmian fashion Vives looked upon the Christian revelation as a moral guidance rather than as an instruction in theoretical dogmas. Consequently, he was firmly convinced that those

---

[73] M, VI, 183; R, II, 478. "... Sed illi ignari sui, ea quaesierunt et scrutati sunt, quae humanum omnem captum excederent, et in his quae assequi non poterant, arrogantissime definierunt multa, non cunctantius, quam si manibus attrectassent, ut de coelis, de elementis, de rerum essentiis, de facultatibus; sed potissimum Plato et Aristoteles, de Auctore mundi, de materia, de opificio universorum, de regimine illius et providentia, de immortalitate animae ... quibus de causis et rationibus, philosophos videas, homines a dubous vitiis longissime impulsos, imperitia, et quam imperitia gignebat, superbia, ea invexisse placita in cognitione naturae, ad quae nec vetulae, nec pueri risum teneant, qualia sparsim recenset Aristoteles ..." (DD., I, 5, 1).

[74] Ibid., 186; 482.

[75] Ibid., 183; 477 b. "In volumine eius de Animalibus primo: Imum ventrem et faciem esse similes corpulentia vel gracilitate, ita crura et lacertos. Cuius rei multa sunt documenta in contrarium; vel hic in Flandria plurimi vix habent suras, brachia tamen musculosa, et succi plena; quod de multis Principibus memoriae est proditum ... et hodie videmus in Francisco Rege Galliarum ..." (DD., I, 5, 1).

who had received such "divine philosophy" had nothing to learn "from
the chimeras of the gentiles." [76] To rely on Aristotle's authority in moral
subjects was to him "to insult the powerful and bright splendor of the
sun with the flicker of trembling candles." [77] Ready as he was to make
some exceptions in favor of the Socratic reliance upon "the natural light
of conscience," the Platonic transcendent morality, and the Stoic synthesis of cosmic order and moral righteousness, Vives reserved the full blast
of his indignation for the intra-mundane, naturalistic and worldly
Aristotelian concept of human happiness. "Nobody should ever doubt
that Aristotle's happiness is opposed to our holy religion and consequently to right reason as well." "It is impossible to serve Aristotle and
Christ at the same time; their precepts are antagonistic." [78]

Vives' most detailed and exhaustive criticism was, however, directed
against Aristotelian logic. Vives' early enthusiasm for the *Organon* became progressively cooler with the passing of the years and a more careful study. Although – as we shall have to explain in another chapter of
this book – Vives' conception of logic was basically Aristotelian, in more
than one important respect he had serious reservations. First of all, Vives
was convinced that logic had to be eminently practical. The length, the
confusion, the obscurity, the unnecessary complications of Aristotle's
logic were a serious handicap to its usefulness. "Nobody has ever found
in the logic of Aristotle a practical instrument to collect arguments for
a given subject, no matter how carefully and extensively he has read
Aristotle's books." [79] In another place Vives complains that "the use of
the tool is more difficult and complicated than any function the tool
tries to perform." [80] Besides this general criticism, Vives evaluated the
books of the *Organon* one by one. The *Categories,* he thought, are out
of place, since they belong to metaphysics. Besides, they are confused,
incomplete, and totally impractical for essential definitions. *On Inter-
pretations* does not belong to the dialectician either, but rather to the
grammarian; moreover, the discussion of modal judgments and future

[76] See the whole book 6, first part, *De disciplinis* (M, VI, 203-222; R, II, 498-510).
[77] *Ibid.,* 210; 500 a. "Quantam facimus soli injuriam quum ad illius juvandum lumen clarissimum et serenissimum, lucernulas admovemus."
[78] *Ibid.,* 213; 502-503. "Aristotelicam felicitatem contrariam esse pietati nostrae, atque adeo rectae rationi, neminem puto dubitare ... Si Aristotelica beatitudo commentitia est, quid laboramus quomodo eam tueamus?"
[79] M, VI, 114; R, II, 428. "Nemo est enim qui quantumlibet diligenter lecta et excussa universa Aristotelis logica, sentiat se instrumentum habere, quo in aliqua ad disserendum materia argumenta in promptu excogitet." (*DD.,* I, 3, 2).
[80] M, VI, 118; R, II, 430 b. "Omnia vero tanta subtilitate dissecat, ut laboriosius sit instrumentum intelligere, quam usum." (*DD.,* I, 3, 3).

contingents is "difficult and bewildering." The *Prior Analytics* is excellent as far as the rules of the syllogism, but useless in much of its subtleties. The *Posterior Analytics* does not belong to Dialectic but to the treatise *De Anima*. Furthermore, the Aristotelian ideal of certain demonstration is beyond the reach of "our weak minds, constantly exposed to error." The *Topics* is more a "jungle of commonplaces" than a practical art, and the "predicabilia" are practically worthless, because of "our indigence in specific differences." Finally, Vives considered the *Sophistici Elenchi* a very practical book, although he thought that any translation would lose much of its value.[81] Vives closes the criticism of Aristotle's dialectical books with the following words:

No art was ever born perfect; not even Aristotle was able to bring to perfection what he had discovered. Often he was more carried by the admiration of the novelties which he found, than by their prudent evaluation. This happens to all the discoverers, even to me, in the small things I brought to light. Therefore I shall not say a word more about Aristotle, whom I respect as is reasonable, but with whom I sometimes disagree, not without a slight touch of blush on my face.[82]

No other school of Greece occupied much of Vives' time and attention. His admiration for the Stoics has already been mentioned and will become more clear in following chapters. Probably, in opposition to Valla's flirtation with Epicurean philosophy, Vives' attitude toward this school was no different from the normal cliché popularized by Christian thinkers in the Patristic age.[83] Moreover, to make more clear his natural aversion to Epicurean thought, Vives totally disjoined it from the Socratic tradition.

Opposite to these [Socratic philosophers], and under irreconcilable banners, are the followers of Epicurus. They obliterated dialectics for the sake of physics, produced legions of atoms, fought for the supremacy of pleasure, and, finally, enslaved virtue, the most beautiful thing on earth, to the brutal passions of the body.[84]

Vives' vision of Greece was obviously from a Roman perspective. In spite of his solid knowledge of Greek, Vives should be classified as one

[81] All this criticism is expounded in Vives' late essay *De Aristotelis operibus censura*. (M, III, 25-37; R, I, 975-977).
[82] M, VI, 124; R, II, 435 a-b. "Nulla ars simul et inventa est, et absoluta; nec ille tam multa potuit unus et primus invenire ac judicare; multa ex iis quae inveniebat nova, admirabatur, inspiciebat provius, necdum tamen satis sibi fecerat familiaria censere ac aestimare ut posset; quod omnibus contingit inventoribus; nec dubito quin idem mihi in iis, quae ipse pario: itaque de Aristotele non dicam plura, quem ego veneror, uti par est, et ab eo verecunde dissentio." (*DD.*, I, 3, 3).
[83] See, e.g., M, I, 18; R, I, 311 a (*Meditationes*).

of the leading Latin Humanists of his century. His familiarity with Roman language, history, literature, philosophy, jurisprudence, and institutions, was matched only by that of Erasmus and, perhaps, Budé. The most characteristic traits of Vives' intellectual personality were of Roman extraction. Vives' distrust of speculation echoes the pervasive influence of Pyrrhonists and Academics upon the philosophy of the Empire, as well as the Roman bent of mind toward the practical and the tangible. Cicero's eclecticism also had a decisive impact upon Vives' thought. In fact, much of Vives' knowledge of secondary Greek authors was actually derived from Ciceronian sources. Occasionally, however, Vives criticized the superficiality of Cicero's philosophical training.[85] From the Roman Stoics, especially from Seneca, Vives learned to evaluate ethics as the supreme part of philosophy, although he found Seneca's moral ideals too rigid and unrealistic.[86] Cicero and Quintilian taught him the rhetorical conception of philosophy; Vives praised Cicero for reorganizing and reducing to an art the topical books of Aristotelian logic, but criticized Quintilian for his exaggerated attempt to identify all human wisdom with the formal precepts of rhetoric.[87] In Roman jurisprudence and legal monuments – which he passionately admired – Vives discovered the intimate connection between the precepts of positive law and the natural righteousness of man. Finally, in Roman history Vives found that political freedom is the condition of that unobstructed verbal communication between men which makes culture possible and civil life a pleasure of the spirit. Vives' *Declamationes Syllanae* and his essay *Pompeius fugiens* are nostalgic eulogies of Republican freedom and peace. For Caesar's imperialistic wars Vives had nothing but contempt.[88] In 1521 Vives wrote a singular appendix to his commentaries on Saint Augustine's *Civitas Dei* entitled *Quinam fuerint Gothi*, in which he discussed the origins of the Visigoths and the process of Roman

---

[84] M, III, 17; R, I, 574 a. "Adversa fronte, atque infestis signis in istos pugnant Epicurei ... qui dialecticam relegantes, ad res physicas tuendas legionibus insectilium corpusculorum, quas vocant atomos, in aciem prodeunt, et de summa rerum pro voluptate dimicantes, etiam praestantissimam et pulcherrimam rerum omnium, virtutem, et subjiciunt, atque illam rerum dominam brutali titillationi foede jubent ancillari." (*De initiis*).

[85] See above, note 25.

[86] Vives thinks that the Stoic ideal of virtue reduced the wise man to a "stupid rock." (M, III, 16; R, I, 573 b. *De initiis*).

[87] See *De disciplinis*, part 2, book 4, chapter 1. (M, VI, 152-157; R, II, 453-457).

[88] See in Adams (*Better Part of Valor*, pp. 285-291) a summary of Vives' ideas on the subject and their relationship to English Humanism.

[89] This essay is not included in Mayans' Latin edition of Vives' works. For a Spanish translation, see R, I, 875-882.

[90] See p. 234, note 23.

decline.[89] This little book shows that, like Saint Augustine, Vives considered the collapse of the Roman Empire as the most calamitous setback in the history of culture.

Much has been already said – and more will appear in other parts of this book – about Vives' judgment of medieval culture. Vives' contempt for the history of scholastic thought – which probably he knew much less than Roman history – was obvious and radical. None of his books gives the slightest indication that Vives was aware of the great moments of medieval thought, of the Neoplatonic revival of John Scot Eriugena, of the controversies of Abelard with Saint Bernard and the humanism of Chartres, of the impact of the Dominican order upon the University of Paris, of the Thomistic synthesis and its criticism by Scotus and Ockham. In fact, Saint Thomas himself is mentioned only two or three times in Vives' books, and always in some secondary position.[90] Ancient and classical languages had been neglected for fear of dogmatic aberrations in the reading of the Scriptures. Poetry was sold to the glorification of violence, war, and obscenities. History had prostituted itself into superstition. Dialectic was basically misunderstood by Petrus Hispanus: instead of deriving general rules from an inductive observation of ordinary language, terministic logic attempted to impose some formal rules upon an outlandish jargon totally irrelevant to life. Grammar and rhetoric were pitifully ignored in medieval education. Natural philosophy was severed from the practical needs of man and lost in a vain speculation. Medicine was divorced from theoretical knowledge and lowered itself to the skill of the practitioners, if not to the fantastic blunders of witchcraft. Astrology had corrupted the noble science of astronomy, and mathematical abstractions had preempted the practical study of measures and budgeting. An endless number of complicated laws written in an intolerable gibberish had crippled the supreme art of jurisprudence into a servile repetition of Decrets.[91] There was no doubt in the mind of Juan Luis Vives that the first step into the future had to be a reform of education, inspired by the achievements of ancient times in order to overcome the aberrations of the recent past.

---

[91] These critical remarks are the core of the first part to the treatise *De disciplinis*, a part which Vives entitled "De causis corruptarum artium."

CHAPTER 9

VIVES ON EDUCATION

"Tota reliqua vita ex puerili educatione pendet"
From *Introductio ad Sapientiam*

The history of pedadogy and the history of thought are inseparably bound together. Educational reformers are thinkers in their own right, or at least they crystallize into a pedagogic scheme the world-views of fashionable philosophers. Bacon's realism was the inspiration of Comenius; Cartesian rationalism lived for years in the schools of Port-Royal; *L'Emile* of Rousseau led the way in romantic approaches to education; German idealism was brought to bear in Schiller's *Letters on the Aesthetic Education of Man*; John Dewey's writings on education are at the same time a summary of his pragmatic theory of knowledge. By the same token, the history of European thought in the seventeenth century remains a puzzle without a thorough knowledge of such educational reformers as Vittorino da Feltre, Guarino da Verona, Rudolph Agricola, Erasmus, Philip Melanchthon, John Sturm, Thomas Elyot, Peter Ramus, Montaigne, Roger Ascham, Richard Mulcaster, and last but not least, Juan Luis Vives.

In the history of education Vives is an exceptional figure because in him the thinker and the doer are perfectly balanced. His educational tracts have all the practical wisdom of such schoolmasters as Sturm and Pestalozzi as well as the depth and universality of such theoreticians as Montaigne and Locke. Vives' pedagogical wisdom was firmly based upon his own ethical, religious, and epistemological principles. In fact a careful reading of Vives' works gives the definite impression that the last twelve years of concentrated philosophical reflection were motivated by an increasing concern with precisely the philosophical implications of the educational reform. As Vives himself repeatedly pointed out, the treatise *De Disciplinis* leads to the psychological book *De Anima et Vita.*[1]

Vives' books of pedagogy center around his residence in England. His first two educational essays, *De Instituione Feminae Christianae* and *De ratione studii puerilis,* were both written the year Vives arrived in England, and were dedicated to Queen Catherine for the instruction of Princess Mary. *De subventione pauperum,* which was not only a social treatise, but also a program for the education of the poor, was written after Vives' second visit to England in 1526; *De officio mariti* was concluded in 1528, the year of Vives' exile from England; finally, the comprehensive volumes of *De Disciplinis* were published only three years later in 1531.

a. General Principles of Vives' Pedagogy

The educational reform in England during the first half of the sixteenth century was indeed the background of Vives' pedagogical work. English Renaissance education was itself the result of several complex ingredients. The first was a direct contact with Italian Humanism. In the middle of the fifteenth century William Grey studied in Ferrara under Guarino da Verona, Thomas Linacre learned Latin from Politian in Florence, Grocyn studied Greek with Vitelli, and for three years John Colet received the inspiration of Ficino and Pico della Mirandola. The second source of English Humanist education was the enlightened pietism of the later Brothers of the Common Life, especially Rudolph Agricola and Hegius. Both tendencies were personified and magnified in the imposing figure of Erasmus of Rotterdam, whose long and repeated visits to England left an indelible imprint upon the culture of the Island.

Vives' ideas on education coincide, at least in part, with the general trends of English Humanism. Like most of the London Reformers, Colet, Lily, Thomas More, and Erasmus himself, Vives set the moral education

---

[1] In *De disciplinis* Vives writes about the diversity of temperamental dispositions: "In unoquoque, ad tradendam ei disciplinam, spectandum est ingenium, cuius contemplatio ad inquisitionem pertinet *De Anima*" (M, VI, 286; R, II, 562 b). In another passage of the same treatise Vives emphasizes that education is based upon a thorough knowledge of man: "noscendus est homo intus et foris." Vives believes that the most important contribution of psychology to pedagogy is the observation of man's passional mechanism: "affectus quibus incitantur rebus, vel augescunt, quibus contra cohibentur, sedantur, tolluntur" (*Ibid.,* VI, 402; II, 658 b).

The best study of Vives' psychological and ethical foundation of pedagogy is the above mentioned work of Díaz Jimenez, *Los fundamentos éticos, religiosos y psicológicos de la pedagogía de J. L. Vives.* See also, Daly, *Educational Psychology of J. L. Vives.*

of the individual as the primary goal of the learning process. As we shall see later the deep roots of Vives' moralizing zeal were derived, perhaps more emphatically than in any of his contemporaries, from a Socratic and Stoic conception of virtue as a proper judgment of values, from an almost Pelagian faith in the perfectibility of the individual, and finally, from a firm persuasion that men make institutions and not vice-versa. This ethical orientation dictates every detail in the pedagogical program prescribed by Juan Luis Vives. When parents bring their children to school for the first time they should be told that "the aim of learning is to make those children wiser, and therefore, better." [2] And Vives adds: "It is absolutely intolerable to see carpenters, shoemakers, farmers, and other people from the lowest levels of society more temperate and self-restrained than many erudite scholars." [3] The choice of teachers is the first important moral decision: "Those assigned to teaching ought to be men of learning and good morals; learning without morality is harmful and indecent; morality without learning, no matter how praiseworthy in itself, does not belong among educators." [4] The same high ethical standard is applied to the selection of reading material. Negatively, the teachers must be extremely careful not to poison the minds of their pupils with immoral readers:

First of all the boy must be kept away from any author who might en-courage vice in general or who might aggravate the defects of the individual. For instance, a lascivious young man should be prevented from reading Ovid, a facetious and whimsical student should avoid Martial, Lucian is not for the cynic detractor, nor Lucretius for the irreligious pupil ... Cicero will be of little help to the conceited and vainglorious child ...[5]

Vives was particularly concerned with the danger that the reading of pagan literature might turn into an aesthetic orgy of the imagination:

The student should approach the reading of pagan writers equipped with a powerful antidote against poisonous plants ... He should keep constantly

---

[2] M, VI, 278; R, II, 556 a. "Litterarum finem esse ut sapientior fiat iuvenis, ac inde melior." (*DD.*, II, 2, 2)

[3] *Ibid.*, VI, 279; II, 556 b. "Ferendum non est moderatioribus esse plerumque affectibus agricolas, et sutores, et carpentarios, et homines de ima plebe, quam eruditos complures." (*DD.*, II, 2,2)

[4] *Ibid.*, VI, 276; II, 554 b. "Qui ad magisteria evehentur, censeantur non ex doctrina modo, sed etiam moribus; doctrina enim cui non respondet vita, res est perniciosa et turpis; vita autem sine doctrina, multum quidem meretur laudis, sed ad docendum non asciscitur." (*DD.*, II, 2, 1)

[5] *Ibid.*, VI, 320; II, 592 a. "Ante omnia arcendus est puer ab auctore, qui vitium potest fovere, ac nutrire quo is laboret; ut libidinosus ab Ovidio, scurrilis a Martiale, maledicus et subsanator a Luciano, pronus ad impietatem a Lucretio, ... gloriosulo non multum conferet Cicero..." (*DD.*, II, 3, 5)

in mind that he is in the territory of gentiles, namely, among thorns, poisonous herbs, and much pestilence; that he is there for the sole purpose of
selecting the useful and rejecting whatever might prove to be harmful.[6]

In this particular respect Vives was even more severe than most of his
fellow humanists. While Erasmus and Thomas More worked hard on
the translation of Lucian, Vives repeatedly recommended his exclusion
from the classroom.[7] Although Beatus Rhenanus, Clichtove, and Bade
were enthusiastic admirers of Ovid, Vives did not hesitate to encourage
a merciless censorship of the Latin poet.

Of course, poets have written much that is sweet, beautiful, great, and
admirable. For this reason they do not need to be put away; it will suffice
to have their books expurgated ... Do you really think that mankind would
suffer an irreparable loss if a few obscene pages by a dirty poet were removed
from his book? ... If the Emperor Justinian decapitated hundreds of jurists,
who will blame me for extirpating those lines which might pervert a youth?
Having lost many monuments of philosophers and sacred writers, will it be a
catastrophe to get rid of Tibulle or the *Ars amandi* of Ovid? [8]

Vives was deeply concerned with the dangers of literature only because he was so well aware of its possible contribution to the moral
education of the child. Like most English Humanists, and according to
the example of Erasmus, Vives looked upon classical literature not only as
a model of diction and eloquence, but primarily as a source of moral
power. For this reason perhaps, Vives has traditionally been classified
among the "moralistic Humanists" rather than among the "stylists" like
Lefèvre d'Etaples or John Sturm.[9] Vives' positive ideal in the selection
of authors was to find those who "will teach not only to learn well, but

---

[6] *Ibid.* "Veniat iam ad lectionem gentilium ,tamquam in agros venenis infames
praemunitus antidoto ... meminerit se per gentiles iter facere, id est, inter spinas,
inter toxica, aconita, et pestes praesentissimas, ut ex eis sola sumat utilia, rejiciat
cetera ..."

[7] M, VI, 336; R, II, 605 b. Vives makes the following judgment of Lucian:
"Asinus est, verborum apparatu instructus ac tumens, rerum inanis prorsus." (*DD.*,
II, 3, 7)

[8] M, VI, 323; R, II, 594 b. "In [poetis] et dulcia, et pulchria, et magna, atque
admirabilia insunt multa, non tolli oportere, sed repurgari ... Scilicet intolerabilem
faciet humanum genus jacturam, si ex spurco poeta partem abscindas obnoxiam?
Detruncavit Caesar Justinianus tot jurisconsultos, et nefas erit ex Ovidio detrahi eos
versus, quibus adolescens fiet nequior? Immo vero, amissa sunt tot philosophorum
et sacrorum auctorum monimenta, et grave erit, ac non ferendum facinus, si Tibullus
pereat, aut *Ars amandi* Nasonis?" (*DD.*, II, 3, 5)
See also, *ibid.*, VI, 269; II, 549 (*DD.*, II, 1, 6).

[9] See, e.g., Frederick Eby, *The Development of Modern Education*, 2nd ed.
(Englewood Cliffs, 1961), p. 42. These labels were taken by Eby from R. H. Quick,
Essays in Educational Reformers (New York, 1924), who does not even mention
Vives.

to live well." [10] Among those authors Vives laid a special emphasis on two particular groups. The first was a selection of Christian poets, whom he constantly recommended.

There are Christian poets like Prudentius, Sidonius, Paulinus, Arator, Prosperus, and Juvencus, who are both interesting and valuable. These writers are comparable to any of classical literature, even in the beauty of style. Of course in their content they are far superior, as divine things are superior to human.[11]

The second group Vives strongly advised were the historians, who offered to the student concrete types of abstract moral standards and notable deeds as told by masters of words.[12] More than any other written word, history, "the nurse of Prudence," was viewed by Vives as a reminder "of what to do and what to avoid." [13]

Although Vives was not always consistent in establishing the relationship between the content of Christian morality and the remarkable exemplars of pagan wisdom he much admired – particularly the Roman Stoics – there is little doubt that the ethical education of Vives' academy stressed Christian ideals and piety.

Children ought to be initiated in the basic principles of our holy religion in their most tender years. They have to learn to know themselves and their weakness, to be aware of their natural inclination toward evil, to keep always in mind that there is nothing they can do without God's help for which they should constantly and faithfully pray... Their unfledged and receptive minds have to be enriched with the true and orthodox idea that man was first an enemy of God and was then reconciled to Him through the crucifixion of His Son. The child should learn to fear God for His power, to respect Him for His constant presence, and to love Him for His gifts and liberality.

Students should be persuaded that the education they are about to receive in the school is primarily the education of the soul ... that it is a blessing

---

[10] M, I, 269; R, II, 326 a. "Quique non modo bene scire doceant, sed bene vivere." (De RSP.) Also, ibid., 265; 323 b: "qui vitam erudiant."

[11] M, I, 269; R, II, 326 a. "Sunt et Christiani poetae, quos jucundum fructuosumque erit legere, velut Prudentius, Sydonius, Paulinus, Arator, Prosper, Juvencus, qui multis in locis possint cum quovis veterum certare, elegantia carminis divina." (De RSP.) Vives' exaggerated esteem of those Christian poets fits well with his preference for Lucanus over Vergil and Horace.

[12] The insistence upon the moral educational value of history was probably one of the most fascinating and revolutionary traits of the pedagogical program of Vittorino de Feltre in Mantua. See Woodward, Studies in Education, pp. 15-17.

[13] Vives calls history "Nutrix Prudentiae" in the second part of his treatise De Disciplinis (M, VI, 388; R, 648 a). See a more detailed presentation of this idea in De Ratione dicendi (M, II, 206; R, II, 781 a).

from Heaven ... and that they should enter the school building with the respect and devotion a temple deserves ...[14]

It would be erroneous, however, to conclude from these and similar quotations that Vives had in mind an ecclesiastical or denominational school. In fact Vives' pedagogical suggestions were never applied to the foundation or reform of any concrete educational institution, Catholic or Protestant. Melanchthon can indeed be considered as the leader of the Protestant educational reorganization in Germany; Aquaviva's *Ratio studiorum* (1594) can be credited with the success of the Jesuit colleges in Catholic Europe and America. Vives' pedagogical programs, although widely imitated by all religious denominations, remained, like his name and his thought, well above the theological or nationalistic controversies of the historical moment. Moreover, since the aim of Vives' pedagogy was the moral and practical training of the individual as the best means to secure the reform of society, the church was not directly involved. Rather, education was the immediate responsibility of the secular powers, a municipal duty of every important city.

Let us establish a center of education in every city: let us gather there a group of teachers of exceptional learning, morality, and prudence. These teachers should be paid from the public treasury ... Senior citizens should be put in charge of the patriotic and civil education of the pupils, as was done in Rome ...[15]

This bold proclamation of the secular character of education, even with its strong Christian emphasis, was not a revolutionary discovery of Vives himself but an inspiring synthesis of Flemish pietism and the Hanseatic tradition of the *burgh* schools financed by the towns without the support, and sometimes even against the opposition, of the local

---

[14] M, VI, 293; R, II, 569 b. "Omnibus initio statim fundamenta sunt tradenda pietatis nostrae, ut noscat se, quam est infirmus, et pronitate naturae malus, ut nihil nec sit, nec potest, nec valet, nisi ope Dei, illum implorandum crebro et bona fide ...; integrae opiniones in vacuum pectus instillandae, nos inimicos Dei reconciliatos illi esse per crucem Filii eius, Deum ut potentem metuat, ut conscium vereatur, ut datorem ac beneficum amet." (*DD.*, II, 2, 4)

Ibid., "Pueri persuasum habeant quae sunt in scholis accepturi cultum esse animi, id est, Patris nostri ...; sic fiet ut eiusmodi cultum ... ut sacrum ac coelitus demissum revereantur, ac adorent, tum in scholas tamquam in templa venerabundi introeant ..."

Vives himself wrote some prayers to be said in the school. (M, I, 131; R, I, 531 b. "Quum ad studium nos paramus," *Preces.*)

[15] M, VI, 285; R, II, 562 a. "Constituatur in quaque civitate ludus litterarius; eo asciscantur praeceptores, viri explorata doctrina, probitate, prudentia; salarium repraesentetur eis de publico ...; mores vero patrios et totam educationem vitae civilis a prudentibus senibus, quemadmodum olim Romae ..." (*DD.*, II, 2, 3)

church.[16] In any case, Vives' contribution to the history of secular education in Europe remains a noble and important one frequently ignored or misrepresented in the history of pedagogy.

In the aspects of Vives' pedagogy we have stressed so far, his main service has been the judicious and eloquent expression of the prevalent trends among English and Flemish Humanists. Vives' philosophy of education, however, presents several features which differentiate him from other pedagogues of the Renaissance and, indeed, place him far ahead of his times. Traditionally, humanistic pedagogy has been characterized as bookish "learning for learning's sake." [17] Even modern historians of pedagogy classify the educators of the Renaissance in three different groups: the stylists, the scholars, and the verbal realists. Common to all was an obsession with the written word. The stylists apply themselves to an aesthetic contemplation of beautiful diction for its own sake; the scholars recommend the study of things in order to understand books; the verbal realists who cared about things themselves, sought to learn them, not directly, but through the reading of books. Vives simply does not fit into this classification. He sought purity and elegance of diction, because of the close association of aesthetic and moral propriety, and also because of the social power of the eloquent word.

Whoever said that justice and language were the two pivots of human partnership had a profound intuition of human nature. Of these two, language is the stronger . . .; words win the approval of other people and control their passions and emotions . . . I do not see anything more relevant to society than the ability to speak properly and eloquently.

Emotions can be set ablaze by the sparks of words; reason is aroused and directed by language. There is no occasion in public or private life, at home or outdoors, with friends or enemies, with superiors, subordinates or equals, where words can be left out. Words can be the cause of great evils and the beginning of incomparable blessings. It is very important, therefore, always to use a decent language, adapted to the circumstances of time, space, and people; to avoid any childish, destructive, or dishonest word. For all these reasons the study of rhetoric has to be directed not to a useless and empty use of words, not to a vain display of well-combed, shiny, and flowery expressions, but to the acquisition of a proper language which will prove that eloquence is a most important part of prudence.[18]

---

[16] For the history of secular education in the Low Countries, see Eby, *Development*, pp. 21 ff.
[17] Thus, e.g., Quick, *Essays*, p. 11. Quick, well known for his unqualified statements, goes on to say that since the Renaissance, "schools have been places of learning, not training." In this respect, like in many others, overgeneralized judgments about Renaissance trends, do not fit well with Vives' patterns of thought.

Vives was as distant from the humanists who believed that literary taste was the keystone of education as he was from those who followed Quintilian in an exaggerated conception of rhetoric as the summary of all arts.[19] Nor can Vives be classified with the "scholars." It is true that what Vives called "philology" included an extensive knowledge of linguistics, geography, history, literature, mythology, and institutions, oriented toward the better understanding of written monuments of the past. It would be false, however, to conclude that Vives' program of studies was reduced to an enlarged course in philology. What makes Vives unique in his age (perhaps with the exception of Rabelais who published his *Gargantua* two years after Vives' *De Disciplinis*), was his insistence upon the necessity of an immediate and practical acquaintance with the things of nature.[20] These *"res naturae"* were not only moral values and standards, but also, although on a subordinate level, the physical objects which man was supposed to control and to manipulate to satisfy his own bodily needs. No other man of his generation had such a vivid conception of the pragmatic character of knowledge and of the importance of immediate sense perception as the source of every human experience.

In the first year of school the child should be presented with the easiest thing to learn, that which he can reach with his senses, the beginning of all possible a picture of all nature: the skies and everything they contain, the elements, fire, air, water, and earth . . . Here no polemic or controversy is in place, only a silent contemplation.[21]

---

[18] M, II, 90; R, II, 689. "Qui humanae consociationis vinculum dixerunt esse justitiam et sermonem, hi nimirum acute inspexerunt vim ingenii humani; quorum duo sermo certe fortior est ac validior inter homines . . .; sermo autem et mentes ad se allicit, et in affectibus dominatur, quorum in totum hominem impotens est regnum et pergrave . . . Ego vero nihil video conducibilius hominum coetibus, quam sit sermo bene institutus, atque educatus." (*De RD.*)

Ibid., VI, 356-357; R, II, 621 a-b. "Affectus animi sermonis scintillis accenduntur, et ratio incitatur, ac movetur . . . Nulla omnino vitae ratio, atque actio, carere potest sermone, publica, privata, domi, foris, cum amico, cum inimico, cum hoste, cum majore, cum minore; is est maximorum et bonorum et malorum causa. Quantum ergo est uti sermone decenti et consentaneo personis, rebus, locis, temporibus, ne quis exeat perverse, pueriliter, indecore! Neque enim alio est tota haec tractatio convertenda, non ad inane verborum studium ut ea compta sint atque splendida, ut concinna suavique structura coagmentata, sed neque dicamus putide, inepte, ac ut minime dici conveniat, ut appareat artem potissimam esse prudentiae portionem" (*DD.,* II, 4, 3).

[19] See, e.g., M, VI, 155; R, II, 455 b – 456 a (*DD.,* I, 4, 1).

[20] According to Quick, *Essays,* p. 25, Rabelais was only "the greatest of the verbal Realists," who being, "a child of the Renascence," in other respect "advanced far beyond it and gave a hint of Realism." In fact, Rabelais did more than that; a short review of his educational devices, however, proves that Rabelais did not significantly progress beyond Vives' suggestions. See, Eby, *Development,* pp. 53-55.

Following this line, Vives recommends the study of geography, astronomy, hydrography, zoology, botany, oceanography, marine biology,
agriculture, and mineralogy. And then Vives adds the following beautiful words:

The study of nature wants a man of diligence and dedication, not a stubborn, proud, or quarrelsome man; a man who will observe and contemplate
nature under a serene sky or in time of storm, in the fields, up on the moun-
tains, in the middle of the forests. A man who will ask others, especially those
who are more familiar with nature: the farmers, the shepherds, the
hunters...; there is indeed no individual capable of observing the huge
variety of nature ... Men like this will be very useful to the rest of mankind,
in the tilling of the soil, the recollection of fruits, and the finding of medicinal
herbs ... just walking around in silent contemplation is both school and
teacher.[22]

In some more concrete instances, Vives' approach to realism in education is amazingly modern. Vives laid great emphasis on the history of
technology which he called "the history of arts and discoveries." [23] He
recommended in this respect that "the student should investigate how
each one of those arts was discovered, improved, and applied," and
gave as typical examples the history of agriculture, transportation (with
special emphasis on navigation), architecture, and medicine.[24] Long
before Comenius and even Rabelais, he indicated that the best means
to learn about the crafts was "to visit the workshops and factories, and
to solicit information and be taught by the artisans and the manu-
facturers who are familiar with them." [25] As a practical example, he
offered and praised the custom of the Lily College in Louvain where

---

[21] M, VI, 348; R, II, 615 a. "Initio exhibenda sunt facillima, id est, sensibus ipsis
pervia, hi sunt enim ad cognitionem omnem aditus; ideo primum inter haec obtinebit
locum expositio quaedam, et velut naturae totius pictura, coelorum, elementorum, et
earum rerum quae sunt in coelis, quaeque in elementis, igne, aere, aqua, terra ut non
aliter summa quaedam sit comprehensa dilineatio, atque orbis universi descriptio in ta-
bula...; nihil est hic opus disputationibus, sed contemplatione naturae tacita..."
(*DD.*, II, 4, 1)
[22] *Ibid.* "Studiosum spectationis huius, ut sedulum ac diligentem requirimus, ita
minime pertinacem, arrogantem, contentiosum; nihil hic jam opus est altercationibus
et rixis, sed aspectu quodam; ita contemplabitur rerum naturam in coelo et nubilo et
sereno, in agris, in montibus, in silvis; tum ex iis quaeret, ac sciscitabitur multa, qui in
illis locis sunt frequentes, quod genus sunt hortulani, agricolae, pastores, venatores...
neque enim unus aliquis potest omnia haec adeo tum multa, tum varia, intuendo
obire ... Magnam hi adferent utilitatem agro colendo, percipiendis et condendis fru-
gibus, esculentis et poculis, medelis ac fomentis in affecta valetudine ... Deambulatio
illa, atque otiosa ipsa contemplatio, et schola est, et magister."
[23] M, VI, 373; R, II, 635 b. "Hominum artes ac inventa." (*DD.*, II, 4, 6)
[24] See *De Disciplinis,* part 2, book 4, chapters 5, 6, 7 (M, VI, 361-386; R, II, 631-
647).
[25] See *De Disciplinis,* part 2, book 4, chapter 6 (M, VI, 374; R, II, 635 b).

sailors, fishermen, farmers, shoemakers, soldiers, and carpenters were invited to the students' meals to share with them the wealth of their daily experience.[26] Although Vives had the typical humanistic aversion to the study of pure mathematics, with vision and insight he encouraged their application to optics, perspective, architecture, and music.[27] Vives was particularly interested in the study of all the auxilliary sciences of medicine, especially botany and anatomy.[28] It is true that in the last two cases Vives was not an innovator, but at least he had the vision to reject in emphatic terms any confusion of medicine with astrology, alchemy, witchcraft, or the suspicious skill of the medical practitioners.[29] Chapter seven of the fourth book, second part, of De Disciplinis is a magnificent document in the history of medical training because of its perfect balance between the theoretical and the practical education of the future physician.[30]

In conclusion we can say that Vives' general principles of education were partly derived from the English-Flemish tradition of his times, and partly original and personal. The moralistic tendency, the emphasis on classical literature, and the basically secular character of education Vives had in common with Agricola and Erasmus, Thomas More and Lily. More his own were the moderation of the Quintilian ideal of eloquent diction and, above all, his insistence on a pragmatic, intuitive, and realistic study of applied sciences and technology.

---

[26] Ibid., 375; 636 a.

[27] Probably in England Vives became acquainted with the works of Grosseteste and Roger Bacon on optics and perspective. See W. Wightman, Science and the Renaissance, An Introduction to the Study of the Emergence of Science in the XVI Century (New York, 1962), pp. 161 ff.

As Gilbert points out in his book Renaissance Concepts of Method, p. 83, it is a historical fact that "the study of geometry and mathematics was not so foreign to the world of humanism as one would expect from the predominantly literary character of that movement." In fact, the humanist educational reformers encouraged the study of these disciplines, which had been greatly neglected by the medieval universities. Agricola, Celtis, Melanchthon, and Sturm were all of them extremely sympathetic to the study of mathematics. This is an aspect of humanist pedagogy which has been greatly ignored.

[28] For the revival of botanic and anatomy in the first half of the sixteenth century, see Wightman, Science and Renaissance, chapter 11, "The Medical Disciplines" (pp. 207-225).

[29] M, VI, 205-206; R, II, 497. In the first part of De Disciplinis Vives attacks the "fraud" of astrology, a position which contrasts sharply with some of the hesitations of his contemporaries, including Melanchthon and Henry VIII.

[30] Ibid., 373-380; 635-641. Lange, Luis Vives, pp. 165 ff, has made a comparison between Vives' comprehensive program of education in medicine with the narrow curriculum advocated by Sturm in Strasbourg. The latter was limited to the Ars parva Galeni and to the Parva Naturalia Aristotelis.

b. Educational Policy

If the aim and the general principles of Vives' pedagogy were immediately derived from his ethical and religious "*Weltanschauung*," the
pedagogical methodology he recommended was a concrete application
of his psychology. Some scholars have even affirmed that Vives was the
founder of a modern pedagogy based on and inspired by observational
and empirical psychology.[31]

Vives placed special stress upon the proper environment of the school
as the first ecological ingredient of the child's sense experience. Vives
wanted, first of all, a salubrious and wholesome location. He warned,
however, against a luxurious or excessively alluring scenic background,
"unless the school be dedicated to the study of disciplines of enjoyment
and delight, like poetry, music, and history." Furthermore, the site of
the school should be far removed from the enticements of the court,
from the vicinity of light-minded young women, and from noisy factories, "like the wheels, cranks, and gearing of the textile industry." [32]
Vives wrote:

> The wisest thing to do will be to build the school outside of the city, es-
> pecially if it is a harbour or a commercial center, provided we do not choose
> a place where the loafers of the region loiter. The school should never be
> built next to a public highway lest the attention of the pupils be distracted
> by the constant traffic. Another location to be carefully avoided is in the
> proximity of international borders, because the constant threat of war de-
> stroys the serenity study requires.[33]

Vives was also concerned that the school provide a diet adapted to
each individual, convinced as he was that "proper food very much aids
the sharpness of the mind and the vigor of memory." Following Galen's

---

[31] Such is, e.g., the characterization made by Woodward in his classical work *Studies
in Education:* "He was the first humanist to submit to systematic analysis the Aristotelian psychology, and to regard the results of his study in their bearing upon instruction" (p. 180). Also: "His interests were those of a humanist and practical teacher,
and his study of psychology was rather the product and accompaniment of this educational activity than its originating impulse" (p. 184).

[32] Vives begins the second part of *De Disciplinis* with a chapter dealing with the site
of the school, the salary of the teachers, and the importance of food, rest, physical
exercise, etc. (M, VI, 272-278; R, II, 550-555).

    According to Woodward, *Studies,* p. 191, Vives was the first European pedagogue
to notice the importance of environment.

[33] M, VI, 273; R, II, 551. "Consultius esset extra urbem constitui gymnasium,
praesertim si vel ea sit maritima, vel mercimoniis dediti incolae; modo ne locus cape-
retur, quo ex urbe consuessent otiosi deambulare animi gratia; nec publico itineri ad-
jaceat, ne animi scholasticorum novitate commeantium avocentur ab opere instituto;
non in regionibus limitibus, qui solent bello infestari, ne is metus non sinat quietos in
studia intendere." (*DD.,* II, 1, 1)

recommendations, Vives urged that "those of dry complexion be given wet food," "the bilious child should be fed in such a way as to debilitate his gloomy humor," and "those who are excessively subtle and sharp should receive greasy and robust nourishment." [34] If Vives' dietetics sound charmingly primitive today in their concrete formulation, they nevertheless reveal a concern with the physical well-being of the individual which stands in sharp contrast to the ascetic self-denial of the monastic Middle Ages. Actually, Vives, like most humanists, was also a champion of modern hygienics. His precepts of bodily cleanliness are as emphatic and descriptive as the propriety of the written word allowed: "The cleanliness of the body ... is extremely important to welfare of both the body and the mind. Every morning you shall wash hands and face with cold water and dry them with a clean cloth. You shall also wash frequently those parts of the body which are connected with the discharge of human waste. These parts are the head [sic], the ears, the eyes, the armpits, and the shameful parts. Feet have to be kept always clean and warm ..." [35] Vives also recommended moderate physical exercises, especially those which "provide pleasure and require effort, like ball games and races"; those which harden the body but do not change man into a beast." On rainy days children can be allowed to play cards or chess games "which sharpen the wit and strengthen the power of memory." [36]

Vives was especially concerned with the control of the child's imagination. Vives' patient observation of mental behavior led him to discover the intimate relationship between imagination and memory in its selective and retaining power, between imagination and the passional thrust of the individual and, finally, between imagination and the appraisal of evidence by the intellect. Because of this important relation – which we shall discuss in more detail in Chapter Twelve – one of Vives' main worries was the proper selection of literary models. He was particularly irritated by the glorification of violence in books of chivalry and the defilement of sex in erotic literature. As Plato expelled the poets from his Republic, Vives was careful to guard against the deleterious influence of poetical imagination upon the formation of the pupil's moral judgments. "The poets sing and praise revenge, hatred, and cruelty. Homer's hero, Achilles, is a brutal savage; Ulysses, who has the reputation of being an exemplar of prudence, was truly a liar and a

---

[34] Vives deals with the importance of food at the end of chapter 4, book 3, part 2, *De Disciplinis* (M, VI, 319-320; R, II, 590-591).

[35] M, I, 8; R, I, 1212. (*Int. ad Sap.*, IV, 88-92)

[36] M, VI, 315; R, II, 591 a-b. (*DD.*, II, 3, 4)

cheater ... And what shall I say about those who glorify their own or
other people's love affairs?" [37]

Vives' attack against violence and erotism was radical and uncom-
promising. Homer, Ovid, Aristophanes, Plautus, Terentius, Catullus,
Propertius, and Martial, all felt the sting of Vives' moral indignation.
The rejection of medieval romance was equally sweeping.

What pleasure can be derived from such unbelievable adventures? This
man killed twenty enemies, all by himself; the other killed thirty. Another
one, pierced by six hundred wounds and abandoned as dead, the next day
arises fresh and healthy, puts up a tremendous fight against two enormous
giants, and gets out of it with so much silver, gold, silk, and jewelry that not
even a galley could transport it.[38]

Modern writers were also criticized by Vives. Boccaccio and Politian
were severely castigated by the Spanish Humanist who, nevertheless,
was generous enough to make an exception of La Celestina because of
its moralistic end.[39]

Another concern of Vives' pedagogical methodology was to improve
by all possible means the performance of memory, whose *modus operan-
di* by association Vives described in a magnificent chapter of his treatise
De Anima. Vives' remarks on the training of memory were dictated by
the general rule that memory grows with exercise. Consequently, Vives
urged that "one should memorize something every day, even a useless
quotation." [40] On the relation of memory's retaining power to bodily
conditions, Vives was amazingly concrete and naive. He was convinced,
for example, that "wine is the death of memory"; he recommended
abstaining from "thick beer" to avoid indigestion and from "sleeping
facing the ceiling." [41] The most exciting part of Vives' memory training

[37] *Ibid.,* VI, 96; R, II, 414 a. "Canuntur et concelebrantur ab eis ultiones, bella, et
exempla omnia crudelitatis; Homero imago optimi Principis expressa est in Achille,
quo nullus fuit truculentior, aut inhumanior; imago sapientis in Ulysse, quo nullus fuit
fraudulentior, aut mendacior ... Quid illi qui vel suos, vel alienos sunt amores perse-
cuti?" (*DD.,* I, 2, 4)

[38] *Ibid.,* IV, 87; I, 1003 a-b. "Quae potest esse delectatio in rebus, quas tam aperte
et stulte confingunt? Hic occidit solus viginti, ille triginta; alius sexcentis vulneribus
confossus, ac pro mortuo iam derelictus, surgit protinus, et postridie sanitati viribusque
redditus, singulari certamine duos Gigantes prosternit; tum procedit onustus auro,
argento, serico, gemmis, quantum nec oneraria navis posset portare" (*De IFC.,* I, 5).
On Homer, see M, VI, 97; R, II, 414 b (*DD.,* I, 2, 4); on Catullus, Propertius, and
Martial, see *ibid.,* VI, 322; II, 594 a (*DD.,* II, 3, 5).

[39] *Ibid.,* VI, 99; II, 416 b (*DD.,* I, 2, 4).

[40] *Ibid.,* I, 271; II, 327 b."Aliquid quotidie ediscendum est, etiam quum non est
necesse." (*De RSP,* II). See also *ibid.,* VI, 310; II, 583 b (*DD.,* II, 3, 3).

[41] Vives' drastic condemnation of wine as destructive of memory is found in his
popular collection of aphorisms *Introductio ad Sapientiam:* "Vinum, memoriae mors."
(M, I, 15; R, I, 1212 b) The more qualified rejection of beer and the recommen-

program was the one inspired by the laws of association which he presented in his psychological books. Vives urged the student to study in a loud voice "because we retain better what we learn through two different senses, sight and audition," also to memorize important texts "right before going to sleep, and to ask ourselves about them immediately after we wake up." [42] Finally, it can justly be said that Vives was one of the early champions of notebooks, files, dossiers, catalogues, and all the other devices still used by today's students and scholars until the computer will have made them completely unfashionable. Vives could not conceive of a student without pen and paper; the time and effort required in writing was taken by him as a guarantee of attention, mental concentration, and interest. He recommended several kinds of notebooks and files. One should be used to classify (not alphabetically) Latin and Greek vocabulary and idioms; another one should be reserved to collect examples or exceptions to grammatical rules; another one could be used to write down all the questions the student should ask the teacher, or all the problems which demanded special attention; sayings, adagia, and aphorisms could be kept together in another file; finally, a larger notebook should be used to make summaries of lectures heard or books read.[43] Of course, Vives warned against the excessive reliance upon written notes according to the medieval saying, *"non in folio, sed in capitolio."*

The last and most important part of Vives' methodology has to do with the control of the human passions which threaten the uprightness of man's decisions. Vives was extremely suspicious of all the scholarly exercises and practices which sought to engage the child's emotions in the process of learning. Of these, the one he disliked most were the public *"disputationes"* which medieval scholasticism had employed with special gusto. Vives reduced their number to "very rare occasions," and forbade them without exception in the early years of school.[44] Only reluctantly he consented to their practice among mature students, al-

dations about sleeping habits, are found in *De ratione studii puerilis,* II. (M, I, 271; R, II, 328 a.)

[42] Most of Vives' suggestions for memory training are included in part II, book 3, chapter 3, *De Disciplinis* (M, VI, 309-315; R, II, 583-587).

[43] On notebooks, see M, I, 272; R, II, 328-329 (*De RSP.,* II). Also, VI, 310-311; II, 583-584 (*DD.,* II, 3, 3). In this chapter Vives states the general principle: "Utilissimum est quae memoria contineri cupimus, ea scribere, neque enim aliter infiguntur stilo in pectus, quam in chartam, videlicet attentio in eo, quod ipsi scribimus, diutius immoratur, itaque magis suppetit tempus ut illud adhaerescat."

[44] M, VI, 275; R, II, 553 b. "Rarae sint disputationes publicae." (*DD.,* II, 2, 1). See also *ibid.,* VI, 3, 4; II, 587-591) (*Ibid.,* II, 3, 4: The whole chapter is dedicated to the subject "Disputationes quando pueris permittendae.")

though he preferred by far the "silent and authentic confrontation of opinions within one's self" according to the rules of Agricola's scrutiny of evidence.[45] To those engaged in public debates he urged again and again an unequivocal definition of the issue, the right use of the proper words, a serene attitude, and, above all, the modesty not to seek a polemic victory at the sacrifice of truth itself.

It is absolutely essential not to become too emotional in a debate, which ought to be a serene confrontation of evidence. For this reason, people who are too irritable, sensitive, or conceited, should never be allowed to participate in such public discussions. People of this kind usually get too irritated to ever hear the objections of their partner or to stop to think about their own answers. Conceited people, on the other hand, are busy observing the faces and the winkings of those in the audience, and do not pay any attention to what is going on in the discussion . . . Sophists are those who do not seek truth but the approval of the gallery.[46]

Vives has been severely criticized for his failure to appreciate the merits of a dialectical encounter of divergent opinions, especially as an educational device to promote the direct involvement of the student. It is true that in this respect he was much more impressed by the abuses than enlightened by the constructive aspects of debate and emulation. Although Vives was clearly aware of the positive role debate played in classical antiquity, he was evidently shocked by the mockery of it which he was forced to witness in the University of Paris. His description of the scholastic disputes speaks for itself. The partners in the debate sought "not the clarification of truth, but the defeat of the adversary"; the dialectical exercise became "a comedy played for the delight of the crowd" in such a way that even the philosophers "danced to please the congregation." Children in the schools "altercate during the meals and after the meals, before and after lunch, before and after dinner; they altercate inside and outside the house, at the table or in the public baths, by the fire, or in the church, in public and in private, everywhere and always." The manners they display in those debates are "worthy of

---

[45] M, III, 78; R, II, 837 a. Vives describes this deliberation as "tacita et vera cuiuscumque secus disputatio." (*De disputatione*)

[46] *Ibid.*, III, 79; R, II, 838. "Conservandum est judicium integrum, minime perturbatum tempestate aliqua affectionum, quae omnes incitatae . . . velut fumum quendam rationi . . . offendunt, quo veri perspicientia impeditur; idcirco biliosi, fervidi, irritabiles, captatores inanis gloriolae, non sunt idonei altercationi . . . incenduntur enim facile et censurae tamquam dejiciuntur de gradu eorum quae dicuntur, ut quid vel antisophista objiciat, vel ipsi respondeant, non attendant; tum studiosus gloriae adeo est observandis omnium vultibus, gestibus, nutibus, occupatus, ut ea quae dicuntur non possit animadvertere." (*De disputatione*)

prostitutes or gladiators." The process of the debate is always the same: "first they scream until they lose their voices, then they begin to call names, to threaten each other ... after the words come the actions, and the real fight follows the symbolic dispute." [47] And so Vives urged that the teachers of the academy "be totally alien to any kind of sectarian litigation, knowing, as they should know, that almost everything is uncertain and obscure, and that it is absolute madness to hate your brother for things which are known well neither to him nor to you." [48] There was, however, a scholastic exercise which Vives approved with enthusiasm: the practice of "repetitio," especially the one conducted by the brightest students for the sake of those left behind "because it is a proven fact that children find it easier to grasp the minds of their equals than the minds of their teachers." [49]

Vives was equally concerned with the restraining of two passions which he thought were particularly in conflict with the right motivation of the pupil. The first was an excessive desire for honors and rewards. Although Vives recognized the value of a moderate word of praise in the right circumstances and for the right person, he was emphatic in removing from his academy any practice which could encourage too much emulation or a destructive rivalry among conceited students or hyperexcitable academicians.[50] With harsh words, he condemned the abuse of academic titles and degrees, the excessive rewards, the comparisons among students, and the practice of having two teachers lecturing on the same subject in the same school.[51] More directly and immediately destructive of true education was, according to Vives, the fear of punishment. Although Vives did not entirely exclude the practice of corporal punishment, he permitted it only as a last resort and with extreme moderation: "as mild as possible, not a harsh punishment like the one inflicted on slaves." Vives masterfully describes the ruinous effect of fear upon the child's attitude:

Fear breeds hatred for the teacher, the only being which stands between the pupil and his wild desires; if this child comes upon a weaker teacher, he will be extremely cruel to him. The fearful child will never do his duty, but only an appearance of it. Fear is the worst possible custodian, it truly turns

[47] This colorful description is included by Vives in *De Disciplinis*, part 2, book 1, chapter 7. (M, VI, 49-57; R, II, 376-382).
[48] M, VI, 277; R, II, 555 a. "Magistri procul abeant a sectis et rixis, qui sciant pleraque omnia in disciplinis obscura esse et incerta, furiosumque esse odisse fratrem propter id quod non magis compertum est tibi quam illi" (*DD.*, II, 2, 1).
[49] *Ibid.*, VI, 310; II, 584. (*DD.*, II, 3, 3)
[50] *Ibid.*, VI, 275; II, 552 b. (*DD.*, II, 2, 1)
[51] *Ibid.*, VI, 277; II, 555.

the child into a corrupted slave; . . . the child loses any interest in anything he is told to do. His body might remain chained to the school bench, but his spirit flies in the wings of his desires . . . If, by some circumstance, the pupil can get rid of his teacher, he imagines to have reached a fantastic victory . . . and feels free to indulge in every whim of his own. Usually he gets involved in all kinds of evil deeds and wild pleasures, like a ship caught in the middle of a storm with a broken rudder . . .[52]

Furthermore, fear is precisely the attitude of mind most opposed to that which Vives considered fundamental in the process of learning. The relations between teacher and student are regulated, according to Vives, by a basic principle which can be stated as follows: learning is essentially a process of imitation and transposition in which the wisdom and knowledge of the teacher is transplanted to and assimilated by the student. "Children have the instinct of monkeys – they mimic whatever they see, but especially the behavior of those persons they admire and respect." [53] In a way, Vives considered the process of learning one's native language, a process of imitation, the pattern and model of all instruction. This transaction requires a warm feeling of admiration on the part of the student, without which, education itself becomes impossible. Vives warns, however, against those who mistake admiration for the easy popularity of the indulgent instructor or the excessive familiarity of the teacher who becomes as childish as the children he attempts to educate.[54] Vives demands on the part of the teacher not only a solid knowledge and a proved honesty, but also a paternal affection for his students and a mature wisdom.[55]

We shall close our review of Vives' methodological pedagogy with one of its more revolutionary and inspiring aspects, the insistence upon guidance and vocational training on an individual basis. Although other educators of the Renaissance, such as Vittorino da Feltre, had previously

---

[52] M, VI, 282; R, II, 559 b. "Hinc odium paedagogi tamquam obicis votorum, et ubi se paullo solutiorem conspicit, asperum se praebet monitoribus . . . tenetur non in officio, sed in officii quadam simulatione, in qua manere eum cogit metus, pessimus officii custos, qui ubi in animo invaluit, reddit illum mancipium nequam . . . ergo non ponit operam in litteris, nec id quod agere videtur, agit; sed praesente corpore, animus ad desideria sua peregrinatur, qui etiam corpus secum eodem rapit, si paullum modo metus abscedat . . .: quod si qua ratione paedagogum queat a se dimovisse, praeclaram videtur sibi nactus victoriam, et liberatus gravi servitute . . . tum vagatur, tum errat solus in licentia omnium flagitiorum . . . non aliter ac navis in summa fluctuum potestate fracto clavo et gubernatore summerso . . ." (DD., II, 2, 2)

[53] M, VI, 280; R, II, 557 a. "Sunt pueri naturaliter simii, imitantur omnia et semper, et praecipue quos propter auctoritatem, et quam illis habent fidem, dignos imitatione judicant . . ." (DD., II, 2, 2)

[54] Ibid., 279; 555 a.

[55] M, I, 271; R, II, 328 a. "Praeceptor non minus amandus . . . quam si esset pater" (De RSP., II).

insisted upon this individualized approach to education and instruction, none of them can be compared with Vives in the practical wisdom of his suggestions.[56] According to Vives' psychology – which we shall be discussing in Chapter Twelve of this book – physical and anatomical conditions, sense perception, memory capacity, imaginative creativity, and emotional balance make up the "ingenium" of each person. The mode of instruction and the professional future of the child is dictated by his particular "ingenium." [57] From this truly humanistic and Platonic emphasis upon individual dispositions and natural talents, Vives derived the urgent need for student guidance and counseling based upon personal knowledge of the child and oriented toward his professional future. This professional orientation should, first of all, be exemplified by the teachers themselves: "the instructor must have a temperament adapted to the art he teaches." For example, "the grammarian should not be an irascible person, the physician cannot be so stubborn as to refuse to learn from others, the moral philosopher should be a man of spotless behavior . . ." [58] Once the child has been accepted into the school, "he should be tested for a few months." This long trial includes not only a theoretical test of memory and wit (especially by means of arithmetical problems), but also the observation of the child in games and during his daily conversation with his fellow students. These observations should be kept as the personal record of each student and should be periodically revised by the members of the faculty. The whole faculty should meet at least four times a year to discuss the progress of each student, individually, so as to be able to direct the individual "according to his own talents." [59]

c. Special Students: Princes, Women, and the Poor

Vives placed extra stress upon several special groups of students. Like almost every other educator of the Renaissance, he believed that "the highest duty of philosophy is the education of the rulers and the prin-

[56] See a summary of Vittorino's theory of education in Woodward, *Studies in Education,* pp. 11-25. Vittorino's insistence upon individual guidance was justified by the enormous differences among his pupils, the children of the Marquis of Mantua and a large number of poor scholars maintained by the generosity of Lady Paola.
[57] See below, pp. 268-269.
[58] M, VI, 274; R, II, 552 a-b. "Magister ingenium habeat accomodum ei, quam profitetur arti . . .; grammaticus ne sit rabiosus, non pertinax medicus quique melius decenti nolit cedere, non moralis philosophus arrogans, et flagitiorum manifestus . . ." (*DD.,* II, 2, 1)
[59] The last chapter of the second book, part 2, *De Disciplinis,* develops all these suggestions in detail (M, VI, 291-298; R, II, 567-572).

ces." [60] Such belief was, no doubt, a sequel to his political philosophy which consisted – as we shall see – of an attempt to moderate and enlighten the existing hereditary monarchies. More theoretically, the persuasion that the intellectual training of the ruler would result in the welfare of the community was indeed an attitude of no little importance in the political history of modern Europe. Unlike Machiavelli, Erasmus, or Melanchthon, Vives never wrote a manual for the education of the prince. His views on the subject appear rather in the dedication of some of his tracts to royal patrons. Such were the treatises *De ratione studii puerilis* (which he dedicated to Queen Catherine of Aragon), *De Disciplinis* (dedicated to John III of Portugal), *Exercitatio linguae latinae* (dedicated to the future Philip II of Spain), *De Concordia et discordia* (which was presented to Charles V), and, finally, *Declamationes Syllanae* (to Ferdinand of Austria). The core of his ideas will be presented later in the context of Vives' political thought.

Vives also took a particular interest in the education of women. He knew well that one of the most controversial issues of the day was the simple question: "Should a woman be educated and learned?" [61] Vives' answer might very well disappoint contemporary champions of feminism and equal rights, but in the first half of the sixteenth century his position was indeed a revolutionary break with the views of medieval education. This is not to imply that Vives was the originator or the leader of such a trend. Probably during Vives' life more books were written in England alone on the subject of feminine education than throughout Europe in all the Middle Ages. If we had to name a leader of this movement, we should probably choose Thomas More whose influence on the matter Erasmus recognized, and whose household made such an impression upon Juan Luis Vives. Vives' association with Catherine of Aragon, however, enhanced his authority and expanded his influence. Even if we considerably toned down Watson's assessment of their joint impact upon English life, there is little doubt that the Spanish Humanist and the Spanish Queen significantly affected the course of women's education in Tudor England. [62]

Vives dealt with this subject in two chapters of *De instituione feminae*

---

[60] Vives puts forth these ideas in *De Concordia*, book 4, chapter 10 (M, V, 373-380; R, II, 229-235).

[61] M, IV, 363; R, I, 1307 b. "Video venisse in quaestionem, an expediat feminam litteras nosse." (*De OM.*, 3)

[62] In his book, *Vives and the Renascence Education of Women*, Watson claims that the Spanish Humanist was "the chief directing and consultative force" of the educational reform in the early years of Henry VIII's reign (p. 1). The same author says that Vives, More, and Thomas Elyott "were all under the spell of Catherine" (p. 11).

Christianae and in one chapter of *De officiis mariti*. Vives' program of women education was dictated by his own ideas on women in general. Like most humanists, Vives believed in the essential equality of men and women, although some of his remarks on the weaker sex were not flattering. However, in spite of the basic similarity of the sexes, Vives was not prepared to recognize any other role for women than their domestic functions. Women education therefore need not be oriented to any professional career, not even to the instruction of children except in their very tender age.

Women should study for their own sake, or, in the best case, for the education of their children as long as they are very little. It is not proper for a woman to be in charge of schools, to socialize with strange men, to speak in public, or to teach at the risk of jeopardizing their own ἀρετή and chastity. The honest woman stays at home, unknown to others. In public meetings she should keep her eyes down, be silent and modest, seen but not heard.[63]

The range of feminine education was consequently planned by Vives on a rather narrow basis. A detailed knowledge of nature, deep theological questions, philosophical controversies of any kind, grammar, dialectic, history, political science, and mathematics were left out of the curriculum entirely.[64] Special care should be taken to prevent women from the study of rhetoric, since, Vives wrote, "silence is the embellishment of matrons." [65] Another general principle of Vives' pedagogy for women was the persuasion that, although women were not inferior to men – a conception against which he fought gallantly – they were indeed more vulnerable, both physically and morally: "Women are rational animals like men, but they have a changeable disposition which bends easily under pressure." [66] The practical result of this belief was a more severe supervision of feminine education, especially in literary training. Books of chivalry and erotic fiction and poetry should be totally removed from feminine hands. More, even so, than in the case of men, the education of women had to be specifically directed to their moral

---

[63] M, IV, 84; R, I, 1001 a. "Sibi uni discat, vel ad summum liberis pueris adhuc ... neque enim scholis praefici feminam decet, nec inter viros agere, aut loqui, et verecundiam pudoremque vel totum vel magna ex parte in publico deterere primum ...; quam si proba sit, domi sedere potius, et aliis incognitam esse convenit, in coetu vero, demissis oculis, pudibundam tacere, ut videant quidem eam sane nonnulli, audiat nemo" (*De IFC.*, I, 4).

[64] Vives deals at length with the program of women education in *De officiis mariti*, chapter 3, "De disciplina feminae" (M, IV, 362-284; R, I, 1307-1325).

[65] M, IV, 370; R, I, 1313 b. "Inter feminae tuae disciplinas silentium numerato, magnum sexus illius ornamentum" (*De OM.*, 3).

[66] *Ibid.*, 364; 1309 a. "Animal est femina ratione praeditum ut vir, sed ingenium habet ambiguum ad utrumque usu et consiliis flexile."

strengthening. Vives saw a protection against feminine vanity and superficiality in intellectual learning: "The ignorant woman does not even understand how silly and vain are the excessive make-up, the expensive clothing, the pretty appearance; she does not realize how dangerous it is to attract the eyes of other people to herself." [67] Moreover, learning was taken by Vives as a safeguard of chastity, the virtue par excellence of future mothers and wives. On repeated occasions Vives expressed the conviction that a woman could not be impure and learned at the same time, although he was slightly disturbed by some embarrassing cases of classical antiquity.[68] The examples he loved to quote were the four daughters of Isabella, Doña Mencía de Mendoza, and the three daughters of Thomas More.

If we add the skills required in domestic affairs to the moral education of woman, we can reconstruct Vives' complete program of women education in the following way: The young girl should first of all learn to read her own vernacular and, if she has talent for it, Latin as well. Her favorite readers should be the Christian poets and the Bible. Thereafter, she should learn the precepts of moral philosophy in the writings of Plato, Cicero, Seneca, and Plutarch; practical examples of moral heroism should be familiar to her through the reading of the *Acta Sanctorum*. She should read Aristotle for domestic economics. Vives recommended Filelfo and Vergerius for child care and education. Finally, all women, "even the queens," should learn to knit, to cook, and to administer rudimentary first aid and medical care. Music, dancing, and drawing are conspicuously absent in Vives' program. The education of women should be supervised by an honest teacher, married himself to an attractive woman (the husband should constantly refine the education of his wife with intelligent conversations). Such, no more nor less, was the revolutionary program of feminine education advocated by Vives.[69]

The third group of students which attracted Vives' attention was the needy and the handicapped. In his social treatise, *De subventione pauperum*, Vives reminded the municipal authorities that it was their direct responsibility to provide for and supervise the education of poor children,

[67] M, IV, 79; R, I, 997 a. "Mulierem non facile invenias malam, nisi quae ignorat ... quam leve ac vanum sit comi anxie, excoli, perpoliri, magno ornari; quam perniciosum aliorum in se oculos et desideria convertere ..." (*De IFC.*, I, 4)

[68] Vives discusses the cases of Sappho, Leontia, and Sempronia, whose virtue he tries to defend with rather amusing arguments (M, IV, 79; R, I, 997 b, *De IFC.*, I, 4).

[69] M, IV, 362-384; R, I, 1307-1325 (*De OM.*, 3) and, *ibid.*, IV, 77-85; I, 995-1001 (*De IFC.*, I, 5).

orphans, and abandoned illegitimate children. Vives was particularly concerned with job training of welfare recipients: "If they cannot be made tailors, they should learn to be shoemakers. If they are too old or incapable of learning those or similar skills, they should be taught to draw water from wells, to dig in the fields, to move things with a little wagon, to run errands for the magistrates of the city, to take care of rental horses . . ." [70] "The textile industry in Bruges and Antwerp," Vives remarked, "was badly in need of apprentices." [71] Vives was also amazingly modern and alert in respect to education of the blind which, according to him, should not be limited to "playing musical instruments or making little baskets," but should be expanded into a higher intellectual training "if they have the natural gift for it, and if there is somebody who can read for them." [72]

d. The Curriculum

We shall conclude this presentation of Vives' pedagogy with a short survey of his ideas on the curriculum and the textbooks of his choice. Regarding the latter, Vives was persuaded that there was an urgent need for an ambitious survey of all the books available, "almost infinite in number," to make an authorized and selective scrutiny possible. "Whoever makes such a critical survey based on his own knowledge and the wit of his judgment will, in my opinion, become a unique benefactor of all mankind." [73] Vives clearly aspired to such a title – "I have taken upon myself this imposing task" – although he was modest enough to realize that his performance would necessarily be deficient and incomplete: "Even if they push me into a dark corner, I shall be happy to watch the advance of human culture from there." [74] It is naturally impossible to summarize Vives' critical review of books and authors within the limited range of this volume. It will suffice here to state that Vives, in his treatise *De Disciplinis,* passed judgment on literally hundreds of first- and second-rank writers; from pre-Homeric literature to the books of Boccaccio and

[70] M, IV, 472; R, I, 1394. "Si aetate sunt idonei, edocendi ad eam artem ad quam dicent se maxime propensos, modo liceat; sin secus, ad similem quampiam; ut cui non licebit suere vestes, suat quas caligas nominant; sin est provectior, aut ingenio nimis tardo, facilior aliqua tradatur, denique ea quam nemo non paucis diebus perdiscat, fodere, haurire aquam, bajulare, monotrochon trahere, apparere magistratui, viatorem esse, aliquo proficisci cum litteris aut mandatis, equos agere perpetuarios." (*De SP.,* II, 3)

[71] *Ibid.,* 472; 1394 b. "Omnes opifices queruntur de raritate ac infrequentia operariorum, et qui serica Brugensia contexunt, conducerent quosvis pueros tantum ad gyrandos quosdan tornulos . . ."

[72] *Ibid.,* 473; 1395 b. "Alii caeci ad litteras sunt idonei, studeant, in nonnullis horum eruditionis progressus videmus non paenitendos."

Erasmus; from the fields of philosophy, theology, history, medicine, jurisprudence, and natural sciences; from Greek, Latin, medieval, Islamic and
contemporary books in the vernacular. More than the specific content of
each judgment – some judgments of which naturally have been fundamentally overhauled and modified by today's scholarship and criticism –
what is truly significant and revealing of the mood of the times is precisely
this global attempt to qualify past achievements for the sake of future education. In this encyclopedic and ambitious project, Vives had no immediate predecessor nor equal in his day. His work is a most eloquent testimony
to the intellectual attitude of that era of change, of reflection, and of
planning.

The curriculum itself was divided into three different stages which Vives
did not label in any specific way. The first lasted eight years, from the
seventh to the fifteenth year of age.[75] It began with the study of Latin,
followed by that of Greek. The training in those languages was itself disposed in three levels: the first was a study of the general rules of grammar
without excessive detail; the second, the reading of models and composition; finally, the study of philology. Vives was less than enthusiastic
about the study of other languages such as Hebrew or Arabic, which he
allowed only after the study of Latin and Greek, and only "if there was
time enough for it." [76] The study of the arts – the University course –
which, in Vives' mind, would take about ten years, followed the learning
of languages, bringing the student to his twenty-fifth year. Such a long
process had to start with the study of the first part of dialectics, roughly
corresponding to the first four books of Aristotle's *Organon*.[77] Immediately
thereafter, the student should begin to learn the rudiments of physics and
the introduction to metaphysics, or "prima philosophia," without subtleties or excessive controversies. Only at this moment could the young student profit by the study of the second part of dialectics or topical invention
and rhetoric.[78] The arts course should close with the study of mathematics,

---

[73] M, VI, 267; R, II, 546 a. "In unaquaque arte et peritia libri debent assignari . . .
Hoc qui faceret, magna scientiarum notitia et acrimonia judicii fretus, nae is mea
sententia ingens in universum hominum genus beneficium conferret . . ." (*DD.*, II,
1, 6)
[74] *Ibid.*, "Neque ullum aliud bonum invidebo generi humano, a quocumque pro-
ficiscatur, et me in postremum, aut etian in nullum rejici locum, jucundissimum mihi
erit intuenti profectus humanae sapientiae."
[75] M, VI, 299; R, II, 575 a. (*DD.*, II, 3, 1)
[76] *Ibid.*, 304; 577. (*DD.*, II, 3, 1)
[77] See *De Disciplinis*, part 2, book 4, chapter 1. (M, VI, 298-304; R, II, 612-616).
[78] *Ibid.*, chapter 2 (M, VI, 304-309; R, II, 617-621).

with special emphasis on applied mathematics.[79] The third and final stage
of education was the professional training of the mature man. This part
should begin with a history of technology common to all students. From
there it should divide into either medicine or jurisprudence, the latter com-
prehending a more profound knowledge of history and moral philosophy.[80]

---

[79] *Ibid.*, chapter 3 (M, 309-315; R, 621-625).
[80] *Ibid.*, book 5, chapters 1 and 2. (M, 386-401; R, 641-658)

CHAPTER 10

INDIVIDUAL AND SOCIAL ETHICS

"Christianus: perfectus et consummatus homo"
From *De Pacificatione*

Vives' ethics are basically a humanistic synthesis of Christian theocentrism and Greek rationalism. From the Judaeo-Christian tradition Vives derives the guiding principle that morality is a normative order demanded from man's free will by the creative action of the Author of Nature. This divine order consists in the subordination of the inferior to the superior part of man. According to the dualistic rationalism of Platonic thought Vives finds in reason the noble component of man, in the body his lower and less dignified part. Moral order, therefore, is the subjection and control of the inferior passions by the intellectual powers. The humanistic emphasis consists in presenting morality as the acme of human perfection: to be moral is simply to be a perfect human being. These views were not entirely new. Indeed, Christian and medieval ethics were but different versions of identical or similar conceptions. What is relevant and worth studying in Vives' ethics is precisely the characteristic slant and emphasis with which he presented them. The first part of this chapter is an attempt to explain the naturalistic, rationalistic, and secularized trends of Vives' moral philosophy.

a. The Naturalistic Emphasis

From a strictly orthodox and Christian point of view, we are struck first by Vives' neglect of the salvational aspect of morality. According to Vives, virtue is not primarily a means of eternal salvation; morality is not exclusively man's obedience to a divine command intended to test human freedom and whose content is in itself as indifferent to human nature as the forbidden tree of paradise. Vives' notion of moral virtue does not exhibit the strong traits of material heteronomy which Kant and his disciples believed to be the unique and accepted view of Christian ethics. This does not mean, however, that the eschatological dimension is absent from Vives' point of view. On the contrary, the unfinished character of earthly perfection and its essential propensity toward the eternal fulfillment is truly a fundamental feature of Vives' moral philosophy. As a Christian, Vives' point of departure was to look at life "as a pilgrimage to eternity," "a journey surrounded by disasters and evils which threatens to end up suddenly for the most unexpected reasons." [1] Vives' repudiation of Aristotelian ethics, as we saw before, was precisely motivated by Aristotle's narrow-minded effort "to seek the whole of human happiness in this life, without reserving anything for the world beyond." [2]

Vives' conception of the ultimate foundation of morality is also a highly significant departure from the fashionable Ockamistic voluntarism of his day. Moral law, according to Vives, is not a divine command exclusively dependent upon God's inscrutable will. Adultery, for instance, is not evil because God has forbidden it; on the contrary, God forbade it because it was evil, namely, a perversion of that natural sexual energy which, in God's plans, secures the propagation of the human race in a reasonable manner. Moral order guarantees the integrity of human nature in the same way physical order is an integral part of the cosmos. Vives' moral philosophy is based upon the premise that virtue is a perfection of man *qua* man and that vice is totally unnatural. Morality is not "added" to man, it constitutes man's very nature. To be human is to be a moral being. The remote and final foundation of morality is the same as the foundation of all possible being, namely the Divine Essence as the model of every creature. Vives' lack of interest in the positive precepts of canonical and institutionalized Christianity springs also from this conception of morality as an internal harmony and order rather than as an arbitrary and incidental ordinance. According to Vives, a virtuous man tunes in with the total created order of the universe: "This is the order of Nature, that Wisdom be the rule of the whole, that all creatures obey man; that in man, the body

---

[1] M, V, 255; R, II, 132. "Vita haec nostra ... via est ad illam aeternitatem" (*De Concordia*, II). See also, *ibid.*, I, 4; I, 1208 a: "Quid aliud est vita quam peregrinatio quaedam, tot undique casibus objecta et petita? Cui nulla hora non imminet finis, qui potest levissimis causis accidere." (*Int. ad Sap.*, 36)

[2] *Ibid.*, VI, 211; II, 501. "Aristoteles in vita hac quaerit beatitudinem, alteri nihil relinquit" (*DD.*, I, 6, 1).

abides by the orders of the soul, and that the soul itself comply with the will of God. Whoever violates this order, sins." [3]

By the same token, a virtuous man becomes similar to God Himself, and, by freely molding his own life according to patterns derived from the Author of Nature, he becomes not only a better man but indeed a man in the full sense of the word: "The body should be obedient to the soul, and in the soul the lower passions should be controlled by reason, which is the queen and governess whose leadership makes us true men and imitations of the Divine Nature." [4] Virtue, therefore, is no accidental luxury of man, but the fundamental condition of true humanity. The moralizing tendency of Vives' humanism is not incidental or temperamental, it springs forth from the very essence of his thought.

Vives' conception of moral virtue as a triumph of reason reflects an exaggerated dualistic conception of man which occasionally borders on crude Manichaeism. Its first manifestation is Vives' constant debasement of the body, "the slave of the soul" and "the vase made of clay." [5] A whole chapter of Vives' treatise *De concordia* is dedicated to prove "how feeble and sordid is the human body." Here are a few of Vives' thoughts on the subject:

What is the nature of this body of ours that people feel inclined to call it a sepulcher, a jail, or, even more fittingly, a rotten cellar and a filthy sewer? One thing I know well, namely that if you dare to open this dirty dungyard covered with a thin skin, it stinks. You yourself can judge by the waste which leaks through the nose, the ears, the armpits, and even through the mouth; not to speak of those shameful parts of the body which pudor forbids to mention . . . [6]

Through its contact with the body, the soul itself becomes split and weakened. It is precisely at this point where Vives' moralism becomes extremely rationalistic and intellectualistic. According to him the soul is divided into two parts. The lower portion:

---

[3] *Ibid.*, I, 11; I, 1216 a. "Hic est naturae ordo, ut sapientia regat omnia, pareant homini cetera quae videmus: in homine vero corpus animo, animus menti, mens Deo. Si quid hunc ordinem egreditur, peccat." (*Int. ad Sap.*, 120)

[4] *Ibid.*, VI, 401; II, 658 b. "Corpus debet obsequi animo, in animo vero motus rationis expertis rationi ipsi dominae ac imperatrici, videlicet unde homines sumus, et ex iis rebus inter quas versamur, conjuctisimaeque Divinae illi Naturae quae regit omnia." (*DD.*, II, 5, 3)

[5] *Ibid.*, I, 8-10; II, 1213-1215. (*Int. ad Sap.*, Chapter 4)

[6] *Ibid.*, V, 345; II, 204. "Cuiusmodi habet corpus, quod alii sepulchrum nominarunt, alii carcerem, verius dici posset putris cuiusdam navis sentina aut cloaca ruinosa. Foetebit si aperias sterquilinium hoc opertum cute; quod quale sit, abunde ostendunt quae per eius omnes meatus perenne scaturiunt, per nares, per aures, per axillas, per os ipsum: quid dicam per ea, quae pudor vetat eloqui non minus quam proferri?" (*De Concordia*, IV, 4)

because of its liaison with the body is deprived of reason, is brutal and blind, more similar to the instincts of the beasts than to human intelligence. It is there where the passions or perturbations of the soul take place, such as pride, envy, hatred, anger, fear, sadness, and greed. This is indeed the most vile section of the human soul, closest to bestiality and most removed from God.[7]

The more excellent part of the soul is "that one which understands, remembers, reasons, and judges. This is the soul proper, which makes us men, similar to God, and superior to the brutes." [8] Vives' description of the virtuous man's enlightened serenity is obviously inspired by the Roman Stoic ideal of the sage which permeates the writings of Seneca, Quintilian, Cicero, and Horace. Virtue, he wrote, "is to have an inner silence"; "to enjoy a spiritual tranquillity far more precious than any wealth or honor"; "to relish a most sweet music and harmony"; to be adorned "with an interior beauty," and protected "with an iron curtain." [9]

The supreme act of reason, as the charioteer of man, is a prudent judgment about the relative and true value of all human choices. The righteousness of this axiological judgment is threatened by man's lower passions; virtue springs forth from "an uncorrupted judgment which assigns to each thing its proper value, a judgment which does not take what is worthless as though it were valuable, nor repudiates what is beautiful as if it were ugly." [10] The main purpose, therefore, of all education and all human learning is precisely the enlightenment of reason: "All human knowledge is healthy and useful as long as it is referred to its final goal which is virtue and the exercise of good actions." [11] Following the example of Socrates, Vives recommended self-knowledge as the first step in the right direction: "All the precepts of moral philosophy are ordained to

[7] *Ibid.,* I, 10-11; I, 1216. "Est altera pars ex coniunctione corporis, bruta, fera, atrox, bestiae quam hominis similior: in qua sunt motus illi, qui sive affectus, sive passiones, sive perturbationes nominantur, Graece πάθη, arrogantia, invidentia, malevolentia, ira, metus, moeror, cupiditas, stulta gaudia. Pars inferior nominatur etiam animus: qua nihil a belluis differimus, et quam longissime discedimus a Deo, extra morbum et perturbationem omnem positum." (*Int. ad Sap.,* 5).

[8] *Ibid.,* "In animo duae sunt partes: illa quae intelligit, meminit, sapit, ratione, judicio, ingenio utitur et valet. Haec pars superior appellatur, et proprio nomine, 'mens,' qua homines sumus, qua Deo similes, qua ceteris animantibus praestamus."

[9] All of these statements are taken from *Introductio ad Sapientiam,* chapter 18 (M, I, 45-48; R, I, 1253-1256) and from *Satellitium animi* (M, IV, 36-38; R, I, 1179-1181).

[10] M, I, 1; R, I, 1205. "Vera sapientia est de rebus incorrupte judicare, ut talem unamquamque existimemus, ne vilia sectemur tamquam preciosa, aut preciosa tamquam vilia rejiciamus, ne vituperemus laudanda, neve laudemus vituperanda." (*Int. ad Sap.,* 1)

[11] *Ibid.,* I, 12; I, 1217. "Reliqua eruditio munda est et frugifera referatur modo ad suum scopus, virtutem, hoc est, recte agere." (*Int. ad Sap.,* 6).

assist human reason. Consequently, it is absolutely imperative to gain a thorough knowledge of man, both internally and externally." [12] Vives' most inspiring treatise, *De Anima,* is precisely a concentrated effort of self-introspection into the interaction of the intellectual and the emotional components of human nature. The first part of *De disciplinis* is a retrospective look into the gradual corruption of culture by the unbridled passions of man.

Let man begin being a true man; let him have a thorough knowledge of himself. The devils do not know themselves, because they refuse such a knowledge; the beasts, because they are incapable of it ... Pride darkened and oppressed the human mind to the point that humans ignore themselves, where and with whom and how they ought to live, the nature and the true value of worldly things ... Let man recognize that he is an animal swollen with pride ... He has a soul, but constantly battered and mishandled by his own passions ... Man worries, fears, hopes, becomes sad and desperate, shrinks into himself or flies on the wings of his fantasy; the slightest breeze shakes him deep inside; a word, a gesture, the opinion of a base human being, impresses and controls him.[13]

One of the most powerful means of moral education, according to Vives, was the reading of proverbial literature, the traditionally Stoic device to lead men to meditation and self-knowledge. The very density and obscurity of the aphorism, the intrigue and finesse of the sparkling short sentences, was believed to bestow upon the written language some of the charm and the galvanic effect of nonverbal symbolism. The extreme popularity of Vives' sapiential books, *Introductio ad Sapientiam* and *Satellitium animi,* testifies to their high quality, especially taking into account the large number of similar writings which the Renaissance produced. The content is also of decidedly Stoic character: the aristocratic character of virtue, the recommendation of moderation and stability, and, especially, the classical reminders in time of adversity such as the shortness of "life's

---

[12] *Ibid.,* VI, 402; II, 658 b. "Ad suppetias ferendum rationi cuncta moralis philosophiae praecepta sunt comparata velut exercitus quidam: quare noscendus est homo totus intus et foris." (*DD.,* II, 5, 3)

[13] *Ibid.,* V, 338; II, 201. "Incipiat iam ergo homo esse homo, id est, nosse se, nam neque daemones se norunt, quia nolunt, nec bestiae, quia non possunt ... Tanta caligine mentes nostras obruit ac oppressit, ut nemo se noscat, nemo quis, ubi, cum quibus, quemadmodum vivat, quae sit rerum natura ... Videat animal hoc superbissimum et consideret, quae sint illa ob quae superbit, et intelliget se sordidum et pannosum de cultu gloriari, infirmum de viribus, egenum de opibus, ...; habet animum, primum quam concussum at agitatum affectuum tempestatibus! Quam discissum, divulsumque illa discordia civili ... Sollicitus, anxius, metuit, sperat, moeret, contrahitur, dilatatur, levissima aurula totus ab immo concitatur ... uno numo, una voce, uno gestu, uno judicio postremi hominis et de faece ..." (*De Concordia,* IV, 3).

comedy," the vanity of wealth and honor, the transient and mercurial character of fortune and fate.[14]

This Stoically inspired identification of virtue with an enlightened and prudent judgment inevitably led to a naturalistic and secularized form of morality itself. On the relationship between the moral core of Christianity and natural ethics, Vives' attitude was, to say the least, ambiguous and insecure. On one hand Vives was extremely emphatic in stressing the paramount superiority of Christian ethics above pagan wisdom. In his treatise *Introductio ad Sapientiam* Vives wrote:

> All human wisdom is nothing but mud and insanity, at least in comparison with Christian morality . . . Whatever was honest, prudent, wise, pure, holy, praiseworthy and admirable among the gentiles, is found in our holy religion raised to the sky above, more pure, more straight, and more bright.[15]

With less vigor, perhaps, but still with an honest conviction, Vives occasionally pointed to the supernatural character of virtue, which "comes from above and is God's gift." [16] Consequently "we must pray to God for it with great devotion and insistence." On the other hand, Vives seems frequently bent on draining the ethical ideals of man of all their Revelational meaning and their supernatural character. Although Vives proclaims *ore tenus* that the recommendations of the *Satellitium* have been "dictated by the law of Christ," it is hard to find therein anything which either Seneca or Quintilian could not have written by themselves. In fact, Vives openly declared that, in his opinion, "no one could find a better Christian than the 'Stoic sage." [17] Even the counsels of evangelical perfection are reduced by Vives to precepts of the natural law dictated by an enlightened self-interest. Vives maintains, for example, that the love of enemies is only a command of the natural law which reason can discover by itself:

> The Christian ought to love even those who are outside the Church and the communion of the body of Christ. What kind of barbarious cruelty is it to think that Christianity is compatible with hatred of the Turks? . . . The Turks have to be loved because they are also human beings. In fact, we must

---

[14] See *Satellitium animi*, 40-142. (M, I, IV, 38-53; R, I, 1183-1194).

[15] M, I, 23; R, I, 1229. "Quicquid grave, prudens, sapiens, purum, sanctum, religiosum; quicquid cum admiratione, exclamatione, plausu, apud gentiles legitur; quicquid ex illis commendatur, ediscitur, in coelum tollitur: id totum purius, rectius, apertius, expeditius invenitur in pietate nostra." (*Int. ad Sap.*, 10)

[16] *Ibid.*, I, 17; I, 1223. "Praestantissima illa rerum universarum virtus, neque dono ab hominibus datur, neque accipitur: divinitus contingit. Idcirco a Deo suppliciter ac pie petenda est." (*Int. ad Sap.*, 7)

[17] *Ibid.*, III, 17; I, 574. "Nullum veriorem hoc sapiente Christianum fore puto." (*De initiis*).

love even those who persecute and hurt us. This is not only a precept of Christ, but also a command of natural law . . . This is also what our own self-interest demands. Is there anything more reasonable and more fitting with our nature than to treat others exactly the same way you would like them to treat you? [18]

In the introduction to the treatise *De pacificatione* Vives writes:

. . . Nobody can be called a Christian, namely a perfect and accomplished man, who is not dedicated to peace, harmony, and kindness; . . . this is also the teaching of the Divine Master of Wisdom and Truth who is at the same time the author and the interpreter of Nature.[19]

These and similar statements of Vives betray an almost Pelagian interpretation of Adam's sin and of the redemptive work of Christ. The fall of Adam introduced into the world an authoritative scandal which disrupted the balance between the blind thrust of our passions and the guidance of reason.

Through sin man's intelligence became dull and obtuse and his reason was obscured by darkness; pride, jealousy, hatred, cruelty, all appetites and desires were set in constant turmoil; loyalty was broken and man lost his natural capacity to love; the body was plagued by diseases and the earth was damned with stink in the air, corruption in the waters, with freezing winters and burning summers.

What is the source of antagonism in human society? People kill each other, steal from each other, cheat each other, hate each other without break nor intermission. There is no doubt: Man has destroyed his own nature; man coveted to be divine and lost his own humanity.[20]

The work of redemption is, therefore, if not exclusively, at least in a very important respect, an act of enlightenment and teaching. Christ seeks to reinstate the order by strengthening human reason with the supreme light of his doctrine and with the power of his tragic example. The core of

---

[18] M, V, 390; R, II, 243. "Quocirca illis qui sunt extra ecclesiam et communionem gratiae corporis Christi non cladem optabit Christianus . . . Quae barbaries est existimare hoc demum esse vere Christiani, si strenue Turcas aut alios Agarenos execretur . . .? Amandi sunt Turcae, nempe homines . . . Non solum hoc erimus affectu atque animo in eos impios, a quibus non laedimur, sed in eos ipsos qui nos persequuntur . . . Hoc naturae lex postulat, hoc Christi jussa . . . hoc nostrae ipsorum utilitates . . ."

[19] M, V, 406; R, I, 257. "Declaratum est neminem non solum Christianum appellari posse, id est perfectum et consummatum hominem, sed nec hominem quidem, qui paci, concordiae, caritati, benevolentiae, quantum ab eo praestari possit, non studeat; huc a natura nos . . . incitari, hic adduci a Magistro divinae sapientiae ac veritatis, ab interprete naturae . . ." (*De pac.*, 1)

[20] See below, p. 229, note 4 and 5.

Christian morality coincides fully with the essentials of natural ethics: the control of human passions.

> Our mind is a victim of its own darkness; our passions, stirred up by sin, have covered the eyes of reason with a thick layer of dust. We need a clear insight, serene and undisturbed . . .
> All the precepts of moral philosophy can be found in the teaching of Christ. Nobody has seen God, but we have Christ, His interpreter and legate, His own Son . . . In his doctrine, and his words, man will find the remedy to all moral diseases, the ways and means to tame our passions under the guidance and the power of reason. Once this order has been secured man will learn the proper behavior in his relations with himself, with God, and with his neighbor; he will act rightfully not only in the privacy of his home, but also in his social and political life.[21]

And even more explicitly in the *Introductio ad Sapientiam*:

> The immediate and direct goal of Christianity is to calm down the storm of human passions, thus to provide the soul with a joyful serenity which makes us similar to God and to the angels.
> The remedies to our moral diseases can be found either in the very nature of things and of man himself, or in God and in the example and doctrine of Christ.[22]

Vives summarizes his thought by saying that, "a Christian is only a man reinstated in his nature." [23] This amazing expression of naturalism in the first half of the sixteenth century is obviously a highly significant fact in the intellectual history of Europe. Leaving aside the individualistic supernaturalism of Luther and the institutionalized Christianity of Trent, Vives' thought forecasts and prepares for the main stream of secularized humanism which carries the thought of Bovillus, Du Vair, Montaigne, Grotius, Lipsius, and Pierre Charron.

---

[21] M, VI, 402; R, II, 659 a. "Mens autem nostra ea tenebrarum densitate obducitur ut id non dispiciat, affectus enim peccato incitati ingentem atque obscurissimam caliginem ob oculos rationis offuderunt; opus est ratione quapiam liquida, et minime perturbata . . . Ergo ex Dei doctrina precepta disciplinae huius erunt nobis haurienda: Deum nemo vidit umquam, Dei interpretem . . . habemus Jesum Christum . . .; Filii interpretes sunt ejus discipuli . . .: ex horum doctrina, et dictis, velut remedia colligentur morbis animi, ut sub rationis manum et potestatem affectiones subdantur: ordinatione hac constituta . . . probe sese homo geret secum ipse, et cum Deo, et cum homine superiore, inferiore, pari, sive privatim, sive in familia, sive in re communi omnium et publica . . ." (*DD.*, II, 5, 3).

[22] *Ibd.*, I, 17; I, 1223 b. "Nec aliud conatur pietas Christiana, quam ut serenitas humanos animos exhilaret: et tranquillitate animorum, compositisque affectionibus simus Deo, angelis quam simillimi. Remedia his morbis, vel ex rebus ac nobis ipsis, vel ex Christi lege ac vita petuntur." (*Int. ad Sap.*, 8)

[23] M, V, 201; R, II, 87 a. "Quid enim est aliud christianus, quam homo naturae suae redditus, ac velut natalibus restitutus?" (*De Concordia*, 1)

b. Virtue and Domestic Society

We turn now to the second important aspect of morality, its social dimension. Vives enthusiastically subscribes to the Aristotelian-Thomistic notion that man is by his own nature a social being. Most of his arguments were obviously a mere repetition of the traditional ones. Such was, for instance, the proof derived from the need of mutual assistance originating in the distribution of individual talents and skills.

Nobody has such bodily strength and sharp intellect that he can suffice to himself if he wants to live like a man.

The individual man needs the service of many other individuals just to satisfy his daily needs: he needs the help of farmers, shepherds, journeymen, weavers, sailors, and many others, depending on his way of life.[24]

Vives places, however, a special emphasis on the proof of man's sociability derived from the natural character of benevolence and sympathy toward others. The Author of Nature, Vives argued, had made man not only dependent upon other men, but also naturally inclined to love and to help them.

Experience proves every day that man was created by God for society, both in this and in the eternal life. For this reason God inspired in man an admirable disposition of benevolence and good will toward other men.[25]

As we shall see later in this very chapter, Vives bases three of his more important social teachings upon this natural benevolence: the social function of private property, the civic obligation of welfare, and, finally, the injustice of war.

The first nucleus of human society, which man's need of mutual implementation and social benevolence seeks to establish and to perpetuate, is the family. "Man searches for the company of a wife in order to have some descent and to secure what he has already acquired. The reason is that no matter how weak and timid the female is, she is by nature a careful and vigilant custodian." [26] Vives' moral teaching on marriage is included in

---

[24] Ibid., IV, 423; I, 1358 a. "Nullus tamen vel corpore validus, vel acer ingenio, qui si humano more ac modo victurus sit, sibi unus sufficiat." (De SP, I, 2).
    Ibid., V, 200; II, 86. "Ad quotidianas necessitates quam multorum sunt labores corrogandi! Agricolae, pastoris, textoris, extructoris, nautae, vehicularii, et aliorum aliis pro cuiusque arte ac ratione vitae." (De Concordia, 1).
[25] Ibid., VI, 222-223; II, 510. "Hominem re ipsa testatur conditum esse a Deo ad societatem, et in vita hac mortali, et in altera illa sempiterna; idcirco et glutinum ei societatis addidit animum ad benevolentiam mirifice appositum." (DD., I, 7, 1).
[26] M, IV, 423; R, I, 1358 a. "Uxorem sibi adiungit prolis gratia et ad conservandum parta, ut est meticulosus sexus ille natura et tenax." (De SP., I, 2).

two different tracts, *De institutione feminae Christianae* and *De officiis mariti*. The first book is divided into three parts dealing with unmarried girls, with the obligations of mothers and wives, and with widows. In *De officiis mariti* Vives repeated the same scheme, insisting upon the obligations of husbands.

Vives' condemnation of premarital sex goes even further than the severe traditions of his time. "The girl who has lost her virginity will live forever in total consternation; or rather she will die every day, being physically alive and morally destroyed." [27] To prevent this disaster Vives recommends to parents an unbelievably rigid discipline. Young girls should, first of all, be denied any social contact with men; their drink should always be "what Nature has provided – clear and fresh water"; [28] the hours of sleep should be short; the use of makeup totally forbidden: "The woman who paints her face is mad if she does it to please herself, perverted if she tries to attract the attention of men." [29] And Vives adds with a certain mean sense of humor:

I have the impression that you are putting on a mask to go hunting for a husband; the problem is that if you please one man with your face hiding behind those pastels you might scare him away whenever you unveil it . . . unless you decide never to wash off such a scab . . .[30]

Young girls should very seldom leave their homes, and, when they do, should always be in the company of their mothers.[31] At home a prudent and chaste matron should always take care of them, never losing sight of the innocent maids.[32] Dances are always risky, especially masquerades which "should be totally forbidden in Italy and in Spain where the maliciousness and ruffianism of young men could prove to be disastrous." [33] Dating, flirting, and romancing were, for Vives, not only immoral, but ridiculous and irrational. Vives made no concessions in his fight against

[27] M, IV, 95; R, I, 1009. "Semper consternata, semper exanimata vivet, immo non vivet, sed privabitur morte corporis, quum toties animo enecetur." (*De IFC.*, I, 6).
[28] *Ibid.*, 97; 1011. "Potus erit ille a natura in commune paratus, liquida et pura aqua." (*De IFC.*, I, 7).
[29] *Ibid.*, 102; 1014. "Equidem audire velim, quid spectet virgo . . ., si sic placere sibi, demens est . . .; si viris, scelesta." (*De IFC.*, I, 8)
[30] *Ibid.*, 103; 1015. "Perinde mihi videre esse, cupere te fuco pellicere virum aliquem ac persona; quem tantum avertes renudata, quantum attraxisti contecta . . . Quando fucum elueris, quomodo eris grata? Nisi forte numquam crustam illam ablatura es . . ."
[31] *Ibid.*, chapter 9. "De solitudine virginis." (M, IV, 116-121; R, I, 1026-1030)
[32] *Ibid.*, IV, 116; I, 1026.
[33] *Ibid.*, 144; 1048. "In Hispania, Italia, et aliis regionibus, in quibus propter ingeniorum acumen plus est calliditatis et vafriciei, verendum est ne magnorum scelerum occasionem praebeant ejusmodi ludicra . . ." (*De IFC.*, I, 12)

erotism; his own relations with Margaret Valdaura were obviously not those of a Latin Don Juan. Few of his pages are more sarcastic, and even cruel, than those in which he described the infatuation, the passion, the yearning, and the behavior of lovers.

The young man approaches his girl in a most humble and charming atti-tude. First he says that he has been captivated by her beauty; a few seconds later he is already announcing that he is about to die in an excess of love ... He calls you beautiful, pretty, discreet, noble; although sometimes there is no trace of those qualities. You are delighted with those lies ... He swears to you that he will die, that indeed he is already in agony. Are you going to believe him? Why do you not ask him to show you to the sepulchers of all the lovers who died of love? And if he dies, is it not better that he dies than for you to die, or for both of you to perish at the same time?

A French young lady who went to Spain with the train of Marguerite of Valois to visit her brother Francis I (at that time a prisoner of Charles) was amazed by the large number of Spanish lovers who were constantly saying they were about to die of love. So, finally, she answered one of them: "Drop dead, then; I want to see at least one *really* dying among the thousands who are *about* to die." [34]

Vives was firmly persuaded that the choice of the bridegroom was not the responsibility of the bride, but the choice of the bride's parents. All he was ready to grant to the female partner was a veto right, after long hours of consideration and prayer.[35]

In the second part of the book, explicitly leaving aside the controversial questions about the relative value of virginity and matrimony, Vives dealt more in detail with the sexual relations of wife and husband. With uncompromising candor Vives displayed his view of marital sex as a brutalizing experience justified only as a means of childbearing and as a remedy to man's concupiscence. The title of Chapter Six is: "On the behavior of a wife toward her husband in their intimate relations." [36] In

---

[34] *Ibid.*, 148-149; 1052. "Aggreditur hic suavis ac blandus, et primum omnium puellam laudat, captum se dicit eius forma, postremo perire prae amore immodico ...; vocat te formosam, venustam, ingeniosam, facundam, nobilem; et forsan, nihil horum es, sed tu mendacia illa libenter audis ... Moriturum se declarat, atque etiam iam mori; credis tu hoc?, demens, proferat tibi ille, quot amore interierint ex tot amatorum millibus ...? Quod si perit, quanto consultius est tibi perire illum quam te? aut etiam unum perire, quam duos?

Puella quaedam Gallica, ex iis quae Margaritam Valensiam comitatae sunt in Hispaniam, visentem Franciscum Franciae Regem fratrem suum Caroli Caesaris cap-tivum, cum a juvenibus Hispaniae subinde audiret: 'Amore enecor': 'morere jam tandem, inquit, ut amatorem aliquem mori videat, ex tot moriturientibus" (*De IFC.*, I, 13).

[35] *Ibid.*, chapter 15. "De quaerendo sponso" (M, IV, 155-172; R, I, 1057-1071).

[36] *Ibid.*, book 2, chapter 6. "Quomodo privatim se cum marito habere debat" (M, IV, 217-223; R, I, 1107-1112).

this chapter Vives did not hesitate to recommend for imitation some rather shocking examples of connubial chastity which might prove today extremely unpopular. Such was, for instance, the case of the Spartan woman who was proud of never having attempted to excite the desires of her husband, or the behavior of a legendary queen who after each act of sex did not allow further intimacies until the oncoming menstruation would make sure she was not yet pregnant. Furthermore, Vives enthusiastically praised both the decision of a former English Queen to give up sex after her first child, and the mutual agreement of many pious couples to abstain completely from any sexual intercourse.[37] This amazing attitude toward sex was not tempered or corrected by Vives' own marital experiences. Vives' moral treatise, *De officiis mariti,* written three years after his wedding, is not significantly different from *De institutione feminae Christianae,* a book written in a hurry to compliment the Queen of England.[38] After having advised the wives never to take the initiative in their sexual relations, Vives writes to the husbands:

Let the husbands keep constantly in mind that as Christians they have given up the world and all its pleasures. Consequently, they should make use of sex only in rare occasions and with extreme moderation, more as a compensation for their fatigue and hard work than as a concession to their passions.[39]

It is hard to imagine the sexual enthusiasm of husbands who had been instructed by the following aphorisms of the *Introductio ad Sapientiam*:

- The pleasure of the body is, like the body itself, vile and brutal.
- Sensual delectation bores the soul and benumbs the intellect.
- Sensual delectation is like robbery, it vilifies our soul. This is the reason why even the most corrupted man seeks secrecy and abhors witnesses.
- Sensual pleasure is fleeting and momentaneous, totally beyond any control and always mixed with frustration.
- Nothing debilitates more the vigor of our intellect than sexual pleasure.[40]

---

[37] *Ibid.,* 222; 1111.
[38] Vives admitted to Cranevelt that he did not have time to correct the manuscript. (*LC.,* 53, v. 54).
[39] M, IV, 377; R, I, 1319. "Maritus cogitet ... christianum se esse, qui mundo et deliciis nuncium miserit: harum rerum omnium causa, oportet in matrimonio pauciores voluptates suscipi, et eas temperatissimas, ut refectio tantum laborum curarumque quaesita esse videatur, non indulgentia cupiditatum." (*De OM.,* 3)
[40] M, I, 7-9; R, I, 1211-1213. "Delectatio corporis, ut corpus ipsum, vilis ac pecudina est. Nihil est quod aeque et vigorem mentis debilitet, et robur ac nervos corporis infingat, ut voluptas. Nec aperte frui licet ...: pariunt enim ignominiam: idcirco tenebras et latebras quaerunt. Quid quod sunt fugacissimae, et momentaneae, nec retineri ulla vi possunt, nec umquam veniunt purae, cuiuscumque amaritudinis expertes?" (*Int. ad Sap.,* 87, 71, 72)

To complete this unpalatable aspect of Vives' matrimonial ethics we can add a few words about Vives' strong patriarchalism. According to the Spanish thinker from Valencia, nature has made man the protector and leader while the "weaker sex" is supposed to be obedient and submissive to the head of the family.

A wife's love for her husband includes respect, obedience, and submission. Not only the traditions of our ancestors but all human and divine laws agree with the powerful voice of nature which demands from women observance and submissiveness.[41]

c. The Body Politic

The second level of mutual implementation and benevolent expansion of the individual is the wider horizon of civil society. Its origin, progress, corruption, and reformation is in Vives' mind primarily a moral issue. Society itself is the result of man's natural and virtuous inclinations; all social evils, especially poverty and war, are passional disorders of individual citizens which have burst forth into the social dimension. Consequently, Vives approaches the study of such theoretical questions as the origin of the State or the ideal form of government in a hortatory manner which might appear slightly superficial to the speculative political philosopher. Nevertheless, some of Vives' ethical recommendations were derived from basic theoretical assumptions which paved the way for the more explicit and revolutionary formulations of later writers.

Vives' description of the origin and progress of civil society follows the traditional guiding lines. Beyond the domestic society, man tends to find other work partners, first because he needs them, and second because he himself feels inclined to help others – hence the clustering of living quarters and the distribution of work according to individual qualifications.[42] This golden age of peace and harmony, to be understood apparently in a historical sense, is disturbed, however, by the disordered passions of a sin-ridden human race. Life in community at that stage is only possible within the structure of society where the precepts of natural law become officially specified and proclaimed, and where the coercive power of the

---

[41] M, IV, 189; R, I, 1085. "Neque vero sic amandus maritus est, quemdamodum amicum amamus, aut fratrem geminum, ut solum sit amor; plurimum, cultus, ac reverentiae, admixtum oportet, plurimum obedientiae, atque obsequii; non modo mores majorum, atque instituta, sed leges omnes humanae ac divinae, ipsa etiam rerum natura clamat, mulierem debere esse subditam marito ac ei parere." (De IFC., II, 4).

[42] M, IV, 424; R, I, 1358 (De SP., I, 2).

State guarantees and reestablishes the primitive order.[43] This basic conception seems to imply that the institutionalized communal life which we call society is nothing but a redeeming device which seeks to repair the moral disorder begotten by sin, and makes possible the pursuance of the same goals for which the original community came into being. The political philosophy of Juan Luis Vives is only an expansion and concrete application of this fundamental view.

First of all, the ruler is viewed by Vives as the man who reestablishes, promotes, and guarantees the moral life of the individual in his community. The ruler, then, shares in the Divine Paternity because he orders the community of men with a power delegated to him by the Author of a well-ordered Nature.[44] Vives seems not to be concerned with the possibility that the paternal character of political authority could prove a source of abuse and tyranny. Vives' insistence, was rather upon the exemplary responsibility of the ruler. He considered the ruler as the model of the moral order which civil authority attempts to secure for the subjects. An immoral ruler is the ruin of a society. History provides tragic examples of ravaging wars provoked solely by the lasciviousness or the greed of the rulers.[45] For this same reason, Vives subscribes with enthusiasm to the Platonic demand that the ruler be an enlightened man. A whole chapter of Vives' treatise *De concordia* is dedicated to prove "How small is the difference between the Prince and the Sage." Vives writes:

> The prerogative of the Prince is only to have a better judgment than the people . . . What else is a true ruler but a sage with public authority? Maybe there is a small difference between the two as far as their power is concerned; but with respect to their reason, judgment, reflection, wit, and will, there is no difference whatsoever.[46]

---

[43] In this conception, then, the coercive power of the State, appears as a consequence of Adam's sin. For a comparison of this view with some of the late opinions of Luther on the subject, see *Luther's Werke*, ed. O. Clemen, 7. vols., 5th ed., (Berlin, 1959), "Vom Weltlicher Obrigkeit," II, 360-394.

[44] M, V, 175; R, II, 27. "Est enim Princeps in republica, quod animus in corpore, et imago quaedam auctoris illius rerum naturae." (*De pace inter Cesarem et Franciscum*).
  Vives applies the idea of "paternal authority" to the Prince, the teacher, and the husband: "Publicus pater est Princeps et magistratus, privatus paucorum est magister, domesticus est maritus, et qui nec patris caret nomine, pater familiae." (M, V, 421; R, II, 269 a, De pac.)

[45] M, V, 255-331; R, II, 132-195. (*De Concordia, III*)

[46] *De Concordia*, book 4, chapter 10: "Quantulum Principem ac virum sapientem intersit." Vives writes: "Illa demum est magnitudo vera Principis, melius de rebus statuere quam vulgus, et primum omnium seipsum moderari, qui tot millia habet in sua potestate . . . Quid est porro aliud verus Princeps, quam vir sapiens cum publica potestate? Ita ut inter Principem et sapientem in potestate erga alios quidem fortassis

Like most humanists Vives attached paramount importance to the education of the Prince and to the alliance of thought and action, scholars and rulers, in the administration of public affairs. One is tempted to see in this humanist trend the early start of the enlightened despotism which was beginning to encroach itself into the European courts of that age. Nevertheless, we should not forget the constant recommendation of moderation which characterizes the political thought of most humanists. Vives' writings betray an ardent love of individual liberty and a sincere respect for the unassailable rights of the people which are absolutely incompatible with any form of tyranny. In the *Satellitium animi* Vives proclaims the three principles of tolerance, freedom, and democracy which inspire each one of his pages: "Thought is free. Only the sheer power of Truth can force our mind. All men are equal." [47] With a profound feeling of personal compassion he deplored the wars between France and Spain as a senseless rivalry between Francis I and Charles V which completely ignored the rights of the suffering population.[48] In the same spirit he attempted to moderate the barbarous innovation in the political theory of his age – according to which the King was not obliged by the laws, *legibus solutus* – without thereby being trapped in the glorification of the right to rebellion. Vives admits that in the initial compact whereby the members of the community agreed upon electing a ruler "it was thought unfitting to bind him to the same laws as the rest of the people." [49] The reason was that "the ruler being honest, it was inconceivable that he would commit an evil action; and being prudent, it was impossible that he would commit a sin of imprudence or ignorance; and being powerful, he could not by any means be coerced." [50] With the corruption of morals, however, this principle was terribly abused, to the point, Vives remarks, "that it became a rule not only that the King was not bound by the laws, but something infinitely worse, that he was allowed to do whatever he pleased." As a result of such abuse, "whoever mentions the welfare of the people, or the liberty of the people, or the

aliquantulum, in judicio vero, ratione, mente, consilio, voluntate, nihil intersit." (M, V, 372; R, II, 229)

[47] M, IV, 60-61; R, I, 1200-1201. "Cogitatus liber. Cogitatus quis coget? Vis veritatis. Homo homini par." (*Satellitium,* 190-192)

[48] The two documents written by Vives on the war between France and Spain abund in this idea. See, *De Francisco Galliae Rege a Caesare capto* (M, VI, 449-452; R, II, 23-27), and *De pace inter Caesarem et Franciscum Galliarum Regem.* (M, V, 175-187; R, II, 27-39)

[49] See *De disciplinis,* I, 7, 1: "De optima primaque institutione ditionis et legum" (M, VI, 222-229; R, II, 510-515).

[50] *Ibid.,* "Ita ut non solum in proverbium abierit 'Principem esse solutum legibus': sed quod pejus est, 'Principi licere quidquid libeat'."

tranquillity of the people, is right away labeled and despised as a reckless insurrect." An then Vives adds: "Of course I am speaking about the legitimate and justified rights of the people, since there is nothing more harmful to the same people than the unchecked libertinism of the mob which breeds sedition and insurrection." [51] Although Vives never theorized on further questions of political theory, it is clear from his writings that his thought pointed more toward the constitutionalism of Alciatus, Buchanan, Althusius, and Hooker than toward the absolute sovereignty of Bodin, Barclay, or even his own friend William Budé.

One of the most important consequences of Vives' moral approach to social ethics was the emphasis upon the responsibility of the public powers with regard to the education of citizens. In his letter to Henry VIII, after the battle of Pavia, Vives reminds the King that one of the first duties of the ruler is to promote the moral education of the subjects.

I am utterly convinced that the Prince cannot do anything more conducive to the common good of the republic than to instill in its youth sound and straight opinions about the use, the value, and the end of everything: money, possessions, friends, honors, nobility, dignity, power, beauty, pleasure, intelligence, wit, ambition, virtue, religion ... Otherwise men will be tempted to subvert the order of priorities, to overprice what is miserable and to neglect what is valuable. In that case they will cause tremendous tragedies to society for the sake of some material profit or for other fantastic dreams of their own making. These are the men who will sacrifice the welfare of the body politic to their own private interest and forge for themselves a stupid notion of civil liberty which will make them evil rather than free.[52]

It was precisely this insistence upon the responsibility of the civilian, not the religious leader, with the moral training of the citizenry which made Vives one of the champions of secular education.

The same moral ideals inspired Vives' thought about the lawmaking power of the State, thoughts which he put together in two short treatises, *Aedes legum* (1519) and *Prelectio in leges Ciceronis* (1519), both written in Louvain probably under the impact of Cranevelt's friendship.

---

[51] *Ibid.,* 227; 514 a. "Civitati nihil est aeque perniciosum ut vulgi libertas effrenata, ex qua nascitur seditio, extremum malorum publicorum."

[52] M, V, 179; R, II, 31. "Quapropter aut ego vehementissime fallor, aut principibus et magistratibus ... nihil magis expedit, quam teneram statim aetatem curare rectis ac sanis opinionibus imbuendam, ut sciant qui sit usus, quod premium, qui finis univscuiusque rei ... pecuniae, possessionum, amicorum, honorum, nobilitatis, dignitatis, imperii, formae, virium, voluptatis, ingenii, eruditionis, virtutis, ac religionis, ne inversis rerum aestimationibus, maxima negligant, minima et abjecta consectentur, de pecunia, de umbris, de somniis, quae ipsi sibi confingant, graves moveant tragoedias ...; his sunt qui ... stultam quandam excogitant imaginem libertatis, qua non fiunt liberi, sed mali" (*De pace inter Caesarem et Franciscum*).

The first is a short, literary essay in which Vives describes in allegorical terms the function of legislation in society. The author envisions a well protected and delightful city, "the seat of human associations and designs, linked together by mutual duties and rights, the seat of justice and peace, humanity, loyalty, hospitality, and of all the virtues which men exercise for the sake of other men." In the very center of the city arises a tower of marble, "beautiful and well built, not excessively luxurious or jovial, but rough and rugged in a few spots, pleasant and welcoming in others." The pinnacle of the tower is the eternal law of God, "the governess of the universe, the Divine Intelligence which commands and forbids according to reason." The occupants of the tower are "justice, temperance, fortitude, love, peace, concord, and faith." The tower itself is the body of positive laws which public authority promulgates and enforces to insure the social life of each individual.[53]

The second book is an introduction to the well-known tract of Cicero. Vives begins with an enthusiastic acceptance of the Roman Stoic notion of Natural Law:

> Natural Law has the same validity everywhere because it was impressed into the heart of every human being even before he was born. All nations profess it immutable and identical with spontaneous and universal agreement... These laws were not ratified by any individual man, were not adopted by any particular assembly, were not promulgated by this or that Kingdom, they were not even agreed upon by mankind itself. These laws were born within ourselves and grew in ourselves without ever becoming obsolete or old-fashioned...[54]

The content of this Natural Law is, according to Vives, more complex and rich than a mere set of moral criteria. It includes a natural inclination toward religious worship and social life together with an almost instinctive aversion toward sin and moral disorder. In fact, this ethical and innate tendency of man is implemented on the epistemological level with an intellectual sympathy toward Truth and some common notions which direct and control man's thinking. Both of them are an integral part of man's natural qualities, directives, and limitations. As specific conclusions

---

[53] M, V, 483-494; R, I, 681-691.
[54] M, V, 494; R, I, 692. "Jus naturale ..., quod habet eandem vim ubique, illud-que est quod habent omnes scriptum in cordibus suis, eduxeruntque secum ex matris utero; idem enim immutabile prorsus habent omnes nationes, sentiunt de illo uno eodemque modo...; nec mirum, quoniam invariabilis eademque est in omnibus hominibus natura...; neque vero quia sic uni homini videtur, nec quia sic uni senatui, uni reipublicae, nec quia sic regno, non denique quia sic orbi, sunt leges illae ratae atque acceptae, sed quia sic nobiscum ortae, nobiscum adoleverunt, non obsolescentes..." (In Leges Ciceronis)

are derived from general principles and common notions, positive laws apply the more general demands of the natural law to concrete situations.[55] The legislator is the enlightened man who interprets those demands and finds the specific means to achieve the final goals. The ruler, with his authority, backs the ordinances of the positive law, and, by doing this, he directs and makes possible the very moral life of the individual citizen. Society is nothing more than a community regimented by law. Public authority reinstates the moral dignity of the individual as a social being.

Vives' concern with the reform of legislation was inspired by this noble vision of the law as the social expression of public morality which remedies the passional disorder of the individual and brings man back from the war in the jungle to the harmony and the delight of the community.

Equity is somehting universal; laws are the consequences and the specific cases. Laws are rivers and channels. Without the constant flow of living water, they are dry and useless. Equity is the soul, the strength, and the vigor of the laws. Without this natural equity, laws collapse. Nothing is more criminal than a law which is not inspired by this natural goodness and equity.[56]

The first quality of the legislator is, therefore, that superior degree of prudence which is granted only to those who have reached a perfect control of their lower passions. Neither fear nor hope, ambition nor hatred are supposed to take control of the man who dictates laws for others; "otherwise they will vitiate the medicine into a lethal poison." [57] Historically, the corruption of legislation has always been preceded by the moral defilement of the legislators themselves.[58] As for the laws, Vives considered them much more a source of moral education than as catalogues of impending punishments.

Since laws were introduced primarily to secure the peaceful harmony and the equal rights of men, their principal aim is to instill in man the proper attitude of mind. Laws should strive to persuade men not to want to do evil,

[55] See *De disciplinis*, part 2, book 5, chapter 4. "De Jurisconsultorum munere." (M, VI, 401-409; R, II, 664-670)
[56] *Ibid.*, 223; 511. "Aequitas, universalitas est quaedam, lex deductio et species; sed iis rivis, et quasi incilibus, aquam continenter ex illo aequitatis fonte suppeditare oportet, sine qua inciles continuo arescunt; est enim aequitas, legum anima, vis, vigor; qua sublata concidant necesse est leges emortuae, nihil enim iniquius est quam leges, quae per aequum et bonum non spirant ac reguntur." (*DD.*, I, 7, 1)
[57] *Ibid.*, 227-514. "Primum legum munus esse debet, ut animum constituant ac forment, fontem actionum omnium, dentue operam, non ut puniant malos, sed ne qui velint esse mali."
[58] M, V, 382; R, II, 236. "Ita medicinam in venena noxia convertunt." (*De Concordia*, IV, 11)

VIVES' THOUGHT

rather than to punish the evil-doers. The first concern of the legislators is therefore the moral education of the child, that they get used to loving what is right and to detesting what is wrong.[59]

Laws and schools were viewed by Vives as the two great social devices of moral education. Accordingly, he gallantly fought for the urgent reform of both institutions. Although Vives was not a professional lawyer, on repeated occasions he pressed for a revision of the existing legislation. If modern education is deeply indebted to humanist pedagogy, modern codification also owes a great deal to the campaign of the humanists for an organized system of law. Vives attacked the endless formalism and the unintelligible jargon of the medieval *Decretalia* with the same unyielding criticism which he displayed in his onslaught against scholastic disputes and distinctions.

Since laws are rules of action, it is extremely important to have few, precise, and clear laws, so that each individual knows exactly how to adjust their own lives to them.

If the laws are multiplied in number, they cease to be guiding marks and become real traps. It is brutally unfair to maintain that ignorance of the law is no excuse, and, at the same time, to have so many complicated laws that nobody can remember nor understand them.[60]

For this overhaul of existing legislation Vives recommended a return to Roman Law which he admired, and a serious philological study of ancient codes as Budé, Nebrija, and Alciatus had already initiated.[61] More important than any reform of the law itself, however, was the wisdom of those, both judges and attorneys, whose function was to interpret the letter of the law to each individual case according to the original intention of the legislator. Vives' spirited defense of Jurisprudence against medieval casuistic and legal positivism is undoubtedly one of the most significant aspects of his social ethics. Vives was convinced that, in the

---

[59] See *De disciplinis,* part 1, book 7, chapter 1: "De optima primaque institutione ditionis et legum; utraque vero quam foede ob ignorantiam et ob pravos affectus corrupta." (M, VI, 222-228; R, II, 510-515)

[60] M, VI, 229; R, II, 515. "Quando lex est velut quaedam regula ad quam unusquisque actiones omnes suas debet accomodare, par est ut leges sint apertae, ac faciles, et paucae, ut sciat quisque quo modo sibi sit vivendum, nec id propter obscuritatem legum ignoret . . .

Iam paucas convenit leges esse. Nam si multa sint, evitari non potest magis crimen, quam casus si multis locis tendantur retia ambulantibus; insidiae sunt tot leges, non condicio vivendi . . . Quae est ergo aequitas ignorantia juris neminem excusari, et tamen leges esse et tam longas, et tam difficiles, ut nemo eas tenere valeat?" (*DD.,* I, 7, 2)

[61] Vives himself mentions these names in *De disciplinis,* part 1, book 7, chapter 3. (M, VI, 234; R, II, 519 b.)

last instance, the most decisive weapon of Justice was a personal decision born out of an enlightened and noble moral sense rather than mechanically produced by the magic device of the law. The social thought of Juan Luis Vives is inspired throughout by this sacred respect for the indispensable character of individual responsibility and moral sense. Legal expertise without prudence can be destructive and criminal. Prudence, however, is not the logical conclusion of a set of premises nor the final reward of an unerring method, but rather a personal achievement. Jurisprudence is moral wisdom applied to the rules which make possible the social life of men. The two chapters which Vives dedicates to this subject in the treatise *De disciplinis* are remarkable examples of eloquence and persuasion.[62]

Vives' emphasis upon the moral aspects of political and social issues prevented him from ever reaching a clear understanding of the impact caused by the economic structural changes of his age. Although the towns of Flanders where he lived typified in a striking manner the rise of modern capitalism and the end of medieval feudalism, Vives remained stubbornly silent about the ethical quality of money-lending upon which the new banking system was being built.[63] There is no doubt whatsoever that Thomas More, the arbitrator of many trade disputes, had a much deeper insight into the problems of the sixteenth century's entrepreneur than Juan Luis Vives, the thoughtful reformer of education. In two cases, however, Vives dealt at length with important socioeconomic problems of his time. The first was a strong defense of private property against the Anabaptist rulers of Münster, which he summarized in his book *De communione rerum* (1535). In this treatise Vives defends and justifies the communistic practices of the Apostolic Church in Jerusalem as a freely chosen way of life made possible by the extremely small number of its membership and under the charismatic direction of the Spirit.[64] On the other hand, Vives bluntly rejects the literal interpretation of the Scripture upon which Anabaptism was founded. Then, in more eloquent terms, Vives attacks the communistic interpretation of human equality:

Will you dare to say that the virtues of the soul are common possessions? Will you pretend that talent, knowledge, experience and maturity, prudence and memory, are common to all men? What about body strength, health, beauty, age, the keenness of the senses? . . . I am a scholar, you are a soldier. Do you think that you are entitled to have a share of my books or that I have

---

[62] *Ibid.*, part 1, book 7, chapter 3 (M, VI, 233-238; R, II, 519-523). Also, *ibid.*, part 2, book 5, chapter 4 (M, VI, 409-416; R, II, 664-670).
[63] See Gilmore, *The World of Humanism*, pp. 120-122.
[64] M, V, 468; R, I, 1416 b. (*De communione rerum*)

to own some of your weapons? Should a child receive the food and the clothing of elder people, or a sick person be treated like a healthy one? ... Some people are masters and some are servants. Do you want all of them masters or all of them servants? ... You say that women should be a common possession ... Not even the wildest beasts do that; father and son cannot have the same female ...[65]

Finally, Vives warns his readers with solemn and prophetic words:

All your possessions, your wife and your children, your liberty and your life, will be controlled by the most ruthless and violent minority, not by the wisest few. Abandoned to their whims and wild desires you will be brutalized by their tyrannical force and gradually robbed of everything which used to be yours.[66]

Vives' defense of private property is, however, only one side of his social theory. In 1525, Vives wrote *De subventione pauperum*, one of the boldest statements of the social function of private property and of the welfare obligation of the State ever written in the sixteenth century. Vives dedicated this book to the magistrates of Bruges in recognition for their courageous and epoch-making program of municipal poverty-relief and for their uncompromising attack against one of the chronic diseases of the time, professional mendicancy.[67] This book is highly significant because of its pioneering effort in unfettering assistance to the poor from the ecclesiastical monopoly of charitable alms-giving and including it among the natural obligations of private citizens and political institutions. Naturally, the clergy of Vives' time fiercely opposed this unheard of attempt to secularize Christian works of mercy. On the other hand, the more conservative champions of irresponsible private ownership have constantly criticized Vives' "socialistic" extravaganzas. The truth is that, in spite of its short-lived popularity and impact, this book has not yet reached the recognition it deserves. It might be added, not without a certain feeling of useless nostalgia, that the modern history of social upheavals in certain

---

[65] *Ibid.,* 475; 1421-1422. "Vis in animo virtutem esse communem? Vis acumen, scientiam, usum rerum, prudentiam, judicium, memoriam? Vis in corpore robur, valetudinem, formam, integritatem, acumen sensuum aetatem ...? Hoccine videtur tibi aequum, ut libri mei sint communes tibi, mihi vero tua arma? Placet dare puero, quae sunt senum, in victu, in cultu, senibus vicissim quae puerorum? Aegris quae sanorum et e contrario ...? Alii sunt heri, alii famuli. Placetne omnes vel heros fieri, vel ministros ...? At uxores videlicet erunt communes. Quid esset causa majorum malorum? Pater filio in hoc non concederet, nec filius patri, nisi inter pecudes ..." (*De communione rerum*)

[66] *Ibid.,* 482; 1427. "Omnia vestra bona, fortunae, uxores, liberi, libertas, sacra et profana concederent in jus et libidinem non meliorum, sed potentiorum, etiam regnum, et tyrannis teterrima atque acerbissima, et latrocinium publicum impunitum receptum pro lege per vim atque arma."

[67] M, IV, 420; R, I, 1355-1356. (*De SP.*, preface)

Catholic countries might very well have been totally different had the social thought of this Jewish exile found more understanding among them.

The treatise is divided into two books. The first is a theoretical discussion of the origin of poverty and of the ethical obligation to help the poor; the second, a concrete program of social assistance and welfare. The first book begins with a somber and depressing description of the misery caused by man's original fall: poverty is indeed a man-made curse, the result of a moral disorder.[68] To remedy this evil each man has to overcome his misdirected self-love; benevolence and help to others have to regain their natural position. The first obligation of the individual is to train others in virtue and to impart to all an "education directed to moral wisdom." [69] In Chapter Nine Vives clearly proclaims the social function of individual ownership. Three hundred and some years before the social encyclics of the Popes, Vives wrote the following lines:

> How many tragedies are caused by the excessive use of the words "mine" and "yours"! In fact, we use them assuming that man has something he can properly call "his," when the truth of the matter is that *everything we have was given to us by God for the sake of others,* even virtue . . . Nobody should, therefore, ignore that man has absolutely nothing for his own exclusive use, no soul, no body, no money, no possessions. We are only administrators and dispensers of those goods for the purpose and goals God assigned to us . . .[70]

The second book presents an amazing program of social welfare, rich in suggestions and recommendations which have not yet lost their actuality and applicability. Vives sees in poverty relief the best guarantee against social disorders, the spreading of diseases, and the corruption of public morality. His first recommendation was to round up all the street and church beggars, and to gather them in public hospitals and orphanages under the direct supervision of municipal authorities. Such action ought to be complemented by a careful census of all the indigent people who live in their own houses.[71] The first and most important welfare measure is to provide everyone able to work with an appropriate job, and

---

[68] *Ibid.,* 421-426; 1357-1360.

[69] *Ibid.,* 427; 1361. "Summum beneficium est, si quis virtutem cuiusquam adjuvet . . . Post virtutem eruditio sequitur tendens ad cognitionem virtutis."

[70] *Ibid.,* 450-451; 1378-1379. " 'Meum' et 'tuum,' quantas inter nos tragoedias excitant . . . ? Quasi vero aliquid ullus hominum possideat, quid merito queat suum appellare; etiam virtutem ipsam a Deo accepit, a quo nobis data sunt omnia, aliis aliorum causa . . . Nemo sit ergo huiusce rei insciens, se nec corpus, nec animam, nec vitam, nec pecuniam habere in usum modo suum et commodum data, sed esse illarum rerum omnium dispensatorem . . ." (*De SP.,* I, 9)

[71] *Ibid.,* 469-470; 1392-1393. (*De SP.,* II, 2)

to train those who are able in more profitable professions.[72] Vives excused neither the blind nor the elderly among the poor from this obligation to work.[73] He was perfectly convinced that there is always a job in the community which fits with the talent, the age, and the physical strength of each citizen. The only excuse he was ready to admit was poor health, but only after a strict medical inspection carried out under the supervision of public authorities.[74] Those who are physically capable of work, but totally unwilling because of their utter moral corruption, should receive just enough food to survive.[75] Vives laid special emphasis upon the social obligation to attend to the mentally retarded and the mentally disturbed.[76] In chapter Six of this second book Vives deals with the problems of financing such a comprehensive program of welfare. First of all, Vives attacks the excessive wealth of the Church: "Bishops and monks converted what initially had been the patrimony of the poor into ecclesiastical rents." [77] Although Vives was far from recommending the confiscation of Church property, since "no amont of money ever justifies any violence," he frankly reminded the clergy that ecclesiastical monies alone could easily alleviate most of the social misery." [78] As secondary sources of income Vives suggested the careful administration of hospital foundations, church collections, loans from wealthy citizens, and last, but not least, the labor of the welfare recipients themselves.[79] Such a program he urged be accompanied by austere fiscal policy of the municipality which had to be willing to give up "banquets, gifts, carnivals, and festivities which frequently lead to moral abuses, pride, and ambition." [80]

d. The International Community

The third and final level of man's social life is the community of nations. The significance of Vives' thought on this subject is measured by

---

[72] Ibid., 471; 1393 (De SP., II, 3).

[73] Ibid., 473; 1394.

[74] Ibid., "Valetudinis habenda ratio et aetatis; sic tamen ne simulatione morbi aut infirmitatis imponant, quod non fit raro, adhibebitur medicorum judicium."

[75] Ibid., 472; 1394 b. "Non occidendi fame, macerandi tamen."

[76] Ibid., 474-475; 1396. Vives recommends that the mentally ill be treated with sympathy and special care in clinics and hospitals. He insists on the specialized treatment that each type of mental illness demands.

[77] Ibid., 478-479; 1399. "Episcopi et sacerdotes caritate pauperum opes illas ad sublevandos inopes collatas iterum in suam curam receperunt."

[78] Ibid., 482-483; 1402-1403.

[79] Ibid., Vives recommends that the administration of the money earned by the poor themselves be in the hands of two clerks appointed by the city magistrates.

[80] Ibid., 482-1401. "Tum civitas ipsa detrahat aliquid publicis sumtibus, velut solemnibus epulis, xeniis, lautitiis, congiariis, annuis ludis et pompis . . ."

the proportions of the European crises through which he was forced to live. It is almost a platitude to say that the first half of the sixteenth century saw a tremendous change in the political structure of Europe. The decay of the Empire and of the Church together with socioeconomic changes of the first magnitude had encouraged the polarization of the Christian kingdoms into modern states closely related to each other, but frequently antagonistic in their territorial demands. Gun powder helped to dismantle the feudal barons from their walled castles. The mariner's compass took man around the world while the printing press had made culture inexpensive and easily available. The intercommunication and the interaction of men had become, suddenly, a challenge of fantasic proportions.

Renaissance historians are more and more inclined to classify the Humanists of the Erasmian circle among the most cosmopolitan thinkers of the day. If the Florentine academicians were the first to rediscover the earthly human vocation of civic responsibility and the delights of social intercourse, Erasmus and his friends were unsurpassed in the farsightedness and maturity of their European vision. Vives was indeed one of their most eloquent, thoughtful, and articulate spokesmen. His correspondence with Henry VIII, with Charles V, with Pope Adrian VI, together with his two beautiful tracts *De concordia* and *De pacificatione* brought to a climactic height the political wisdom of Flemish and English Humanism – the vision of a unified Europe linked together not by Church or Empire but by natural tolerance, mutual respect, and enlightened self-interest. Vives, the Jewish exile forced to live in the central stage of European politics, learned to love Europe without any nationalistic limitation.

Vulgar people make their judgments led by blind passions, instead of being guided by a serene contemplation of truth. Partisan spirit is misleading, exclusivistic, and sharp as a knife. The Spaniard believes that everything Spanish is beautiful and acceptable; the Frenchman thinks the same about French achievements. For almost thirty uninterrupted years these two nations have been at war ... Spain has conquered Naples, Navarre, Milan, and the Rousillon; Spain has defeated powerful French armies and captured the French King. Nevertheless, the French peacock struts around as if the French army had crushed the Spanish soil from the Pyrenees to Cadiz. I want to make clear, however, that this is not meant to be a praise of Spain. On the contrary, I would much more prefer to see my country crowned with other laurels than these military victories which are nothing but plunder and cruelty ... Oh Lord, grant to these sad eyes of mine to see these two nations, my beloved Spain where I was born, and my sweet France where I was educated, competing with each other in more worthwhile enterprises . . .[81]

His prayer was not heard. Vives' "sad eyes" never saw the dream of peace become a reality. His entire life was a constant struggle between his firm hope that man's reasonableness would prevail and the growing despair which the incurable disease of European nationalism provoked in his soul. The books of Vives abound in tragic visions of European wars, religious fanaticism, hatred, and confusion. In his dialogue *De Europae dissidiis* Vives wrote:

Never before in any part of the world has man hated more than in Europe today. It is true that in ancient times some nations from Asia abhorred the peoples of Europe, but at least there was a sea between them . . . Today, however, neighboring nations hate each other without hope of reconciliation. Italians hate trans-Alpines as wild barbarians; Frenchmen spit upon the face of the English; Englishmen hate the people from Scotland and France; a terrible tradition of internecine wars separates France from Spain . . . The layman fights against the clergy, people fight against the nobility, subjects rebel against the rulers, and the rulers despise their subjects. Lutherans and anti-Lutherans hate each other seeking annihilation rather than correction. Among the Lutherans themselves there is no trace of harmony and love . . . The same happens even among the Brothers: the monk tortures the mendicant orders, the minorite insults the dominican priest . . .[82]

In the dedicatory of *De Concordia* Vives wrote to Charles V:

[81] M, V, 283; R, II, 155. "Rudium hominum et vulgarium judicia ex affectu nascuntur, non ex veri dispicientia . . . Res studiis et tamquam factione scinditur, ut propre omnia in vana et levi multitudine; Hispano omnia Hispanica probantur, Gallo Gallica; per triginta annos perniciosum christiano nomini Gallia cum Hispania bellum gerit paene continens: ademit Hispanus Gallo Neapolim, Mediolanum, Navarram, Ruscinonem, tot alii clades attulit, tot exercitus obsidione occidit, Regem ad ultimum cepit, et tamen post haec omnia Gallus domi triumphat, se pro victore . . . gerit; ita loquitur, ita scribit, ut videatur totam Hispaniam a Pyreneis ad Gades victor proculcasse: non hic cano Hispaniae encomium, aliis ego illam rebus laudatam vellem . . . Faceret Christus . . . ego aliquando et Hispaniam quae me genuit, et Galliam quae aluit, florentes vigentesque et in certamen pulcherrimum adductas aspicerem! O si id ego videam antequam ex hac vita migro . . ." (*De Concordia*, III)

[82] M, VI, 454-455; R, II, 41-42. "Nulla aetate, nulla natione, tanta fuerunt odia quantum nunc inter nos: olim odia erant inter gentes Asiae atque Europae, quod mari viderentur diremptae . . .; nunc inter provincias odium publicum et irreconciliabile . . .: Italus Transalpinos omnes tamquam barbaros fastidit, atque odit; Gallus ad Britanni nomen despuit; hic non admodum caros habet Scotos et Gallos; inter Gallos et Hispanos memoria nostra bella gesta non citra ingentes clades . . . Profani homines infensi initiatis, plebes optimatibus, subditi ei qui praestat . . . Inter Lutheranos et Anti-Lutheranos minus miror esse tanta odia; illud magis dolet alteros sic esse in alteros animatos, ut perditos et excisos velint, non emendatos; nec inter Lutheranos ipsos est amor et concordia . . . Monachus in mendicantem, Minorita adversus Dominicanum, Minorita claustralis in Observantem, quae expulsiones, qua convicia, minae, insectatio . . ." (*De Europae dissidiis*)

Europe has suffered terrible damages ... We can see the fields dry-as-dust and abandoned, the dwellings destroyed, the cities either devastated or deserted, the food scarce or terribly expensive, education neglected, morality poisoned, the jugdment of human beings totally subverted ... .[83]

Like most humanists, Vives saw Europe weakened from within by nationalistic wars and threatened from outside by the imperialism of the Turks. Vives' moral indignation against the internal wars of European nations was inspired not only by his sincere pacifism, but also by his passionate concern with the Moslem expansion in the Eastern Mediterranean Sea, the weak flank of Europe. Surprisingly enough the discovery of the New World and the Conquista failed to impress Vives in a decisive manner. Probably because of his strong feeling against a Moslem state, Vives could not see the necessity of a policy of accomodation and appeasement with the Ottoman Empire. Instead he became one of the idealistic crusaders and alarmist prophets who constantly demanded a European alliance against "the invading hordes from Asia." [84] His Christian pacifism did not stretch enough to cover the soldiers of Suleiman, whom he considered as the scourge of God and the perdition of European Christianity. All he could do to retain the noble image of Christian mercy was to recommend a war without hatred, "because, after all, the Turks are still human beings." [85] Moreover, alarmed as he was by the increasing number of concessions and arrangements made between Christian princes and the Turks – a policy which ultimately led to the integration of the Turkish Empire into the European state system – Vives wrote a violent denunciation of any "detente" in a short pamphlet entitled *De conditione vitae Christianorum sub Turca*.

In his dialogue *De Europae dissidiis* Vives presents a colorful sketch of the origin and progress of Europe's dynastic wars. Vives believed that the source of all the troubles was the ambitious plan of the French, the Spanish, and Papal states to take advantage of the smaller units of power in Italy. The fatal sign was given by the conquest of Naples by Alfonso V of Aragon and by the invasion of Italy in 1494 by the French armies

---

[83] M, V, 187; R, II, 75. "Ingentes cuncta Europa clades accepit ... excisos videmus ac depopulatos agros, aedificia diruta, urbes alias aequatas solo, alias exinanitas prorsus ac desertas, alimenta et rara et precii intentissimi, studia litterarum segnia et paene amissa, mores pravissimos, judicia tantopere corrupta ..." (*De Concordia*, dedication to the Emperor)
[84] M, V, 462; R, II, 20. (*Epistola Episcopo Lincolniensi*)
[85] M. M, V, 390; R, II, 243. "Amandi sunt Turcae, nempe homines" (*De Concordia*, IV, 12).

under Charles VIII, "that ugly and little beast." [86] Popes Julius and Leo, succumbing to the temptation of power, entered the dirty game with a devilish array of Swiss mercenaries and ecclesiastical excommunications. The confrontation between the French and the Spanish dynasties reached its climactic moment during the rule of Francis I and Charles V. Vives has been frequently criticized for his partisan line in favor of the Emperor.[87] It is true that after Vives returned to Bruges in 1528, for a short period of his life, he was strongly affected by the Erasmian imperialists of the Spanish Court who saw in Charles V the divine instrument of Spanish supremacy and the only salvation against Lutheran heresy and Turkish invasion. Nevertheless, exception made for those years, Vives remained always neutral and detached from any nationalistic passion. He considered the Imperial Crown of Charles "a merchandise bought with huge amounts of money and terrible intrigues." [88] He accused both Francis and Charles of juvenile irresponsibility and criminal ambition: "The wound of Europe could easily heal if these two lads would content themselves with the dominions they already have." [89] In fact, for many years Vives showed some preference for Henry VIII, whom he considered a promising third power to keep the balance between France and the Empire. The tragedy of the divorce and the games of Wolsey were a terrible disappointment to Vives. With severe words he warned European princes against the new breed of Machiavellian diplomats and professional secretaries who concocted leagues and alliances in a dangerous gamble of secret diplomacy.[90]

Vives' internationalism is a strange mixture of prophetic insight and conservative shortsightedness. He exaggerated the Turkish threat and failed to evaluate the accomplishment of Moslem civilization. His crusading spirit was old-fashioned and dangerous. He failed to see that the colonization of America was also a European affair and that ultimately the resources of the new world were bound to change the structure of European society. He did not have the insight to see that the economic changes of the moment were about to create a new type of society where man had to be different. On the other hand, few people saw more clearly

---

[86] M, VI, 457; R, II, 42. "Tale animalculum, tam pusillum, tam deforme, tantos exciebat motus." (De Europae dissidiis).

[87] See, e.g., Bataillon, "Du nouveau sur L. Vives," p. 105. The author describes the situation as a "mirage imperialiste."

[88] M, VI, 460; R, II, 45. "De Imperatore deligendo, ambitu et profussissimis largitionibus apud electores a Carolo et Francisco certatum, quasi mercimonium licerentur, non regnum." (De Europae dissidiis)

[89] Ibid., 480; 60 b. "Plaga sanaretur si juvenes duo, contenti latissimis imperiis quae possident, amice inter se et concorditer vivere animum possent inducere."

[90] M, V, 219-220; R, II, 103 (De Concordia, I).

than Vives that European unity was not to stand any more upon religious creeds but on natural values and morality. Although he never wrote a book of International Law, he did probably inspire others to do so. Moreover, he was a man of peace and compromise in a time of religious fanaticism and destructive nationalism. Few people have spoken more eloquently than Juan Luis Vives against the tremendous absurdity of war as a means of solving human problems. With warm compassion and penetrating intellect Vives wrote magnificent pages about the causes and the effects of war, about the moral and material consequences of war, about the senselessness of militarism and the terrible price of warlike victories.[91] In this respect, like in many others, the writings of Vives have, unfortunately, an amazing actuality.

[91] The first three books of *De Concordia* are an eloquent attack against the insanity of war. (M, V, 193-331; R, II, 80-195)

CHAPTER 11

RANGE AND PURPOSE OF HUMAN KNOWLEDGE

"Tantum scis quantum operaris"
From *Satellitium animi*

People with little sympathy for the work of philosophers have claimed that the capital invested in philosophy is itself not philosophical, and that philosophical doctrines are born from unphilosophical prejudices. Philosophers as a group reject this accusation and proudly point to the exceptional achievements of some individual minds entirely independent from their historical environment or their educational background. As a rule, however, one is inclined to agree that in most cases the starting positions of a thinking man are rather received than created, more an implement of thought than thought itself. The sceptic frowns upon human knowledge because it does not satisfy the requirements which he, beforehand and arbitrarily, has decreed to be the minimal ones. The Cartesian rationalist overcomes scepticism because, before any meditation, he has already decided to accept the strongest available evidence as evidence itself. Kant denied the possibility of metaphysics as a science simply because he was convinced that Newtonian physics was the paradigm of all scientific knowledge.

Keeping these and similar examples in mind will undoubtedly help us to approach with a certain sympathy the study of Vives' attempt to find an intelligent solution to the central issue of Christian philosophy, the relationship of faith and reason. To this subject we shall dedicate the first part of this chapter.

a. Faith and Reason

Evidently the case of the Christian philosopher seems to be an acute example of unphilosophical prejudice. The Christian who takes his faith seriously but wants also to play the philosopher, finds himself in an embarrassing situation. Faith dictates to him theoretical conclusions he cannot deny and facts the historicity of which he is obliged to accept. To make things worse, the fact that the very eternal fate of the believer depends upon the acceptance of those very conclusions puts an additional pressure upon the mind of the searching Christian. Vives confesses with candor: "It is very dangerous to uphold falsity instead of truth; particularly when it reflects upon Religion which is the corner-stone of our whole life." [1]

In spite of the growing doubt and perplexity of those days, the humanists of Northern Europe were, I believe, sincere and serious Christians.[2] To the best of my knowledge, Vives' religiosity might have been exaggerated, but it has never been denied.[3] There are three religious beliefs which are particularly inseparable from the basic structure of his thought: first, man's transcendental dependence on God, his first and final Cause; second, the constant awareness that each individual belongs to a human race weakened by an original sin; and, finally, a boundless admiration and affection for Christ, the teacher of an incomparable way of life. Vives' religious beliefs do not comprehend more than that, but, without these revealed adminicles it is impossible to understand a single page of Vives. As a creature of God, man is basically good, although finite. As the son of sinful parents, man has been punished with a weakening, not a loss, of his natural powers. As a Christian, man is granted the help of grace as long as he freely decides to accept it. This religious conception of man explains both the origin of all human miseries and the way to recovery. Even poverty and social evils are a divine punishment:

> Through sin man's intelligence became dull and obtuse, and his reason was obscured by darkness. Pride, jealousy, cruelty, all appetites and desires were set in turmoil and disorder; loyalty was broken; man lost his capacity to love: the body was plagued by diseases and the earth was damned, stink in the air, corruption in the waters, freezing winters and burning summers ...[4]

---

[1] M, VI, 214; R, II, 503 b. "Periculosum est contra veritatem pro falso stare, quanto periculosius in re tanti momenti, de cardine in quo vita universa volvitur!" (*DD.*, I, 6, 2).

[2] In general I agree with the main thesis of P. Fèvre's book *Le problème de l'incroyance au XVIème siècle* (Paris, 1911), that a radical attitude of godlessness was almost psychologically impossible in Vives' time. Nevertheless, contemporary scholars have questioned the religious sincerity of such people as Erasmus of Rotterdam. For the two sides of this particular case see S. A. Nulli, *Erasmo e il Rinascimento* (Torino, 1955) as opposed to the more traditional views of A. Renaudet in his brilliant essay *Erasme, sa penseé religieuse et son action (1519-1521)* (Paris, 1921).

[3] See below, pp. 293-294, the different appraisals of Vives' religious attitudes.

[4] M, IV, 422; R, 1356 a. "Homo ipse innocentia exutus, omnia secum in exitium

And again:

What is the source of so much antagonism in human society? People kill
each other, steal from each other, cheat each other, hate each other, with
no break nor pause for a single instant. There is no doubt: man has destroyed
his own nature; man coveted to be divine and lost his own humanity.[5]

Human reason, vitiated by sin, seeks aid in Revelation. Unfortunately,
Vives never explained in theoretical terms the boundaries of human
reason after the fall, nor the character of the divine assistance. His solution
to the problem has to be found in *his* own example rather than in explicit
theories. We intend to define his position by contrasting it with some attitudes which were fashionable among his contemporaries.

Vives was, first of all, clearly opposed to any form of dualistic Averroism. When Vives arrived in Paris, the golden days of John of Jandun
were well behind. But the impact of Latin Averroism was still widely felt.
Averroes himself was still enjoying repose in that secluded corner of the
Inferno which Dante had been careful to provide for him.[6] Since the
thirteenth century the Commentator had reigned supreme in the interpretation of Aristotle.[7] In 1473 Louis XI promulgated an Edict forbid-
ding the teaching of Nominalism at the University of Paris: in it Averroes is mentioned before Saint Thomas and Saint Bonaventura as the best
guide for the understanding of Aristotle.[8] At the end of the fifteenth century the last refuge of Latin Averroism was the University of Padua under
the leadership of Vernia de Chietti.[9]

---

rapuit; retusa est mens, obscurata ratio; superbia, invidia, odium, saevitia, cupiditates
multiformes, et perturbationes reliquae, ceu tempestates quaedam excitatae undis
austro percitis; dissoluta fides, refrigeratus amor ... simul afflictum corpus ...; in
aere foedi ac pestilentes aures, insalubres aquae, periculosa navigatio, molesta hiems,
molestus fervor ..." (*De SP.,* I, 1)

[5] *Ibid.,* V, 201; II, 87. "Unde ergo tantum per universum hominum genus dissi-
diorum, tantum inimicitiarum ...? oderunt, rapiunt, spoliant, fallunt, fraudant,
caedunt, tollunt invicem, nec in his ista exequendi vicibus modus ullus, aut requies?
Quid aliud existimandum est quam defecisse hominem a natura sua? Ita necesse
est ... non fuit homo humanitate contentus, divinitatem expetivit, idcirco et hu-
manitatem, quam relinquebat, amisit, nec quam affectarat divinitatem, est conse-
cutus ..." (*De concordia,* I, 1).

[6] *Divina Comedia,* IV, 119-120.

[7] On the impact of Averroes on medieval thought, see F. Van Steenberghen,
Aristote en Occident: les origines de l' aristotelisme parisien (Louvain, 1946).

[8] See Renaudet, *Préréforme et Humanisme,* p. 93.

[9] The Averroism of Padua is of extreme importance in the history of Humanism
because it ignited the discussion on the immortality of the soul between Pomponazzi
and Marsilio Ficino. Vives mentions Ficino (and Ermolao Barbaro) in his books but
ignores Pomponazzi altogether. Vives, who never visited Italy, came in contact with
Italian Renaissance through the intellectual activities of Lefèvre d' Etaples. At least
Vives' knowledge of Italian Humanism seems to coincide with Lefèvre's preferences.
On Lefèvre, see Renaudet, *Préréforme et Humanisme,* pp. 366 ff.

The humanists in general reacted very sharply against the pagan rationalism of Averroes, the "rabid dog," as Petrarch called him.[10] At Paris, Lefèvre was conducting a relentless attack against Averroism when Vives was still a student at Montaigu. Lefèvre was not a very original thinker, but in his anti-Averroistic crusade he helped to make known in Paris the writings of Hermolao Barbaro and Marsilio Ficino.[11]

Against this historical background Vives wrote the chapter of De disciplinis entitled: "Invective against Averroes. Shameful defeat of the philosopher who was believed by the men of his age to be equal to Aristotle or Saint Thomas." [12] In the first part of this chapter Vives accumulates all the blunders of Averroes in interpreting Aristotle, and concludes with the following biting remark: "You, Averroes, are the most distorted, the most uneducated, and the most revolting writer I have ever read." [13] However, the real cause of Vives' indignation was not Averroes' false interpretation of Greek thought, but rather the impious character of his doctrine. According to Vives the dualism of Averroes would split the Christian thinker into a blind believer without reason and a proud rationalist without faith: "Your doctrine is perverse and blasphemous. It is inevitable that whoever reads your books with vehement passion shall become impious and sink into the forlorn, cold, and dark night of atheism." [14] Moreover, Averroes' double standard of reason and faith is absolutely incompatible with the unique source of all truth both natural and supernatural, which is God, the author of nature and of revelation:

Thus the sacrilegious distinction was born between the light of reason and the light of faith, in such a way that what is true by one can be false by the other, and vice versa. Who else but an impious and stupid man could thus dissociate two extremes which in reality nature itself has linked together? Is there more than one truth? . . . Besides, who can define the limits of natural

---

[10] Petrarch initiated the Humanist attack against Averroes. Vives shows a great admiration for the Italian writer whom he praises as one of the renovators of classical Latinity (M, VI, 340; R, II, 608 b, II, 3, 9) and whose book De remedio utriusque fortunae he recommends together with Boethius' De consolatione philosophiae (M, VI, 404; R, II, 660 b., DD, II, 5, 3).

[11] In 1492 – the year of Vives' birth – Lefèvre visited Italy. Shocked by the Averroism of Padua, Lefèvre was reassured by Ermolao Barbaro and Ficino, whose writings he propagated in Paris. See Renaudet, Préréforme et Humanisme, pp. 137, 379.

[12] M, VI, 191; R, II, 485 b. The title of the chapter – written not by Vives but by his publisher – is: "Irruit in Aberroem, et quem non modo Aristoteli sed et D. Thomae aequiparandum sua aetate homines arbitrabantur, foedissime prosternit, id est, ignarissimum ostendit, et atris coloribus pingit metaphysicam Avicenae." (DD, I, 5, 3).

[13] Ibid., 196; 488 b. "Nihil potest esse illis indoctius, insulsius, frigidius."

[14] Ibid., "Te nihil est sceleratius aut irreligiosius; impius fiat necesse est, et atheus quisquis tuis monimentis vehementer sit deditus."

power and decide that it reaches such a point and not further? It is ridiculous to say that where the thinking man stops there Nature ends, to transfer to Nature itself the feebleness which is ours.[15]

If Vives rejected the Averroistic incompatibility between the dictates of human reason and the Christian dogma, he was equally careful to avoid the right wing rationalism of Raymond Lully and Sabiunde.

Suprisingly enough Vives mentions neither one in his writings, although one could at least expect Vives' sympathy for the voluntaristic overtones and the independent mind of Lully.[16] I can think of some reasons, however, which seen to explain Vives' attitude. Perhaps the strong anti-semitism of Lullius, together with his pro-Arabic missionary dreams, were not entirely pleasing to Vives, the Jewish convert. Besides, Vives might have been reluctant to confess how much he himself was under Lully's influence. From him Vives accepted the basic notion that between the conclusions of human reason and the Christian dogma no conflict was possible, simply because both had one and the same source. The radical difference between Vives and Lully was that the latter was an optimistic rationalist with mystical reveries, while the former had a much more modest conception of man's natural ability. Where Lully (and Sabiunde) speaks of "demonstrating the dogma," Vives was content with an effort to assert its "reasonableness." Chapters three and four of the first book of De veritate fidei contain the most explicit formulations Vives ever wrote concerning the relationship of reason and faith. Vives tries to justify his own apologetical book against those "pious men who believe that one should not attempt to back faith with reasons." [17] Human knowledge, Vives contends, is a finite participation of the Divine Intelligence. As finite, human knowledge never exhausts the truth of reality, it is always fragmentary and incomplete. This knowledge is most clear in those matters which are indispensable to man's eternal salvation. The sin of Adam obscured our knowledge of such matters. Revelation finds, therefore, a willing echo in the human mind. We rediscover with new clarity what sin had only darkened. Human persuasions become objects of faith. When Revelation deals with mysteries, our natural powers react

---

[15] M, VIII, 18; R, II, 1339 a. "Hinc nata est importunissima illa distinctio de lumine fidei et lumine naturae, quod alia vera sint hoc lumine, falsa sint illo, alia e contrario. Quis haec re et natura conjuncta discrevit, nisi homo aliquis impius et imperitus? An est in rebus nisi una veritas? ... Age vero, quis est tanto ingenio, tanta eruditione, et usu rerum, qui metas possit naturae assignare, ut confirmare certo audeat non ulterius naturae vim se porrigere?" (De VFC., I, 3).
[16] T. Carreras Artau, Historia de la filosofía española, pp. 177-199, makes a penetrating study of this aspect of Lully's thought.
[17] M, VII, 5-22; R, II, 1328-1343.

sympathetically to them in the sense that they discover the harmony of the revealed mystery with the trends and inclinations of natural knowledge. On the Trinity Vives writes:

> Before Christ discovered this Truth, no human mind ever thought of it, not even of its possibility. However, after we were told of this mystery by our Divine Master, we began to think of many reasons which we intend to discuss now.[18]

In other chapters of the same book, Vives deals with the "reasonableness" of Christ's Incarnation, the resurrection of the flesh, and with the natural perfection of Christ's moral law. If man were able to discover the convenience of the Christian mysteries, Vives thought that he would be equally able to prepare himself to receive the mystery. Vives rejected the radical solutions of Lully. If he refused to accept man's power to "prove the dogma," he was equally suspicious of Lully mysticism. On the contrary, he believed that man should control his passions to reach "that Wisdom which consists in the right evaluation of everything in virtue of an uncorrupted judgment." [19] There is no missionary zeal in Vives, no mysticism. Lully's naivete has been replaced by a mental attitude much closer to our contemporary criticism than the massive, impersonalized commitment to a system of rational thought which characterizes the author of the *Ars Magna*.

Nobody can expect to find in Vives that exact delineation of the boundaries between Philosophy and Theology which characterizes a contemporary manual of Scholastic Philosophy. After all, Vives wrote twenty years before Trent and four centuries before the first Vatican Council. Nevertheless, a modern reader of Vives will be inclined to resent the long, boring pages on the "metaphysics of the angels," the "philosophical convenience of the Blessed Trinity," and, even worse, the biblical proof of Aristotle's heavenly matter.[20] There is no doubt that in these unwelcomed pages Vives paid an expensive tribute to that unbroken medieval tradition which started with Chartres, and which Florence had brought back to life.[21]

---

[18] *Ibid.*, 141-142; 1436 b. "Antequam veritatem eam Christus retegeret, neque veritatis neque rationum venisset ulli hominum in mentem; sed postquam veritatem a coelesti seu potius magistro Deo accepimus, rationes se nobis coeperunt ostendere atque aperire, quarum nos aliquas ex grandi numero proferemus." (*De VFC.*, II, 2).

[19] M, I, 1; R, I, 1205. "Vera sapientia est de rebus incorrupte judicare." (*Int. ad Sap.*, 1).

[20] According to Vives the "divine philosopher" – that is, God – taught the same as Aristotle in the words of Genesis, "In principio creavit Deus coelum et terram." (M, III, 199; R, II, 1069 a, *De prima philosophia*)

[21] Although Vives never mentions the writings of the philosophers and Humanists

Vives' opposition to Lullian rationalism brought him much closer to the Augustinian than to the Thomistic tradition. This statement, however, should not be understood in the sense that Vives actually made a choice between two well-defined schools of thought. Augustinism, of course, was always much more of an approach or an attitude than a philosophical system.[22] The word "Thomism" on the other hand – as used in modern manuals of History of Philosophy – conveys a false impression: in fact, throughout the Middle Ages, Saint Thomas himself never had a towering and central position in the philosophical consciousness of the Schools. His name appears in Vives' work infrequently and then only with moderate praise.[23] The reason for this historical fact is very clear. As we pointed out before, the core of early Renaissance education in most northern European universities was an arts course in Aristotle supported by a Logic-and-Physics context much more than by a Metaphysics-and-Theology one. The metaphysical-theological Aristotelism, which many students of medieval philosophy identify with medieval thought as such, was not more than the "hortus clausus" of the monastic orders. Vives never had a close contact with such a branch of Scholasticism. Besides, at the time Vives was in Paris, these philosophers-theologians were lost in a sterile exposition of Peter Lombard and such unphilosophical issues as the controversies around the Immaculate Conception. A few years later there was indeed a partial revival of studies on Saint Thomas due to the influence of Pierre Crockaert and the Dominicans of the Saint-Jacques convent. But there is no trace of this movement in Vives' works.[24]

of the school of Chartres, the reading of Marsilio Ficino (whose relationship to William of Conches has been investigated by R. Klibansky in *The Continuity of the Platonic Tradition* [London, 1939], pp. 59-61) probably gave to him some knowledge of the most significant Chartrian contributions to the cause of an integral Christian Humanism.

[22] Both the word "system" and the abstracts in "-ism" are relatively modern, at least when used to mean a body of doctrine. In Vives' time the classical expression was rather "via Sancti Thomae," "via nominalium," etc. See N. Gilbert, *Renaissance Concepts of Method*, pp. 178-179.

[23] In two or three cases the name of S. Thomas appears in general lists of scholastic masters together with such second-rank writers as John Dullaert and Geronimo Pardo. (M, VI, 149; R, II, 451 b, *De disciplinis*, I, 3, 7). The longest, but still moderate praise of S. Thomas is the following: "This doctor is the most acceptable of the schools, and indeed no inept. His books present opinions commonly accepted. In many pages the reader might have the impression that the author follows the judgment of somebody else rather than his own, a procedure which was frequent among scholastic writers." (M, VI, 404; R, II, 660 a, *DD.*, II, 5, 3).

[24] Pierre Crockaert, from Montaigu College, converted to the "via Sancti Thomae" and joined the Dominican Priests of Saint-Jacques in 1504. Five years later Crockaert published a commentary on S. Thomas' *De ente et essentia;* in 1512, and in cooperation with his well-known disciple, Francisco de Vitoria, Crockaert published the *Secunda secundae*. (Renaudet, *Préréforme et Humanisme*, pp. 464, 594, 658). Ong., *Ramus*, p. 147, presents the conversion of Crockaert and his continuous acceptance

If we compare Vives with contemporary Neo-Thomism and its clear-cut distinction between the natural and the supernatural, we will better understand the radical difference in their approaches. A Christian Philosophy "in puris naturalibus," based upon an abstraction from man's fall and redemption, would have been rejected by Vives as a barren and useless speculation. Vives never condemned this abstraction with a specific refutation, but his whole intellectual attitude moves in such a concrete, historical, and personal level that it would have made it impossible. Particularly, the pretended historicity of the original sin is absolutely inseparable from his thought. Significantly enough, Vives, faithful in this point to an Augustinian teaching which Catholic orthodoxy has tried to explain away, "proves" the historical fact of man's original sin "ex experientia":

> We ought to believe that man was endowed by God with all the excellent faculties which are in order for attaining his high destiny . . .
> Now, however, when we see man with a sick and weak body – enslaved to the same creatures God had given him as his servants, slow in understanding and depraved in his will – there is no doubt that the man we see is nothing else but a corruption of the noble creature God created as the king of the Universe. We do not hesitate to say that the cause of this is the sin which separated him from God, his Master. And, indeed, there were philosophers who, by a natural process, arrived at the conclusion that the souls of men are prisoners of their bodies in expiation for past crimes.[25]

This proof is hardly compatible with more modern and precise formulations of Catholic dogma. The loss of the "supernatural" cannot be a "natural" experience; man cannot ever miss a gift for which he has neither desire nor inclination. Of course, by "proving" the original sin from ex-

by the community of Montaigu as a proof that in those days St. Thomas was a symbol of a theologically oriented speculation (in opposition to the logicians of Montaigu) rather than the leader of the realists (in opposition to Ockamistic nominalism). On the acceptance of Crockaert by Montaigu, see Villoslada, *La Universidad de Paris*, p. 47. Although the publication of S. Thomas by Crockaert took place precisely the same year Vives arrived in Paris, this (and similar) fact was never mentioned by Vives, who never became truly interested in the inner activity of the schools.

[25] M, III, 189; R, II, 1061 b. "Sed hominem hunc ... instructum fuisse praeclarissimis a Deo ad tanta munera facultatibus credi par est ... Nunc vero quum et corpore hominem cernamus morbidum, et servum eorum quae illi Deus subjecit, tum intelligentia tardum, et consilii tenebrosi, et voluntatis pravae, indubie degenerasse apparet ab illo homine qui ... huic mundo erat a Deo praefectus; nos peccatum scimus esse causam ...; quidam philosophorum naturae progressu eo pervenerunt, ut dicerent animas hominum in istis corporibus tamquam in ergastulis vinctas, magnorum scelerum poenas dare." (*De prima philosophia*).

At the beginning of chapter 17, book 1, *De veritate fidei Christianae*, Vives wrote: "Corruptam esse naturam nostram, tam manifesto ipsamet ostendit et proclamat, quam aegrotare se, quum tenetur gravi morbo." (M, VIII, 123; R, II, 1421 b).

perience, Vives assumed it as a historical fact known by human reason, and the point of reference in the history of mankind.

The man whom Vives is trying to regenerate lives "in a storm of darkness," "enslaved and muzzled by sin," "worse than the beasts." Man is not the "unum per se" of an "anima rationalis and materia prima." [26]

This vital humanism postulates an equally dramatic God: a personal God who creates from nothing, redeems, and punishes. Vives, like many other humanists, rebels against the Aristotelian First Mover as a caricature of the Christian God. The Aristotelian God does not create, he rather coexists with a world equally eternal; thus, Peripatetic philosophy makes the world "similar to its creator." [27] The First Mover has no freedom, the radical condition of any moral dignity and the very essence of personality:

Aristotle steals from God what is more valuable in rational beings, freedom; and in doing that he transforms the Maker of Nature into its servant ... Enslaved to necessity, the God of Aristotle is deprived of worship, gratitude, affection. How can anybody be grateful to an agent which acts necessarily? Do we thank the fire because it cooked our meal or boiled the water? [28]

Unmovable and unmoved, the Peripatetic "god" solves the mystery of an immutable and provident God by destroying the only lovable part of that secret, namely the love and freedom of an infinite being. Above all, Christian prayer becomes completely ridiculous:

If anyone prays to the Aristotelian God and begs with great desire for the granting of a special benefit, what, do you think, will that God answer to him? He would indeed say: "You are wasting your time; it is not in my power to give it to you because I myself obey the laws of Nature ...; if you get what you want, use it; if not, tolerate your necessity like I tolerate mine." [29]

This concentrated attack against Aristotelian theology was a very significant rebellion of Christian sincerity against the medieval pretense that the wisdom of old Greece was not only compatible, but also perfectly

[26] The first book of the treatise *De concordia et discordia* (M, V, 193-228; R, II, 80-110) presents an existentialistic description of man's miseries and anxiety.
[27] On Vives' rejection of Aristotelian theology, see T. Kater, *J. L. Vives und seine Stellung zu Aristoteles.*
[28] M, VIII, 81; R, II, 1389 a. "Adimit Deo Aristoteles id, quod in entibus ratione atque intelligentia praeditis est optimum, libertatem; et ex principe mundi facit ministrum naturae cui in agendo serviat ... Jam quod sepsit necessitatem abstulit ab eo cultum omnem, caritatem, gratiam; quis enim ei quicquam debeat, qui quae agat, non possit aliter agere? quis igni habet gratiam, quod carnes coxerit et aquam fervefecerit ...?" (*De VFC.*, I, 10).
[29] *Ibid.*, 82; 1389 b. "Si quis Deum illum Aristotelicum imploret ... quid censetis illum responsurum? 'Tu vero frustra consumis tempus et verba, qui mihi supplicas; non enim ea quae tu poscis, in manu mea est tribuere; legibus definitis, praefixisque vado, nec minore premor necessitate in agendo quam tu in patiendo.'"

adaptable to Catholic dogma. Of course, there was a reason for the "Aristotelian temptation" of the Christian mind. The clear and precise definitions of Aristotelian metaphysics, so the Church thought, provided the ideal language for the formulation of the Dogma. Even Melanchthon, especially at the end of his career, succumbed to the spell of Aristotelian *"perspicuitas and proprietas sermonis."* [30] After all, the challenge of Cajetanus' subtleties had to be met with the canons of the Augsburg Confession. With Vives, among others, a trend begins which Christians the world over have not yet been able to master: the trend to think and to speak about God, not with the conceptual apparatus of a pagan rationalist but in strictly Christian terms. The Council of Trent, to be sure, did not help much in this direction.

Although Vives shared with the Augustinian tradition the persuasion that man's intellectual faculties had been vitiated by the sin of Adam, and that this initial disaster was known to us as a historical fact by reason alone, it would be totally misleading to picture Vives as a forerunner of the Jansenists at Louvain, two generations later. No matter how devastating the results of man's original fall might have been, Vives was still convinced that God's punishment had not rendered completely useless the faculties He, Himself, had given to man. Instead of imploring the Divine Assistance in the desperate, helpless, and dramatic manner of Cornelius Jansen, Vives concentrated all his personal effort on making the best possible use of the natural power spared by God's chastisement. Then God has indeed made it more difficult for our intellectual faculties to reach the purpose for which they were granted to man, but not completely impossible. Furthermore, the return of the supernatural gift through Christ presupposes the right use of the natural. Consequently, Christian perfection is not the denial, but the fulfillment of natural wisdom and virtue. Man cannot be a Christian if he is not an *"homo bonus."* More important than the reform of the Church is the improvement of society through the education of the individual.

In this fundamental issue, as in many others, Vives takes a delicate, eclectic position which can – and has been – easily misrepresented. It is a middle way between Augustinism and Pelagianism, Rationalism and Fideism. Knowledge at the natural level is still possible because it is "a divine gift"; but it is also weak and limited because this gift belongs to a man who is now, historically, under the punishment of God. In the fol-

---

[30] See Karl Hartfelder, *Philip Melanchthon als Preceptor Germanaiae* (Nieuwkoop, 1964), pp. 375 ff.

lowing section we intend to specify the degree of reliability assigned by
Vives to the noetical powers of the *"homo lapsus."*

b. Knowing as a reliable instrument of action

Vives builds up his epistemological theories upon the simple but far-
reaching principle that human knowledge is reliable only and insofar as
it is applied to the end assigned to it by the Providence of God within the
total harmony of the Universe. Man is supposed to use his knowledge only
as an instrument in the pursuit of his God-given destiny which is God
Himself after the test of human freedom in this earthly life: "Original
sin has not obscured human reason to the point of making impossible the
knowledge of those truths which are indispensable to man as such." [31]

From this principle Vives derives the first negative determination as
to the trustworthiness of human knowledge. Knowledge has not been
given to man to satisfy his unbridled and proud curiosity about himself,
nature, and God. When knowledge is abused for the sake of vain speculation it yields only error and passionate disputes:

> The philosophers, although perfectly aware of their weakness and poverty,
> refused to stick to this earth and to be contented with those things they could
> easily reach. On the contrary, unable to understand themselves, they tried
> to search and to pry into mysteries which by far exceed all human capacity.
> The less they knew the more they defined with bold arrogance about the
> heavens, the elements, the essences of things, the faculties; especially Plato
> and Aristotle authoritatively spoke about God, matter, immortality...
> Finally the philosophers introduced in the knowledge of Nature notions that
> children and elder women would find hopelessly ludicrous.[32]

This ethical condemnation of purely speculative philosophy as an evil
product of proud curiosity is typical of Vives. All his pages present a stubborn reluctance to get involved in a subtle discussion of traditionally
controversial issues of Scholastic philosophy and the interpretation of
Aristotle. Speaking about the *Metaphysics* of Aristotle Vives recommends
a sober interpretation, because "they contain so many subtleties and such

---

[31] M, 185; R, II, 1058 b. "Neque vero usque adeo mentis nostrae acies retusa est,
quin veritates prospiciat quatenus humano generi conducit." (*De prima philosophia*).
[32] M, VI, 183-184; R, II, 478. "Philosophi, ignari sui, ea quaesierunt et scrutati
sunt quae humanum omnem captum excederent, et in his quae assequi non poterant,
arrogantissime definierunt multa, non cunctantius quam si manibus attrectassent, ut
de coelis, de elementis, de rerum essentiis, ac facultatibus; sed potissimum Plato et
Aristoteles, de Auctore mundi, de materia, de opificio universorum, de regimine illius,
de immortalitate animae... et ea invexisse placita in cognitione naturae, ad quae
nec vetulae nec pueri risum teneant..." (*DD.*, I, 5, 1).

puny details that they just break down our brains, and have given to many people an excuse to investigate things which simply do not exist . . . like those people who see stars on a clear, bright morning . . ." [33] In exactly two lines Vives disposes of the thorny dispute about the conciliation of human freedom with the Providence of God, an issue to which Suárez, Molina, and Bellarmino dedicated entire volumes: "God's knowledge of the future does not deprive me of liberty any more than the presence of a witness impedes the execution of an action." [34] In 1531 Vives wrote a short treatise, De prima philosophia, which several scholars have used to prove Vives' traditional Aristotelism.[35] However, this book is not an exception to the anti-speculative trend of Vives, but rather a confirmation. All that Vives intended by this little essay was to offer a short summary of Aristotelian philosophy in non-technical language, as a sufficiently reasonable "conjecture" to satisfy a minimum of legitimate curiosity. Centuries of medieval speculation are thus reduced to some basic schemes: the pages on the hylomorphic system, the theory of substance and accident, and the analogy of being are good examples of Vives' simplifying action.[36]

One of the most important and far-reaching "reductions" made by Vives was the exclusion of the investigation of particular final causes. According to him, God has assigned an end to each creature within the total created order of the Universe, but it would be complete foolishness on our part to try to investigate the "secret designs of His wisdom":

God, as a most wise agent, ordained everything to its proper end . . .

We, because of the dullness of our intelligence, completely ignore the beginning, the progress and the end of everything; but it is absolutely impossible that God has not provided an end even to the smallest creatures; nevertheless, God's purposes and intentions are totally hidden from us. Therefore, it would be complete foolishness to try to investigate the causes of things which have not been revealed to us.[37]

---

[33] Ibid., 352; 617 b. "Illae Aristotelicae subtilitates, atque adeo non raro quoque praetenues minutiae frangunt ingenii aciem ac retundunt; praebuit etiam nonnullis ansam, ut quae nusquam essent inquirerent, et ex diligentia . . . immodica aliquid se invenisse crederent, quae non viderent . . . non aliter quam si sudo atque sereno coelo de medio die querunt astra . . ." (DD., II, 4, 2).

[34] M, VIII, 386; R, II, 1217 b. "Ceterum Dei praevidentia non magis libertatem mihi mean adimit, quam aspectus tuus, dum me aliquid agentem intueris." (De anima, II, 11).

[35] See, for instance, Bonilla, Luis Vives, II, 15 ff; also Monsegú, La filosofía del Humanismo, chapter 8, pp. 197-229.

[36] M, II, 196-215; R, II, 1068-1081. (De prima philosophia, 1).

[37] Ibid., 186-187; 1059 a – 1061 a. "Ergo quia sapientissimus est, omnia in finem aliquem constituit, et quia optimus, in finem bonum . . .; nobis quidem propter tarditatem ingeniorum, et maximarum rerum inscitiam, ortus, progressus, exitus, et causae

Vives believed that human reason "spoiled by the sin of our fathers" is only capable of formulating certain conjectures subject to correction, but powerful enough to make man the "King of the Universe": "In the realm of nature, man's investigation can reach certain conjectures, but no scientific knowledge, which we do not deserve, impaired as we are by sin and oppressed by the heavy burden of the body. It is true, however, that such scientific knowledge is not even necessary to us, as we see that, without it, man has become the King and the Master of the sub-lunar universe." [38]

As far as I know, Vives was one of the first to formulate in such precise terms this conciliatory position between the Christian belief in a God-given order of the Universe and the mechanistic banishment of particular final causes. Vives' attitude is faithfully (almost literally) reflected in the books of Telesio, where Bacon and Galileo, as is generally accepted, found a great deal of inspiration.[39]

After having condemned theoretical speculation as proud curiosity totally strange to the purpose assigned by God to human knowledge, Vives proceeds further to establish in a positive way the goal of our cognitive faculties. First of all, knowledge has been given to man for the mastery of nature oriented to the satisfaction of his material needs. In a very striking formula Vives expressed this idea by saying that "man knows as much as he can operate." [40]

Vives' condemnation of speculative philosophy and his insistence upon the pragmatic character of human knowledge has impelled many of his biographers to join his name with the aureola of glory which scholars have so lavishly granted to Bacon.[41] Even Ortega y Gasset, in his otherwise interesting lecture on Vives, simply takes for granted that Bacon

singularum ignorantiae sunt; fieri tamen non potest quin ille maximas habeat et in minimus rebus causas ... verum illius sanctae et reconditae voluntatis rationes ac consilia occulta sunt nobis." (De prima philosophia, 1).

[38] Ibid., "In quibus conjecturas quasdam invenit hominum inquisitio, nam scientiam non meremur et peccato contaminati et proinde gravi mole corporis oppressi; sed neque est nobis necessaria, nam videmus omnium quae in hoc sublunari sunt mundo principem esse ac praesidem hominem constitutum."

[39] For Telesio's position see N. Abbagnano, Bernardino Telesio (Milano, 1941), pp. 106, 209. Telesio takes a further step: since God is the explanation of the whole as such, He does not explain anything in particular. Telesio's mechanicism is presented as Christian and orthodox. On the influence of Telesio upon Bacon, see Charles Remusat, Bacon, Sa vie, son temps (Paris, 1887), p. 383; also F. H. Anderson, Francis Bacon, His Career and His Thought. The Arensbergh Lectues, ed. W. H. Werkmeister (New York, 1962), pp. 344-346. On Galileo, see A. Burth, The Metaphysical Foundations of Modern Science, 3rd ed. (New York, 1955), pp. 50-53.

[40] M, IV, 63; R, I, 1203. (Satellitium).

[41] See, e.g., Menéndez y Pelayo, Ensayos de crítica filosófica, pp. 168-169; also Monsegú, La filosofia del humanismo, pp. 167-168.

learned from the Spanish Humanist the very foundations of empirical science.[42] Günther, in his doctoral dissertation on the subject, comes to the surprising conclusion that "without any doubt Vives was one of the most important sources of Bacon's thought." [43] I believe that these exaggerations have to be radically tempered. I hasten to say that Bacon never mentions Vives' name. In fact, the Lord Chancellor was not particularly interested in the writings of the humanists.[44] It is true that Bacon was not the type who would be eager to dispense words of acknowledgment. The phrase *"nullius vestigia sequuutus"* (I have not followed the steps of anyone) was one of his favorite expressions of inborn modesty. Actually, between Bacon and Vives there were undoubtedly striking similarities. Both believed that the end of science is the use, not the explanation, of nature. Both reacted against slavery to authority and the dangers of hasty generalizations.[45] But these ideas were already part of European culture at that time, not the exclusive property of Juan Luis Vives. Besides, Bacon's reputation was not only due to the magnificent vigor with which he proclaimed that message, but especially to his highly unpractical but extremely suggestive methods of induction which never crossed the mind of our Spanish Humanist. Bacon's analysis of the faulty habits of the human mind was much more penetrating than the simplified ethical condemnation given by Vives in his *De disciplinis*. And in many instances, what in Vives is a passing remark or just a hint, in Bacon appears as a fully developed philosophical doctrine. Furthermore, in a very important respect, Vives and Bacon stand in complete antagonism. According to Vives, knowledge is not primarily an instrument for the use of the world, but a weapon for the conquest of human passions. The most important goal assigned by God to human knowledge is to guide a free but blind will in the pursuit of good. Bacon, on the contrary, laid such emphasis upon the pragmatic bearing of knowledge that he almost identified philosophy with the methodology of the natural sciences. He completes this reduction by denying the possibility of natural theology and by placing psychology and ethics "within the prerogative of revealed theology." [46] Consequently, Bacon's *"nova inductio"* primarily applies to physics, the

[42] Ortega y Gasset, *Vives y Goethe*, p. 87.
[43] R. Günther, *Invieweit hat L. Vives die Ideen Bacons von Verulan vorbereitet*, p. 67.
[44] In the *Novum Organon* Bacon mentions Erasmus twice (*Works of Bacon*, ed. R. L. Ellis, I, 451), once Sturm (*ibid.*, 451), Comines (*ibid.*, 717) and Ascham (*ibid.*, 451). The only man of the sixteenth century Bacon warmly praises is Telesio, whom he calls "primus novorum hominum." (*ibid.*, 453).
[45] On Vives' independence from authority see above, p. 154. On Vives and the dangers of hasty generalization, see below, p. 286.
[46] See *Novum Organon*, ed. Ellis, I, 96; *De augmentis scientiarum* (*ibid.*, II, 2, 6).

realm of the *"magna instauratio."* In all of Bacon's books there is only one isolated and unconvincing remark about the possibility of applying the same methods to logic, ethics, and politics. Psychology was totally excluded. There is no doubt, then, that in their general conception of the content and the goals of philosophy, Vives and Bacon were diametrically opposed.

Bacon expected from science the "relief of all human miseries"; Vives was totally dedicated to the "improvement of society through the reform of individual ethics, not to the contemptible delight of material prosperity":

> That great man Socrates was convinced that it is improper to search for material things we can easily dispense with, and to forget the others the ignorance of which is criminal and shameful ... So this man, acclaimed everywhere as the wisest of all mortals, declared and confessed his ignorance on Natural Philosophy, in order to persuade his fellow man not to get excessively attached to those material objects in detriment of their moral life.[47]

This conception of knowledge, not as an end in itself, but almost exclusively as an instrument for action – moral action especially – might appear both relativistic and sceptical.[48] Usefulness seems to have replaced the notion of truth. Of course, Vives never drew such a radical conclusion. However, on his own premises, a scientific theory which at a certain time and under certain conditions helps man to subdue Nature is the result of the right use of our God-given power of knowledge. Whether that theory is an apodictic conclusion or a firm belief is totally irrelevant, as long as it works. Similarly, a moral persuasion which factually motivates man's behavior is based upon "true" knowledge, even if mathematical evidence in the moral world proves to be a rare commodity.[49] What differentiates Vives from more recent forms of pragmatism is that for him the instrumental power of human knowledge is guaranteed by the divine ordination of man's faculties to the end for which he was created. Human knowledge is not reliable when and if it works; it rather works because it is the gift of a reliable God:

[47] M, III, 15; R, I, 572 b. "Divinus ille vir congruum existimabat ea magno labore quaeri, quae nullum afferrent malum, illa vero ignorari, quae nesciri grande flagitium nefasque esset ... et quum esset unus omnium consensu et approbatione rerum ejusmodi scientissimus, affirmavit tamen, se illorum omnium ignarum esse ut ceteri desperata, tanto auctore, naturae arcanorum scientia, illis relictis, ad morum compositionem totos se converterent." (*De initiis*).

[48] Vives occasionally recognizes the value of pure contemplative knowledge. (M, III, 341; R, V, 1182).

[49] Vives' position is that our moral obligations can be based upon firm persuasions in the same way science can be perfectly useful with working hypotheses. Vives' attitude can therefore be compared to the position of Father Mersenne. See below, p. 288.

We have to believe that man, as the lord of the material world and holder of such sublime Destiny, was endowed by God with as much power as is needed for the attainment of his noble end. Consequently, man was given a swift intelligence to explore both the human and the divine, a clear judgment to appraise the things of which he was the master . . .[50]

This basic reliance upon the divine origin of our cognitive faculties, however, does not preclude a distressing and painful awareness of the limitations of human knowledge. In contrast with the optimistic words just quoted, Vives' writings are filled with complaints about the weakness of human knowledge which might seem to have been written by David Hume himself in those somber hours of doubt which preceded the relaxed moments of the backgammon game.

Vives, naturally, explains human indigence as a result of the original fall of man: "there is no doubt that the man we see now is only a corruption of that one to whom God subordinated the whole universe." [51] First of all, sense knowledge, which seems so reliable, is extremely untrustworty.

We enter into knowledge through the gates of the senses; common people believe that sense knowledge is the most certain, and that we cannot be deceived by it . . . But it happens every day that the eyes and all the senses, even the sharpest and most attentive are wrong because of some internal defect, or because of the "medium" or the object.[52]

To make things even worse, sense knowledge can be jeopardized by the disturbing effect of a strong passion: "Sometimes this passional blindness is so overwhelming that people say they do not see nor hear the very things they do see and hear; such is the alienation of the judgment that it precludes the proper use of the senses." [53]

[50] M, III, 189; R, II, 1061. "Hominem hunc sive jam tantarum rerum dominum, sive tantis bonis destinatum, instructum fuisse praeclarissimis a Deo ad tanta munera facultatibus credi par est, nam qui sapientissimus jussit finem peti, idem optimus facultatem et instrumenta finis consequendi voluit attribui, potentissimus tribuit . . . Fuit igitur ornatus . . . celeritate intelligentiae qua mundana et divina facile percurreret . . . tum luce judicii ut qui et cuius quidque esse pretii . . . censeret . . ." (De prima philosophia, 1).
[51] See above, p. 235.
[52] M, III, 193-194; R, II, 1064 a. "Ingredimur ad cognitionem rerum januis sensuum; nec alias habemus clausi hoc corpore." (De prima philosophia). See also, ibid., 84-85; 981. "Primam fidem arbitramur esse sensuum; hanc vulgus certissimam esse ducit, nec falli se ab illa posse . . .; sed falli nonumquam oculorum obtutum, et aliorum sensuum aciem, res est quotidiana, vitio suo, aut medii, aut objecti, aut communis sensus, qui nisi advertat, nihil percipietur recte." (De instrumento probabilitatis, I).
[53] Ibid., "Interdum quoque tanta est caecitas, ut qui perturbationibus tenentur, videre vel audire negent, quae vident atque audiunt . . . ita enim judicii vim voluptas occupat ut nihil sinat agere."

Unfortunately, these very senses are the only source of all human knowledge, not because Vives denies any rational power to man, but because
all our intellectual knowledge is derived from and leans upon previous
sensations:

Like those who live in a basement, with only one little window to the outside, do not see except through that window, thus we see nothing except
through our senses. Nevertheless, we peep into the outside and with our mind
we infer the existence of something beyond our senses, but only as much as
our senses permit us to do. Our mind rises upon the senses, but is based upon
the senses. The senses point to the way, nor is there any other. The mind
infers the existence of something, but it does not see it. Therefore, when we
say that something is or is not, that it is this or the other way, we guess if
from the feeling of our own soul, not from the things themselves, because
they are not their own measure but our mind is.

Because of all this we have to judge things not according to their own
characteristics, but according to our own appraisal and judgment.[54]

These words are indeed a most dramatic expression of Vives' vulnerability
to sceptic hesitations. Nevertheless, in all fairness to their author, they
need to be explained with reference to other passages scattered throughout Vives' work. If the reader expects an explicit and systematic answer
to such questions as whether metaphysics is possible or whether the Aristotelian ideal of science is within human grasp, he might be sligtly disappointed. However, a careful selection of Vives' remarks can provide us
with enough evidence to clarify his thought.

First of all, according to Vives, our knowledge of the essence of things
is only an approximate guess based on their sensible operations after a
careful induction which Aristotle theoretically recommends but practically neglects. Vives gives a definition of the "universal" which sounds
perfectly scholastic: "the essential similitude of those things which belong
to the same species." [55] The problem is that "we know this essence not
in itself, but only through our senses, namely through their sensible actions
and operations." [56] The knowledge of the essence is therefore nothing

[54] M, III, 193-194; R, II, 1064-1065. "Ut qui in cubiculo tantum habent speculare
unum, qua lux admittitur, et qua foras prospiciunt, nihil cernunt, nisi quantum speculare illud sinit, ita nec nos videmus, nisi quantum licet per sensus, tametsi foras
promicamus, et aliquid ulterius colligit mens, quam sensus ostenderunt, sed quatenus
per eos conceditur; assurgit quidem supra illos, verum illis tamen alia intuetur; ergo
nos quae dicimus esse aut non esse, haec aut illa, talia non talia, ex sententia animi
nostri censemus, non ex rebus ipsis, illae enim non sunt nobis sui mensura, sed mens
nostra... quocirca censendae sunt nobis res non sua ipsarum nota, sed nostra
aestimatione ac judicio." (De prima philosophia, 1).
[55] M, III, 122; R, II, 1041 a. "Similitudo essentialis in multis." (De explanatione).
[56] Ibid., "Essentiam vero uniuscuiusque rei non per se ipsam cognoscimus, sed per
ea quae de illa sensibus usurpamus."

more than a "verisimilitude," a "conjecture," "a glimpse from afar" or "a probability." This knowledge is such that Vives feels entitled to say that "the nature of the soul is basically unknown." [57] The Aristotelian essential definition through genus and species is only a theoretical and mostly inexpedient one, for the simple reason that "we have a very annoying shortage of specific differences." [58] Except for extremely rare cases, our knowledge of the specific is only a "close approximation." [59] The whole essay *De explanatione cuiusque essentiae* is a critical presentation of the Aristotelian notion of generic and specific knowledge: "To differentiate the categories is as difficult and unfeasible as it is to separate the things signified by them." [60]

In the second place Vives expressed serious doubts about the "first and necessary principles" according to which the Aristotelian demonstration is said to proceed:

The part in which Aristotle deals with the demonstration is extraordinarily complicated and confused, therefore useless in practice ... Tell me, Aristotle, are you thinking of us or of Nature itself? ... I do not understand according to Nature but according to myself. You do the same. We are human beings; our minds are weak and exposed to error; Nature has an infallible intelligence. How can I know what is first and immediate in Nature when I even ignore myself? [61]

The conclusion, therefore, is that:

---

[57] Vives uses the expressions "viam similutidinis" and "notiones finitimae et proximae." (M, III, 122; R, II, 1041). The very title *De instrumento probabilitatis* indicates that metaphysical knowledge in Vives' mind does not exceed a high probability. In *De anima* Vives declares: "Nihil est magis quam anima reconditum, magisque ad omnes obscurum et ignoratum." (M, 299; R, II, 1148 a).

[58] M, III, 123; R, II, 1042 a. "Quarum differentiarum nos ingenti laborare penuria merito Aristoteles est conquestus." (*De instrumento probabilitatis*).

[59] Vives admits that in most cases we do not reach the specific difference: "Si assequimur, bene habet; sin minus, consectamur, quantum possumus, propria." (M, III, 126; R, II, 1044 b, *De instrumento probabilitatis*).

[60] In spite of his critical attitude, Vives was sharply criticized by one of his own admirers, Nizolio, in the book *De Veris principiis et vera ratione philosophandi contra pseudo-philosophos*, ed. Q. Breen (Rome, 1956). Nizolio writes: "Oh Ludovicus, more silly than the rest of the philosophers ..." (p. 95). In other pages, however, Nizolio praises Vives with enthusiasm. Since Nizolio was carefully investigated by Leibnitz (see B. Tillman's book, *Leibnitz'z Verhältnis zur Renaissance im allgemeinen und zu Nizolius im besondern* [Bonn, 1912]) we can conclude that the German philosopher knew at least Vives' name.

[61] M, VI, 118; R, II, 431. "Quae vero de demonstratione, praeterquam quod sunt involuta et mire intrincata, nulli sunt usui ... Cedo, respicis nos et captum nostrum, an rerum naturam? ... Neque enim ego pro captu naturae intelligo – ac ne tu quidem – sed pro meo; nos sumus homines, id est, ingeniis errori obnoxiis et infirmis; natura habet intelligentiam non errantem. Qui scio ego quae sint prima, quae sine medio, quae necessaria naturae? Quae sint mihi talia vix scio ..." (*DD.*, I, 3, 3).

Your [Aristotle's] long dissertation about the demonstrative process is completely useless and a waste of time. If you, Aristotle, are speaking to men you will never reach a universal form of argumentation, because for some people some propositions are "immediate and necessary," while others are only persuaded by way of verisimilitude. Some, like the Academics, do not trust even the senses, others trust only the senses, like the Epicureans ... Your demonstration is like a Lesbian norm, which adapts itself to the building, not the building to the norm ...

You, Aristotle, require necessary principles, namely those which cannot be otherwise. How and where can we know them? The universals are known to us only through an inference from the individuals which are almost infinite; and if one individual remains unknown the universal itself vanishes.[62]

In this attack against the Aristotelian theory of syllogism Vives becomes sarcastic and bitter: "Are you making fun of us? You are like one of those doctors who prescribes a medicine made out of three ingredients: one to be found in China, the other in India, and the third in the nest of the Phoenix." [63]

Having read these and similar lines one finds it hard to believe the attempt of some scholars to classify Vives as a basically Aristotelian thinker without further qualifications. Even a man as conservative as Bonilla understood the implications of Vives' words: "With all these arguments, Vives seems to deny the very possibility of science as such, then this is what follows from the denial of the possibility of argumentation in the form given by Aristotle." [64] What is bewildering in the case of Bonilla is that, after having reached one of the most difficult points in the interpretation of Vives, he abandons it without further investigation. On the other hand it seems to me that it would be false to characterize Vives as a forerunner of Sánchez or Pierre Bayle, without further qualification. Scepticism is a radical attitude of mind, and Vives was not a radical. Scepticism is incompatible with Christianity, except on the basis of a total fideism, and Vives, the bitter opponent of Averroism, was desperately trying to find a natural basis for Religion. Although Vives candidly acknowledged the feebleness of human knowledge, he constantly reiter-

[62] *Ibid.* "Inanis est ergo tota de demonstratione traditio et sine usu ... Quod si homines doces, non erit tibi una et perpetua demonstratio; aliis enim alia sunt immediata et prima; alii verisimilibus tantum capiuntur; alii nec evidentissimis, et de quibus sensus testificantur, satis fidunt ut Academici; alii omnia credunt sensibus, ut Epicurei ... erit ergo demonstratio quasi Lesbia norma, quae se aedificio accomodat, non sibi aedificium ..."

[63] *Ibid.*, 119-432. "Quid agis? Ludis ne nos? ... Facis perinde ut qui ad morbum gravissimum et deploratum, medicinam promittunt confectam ex tribus, aut quatuor simplicibus, quorum unum est in India invenire, alterum apud Seres, tertium in Riphaeis montibus, quartum in nido Phoenicis ex cineribus prioris nascentis."

[64] Bonilla, *Luis Vives,* II, pp. 109 ff.

ated the optimistic contention that it is perfectly rational for a limited mind to operate on the basis of limited evidence. Without being a professional sceptic, Vives did certainly endure the pressing siege of anxious perplexity and insistent doubt which sets him apart from those medieval thinkers who in their *"tranquilla possessio"* wasted their time in excited disputes about unexciting questions. Vives was intelligent enough to feel the doubt, but wise enough not to succumb to it. His attitude was expressed by himself in a very intensive formulation. *"Qui nescit ignorare, ignorat scire."* (Whoever does not learn to ignore something, ignores how to learn anything).[65] Vives' way out from total scepticism was based upon exactly the same subtle, vicious circle as Descartes' meditations. Our knowledge has to be reliable, Vives says, because it has been given to us by an infinitely reliable God:

Because of original sin man lost his mastery over Nature; nevertheless, God did not deprive him of his final destiny. Therefore, God did not deny him the instruments which are needed to arrive at such an end, and left to him as much light as was required to find the path of happiness . . .

There was never a nation so ignorant nor an age so dark in which men ignored those moral principles which could lead them to eternal happiness . . .

We lost indeed our riches and the control over the world, but we kept the true and lasting possessions. God left in us as much power as was indispensable to maintain our life, although now with much pain, attention, and personal effort.[66]

The very weakness of our knowing faculties is a clear proof of the original fall of man. From this (dogmatic) fact Vives draws a basic conclusion. The fundamental ethical attitude in the search of truth is to accept those very limitations with Christian humility and modesty. The first book of his treatise *De disciplinis* is, as a whole, a severe condemnation of philosophical pride. The humble philosopher does not attempt to speculate on the mysteries of Nature: he merely observes Nature in order to draw a practical benefit for himself and his fellow-man. The

[65] M, IV, 63; R, I, 1203 a. (*Satellitium*, 209).
[66] M, III, 190; R, II, 1061. "In illo utique scelere dominatum amisit orbis, non tamen . . . penitus eum rejecit Deus a fine; idcirco nec instrumenta et veluti viaticum sustulit quo ad eum perveniret, tantumque ei reliquit luminis, quantum sat esset ad ingrediendum illa via, qua recta ad felicitatem duceret . . .; numquam enim fuit ulla vel tam stupida et socors natio, vel tam caeca aetas et caligine oppressa, in qua homines ignorarint illa, quorum scientia ad felicitatem eos perduxisset . . .; perdidimus ergo res et imperium, sed nobis vera bona divino beneficio . . . relicta sunt; ad cognitionem rerum naturae id reliquit facultatis, quo assequeremur quod vitae huic tuendae satis esset, sed labore tamen, cura, intentione magna animi . . ." (*De prima philosophia*, 1).

same modesty dictates to him the rule that he should be contented with high probability where better evidence is not available. After all, "All Philosophy is based entirely upon opinions and verisimile conjectures." [67] The occasional error of the senses is not reason enough "to deny them our trust, like the Academics did." The fact that our knowledge misses the essence of things "does not justify Protagoras' total relativism." [68] In a word: the humble philosopher accepts knowledge with its limitations because it is the only one which befits God's creatures. Of course, this solution is basically fideistic. An infinitely reliable God guarantees the knowledge of a limited creature who recognizes his total dependence on Him. The problem is to find a motivation for trust and humility in the very rational search for God Himself. To this problem Vives does not offer any solution. Less religiously-minded philosophers, like Hamilton, have also insisted on the demand for a humble acceptance of human limitations based more on factual self-knowledge than on a transcendental relationship to God.[69] Still, the basic decision to be contented with the available and (poor) evidence coincides with Vives' unconscious fideism in being a prephilosophical intellectual mood without any reasonable basis. Scepticism is also a choice of the same kind. According to Vives, it is not true that the sceptic is the only "wise fellow" who discovers the weakness of the evidence others are ready to swallow. In fact "there is nothing easier than to raise all kinds of questions even in the most transparent issues." [70] The difference between the sceptic and the prudent philosopher is that while the latter accepts the weakness of his own knowledge, the former rebels against it in a kind of personal vendetta against human limitations:

---

[67] M, VI, 417; R, II, 671 b. "Philosophia tota opinionibus et conjecturis verisimilitudinis est innixa." (DD., II, "De vita et moribus eruditi").

[68] In De prima philosophia Vives propounds the remedies to the "errors" of the senses: the error we make today is corrected tomorrow by another experience, or by the judgment of other people, or by our own judgment, which "supplements the senses." Vives insists that there are very few cases where the senses err "because of their own nature." (M, III, 194; R, II, 1064 b).

In the same place Vives overtly condemns Protagoras' relativism: "Nec sententiae accedimus Protagorae Abderitae qui talia esse dicebat qualia a quoque judicarentur . . ."

[69] According to R. Turnbull, in the introduction (p. xlviii) to the works of W. Hamilton (New York, 1855), the central idea of Hamilton's thought is precisely humility, not only as the cardinal virtue of revelation, but of reason. In fact, in his book Discussions on Philosophy and Literature, Hamilton collects testimonies of philosophers such as Petrarch, Scaliger, Grotius, Melanchthon, and Bacon, who emphasized the limitations of human knowledge.

[70] Vives develops these ideas in De disciplinis, part 1, book 1, chapter 3. (M, VI, 17-27; R, II, 350-358).

Some philosophers seek problems and objections even where there are none, to impress others with their sharpness and depth. This way they do not only dispossess the ignorant from their false opinions, but also the learned men from their true knowledge. There is nothing beyond doubt and controversy when it is submitted to an immoderate analysis. There are some thinkers who demand an evident proof for everything; these are the same who despise and scorn the effort of those who dare to try to convince them.[71]

In spite of this realistic and sober description of man's intellectual powers. Vives was far from being one of those die-hard sceptics who feel insulted by the very possibility that their doubts might be overcome.

c. The "Notiones Communes"

One of the most significant manifestations of intellectual modesty according to Vives is to accept the fact that the search for truth is not an individual effort but a cooperative undertaking, subject to the law of constant historical progress. In a typical Christian interpretation of fundamentally Stoic attitudes, Vives believes that the original fall of man has indeed impoverished each individual human reason, but has not silenced the voice of Nature as reflected in the common notions about which all men constantly agree. The importance of this doctrine calls for a closer analysis.

The reliance upon the "ἔννοιαι κοιναι" or "notiones communes" was widely spread among Renaissance Aristotelians. The main source of this essentially Stoic belief was the eclectic writings of Cicero. In his books De Officiis, De Finibus and, especially, the Quaestiones Tusculanae, Cicero tried to find in the "ratio naturalis" or "lumen naturale," first, a solid foundation to the ethical order, and second, a universally accepted criterion for the "perspicientia veri." [72]

The predominantly ethical approach of Cicero was extended to the domain of scientific knowledge by the powerful influence of Galen upon the humanists of the sixteenth century. The fact that, according to Galen,

---

[71] M, VI, 23-24; R, II, 355-356. "Philosophi ... scrupulos, ubi nulli sunt, quaerunt ... qui videantur altius rimari et subtilius omnia examinare; nec solum ignaris inviderunt suam peritiam, sed ejusdem artis studiosis ac peritis. Fuere qui quo magis premant alios, ... eorum quae dicunt rationem in omnibus evidentem postulent ...; quasi vero id ubique praestari possit, aut ulla sit res, quae controversa non queat reddi nimium inquirendo, non veritatis vitio, sed nostrorum ingeniorum ... Admonitioni cuicumque ferocem se superbus praebet ... quem ergo errorem ipse utcumque mutaret abs se deprehensum, si alius indicet magis infigitur et pertinacius ..." (DD., I, 1, 3).

[72] Dilthey, Weltanschauung und Analyse, pp. 175 ff., emphasizes the importance of Cicero's teaching in the revival of Stoicism during the sixteenth century.

the Geometrical axioms were called ἔμφῦτοι by Euclides reinforced the wider interpretation of this doctrine.[73] Dilthey has made a careful study of the importance of the *"communes notiones"* in the intellectual work of Melanchthon. In particular, he pointed out the kinship between this Stoic-Ciceronian belief in the common notions and the Christian faith in a *"lumen naturale."* In this basic approach Vives agreed entirely with the German Humanist.[74] Vives, however, insists upon the fact that, after the original sin, such light has been preserved by God as a minimal guaranty for the intellectual guidance of man:

> We will accept as true whatever is recognized as such by the totality of mankind because, even after the original fall of man, God left in our minds as much light as is needed for our pilgrimage... As Nature gave to the animals stimuli and instincts which preserve them from harm, in the same way God impressed into human minds those notions which are needed for their life... What can be more certain than what men is forced to believe with an instinctive and natural impulse? [75]

This *"lumen naturale"* is, first of all, a solid and firm moral sense which "sometimes directly, other times indirectly, leads us always to the good, the true, the approval of virtue and the rejection of vice." [76] With Saint Jerome, Vives is inclined to identify this natural light with the Christian notion of "moral conscience." [77] Together with this natural moral sense, God has given to man "an innate aptitude and inclination toward the True," where in some way, all the seeds of science are included: "As the soil contains a certain power to produce plants of all kinds, our soul holds the seed of all arts and disciplines together with a most simple and spontaneous inclination toward them... exactly the

---

[73] See Gilbert, *Renaissance Concepts of Method*, pp. 11-13, 102-105.

[74] The verbal expressions of both Humanists is in many cases strikingly similar. Melanchthon was five years younger than Vives, but he lived much longer (he died at the age of 63, in 1560). Twice Vives praises the work of the German Humanist. The name of Vives, on the other hand, is never mentioned by Melanchthon. As far as I know there is no evidence whatsoever of any personal and direct relationship between the two men, although, in many respects, their thought runs very close to each other.

[75] M, VIII, 25-26; R, II, 1345. "Deus in humanos animos de sua luce lucem derivavit, etiamque post naturae casum, tantum reliqui fecit nobis, quantum... in via nos profecto sistere salutis... Nam quemadmodum multis animantibus concessi sunt a natura stimuli quidam instinctusque quibus ad utilia impellantur... ita in hominum mentibus inditas atque informatas esse notiones credibile est, quibus ad ea quae sibi profutura sint, adducantur... Quid ergo dici potest probabilius quam esse hominibus naturale, quo nutu suo omnes homines ferantur?" (*De VFC.*, 1, 4).

[76] M, III, 356; R, II, 1194 a. "Haec mentis nostrae lux, sive censura, qua recte, qua oblique, semper tamen ad verum et bonum devergit..." (*De anima*, II, 4).

[77] *Ibid.*, 357; 1194 b.

same way the eyes seek the refreshing greenery and the ears a beautiful melody." [78] Unlike Melanchthon, Vives remains here extremely vague and obscure. One has the distinct impression that Vives does not have in mind particular truths or principles, but rather a general sympathy and inclination toward basic and fundamental ideas of both the moral and the theoretical level. Another difference between Vives and Melanchthon is that our Humanist tries very hard to convey the impression that the belief in common notions has been a constant teaching of every philosophical school. The Aristotelian δύναμις, the Stoic κατάληψις, and even the Neo-Platonic "ἀνάμνησις" are one and the same thing in Vives' eclectic interpretation:

> The human mind, which is the faculty of Truth, has a certain sympathy with those primordial truths from whence, as from a seed, the others proceed. This sympathy is called "anticipatio" or "information," by the Greeks κατάληψις. This is the source of Plato's opinion that we do not learn but remember . . . This happens, though, only in the same way that the eyes have the colors before the foetus is born: they have only the potency, not the act. [79]

Vives propounded this theory with such conviction that among the representatives of the Scottish School he was considered one of the forerunners of "common sense" Philosophy. [80]

Besides the reliance upon the common notions approved by a universal consent, individual reason has to depend "on the testimony of the best, the most talented." In this point Vives is simply a reflection of the general trend among humanists to widen the knowledge of all the Schools of Greek and Roman thought beyond the limits of a narrow Aristotelism. [81]

It is easy to see that from this fundamental conception of Philosophy as a progressive and collective human effort in the search of Truth, Vives' radical eclecticism follows as a natural conclusion.

Eclectic philosophers have never been too fortunate in world opinion.

---

[78] M, VI, 250-251; R, II, 532 b. "Quemadmodum vis quaedam indita est terrae ad producendas herbas omnis generis, ita animae nostrae velut potestate quadam omnium artium ac disciplinarum sunt indita semina et ad prima illa ac simplicissima pronitas quaedam quo nutu suo fertur . . . quemadmodum acies oculorum ad viride, et auris ad concentus . . ." (*DD.*, II, 12).

[79] *Ibid.*, III, 82; II, 979. "Mens humana . . . naturalem quandam habet cognationem . . . cum veris illis primis et tamquam seminibus unde reliqua vera nascuntur, quae 'anticipationes' atque 'informationes' nominantur, a Graecis καταλῆψεις: hinc Platonis orta est opinio recordari nos, non addiscere . . . sed profecto non magis quam habent oculi notitias colorum, priusquam ex matris utero in hanc lucem prodeant: potestas ea est ad ista, non actus." (*De instrumento probabilitatis*).

[80] See below, pp. 282-283.

[81] See Garin, *La Cultura filosofica*, pp. 72-87.

Their eclecticism is often attributed to lack of originality or even to some
hidden streak of mental laziness. The eclectic does not coin a new philosophical language, does not raise a new philosophical flag, does not preach
the Gospel of a *Magna Instauratio*. The fact that most of them were
great pedagogues – like Hamilton or Victor Cousin – has strengthened
the opinion that they are more gifted in summarizing, in criticizing, and
in teaching what others have created, than in bringing forth their own
creations. Maybe there is some truth in these censures. However, it takes
indeed a certain courage to give up the glamour of originality for the sake
of an unbiased and generous understanding of the achievements of others.
Vives' eclecticism is deeply based on the solid, optimistic view that every
human effort contains a bright aspect from which all can learn. All his
life was dedicated to a fight against narrow sectarianism. Vives was even
afraid that someday he himself would have some disciples:

> Speaking about myself I must say that I would hate to see somebody fol-
> lowing me. I refuse to be the founder of a sect or its preacher. If you agree
> with some of my advice, follow them, not because they are mine, but because
> they are true. Leave me with my Judge to Whom alone I will give an ac-
> count of my conscience... Aristotle demanded recognition for his dis-
> coveries; I will be pleased with obtaining forgiveness for my omissions. No
> art was found and perfected at the same time.[82]

In his little symbolical essay *Veritas Fucata*, Vives presents a gathering
of "Lady Truth" with her lovers. After long discussions with poets,
orators, and politicians, Lady Truth, finally, calls upon the philosophers.
But they also

> were unable to speak, because of the deafening scream of the adversaries; as
> soon as any in particular would dare to say something, the representatives
> of other schools, without any consideration for Lady Truth, would start
> yelling against him. Every one prefers to see Truth not praised at all, than
> to see it praised by the philosophers of other schools.[83]

---

[82] M, VI, 7; R, II, 342. "Ut de me uno loquar, nolim quemquam se mihi addicere;
nec auctor umquam sectae, nec suasor ero, etiamsi in mea verba jurandum sit; si
quid vobis, o amici, recte videbor admonere, tuemini illud quia verum, non quia
meum... Me vero... relinquite meo Judici, cui uni conscientia mea satisfactura
est... Quemadmodum Aristoteles pro inventis a se reposcebat gratiam... ita ego
voluntatem meam oro consulatis boni, erratis autem... ignoscatis." (*DD.*, preface).
[83] M, II, 520; R, I, 885 b. "Accersiti philosophi, sed nullus potuit dicere prae
strepitu immodestissimo inimicorum; nam, ut quisquis coeperat aliquid praefari,
continuo a reliquis omnibus nationibus reclamabatur, nullo respectu dominae Veritatis... mallebantque vel non laudari Veritatem, quam ab homine laudari diversae
factionis." (*Veritas fucata*).

It was Vives' fate to live in an age when Christian unity split into sects, when Europe was divided by national frontiers, and when human thought became atomized in a bewildering individualism. His glory was to lead without pretense and to learn from man's disputes without joining the screaming crowds.

CHAPTER 12

THE PROCESS OF KNOWLEDGE

"Philosophia tota . . . conjecturis est innixa"
From *De Disciplinis*

The exceptional importance of Vives' treatise *De Anima et vita* lies in the paradoxical fact that its content has little to do with the title of the book.[1] *De Anima* does not say much about the soul itself, the nature of which it professes to ignore: "It is not important for us to know what he soul is, but it is essential to know which are its operations." [2] We are even unable to know the operations themselves "and to define them in an absolute way"; [3] Vives' real concern is to investigate "how these operations are conducive to the reform of our morals." [4]

Vives' *De Anima* is not a scholastic treatise on *psychologia rationalis*. Those who have interpreted it this way have completely falsified the thinking of Vives. Naturally it is possible to trace much of Vives' terminology back to Aristotle and to Saint Thomas, as Monsegú has done rather superficially, and Hoppe and Daly have done with more patient research.[5] Still it is possible to expurgate from the book any passing reference to such metaphysical notions as *forma substantialis, facultates,*

---

[1] In the sixteenth century, editors and publishers were normally one and the same person, frequently business-minded intellectuals like Froben or Estienne. The editor had full authorization to change at his will the titles of books and chapters, to make them more sensational and attractive. This is the reason why so many of those titles sound today ridiculously conceited. In his correspondence with Cranevelt, Vives complains about his bad luck in this respect: "I am the victim of Fate; my books always display titles which do not recommend them to my friends and invite the hatred of my enemies and the contempt of those who do not know me."

[2] M, III, 332; R, II, 1175 a. "Anima quid sit, nihil interest nostra scire. Qualis autem et quae eius opera, permultum." (*De Anima*, I, 12)

[3] *Ibid.,* "Neque de iis ipsis operationibus potest semel in totum definiri."

[4] *Ibid.,* ". . . de actionibus ad compositionem morum, ut vitio expulso, virtutem sequamur."

[5] Monsegú, *Filosofía del humanismo,* pp. 115-137, 187-229.

habitus, and their like, without any harm to it. The emphasis, the originality of this book, its significance in the history of thought, is that Vives,
instead of working with "metaphysical trappings and bagatelles," observed and described the mechanism of human actions from its inception
in sense knowledge to its completion in the decisions of the will. Vives
wanted to observe man, to know him better, and to educate him. In the
book's dedication to the Duke of Béjar, Vives wrote:

> The soul is the spring of all our blessings as well as the source of all our
> evils. We must, therefore, know our soul as deeply as possible; then by puri-
> fying the fountainhead we can secure a constant flow of clean and pure
> operations. Without self-knowledge man cannot learn to govern himself.[6]

The observation of man's operational process was the cornerstone of
Vives' educational and moral reform. This return to the intimacy of man,
initiated by Petrach in the fourteenth century, was humanism's greatest
contribution to the history of European thought .Without it, one cannot
understand the literature of that age nor the stream of psychological introspection which goes from Montaigne and Grotius to Pascal and Spinoza.

When I say that in this book Vives relied upon his own observations
and introspection, I do not mean that he followed this empirical method
in a consistent way. On the contrary, observation and metaphysical con-
struction are used in confusing comradeship. While some pages are rich
in inductive generalizations, others are abbreviated summaries of Thomistic conceptions. Nor is there a total consistency of thought. Vives'
eclecticism led him to make assertions which sometimes do not seem to fit
well together. Finally, the reader is often disappointed by the vagueness
and obscurity concerning issues which today seem to us of primary importance. Such is, for instance, the decision about the possibility and extent of metaphysical knowledge, or the possibility of an intellectual intuition. Frequently Vives gave the impression that he was not able to think
his way through a problem, or that he gave up his effort at the most critical moment. His strength was in the brilliant passing glimpse, not the
insistent and relentless method of investigation.

[6] M, III, 298; R, II, 1147. "Illic fons est atque origo bonorum omnium nostrorum,
et malorum, nihil est conducibilius, quam probe nosci, ut purgato fonte, puri di-
manent rivuli omnium actionum; neque enim poterit animum gobernare ... qui se
non explorarit." (*De Anima,* preface)

a. Vegetative and Sense Operations

The first two chapters of the first part are dedicated to the vegetative acts of man: nutrition, growth, and reproduction. The content is basically derived from the study of these operations in the first book of Aristotle's *De Anima,* and basically coincides with the typical views exposed in any medieval treatment of the subject. Life is explained in terms of the effect of heat and humidity upon the four elements, fire, air, water, and earth. Thirst is a want of humidity, and hunger an exigency of heat.[7] Digestion is a reduction of humidity by a constant process of concoction, the products of which leak through "a multitude of pores which punctuate our bodies." [8] An increase in humidity and a decrease in heat accounts for the fect "that fish is larger than earthly animals, and these again larger than birds; for the same reason, Northern people are more corpulent than the Southerners." [9] Even the sexes are determined by a different proportion of heat and humidity, the male having more heat than humidity and the female the other way around. In fact, females are nothing else but "imperfect males with a lack of proportioned heat." [10] Rats can be born through sexual intercourse or "from garbage by spontaneous generation"; birth defects among Dutch children are explained by an "excess of beer and cabbage" in the diet of pregnant women; wheat grows naturally in Sicily without any sowing.[11] These and similar examples strike a sharp contrast indeed with the modernity of Vives' philosophical thought.

Chapters Three to Eleven deal with the senses, both internal and external. The difference between the two is that while the outer senses are purely passive receptors of the stimuli reaching the subject through a medium from an external object actually present, the internal senses never need a present object and, sometimes at least, are active. "Our outer senses are disposed by God to be like receptacles of whatever happens in the outside world. They receive, but they do not project anything." [12] The passivity of the outer senses is proved by the concave shape of the sense organs. Such a passivity has to be understood as the complete de-

---

[7] *Ibid.,* 301; 1150 b.

[8] *Ibid.,* 305; 1152 b. "Universum animantis corpus meatibus est quasi perforatum."

[9] *Ibid.,* 307; 1155 a. "Humor enim auget corpora, eoque majores sunt marinae beluae quam terrestres, et hae quam volucres, et in locis humidis ampliores homines quam in arentibus" (*De Anima,* I, 1).

[10] *Ibid.,* 310; 1157 b. "Nihil enim aliud est femina quam mas imperfectum, nempe cui non justa fuit caloris mensura." (*De Anima,* I, 2)

[11] *Ibid.,* 308-311; 1156-1158.

[12] *Ibid.,* 323; 1166 b. "Sensus nostri omnes ita sunt a Deo compositi instructique, ut ceu receptacula essent eorum, quae foris inciderent, hauriunt enim illi manifesto extrinsecus, non emittunt." (*De Anima,* I, 9)

pendence of sensation upon the impact of an external object. Naturally Vives does not mean to say that our senses do not react to such external impulse. The inner senses, on the other hand, are not "reactions" in the proper sense of the word, but immanent operations of the self. What Vives said about the "stimuli" should not be confused with the metaphysical question about the *species impressae,* a discussion he dismissed as both too controversial and of little use.[13] As for the "medium," Vives assigned light to vision, air to audition, and the flesh of the body to the sense of touch. Typical of his careless style was the omission of the medium to be allocated to the olfactory sense.[14]

Vives' study of the outer senses is a puzzling mixture of old and new conceptions. Under the disguise of traditional terminology the book suggests a corpuscular theory of sensation, especially in the case of audition and vision. Vives imagined the operation of sight as a pyramid, the base of which is the object itself, while the cone "touches" the pupil of the eye.[15] Sound was for him "the clash between the bodies which push the air into the ear propagated in the same way as the circles formed on the water when we throw a stone." [16] The basic assumption is that "always something proceeds from the sensible object to the organ of sensation." [17] This "something" has, therefore, to cover a certain distance. The relation between the impulse of the stimulus and the distance it must travel in the medium is of extreme importance in the study of outer sensation. Distant objects, for example, affect the eye in peculiar ways, "because light has to cover almost instantly enormous distances." [18] Together with this revolutionary updating of Democritus' conceptions, Vives presented Aristotelian theories well established in medieval traditions. Such is the correspondence between the five senses and the four elements, hearing and smelling sharing one common element, the air. Vives also made frequent use of Galen's physiology of "temperaments" – combination of the four

---

[13] *Ibid.* "Dubitatum est, anne species aliquae a rebus venirent ad sensoria: Quaestio non tam necessaria, quam rixosa, ideoque circulis scholarum, et loquacitate contentionum mire plausibilis."

[14] *Ibid.,* 322; 1165.

[15] *Ibid.,* 314; 1160. "Princeps visile ... est lux; et quae videntur reliqua ... nempe radiatione in formam pyramidis, cuius basis est quod spectatur, conus autem attingit pupulam." (*De Anima,* I, 4)

[16] *Ibid.,* 315; 1161. "Sonus ... gignitur ex plaga duorum corporum, qua aer pellitur usque ad aurem ...; nec aliter in aere fit sonitus quam orbes illi in aqua jacto in eam lapide." (*De Anima,* I, 5)

[17] *Ibid.,* 323; 1168 a. "Venire aliquid ex sensibilibus ad sensoria manifestissimum" (*De Anima,* I, 9).

[18] *Ibid.,* 324; 1169. "Dictu quidem mirabile, venire aliquid a corpore ad oculum tanta celeritate, ut momento temporis videatur longissima spatia penetrare." (*De Anima,* I, 9)

elements, their qualities ("humors") – blood, phlegm, black and yellow bile, and the natural, vital, and animal "appetites." As a whole, however, these chapters on the outer senses are neither original nor constructive. Vives seemed to be relatively uninterested in the subject: "the outer senses cannot be educated, being as they are the products of nature." [19] On the other hand, since they are "the gates of our knowledge," the educator will be primarily concerned with providing the sense organs with the right environment and a rich experience of the world. We have insisted upon this point in our chapter on education.

The inner senses are much more important from Vives' point of view because, being as they are under the partial control of man's free will, their exercise almost always involves a moral choice. Besides, they are in a much closer relationship with the intellectual process itself. Vives' study of the inner senses displays a wealth of observations concerning the direction and the possible deviations of our mental operations. Vives, the moral pedagogue, was "unique in his powerful description of states of the soul; he seeks their chronological and causal relationship to win a total picture of their structural interconnection" (Dilthey).[20]

Vives distinguished four "functions" of the inner senses: the function of receiving the sense images (imagination), the function of retaining them (memory), the function of combining them (fantasy), and finally, the function of assessing them (estimative).

If we compare this scheme with the traditionally Thomistic scheme, we notice some significant differences. First of all, as Vives cautioned, one should not lay too much stress upon the name "functions." Vives was somehow reluctant to use the word "faculty" (although he used it sometimes) because of its association with a scholastic metaphysical speculation which he disavows. In the introduction to this book Vives openly declared his intention to avoid in as much as possible any philosophical jargon.[21] At the beginning of the second part, dealing with the "faculties" of the soul – memory, intelligence, and will – Vives wrote:

Thus the human soul is provided with three functions or faculties or powers or, as others say, potencies and parts. We should keep in mind, however, that what is indivisible has no parts at all . . . It is very hard to investigate the operations of those faculties. God wanted us to use those powers, not to speculate about them; we are only simple workers who utilize the in-

[19] *Ibid.*, III, 321; II, 1166. (*De Anima,* I, 9)
[20] "Die Funktion der Anthropologie," p. 429.
[21] M, III, 299; R, II, 1148 b. (*De Anima,* preface)

struments. Nevertheless, it is a most beautiful occupation to study the operations and power of our intelligence for the control and discipline of our spirit.[22]

In the second place, Vives reduced the *sensus communis* of Saint Thomas to a combination of imagination and fantasy. This reduction is not a very fortunate one, and reveals Vives' lack of interest in the purely epistemological problem of how to account for the wholeness of perceptual phenomena.[23] Finally, Vives placed great emphasis upon the distinction between imagination and fantasy, a distinction generally neglected by the Scholastics. "I am well aware that many writers confuse imagination and fantasy, and that they use those names without any distinction." [24] Vives was concerned with the extraordinary creative power of human fantasy: "Fantasy is prodigiously unrestrained and free; it can form, reform, combine, link together and separate; it can blend together the most distant objects or keep apart the most intimately associated objects." [25]

It is not difficult to realize that Vives has reached here the first source of disorder within man: "If the fantasy is not controlled by reason, it can agitate and toss the soul like a storm beating the ocean." [26] Unfortunately, Vives never made a detailed study of the unpredictable ways of human fantasy, although he made some significant remarks on the subject. On the interaction between fantasy and memory Vives wrote: "Those things which the fantasy has joined together are bound to be remembered together." [27] As we indicated before, Vives was equally impressed by the impact of our fantasy upon man's emotional life. On several occasions Vives warned against the interference of an unbridled fantasy with the

[22] *Ibid.,* 341; 1182. "Ita hominis anima ... ex tribus constat praecipuis, sive functionibus, sive facultatibus, sive viribus, sive mumeribus, ac officiis, sive (ut alii appellant) potentiis ac partibus, non quod partes habeat quod est insectile, sed partes pro officio et munere usurpamus ... Quae sint harum facultatum actiones ... perscrutari longe arduissimum ...; Deus quoque facultates has nobis magis concessit ad usum nostrum quam ad notitiam earum ...; sed pulcherrimum tamen est (qui de re pulcherrima, ac praestantissima, adque animum componendum in primis conducibile) quae sit mentis nostrae qualitas ... perscrutari ..." (*De Anima,* II, preface)

[23] Vives deals very perfunctorily with the "sensus communis." (M, VII, 327; R, II, 1171 b., *De Anima,* I, 10). Scholastic philosophy, on the other hand, gives a great deal of attention to this problem. See, e.g., R. E. Brennan, *Thomistic Psychology,* (New York, 1963), pp. 120-126.

[24] M, III, 327; R, II, 1170 b. "Equidem haud sum nescius, confundi duo haec a plerisque." (*De Anima,* I, 10)

[25] *Ibid.,* "Phantasia est mirifice expedita et libera: quicquid collibitum est fingit, refingit, componit, devincit, dissolvit, res disjunctissimas connectit, conjunctissimas autem longissime separat."

[26] *Ibid.,* "Itaque nisi regatur et cohibeatur a ratione, haud secus animum percellit ac perturbat quam procella mare."

[27] See below, p. 261.

delicate process of reasoning and the final act of judgment. For these reasons Vives strongly recommended the training of the child's fantasy as one of the most important aspects of education. Vives' severity in regard to the world of literary fiction also revealed his fundamental distrust of the erratic powers of human fantasy.

After fantasy, Vives dealt with memory, in one of the most interesting sections of the book. Besides the physiological considerations about the location of the memory in the back of the neck, and the influence of the different "humors" on the power to retain images of the past – considerations which Hoppe has shown to be almost literally taken from Galen – the rest of the chapter is exclusively based on original observations.[28]

Most important is the study of the different kinds of memory. Some people retain words, others retain facts. For some it is easier to remember the extraordinary, for others the little details of daily routine. Old events stick in the memory of some people, while others can only remember the very recent ones. It is easier to "recognize" than to "recollect": "many people understand a foreign language much better than they can speak it." Some people memorize quickly but do not retain long; although, as a rule, they are able to refresh their memory in a very short time.[29]

Vives' originality consists in having applied these distinctions to his pedagogical program. A professional orientation based upon personal characteristics and natural aptitudes is, as we have already pointed out, one of the striking innovations of Vives' pedagogy.

The philosophical background of these educational guidelines is the Humanistic conviction that man himself, his "attitude," is decisive in the rational search for truth. Memory is an integral part of that "attitude," because as "the armory of man" it exerts its influence through the selective recollection of past experiences, educational environment, individual and social circumstances, intellectual and passional episodes. The working of the memory, its "mechanism," is, therefore, of great importance in education. Vives conventrated his effort upon the study of the rules which memory follows. He observed the relation between memory and physical health; the importance of attention and the paradoxical effects of passional commotion; the possibility of strengthening the memory with exercise, order, and method; the different kinds of oblivion; the laws

---

[28] G. Hoppe, *Die Psychologie des J. L. Vives*, p. 51, has stressed the originality of Vives' study of memory by comparing his work with that of Melanchthon, who in 1540 published a treatise entitled also *De Anima*. In spite of Melanchthon's lack of fresh ideas, his book was published thirteen times between 1540 and 1590. On Melanchthon's ideas on memory, see Hartfelder, *Melanchthon*, pp. 240-242.

[29] *De Anima*, book 2, chapter 2, "De memoria et recordatione" (M, II, 345-352; R, II, 1185-1191).

of association, and their practical application to the art of mnemotechny; false associations and their source; the special quality of childhood recollections; and the importance of reflection.[30]

Vives enriched this old Aristotelian doctrine of memory-association with a wealth of new and significant observations. For example, on the circuitous path followed by memory in the process of remembering:

From the ring to the craftsman, from the craftsman to the necklace of a Queen, from the Queen to the war her husband waged, from the war to the generals, from those to their ancestors and children, from the children to the studies they made, and so without end. This process follows many different connections: from the cause to the effect; from the effect to the instrument; from the part to the whole; from the whole to the part; from the location to the person; from the person to his ancestors, his descendants; and in general from anything to similar and contraries in endless combinations.[31]

With marvelous introspection Vives observed the importance of the emotions in the direction of the process:

In this process of remembering it frequently happens that the lesser thing reminds us of the better one, but not the contrary. Here in Bruges there is a mansion not far from the Royal Palace where my friend Idiaquez used to live and where we spent together hours of most pleasant conversation. Every time I see this house the memory of Idiaquez comes vividly to my mind. However, when I think of Idiaquez I do not always remember his house.[32]

These examples of Vives' style in this book are sufficient to indicate, I think, that its scholastic scheme and appearance are nothing more than a "scaffold" used by the author. Unfortunately, Vives never attempted to systematize these suggestions into a body of doctrine.

The third and last inner sense considered by Vives was the *vis aestimativa*, which roughly corresponds to the προαίρεσις of Aristotle and to the "instinctive prudence" of Saint Thomas.[33] Although Vives did not dedicate more than passing remarks to it, he insisted upon the function of the

[30] *Ibid.,* 350-352; 1187-1191 a.

[31] *Ibid.,* 349; 1188 b. "... ab annulo in aurifabrum, ex hoc in monile reginae, hinc in bellum quo gessit vir eius, a bello in duces, a ducibus ad eorum progenitores aut liberos, hinc ad disciplinas quibus studebant, in quo nulla est ad sistendum meta; ... a causa ad effectum, ab hoc ad instrumentum, a parte ad totum, ab isto ad locum, ab hoc ad personam, a persona ad priora eius, et posteriora, similia, ad contraria, in quo discursu non est finis." (*De Anima,* II, 2)

[32] *Ibid.,* 350; 1189 b. "Illud usu evenit... ut ex re minore veniat nobis de majore...; ut quoties aspicio domum quae Brussellae est e conspectu regiae, venit mihi in mentem Idiaquaeus, cuius illud erat hospitium... non tamen quotiescunque Idiaquaeus observatur animo, de aedibus illis cogito..."

[33] See *Ethica Nichomachea,* 1141 a; Saint Thomas, *Summa Theologica,* p. 1, q. 88, art. 1.

estimative power which is, according to him, to direct the senses toward
the conservation of the self. The very defintion of this "faculty," which
"starting with the sensations produces the act of judgment," means that
already at the sensitive level man is equipped with an ability to recognize
biological values immediately related to the integrity of the species and
the individual. This sensitive differentiation of the useful and the harmful
is an integral part of the total dynamics of human action, and has, therefore, an important part in the final judgment which precedes the free
choice of the will.[34]

b. Intellectual Process

After consideration of the senses, Vives turned his attention to intellectual knowledge. The scholastic apparatus of this part becomes so insignificant that it can simply be left out of consideration. Vives did not
waste a single line on any of the controversial issues of scholastic metaphysics: the distinction between the agent and the possible intellect, the
conversion to the phantasm, the mediatory quality of the intelligible
species, etc. On the contrary, the approach here was entirely original and
personal. Vives' solution was somewhat complicated and incomplete, but
rich in suggestive observations.

As sensitive knowledge has been given to man for the sake of self-conservation, intellectual knowledge has been given to him as a guide to his
supreme faculty, a free but blind will. "Since man was created for eternal
happiness, God gave him the power to desire his own good . . . But man
cannot desire without knowledge. Hence the existence of another faculty
which is called intelligence." [35] And a little further on: "All knowledge
has been given for the sake of desiring what is good; sensitive knowledge
for the sake of sensible good, intellectual knowledge for the sake of the
good which is itself intelligible." [36] This does not mean that Vives entirely
rejected the speculative side of human intelligence. In fact, he clearly
distinguished between the speculative reason, the end of which is the

---

[34] Vives' insistence upon the instinct of self-conservation as an integral part of man's
internal mechanism was incorporated into Telesio's philosophy, and through Telesio,
it had an indirect but significant role in the formation of Hobbes' thought. See
Dilthey, *Weltanschauung und Analyse,* p. 428.

[35] M, III, 341; R, II, 1182 a. "Homini, quod ad sempiternum illud bonum sit
conditus, facultas est tributa expetendi, ut bono se cupiat applicare et adjungere,
quae facultas, voluntas nominatur; non expetet autem, nisi intelligat, unde altera
existit facultas, quae intelligentia nominatur." (*De Anima,* II, preface)

[36] *Ibid.,* 382; II, 1214 a. "Cognitio omnis propter bonum expetendum est tributa,
sensualis propter sensuale, mentalis propter mentale." (*De Anima,* II, 11)

True, and the practical reason oriented toward the Good.[37] Furthermore, Vives acknowledged that the theoretical contemplation of Truth in itself through the reflective activity of the mind, produces a natural delight: "This enjoyment is born form the congruity between the object and its faculty, because there is nothing more fitting to our intelligence than Truth." [38] Nevertheless, there is no doubt that the emphasis lies with practical reason which enables man to subdue Nature with the arts, and to reach moral perfection in his free choices.[39]

Vives divided the intellectual process into three different steps. Some of the problems connected with Vives' theory of knowledge proceed from this unwarranted hypostatization of the different aspects of our cognitive activity. Vives called the first step *simplex intelligentia,* "simple intelligence." Vives described it as "the first and simple reception of those things which are offered to our mind," and it relates to the whole of intellectual knowledge in the same way sight relates to sensitive knowledge.[40]

Although Vives remained hopelessly vague, it seems that the simple intelligence is only an intellectual apprehension of the singular as it is presented in the actual sensation, or as it is recollected from the images stored in the memory through an act of "reflection." The first group is called by Vives the *sensibilia,* while the second is called the *fantastica.*[41]

The important point here is that Vives abandoned the Thomistic conception according to which the *intellectus agens* apprehends the universal form in the singular by abstracting it from the *materia signata quantitate.*[42] Intellectual knowledge according to Vives does not begin with a preliminary abstraction (a term which Vives practically ignores), but with an intellectual grasping of the individual and singular. In this re-

---

[37] M, III, 355; R, II, 1193 a. "Duplex existit decursus, ratio speculativa cuius finis est veritas, et ratio practica, cius bonum." (*De Anima,* II, 4)

Menéndez y Pelayo (*Ensayos de crítica filosófica,* "De los orígenes del criticismo y del escepticismo," p. 175) lays a great significance upon this distinction, and sees in these pages of Vives the dawn of Kant's philosophy. Actually, the distinction is as old as scholastic philosophy itself. See, e.g., *Summa Theologica,* p. 1. q. 79, art. 11.

[38] M, III, 381, R, II, 1213 b. "Delectatio omnis nascitur ex proportione quadam congruentiaque objecti cum facultate, nihilque est menti congruentius quam veritas." (*De Anima,* II, 10)

[39] See below, pp. 283-287.

[40] M, VI, 343; R, II, 1183 b. "Est prima et simplex apprehensio eorum, quae menti proponuntur, nec aliter se habet in mente, quam oculus in corpore." (*De Anima,* II, 1)

[41] Vives uses the term "reflectio" in a double sense: first, as synonymous with theoretical contemplation; second, as the act of recollection.

For the distinction between "sensibilia" et "phantastica," see M, III, 194-195; R, II, 1065 a-b. (*De prima philosophia,* I)

[42] *Summa Theologica,* p. 1, q. 75, arts. 2, 5; q. 76, art. 1; q. 78, arts. 1-6; q. 85, arts. 1, 2. *Summa contra gentiles,* II, cc. 59-78.

(M, III, 197; R, II, 1067 b – 1068 a.).

spect Vives belongs to a secondary scholastic tradition which goes from Scotus to Suárez, and which is, not only incompatible with a rigid Thomism, but is also more Stoic than Aristotelian.

The problematic part of this solution is the explanation of the content of such an intellectual grasping of the singular. Vives insisted that the simple intelligence of the individual is nothing else than the intellectual knowledge of the "sensible appearance of the singular." He also drew a very clear distinction between this *sensibilis aspectus* and what lies beyond and underneath it, namely the *sensatum*.[43] The latter is described as "something internal" or "latent power" which is "veiled and concealed" and completely "inaccessible to the senses." [44]

Hause, Bonilla, and Menéndez y Pelayo have discovered in these texts a hint of "premature Kantian Philosophy." [45] In my opinion, there is no justification for such a suggestion, for the simple reason that Vives' concern in these and similar lines has nothing to do with the distinction between the phenomenon and the noumenon, but rather with the distinction between accident and substance. In fact these pages force me to think more of Locke than of Kant.

There is only one passage which could be interpreted in a more Kantian sense, but, strangely enough, none of the above mentioned scholars has paid any attention to it. In *De instrumento probabilitatis* Vives wrote: "As our intelligence is born from the sensations, thus the knowledge of the essence, which is intellectual, is born from the knowledge of the accidents, which is sensible." And then Vives added the following mysterious remark: "This happens not only in the knowledge of the essence of the substance, but also in the knowledge of the essence of the accidents themselves." [46] Although this remark can be understood as a rather contorted way of saying that the knowledge of an accident is not the accident itself – a statement which the most realistic philosopher could approve – it can also be interpreted as implying that man does not even know the accidents themselves but only their subjective appearance. In spite of this passing and isolated remark, however, I am convinced that Vives was concerned with the old philosophical problem between em-

[43] See *De prima philosophia*, I (M, III, 197; R, II, 1067 b – 1068 a.).
[44] *Ibid.* "Id quod sensili est tectum et quasi convestitum, quod appellemus sane sensatum ... in eo est sensile, et moles illa exterior, quam sensile operit, tum quiddam intimum esse necesse est, quod nec oculis, nec ulli sensui est pervium."
[45] P. Hause, *Die Psychologie des J. L. Vives*, pp. 17-19. Bonilla, *Luis Vives*, II, 23; III, 98, note 11.
[46] M, III, 122; R, II, 1041 b. See also M, III, 192; R, 1065 (*De prima philosophia*).

piricism and rationalism, namely, whether man is endowed with a power superior to the senses through which he transcends sense knowledge.

The answer to this problem cannot be found in the simple intelligence. Like the Stoics before him, Vives simply did not find words to express the difference, if any, between a sensation and the "simple intelligence of the individual sensible appearance." If there is a positive answer, it will be found in the second stage of human knowledge, the reasoning process. Perhaps man reaches through demonstration what he cannot reach through a simple intellectual "sight."

After the initial act of intellectual apprehension, then, knowledge sets in motion the "reasoning process." In general "reasoning" is a "transition from the better into the less known," through "scrutiny," "comparison," or "inferential discourse." [47]

From the outset Vives emphasized the idea that reason gravitates toward the unknown, the hidden. There is no trace of Platonism in this: sense knowledge is the same point of departure, and, in spite of occasional failures, the very standard of evidence and certainty. Through reasoning, however, man transcends sense knowledge. Vives explicitly condemned any form of empiricism:

If we give credit only to the senses, and all we know is included within their narrow boundaries (as it seems to some philosophers who take such radical and rough steps), we would not know the existence of the soul in animals because we neither see it nor perceive it through any sense. Furthermore, we will deny the existence of form in any object, and finally, we will believe only in the existence of this mass which we can see and touch: a conclusion which is totally unscientific and absolutely repulsive to the human mind.[48]

What is new and original in Vives is the large number of restrictions and limitations imposed upon reason's drive to transcend the knowledge which is acquired through the senses. In the last analysis, however, Vives failed to make clear the exact extent of transcendental knowledge. Only one thing remains certain: beyond sense experience, knowledge for Vives became highly problematic.

[47] *Ibid.*, "Notitia humana est ab iis, quae sensibus sunt cognita, ad ea quae animo et mente, nempe a singularibus ad universalia, a materialibus ad spiritualia, ab affectibus ad causas, a promtis et patentibus ad recondita." (355-1192 b.).

[48] M, III, 405; R, II, 1232 a-b. "Si solis sensibus habetur fides, et intra illorum limites concluduntur omnia, ut quibusdam videtur nimis crasse de rebus statuentibus, nec animas tribuemus mutis animantibus, quippe quas nec cernimus, nec sensu ullo percipimus; neque effectiones sive formas esse in rebus naturae censebimus; nihil denique praeter molem hanc, quam aspicimus et attrectamus; quod est disciplinae omni contrarium, tum ab omni judicio humanae mentis vehementer alienum ac abhorrens." (*De Anima*, II, 19)

The first tendency of reason is to reach the universal. Since the "simple intelligence" ist only an intellectual perception of the singular, Vives drew the conclusion that "the universal is only reached through discourse." [49] Although Vives did not use the word "abstraction," it appears that, according to him, reason reaches the universal or "essential similarity between things which are specifically the same" through a comparative discourse based upon abstraction. This is the way he was understood and attacked by Nizolio. What Nizolio (and many other commentators on Vives) failed to see, however, is that according to Vives, the universal, at least in most cases, *is rather a tendency than an accomplishment* of human nature. "If we reach it, fine; if we do not, we follow step by step as close as possible." [50] The main reason for our frequent failure is that many times "from similar forms proceed different actions, and similar actions from different forms." [51] Consequently, except for the extremely rare cases where we reach accurate universals we must be content with border-concepts or "approximations." [52]

Thus we have arrived at a doctrine which is fundamental to the understanding of Vives. Probability, verisimilitude, conjecture, guessing, approximation are the best words to describe our knowledge of the universal. Philosophy begins to lose its precise, mathematical contours.

The second route from the known to the unknown is the transition from the effect to the cause, and from the cause to the effect.[53] Vives never discussed the ontological value of the principle of causality; he takes it for granted. He was much more concerned with showing that the conclusion that the cause exists is not the same as the knowledge of the essence of the cause. Vives made an important distinction between causes which are "apprehended" from the effect, *apprehensa,* and causes which are "implied," *indagata.* The apprehended causes are those "which consist exclusively of things of this external nature." [54] These, he said, can be

---

[49] *Ibid.,* 379; 1211 b. "Universale tantummodo a ratione discurrente attingitur." (*De Anima,* II, 9). See also 354; 1192 b. "Ratio enim ex singulis eruit universalia" (*De Anima,* II, 4).

[50] Nizolio, *De veris principiis,* p. 94, attacks the position of Vives and Agricola on universals: "Vives et Agricola, alioquin doctissimi, in idem peccatum occiderunt." See *De instrumento probabilitatis,* II (M, III, 122-124; R, II, 1044-1046).

[51] *Ibid.,* 122; 1042 a. "Saepe ex similibus sive affectionibus sive formis diversae nascuntur actiones, nonumquam contra."

[52] *Ibid.,* "Vel ipsas veras et germanas tenemus notiones, quod est sane quam rarum, vel, quantum possumus, finitimas et proximas."

[53] See *De prima philosophia,* I (M, III, 195; R, II, 1066-1067).

[54] *Ibid.,* "In rebus quae omnino exterioris huius naturae constant opere, quae a nobis dicantur deprehensa. Sunt quae mens ardua quadam assurectione supra sensus, et magna indagine investigavit, non solum recte, sed oblique et ambagiose ...: huius generis sunt ... quae dicantur indagata, sive inquisita."

reached with a straight and short argument. Vives did not offer any example, but it is not difficult to imagine what kind of causal connections he had in mind: from the sight of a burned tree we easily infer the existence of fire. Both the burned tree and the fire belong to the physical world. The real issue here concerns the *indagata*. To decide whether and how reason transcends the "things of this external nature" is simply to decide whether and how far metaphysics is possible.

I have already suggested Vives' answer to the problem. Reason transcends the senses, but only as much as the senses allow, or in Vives' own words, "leaning upon the senses." It is difficult, however, to understand what kind of knowledge man can have of God, the soul, and other beings which belong to the group of the *indagata* by "leaning upon the senses." The same lack of precision applies to the third activity of our discursive reason: the inference from accident to substance. Here Vives insisted that what we call an essential definition is only a "description from the accidents."

In conclusion we can say that Vives maintained the possibility of metaphysical knowledge, not as a contemplative grasping of essences which transcends sensible appearances, but rather as a conjecture into the unknown, a glimpse ordained to action. The reliability of such a leap is guaranteed by the natural and innate inclinations of human reason – a creature of God – and also by the common notions of mankind as a whole. Such knowledge is evidently capable of constant progress and patient revision. Metaphysics is an approximative knowledge of essences which provides the general framework for our involvment with nature and our moral actions.

After the comparative scrutiny of the reasoning process, comes the act of judgment. The judgment is an act of choice or approval. The parallel to the forensic process was for Vives far more than a matter of words, it is a real comparison. Reason presents the evidence to the judgment exactly in the same way the attorney presents his evidence to the judge or the jury. "When reason has performed its duty, the judgment first appraises the inference itself, then the matter of the discourse. If it approves both, it cannot refuse the conclusion." The approval of the judgment is called "assent or opinion or estimation"; the disapproval is called "dissent." [55]

---

[55] M, III, 362-363; R, II, 1198-1199. "Dum ratio est in censura sua, quiescit judicium; ea ubi functa est suo munere, exsurgit censura, et judicat primum de connexione, hinc de discursu, quem si approbet, non potest reprobrare clausulam ... Itaque si judicium censeat conclusionem esse veram ... et eam complectitur tamquam sibi congruentem, quae complexio assensus ... dicitur; sin, falsam, aversatur, quae est dissensio." (*De Anima*, II, 5)

In most cases the problem does not arise from the formal aspect of the procedure itself: the formal rules of the syllogism can be easily handled if conveniently summarized.[56] The suspense of the judgment is due in most cases to the different estimation of the alleged evidence. In fact there are very few cases (Vives did not mention any) in which the evidence of the premises is such that they force man's reason to pass this or that judgment. This is the explanation of Vives' blunt statement that "philosophy is entirely based upon conjectures and verisimilitude." [57] The task of human reason is to provide the judgment with all the evidence available to increase the probability of the conclusion, the same way a good attorney accumulates all the possible evidence for the sake of his client. The search for such evidence is facilitated by the art of dialectic with its armory of different "topics" or "loci." Once this evidence has been presented, it is up to the judgment to give the final decision. This is the crucial moment in the truth-finding process. In this decision the essential part is man himself, his personal disposition or *ingenium,* and the influence of his passions on the judgment he is about to pronounce.

Vives' chapter on "ingenium" is indeed one of the best in *De Anima.* Vives made two basic assumptions: first, that the physiological features of the individual are a decisive ingredient of his temperament and character; second, that temperamental dispositions are of paramount importance in regulating man's intellectual powers.[58] The fact that Vives' physiology is merely a repetition of Galen's spirits, biles and phlegms does not jeopardize in the least the novelty of this part of the book. Where Vives truly excelled is in the concrete description of intellectual habits as patterned by the individual "ingenium."

Some people have a robust temperament. They are capable of hard and constant work, like the phlegmatic and melancholic ... People of this type are excellent in the art of mechanics where impatience can invalidate in one moment the effort of a long period ... Others are weak and cannot persevere in one job for a long time, like the bilious people or those with hot blood. To this group belong the inhabitants of very warm countries. Such people can display an enthusiastic effort, but are lacking in tenacity. Many people are unable to concentrate their attention on one job, sometimes because they are overweight, or because they are not used to it ... Some people are very gifted in one particular field, but totally helpless in others.[59]

[56] See below, pp. 277-280.
[57] M, VI, 417; R, II, 671 b. "Philosophia tota opinionibus et conjecturis verisimilitudinis est innixa." (*DD.,* "De vita et moribus eruditi").
[58] See *De Anima,* book 2, chapter 6, "De ingenio" (M, III, 364-369; R, II, 1200-1204).
[59] *Ibid.,* 367-368; 1202-1203. "Quidam habent vires ingenii validas ad laborem

The treatise *De Anima* needs to be supplemented in this respect with Chapter IV, Book II, *De disciplinis*. Together they contain an extraordinary wealth of observations concerning the intellectual mood of different individuals: the optimistic, the shy, the simple-minded, the avaritious, the proud, the melancholic, the bilious, the coleric, the sanguineous, the methodic, the impulsive, the enthusiastic, the apathetic, the young and the old.[60] Vives' perceptive and keen remarks had a powerful influence upon many similar writings which innundated European libraries in the second half of the sixteenth century. Moreover, Vives' pratical ability to formulate a program of student guidance and counseling, based upon the humanist respect for individual talents and dispositions, had an enormous impact upon the development of pedagogical theory and practice.

c. The Passional Interference

The study of temperament led Vives to the consideration of human emotions and the important role they play in one of the most decisive moments of the intellectual process: the evaluation of evidence. Vives' point of departure was the pessimistic view that human emotions are a cumbersome hindrance to be overcome rather than a positive implement of man's activity. "The more pure and lofty a judgment is, the less passion it tolerates; such a judgment examines with much care the possible good aspects of each object and does not accept any excitement, except on rare occasions and with serene moderation." [61] Vives described the sage in the following terms: "The wise man is not governed by the events. He governs them and keeps them straight and well within his jurisdiction. Whenever a passion crops up with all its natural power, the wise man represses it with the control of reason and forces it to withdraw in the face of a prudent judgment." [62]

From these and similar quotations it is easy to see the importance which

ferendum ... ut melancholici et phlegmatici ... ideoque hi artibus manuariis sunt apti, in quibus opus est patientia experimentorum ... Alii leves atque infirmas habent vires ... ut biliosi et calide sanguinei, tum populi ferventium regionum, et alii per aestum, valent enim impetu, non constantia; alii refugiunt laborem attentionis, ex gravi et crassa materia; alii ex deliciis, aut insuetudine, vel desuetudine ... Aliqui in uno quolibet acutissimum, in multis perturbantur ..."

[60] See below, p. 291, on the influence of Vives' work upon similar treatises in the second half of the sixteenth century.

[61] M, III, 425; R, II, 1247 a. "Quo est autem purius judicium, et celsius, eo pauciores et magis leves affectus admittit, tanto scilicet accuratius despicit quid quaque in re sit bonum et verum." (*De Anima*, III, preface)

[62] *Ibid.*, "Multo sunt omnia in sapiente diversa, is enim nec in eligendo bono fallitur ... nec permittit se regendum negotiis, sed regit ipse negotia, habetque se

Vives attached to the study of human emotions. In fact, almost half of the treatise *De Anima* is dedicated exclusively to this subject. Vives considered such a study "the foundation of all ethics, private and public." [63] With an air of immodesty, very rare in him, he claimed for himself the glory of being the first to deal with these matters in an adequate manner, and he included in this accusation not only the Stoic philosophers, but primarily Aristotle himself.[64]

It is no easy matter, however, to convey in a few pages a fair impression of Vives' perceptive and trenchant description of man's emotional life, of the motivation and degrees of human passions, of their interrelation and effects. The powerful introspection which Vives displays in these chapters is not always matched by a clear and orderly presentation. Notwithstanding, Vives' book on emotions is a significant part of European thought, and well-known scholars have not hesitated to point to it as a possible source of similar pursuits by Montaigne, Descartes, and Spinoza.

By "passions" Vives understood a generic notion which includes all human aversions and attractions, likes and dislikes, feelings, emotions and moods. "Passions and affections are the acts of those faculties of our soul by which we follow the good and avoid the evil." [65] Vives classified them in several categories according to different considerations. The first distinction is made on the basis of their intensity.

As the motions of the sea can be caused by a mild breeze, a strong wind, or a wild storm . . . in the same way these turbulences of the soul can be light as the soft wind which precedes the storm, or powerful enough to jolt and shake the soul, to deprive it of judgment and reason. The first ones are usually called "affections," while the second are called πάθη in Greek, and "passion" in Latin.[66]

The second classification divides human passions into two groups:

in suo jure ac potestate, ut surgentem vi naturae affectum, statim rationis freno compescat, cogatque recto judicio cedere."

[63] *Ibid.*, III, 299-300; II, 1148-1149. "Quod est de affectibus speculatio, quae tertio libro continetur, fundamentum universae moralis disciplinae, sive privatae, sive publicae." (*De Anima*, preface)

[64] *Ibid.*, 421; 1244 a. "Tractatio haec non satis diligenter a veteribus sapientiae studiosis vel animadversa, vel tradita; Stoici, quos Cicero secutum se profitetur, omnia haec argutiis suis perverterunt; Aristoteles in Rhetoricis tantum de materia hac exposuit quantum viro politico arbitratus est sufficere . . ."

[65] *Ibid.*, 422; 1244 b. "Ergo istarum facultatum, quibus animi nostri praediti a Natura sunt ad sequendum bonum vel vitandum malum, actus, dicuntur affectus sive affectiones, quibus ad bonum ferimur, vel contra malum, vel a malo recedimus."

[66] *Ibid.*, 424; 1246 b. "Quemadmodum in maris motibus est alius aurae tenuis, alius concitatior, alius vehemens quique horrida tempestate mare omne a fundo verrat . . . sic in his animorum agitationibus, quaedam sunt leves quas velut initia quaedam dixeris surgentis motus, alia sunt validiores ,aliae animum universum concutiunt, deque rationis sede ac statu judicii depellunt . . .; primas illas 'affectiones' rectius

those "which precede the resolution of the judgment, and those which follow it." To the former group belong the "movement of the soul which can be considered as the natural impulses resulting from organic changes, such as the appetite for food resulting from hunger, or the appetite for drink resulting from thirst . . ." [67] The passions which follow a noetic evaluation of the object can be divided into two groups: those which follow and presuppose an act of judgment, and those which succeed "a representation of the imagination." [68] Naturally Vives considered the second group a powerful threat to the supremacy of reason: "As soon as the fantasy provokes into action this turbulent pretence of judgment, man finds himself at the mercy of all kinds of soulful disturbances: we fear, we rejoice, we cry, we feel sad." [69] Vives also distinguished passional acts and "those passions which by frequent repetition have become diseases of the soul"; and between the latter and those which are neither isolated acts nor vicious habits but transitional stages, such as pudor, "which is begotten by shame." [70] The most ambitious classification of emotions, however, is arranged according to a triple concideration of intensity, formal object, and temporality, in the following manner: (Roman numbers refer to Chapters of Book Three, *De Anima*.)

	Initial Stage	Strong	Consuming
1. *Movements toward the good: attractions.*			
Toward the present (or the present memory of the past)	Complacency	Delight (IX) Pleasure Laughter (X)	LOVE (II-IV) Favor (V) Respect (VI) Mercy (VII)
Toward the future		Desire Hope (XXII)	
2. *Movements away from evil: aversions.*			
Away from the present	Disgust (XI) Contempt (XII) Anger (XIII)	Sadness (XIX) Tears (XX)	HATRED Envy (XV)
Away from the future		Fear (XXI) Pudor Audacity	Jealousy (XVI) Indignation (XVII) Cruelty (XVIII) (Pride) (XXIV)

dixeris, alteras 'commotiones' seu 'concitationes,' quae Graeci πάθη nominant, quasi 'passiones' . . ."

[67] *Ibid.*, "Sunt quidam animorum motus, seu impetus verius, naturales, qui ex affecto corpore consurgunt, ut edendi cupiditas in fame, bibendi in siti."

[68] *Ibid.*, "Non semper ad affectum excitandum opus est judicio . . .; illud sufficit, et est frequentius, quod imaginationis movetur visis."

[69] *Ibid.*, "Itaque sola phantasia trahente ad se tumultu sub specie quadam opinionis et judicii quod bonum sit, aut malum, quod est ei objectum, in omnes animi perturbationes versamur, timemus, laetamur, flemus, tristamur . . ."

[70] *Ibid.*, 425; 1246 b. "Sunt affectus nonnulli in transitu, tamquam pudor ex verecundia . . ."

Vives considered equanimity not as an emotion, but a lack of emotion; bodily manifestations of emotion, like laughter and tears, are included in this scheme because of their close connection with emotions themselves. Pride is considered by Vives a poisonous mixture of different emotions.[71]

The definition of each passion is not the most original part of Vives' work, but rather a repetition of traditional (mostly Aristotelian and Stoic) formulations. Love is an inclination of the will toward the good; favor is inchoative love; compassion is pain for an undeserved evil; joy is the motion of the soul in the presence of a possessed good; pleasure is the acquiescence of the will to a good actually enjoyed.[72] Vives' original contribution to the study of human emotions began with his frequent observations about their complicated interrelations. According to Vives, passions can, first of all, weaken or even neutralize other passions. Thus, for instance, contempt can reduce the bitterness of hatred or envy; anger, envy, and even love can invalidate the emotions of respect and veneration; the feeling of trust mitigates the emotion of desire, and, in general, the strongest passion tends to neutralize the weaker emotions and feelings.[73] On the other hand, certain passions help to excite and sharpen other movements of the soul. Love provokes fear; "friends fear for their friends, fathers for their sons, wives for their husbands, and husbands for their wives"; [74] envy is aroused by the love of concupiscence, and favor is occasionally stimulated by hatred," which makes us lean toward the enemies of our enemies"; [75] frequent anger and obsessive envy help to swell hatred and pride.[76] On occasion passions change direction or intensity on account of external events or other causes. Sometimes "envy can turn into compassion when misery succeeds happiness." [77] For this reason envious people are compassionate and compassionate people are inclined to envy; jealousy can turn into hatred and favor.[78]

With special care and attention Vives observed the beginning and the different stages of the passional process through its violent peak to the final fading away of the storm. He pointed to the special relevance of the

---

[71] See book 3, chapter 24, "De superbia" (M, III, 514-520; R, II, 1315-1323).
[72] M, III, 428, 453, 458, 463; R, II, 1249 b, 1268 b, 1272 b, 1277 a (De Anima, III, 2, 5, 7, 9).
[73] Ibid., 427, 437, 453, 490; 1248 b, 1256 b, 1271 b, 1284 b (De Anima, III, 1, 3, 5, 16).
[74] Ibid., 445; 1262 b. "Amor pro iis quos caros habet, meticulosissimus est, et anxius... amicus amico timet, pater filiis, maritus uxori, uxor marito..." (De Anima, III, 4)
[75] Ibid., "Favor non raro ex odio suboritur, ut in adversarium eius quem odimus inclinet, vel in eum cui non favet inimicus noster..." (De Anima, II, 5)
[76] Ibid., 485; 1292 b (De Anima, III, 14).
[77] Ibid., 489; 1296 b (De Anima, III, 15).
[78] Ibid., 492; 1298 b (De Anima, III, 16).

environment in brewing the emotional disturbance. With a typical southern bent of mind, the Spanish scholar remarked that the men of the North react more mildly to the threatened honor of a wife; [79] and that people in Spain and Italy are less inclined to a morbid sadness than those "who live in cold and wet places, especially in the fall and winter, and fall prey to these emotions during the melancholic and long hours of the night." [80] Other external conditions which affect man's emotions are his dwelling, clothing, friends, and social relations. Of special importance is the profession of the individual. "To a soldier there is no greater dishonor than cowardice; to a merchant, poverty is the worst disaster; to a scholar, ignorance is shameful." [81] Bodily condition is also a relevant consideration: "Young people seek pleasure, mature men seek honor, sick persons desire health, those in power covet more power and fame." [82] Vives dedicated special attention to the interrelation of temperament and emotion. Warm temperaments are restless, impatient, and noble; cold temperaments are stubborn, serene, and more selective in their desires; those who have a large heart but little blood are apt to be cowardly; sadness causes black bile and black bile increases sadness. "Melancholic people find themselves in depressive sadness for no apparent reason." [83] In close relationship with the temperamental aspect of our emotional lives are the organic effects of strong emotions upon the human body. Vives' picturesque and vivid remarks concerning the bodily manifestations of fear, sadness, and joy were compiled in two magnificent chapters dedicated to laughter and tears.[84]

This wealth of descriptive psychology is designed primarily to enable us to guard against a harmful impact of emotions upon knowledge. We have mentioned Vives' concern with the disruptive effect of strong passions upon the activity and accuracy of the senses, both external and internal. Strong passions, however, can even distort reason. Jealousy renders a realistic evaluation of evidence impossible, shame confuses the

---

[79] *Ibid.*, 491; 1297 b.

[80] *Ibid.*, 499; 1303 b. "Affectio haec ... invalescit in frigidis temporibus et locis, omninoque in iis quae obtinent ingenium melancholicum, ut in autumno, et hieme, et tempore nubilo, et de nocte, tum ad Septentrionem, in quibus regionibus plures absumit moestitia quam in Hispania, vel Italia." (*De Anima*, III, 19)

[81] *Ibid.*, 510; 1312 a. "Militibus nihil est probrosius ignavia, negotiatoribus paupertas, studiosis litterarum inscientia..." (*De Anima*, III, 23)

[82] *Ibid.*, 437; 1256 b. "Juvenili animo conducibilissimum videtur voluptas, viro decus, aegro sanitas, seni victus, principi gloria, cuique ut est, vel corpore, vel animo, affectus." (*De Anima*, III, 3)

[83] *Ibid.*, 498; 1303 a. "Videas melancholicos homines moestos ... nec ipsi moestitiae suae causam possent reddere" (*De Anima*, III, 19).

[84] See *De Anima*, III, chapter 10, "De risu," and chapter 20, "De lacrimis." (M, III, 469-471, 500-502; R, II, 1280-1282, 1304-1305)

mind, and pride stupifies human reason.[85] Anger and love make men blind to the good and bad qualities of the object.[86] On the other hand, love can increase the depth of our intellectual grasp: "Before we love anything we must know it . . . However, as soon as we love it we know it better, more closely, with more enjoyment." [87] The result of love is fruition, "which is not only a pleasure of the will, but a perfection of knowledge itself." The secret of wisdom is to remember that through knowledge man can keep his emotions under constant control.

---

[85] M, III, 488, 513, 517; R, II, 1295 a, 1314 b, 1317 b (*De Anima*, III, 15, 23, 24).

[86] *Ibid.*, 441, 481; 1259 a-b, 1286 (*De Anima*, III, 4, 13).

[87] *Ibid.*, 448; 1264 a. "Cognoscitur res primum ut ametur . . . ubi vero cum re cara sumus connexi, melius eam novimus, nempe proprius, et tunc fruimur." (*De Anima*, III, 4)

CHAPTER 13

THE SIGNIFICANCE OF VIVES' THOUGHT

I want to end this study of Vives' thought with a modest attempt to formulate some conclusions regarding its significance in the history of European culture. The task is not a simple one. The immediate background of Vives' intellectual performance was characterized by the enormous diversity of its components, the complex tension between medieval and modern patterns of thought, and, in many cases at least, an amazing lack of awareness of what the age was achieving. Many of Vives' contemporaries felt indeed the excitement of the adventure, but, like Columbus, failed to sec in the new shores ahead the boundaries of a virgin continent. These characteristics were mirrored in Vives' life and work. Born in Spain, educated in France, a resident of Flanders, and a professor at Oxford, Vives was exposed to many and different trends of thought. The cosmopolitanism of Humanistic culture is evident in his work. On the other hand, he also paid a high tribute to the hesitations of the moment. Committed as he was to a rebellion against the jargon of the schools, he was never able to create a fitting philosophical vocabulary of his own. Here and there one can feel his reluctance to derive all the consequences of an initial set of premises, to think out a problem in all its implications. Finally, like many of his contemporaries, Vives suggested much more than he said. His books were no bold manifestos of a cultural revolution, but they were rich in innuendos, suggestions, and critical remarks which reveal a philosophical mood, a bent of mind which would have been unbelievable fifty years before him and was an accomplished fact fifty years later.

Vives somehow stands alone, a citizen of the republic of letters without any flag above him, under the sign of no religious denomination. Although he is generally considered a product of the Northern Renaissance – to the dismay of some Spanish scholars – his peculiar characteristics set him apart. His life was a constant struggle against the forces of political, religious, and philosophical sectarianism. For this reason his name and his reputation were never taken under the protective wing of any faction, any nation, or any religious group. Elizabethan England never forgave him for his close association with Thomas More and Catherine of Aragon. The Germans resented his lack of enthusiasm for the Lutheran Reform. The Jesuits and the Spanish Inquisition found him too close to Erasmus. Vives' apparent detachment from Italian culture explains the widespread neglect of his name in modern Italian scholarship. The French cannot forget that, at least for a time, Vives saw in Charles V the only hope of a Christian Europe. Prejudice led some scholars to underestimate his thought and pushed others into an excessive praise. Moreover, the fame of the pedagogue has, in many cases, overshadowed the significance of the philosopher. The encyclopedic character of Vives' writings, the total lack of systematic formulations, the overriding eclecticism of his thought, and the prolix and often careless style are further obstacles in any attempt to define the impact of his ideas upon those who followed him. There is abundant evidence, however, that his books were not only widely read – remember our introductory chapter – but also that they were frequently plagiarized and imitated. On the whole, however, his influence, while widespread, cannot be clearly defined.[1] His suggestions became predominant attitudes; his premonitions were, one hundred years after him, the fashions of the day. I do not pretend to establish a personal and direct relation between Vives and each one of the later writers we are about to mention in this chapter; I claim, however, that Vives occupies a symbolic and significant position in the history of European thought.

Vives divided philosophy in three parts. The first deals with words, *de verbis*; the second with things, *de rebus*; and the third with morals, *de moribus*.[2] Vives' thought in these three branches of philosophy was intimately related to the revival of three disciplines during the Renaissance period: rhetoric, medicine, and jurisprudence. Quintilian and Cicero were the masters of a powerful and beautiful word, Galen was the teacher of the practical art of healing, and Stoic ideals inspired thoughts on legal reform and an ethical conception of human existence. Vives' understanding of logic, science, and wisdom was profoundly influenced by these

---

[1] Lange, *Luis Vives*, p. 14, writes that, as an encyclopedic writer, Vives has been more plagiarized than quoted.

[2] This is the general outline of Vives' *De disciplinis*. Both parts of this treatise are divided in three sections: the first deals with the language-disciplines (grammar, rhetoric, dialectic): M, VI, 77-171; R, II, 399-475; the second with the philosophy of nature (physics, medicine, mathematics): M, VI, 181-203; R, II, 475-498; the third with moral philosophy: M, VI, 208-243; R, II, 498-526. In the second part of the treatise, "*De tradendis disciplinis*," the three sections are: M, VI, 298-745, 351-386, 386-416; R, II, 573-608, 609-641, 641-664.

heroes of classical antiquity whom the Renaissance had brought back to life. Vives' educational program was first and foremost an attempt to perpetuate these great lessons of the past. Consequently, we shall divide our study of Vives' influence into four parts: the rhetorical ideal, science as an art, moral wisdom, and education.

a. Rhetoric and the Logic of Persuasion

The discovery of the complete works of Quintilian in 1416 was a decisive fact in the history of modern European education. Early humanists were profoundly impressed by the Quintilian ideal of the *orator* as the honest man who knows how to speak well. Quintilian's rhetorical conception broadened the horizons of Cicero's *De Oratore* into a comprehensive program of education beginning with moral principles and including not only the formal rules of speaking, but also the material content of the speech. The *orator* speaks well because he knows *what* to say and *how* to say it. In the works of Quintilian, then, rhetoric and pedagogy are practically identified.

Noble as this project was, it contained obvious exaggerations which did not go unrecognized, especially by the Humanists of Northern Europe. One of the most explicit and influential critics of Quintilian was Rudolph Agricola, a disciple of the Brethren of the Common Life, but also the pupil of Theodore Gaza and Battista Guarino in Ferrara in the second half of the fifteenth century. Although Agricola's works were written during the incunabular period, they were printed in the first quarter of the sixteenth century and soon reached a tremendous popularity. Agricola's publisher in Louvain was Bartholomew Latomus, a personal friend of Vives.[3] Johan Sturm introduced Agricola to the University of Paris in 1529. Thus the history of humanistic logic runs without a significant break from Agricola to Ramus; in this process Vives played a modest but significant role. Agricola accepted from Quintilian the notion that grammar, rhetoric, and dialectic are the three parts of the art of human discourse; but he was very eager to make a clear distinction between the realms of rhetoric and dialectic. Rhetoric, according to him, is concerned only with ornamentation. The art of "invention" is, on the other hand, within the jurisdiction of dialectic. Furthermore, the rules of *inventio* are the most important part of the dialectical art, yielding a methodical guide to the finding of arguments on any subject. This guide is produced by a formal classification of all possible sources of information under certain

[3] On Latomus, see above, p. 57, note 23.

headings of key notions which Agricola – following Cicero's example – calls *loci communes* or *communia capita*.[4] This is the first part of dialectic; the second (about which Agricola never wrote) is called *iudicium*. According to Agricola, the ultimate and direct objective of all discourse is teaching.

Vives accentuated and clarified some of the implications of this approach to logic. First, Vives saw clearly that the exaggerations of Quintilian's rhetorical ideals were due to a confusion of form and content. In *De disciplinis* Vives wrote:

> Quintilian indignantly protests against those who cut off from the realm of rhetoric the contemplation of nature and the study of morals . . . However, everyone can clearly see that to speak of the heavens, the elements, and the angels is not the orator's concern. The fact that one discipline helps another does not make the former a part of the latter . . . It is indeed better if an architect is also a philosopher. Nevertheless, this does not make philosophy a part of architecture.[5]

From Aristotle, Vives learned the purely instrumental and formal character of both rhetoric and dialectic. In fact, Vives went beyond Aristotle in abiding by this, and criticized the inclusion of the categories in the *Organon* as an invasion of metaphysics, and of the *Posterior Analytics* as an intrusion of psychology into dialectic. Vives' emphasis upon the formal character of dialectic does not entail, however, an abandonment of the typical humanist position that dialectic is a theory not so much of thought as of statement. Precisely because dialectics is a theory of verbal communication more concerned with linguistic phenomena than with abstract mental operations, Vives rejected with the same acrimony the artificial jargon of terministic logic and the attempts of his Montaigu professors to find an adequate algebraic or geometric symbolism for the formal rules of thought.[6] In his youthful treatise *In pseudo-dialecticos*, Vives insistently demanded that dialectical rules be derived

---

[4] Cicero's influence upon Agricola is brilliantly presented by Ong, *Ramus*, pp. 98-130.

[5] M, VI, 155; R, II, 456. "Clamat Quntilianus et indignabundus . . . amputata esse de rhetorica per homines desidiosos quae ad naturae contemplationem, quaeque ad componendos mores attinerent . . . Quis non videt non esse rhetoris de coelo, deque elementis dicere, de angelis, de pyramide? . . . Non unaquaeque ars alia quavis adjuvetur, nec protinus pars est illius . . . Architectus melior, si sit philosophus; quid ergo philosophia pars est architecturae?" (*DD.*, I, 4, 1).

[6] Vives directs this attack in his early treatise *Adversus pseudo-dialecticos*. (M, III, 44, 46; R, II, 296 b, 300, 302).
Ong (*Ramus*, pp. 74-83, "The Logic of Space") gives a condensed presentation of the geometrical symbolism in the work of Lefèvre d' Etaples, Tartaret, Major, and Celaya. See also in Estelrich, *Vivés*, pp. 5-14, the significant titles of the logical treatises of Juan Dolz, Gaspar Lax de Sariñena, Juan de Celaya, and Antonio Coronel.

from linguistic habits rather than imposed upon them.[7] On the other hand, Vives was painfully aware of the limitations of ordinary idiomatic languages as possible expressions of universally valid dialectical rules.[8]

The humanistic conception of dialectics as an art of discourse rather than as an art of reason is intimately bound up with humanism's instrumental and pragmatic functionalism. Grammar, rhetoric, and dialectic are the tools which can convert a man into an influential teacher, a powerful political speaker, a persuasive diplomat, or a wise interpreter of the written laws. Vives' concern with the power of the word in man's social dimension broadened the horizons set by Agricola. At the beginning of Book Four, First Part, of the treatise *De disciplinis*, Vives wrote:

> The main bonds of man's society are justice and language. All communal life, both private and public, is impossible without both. Nobody can associate with his fellow man if he is unable to understand him. Justice and language are the twin rudders of human society. Justice's power is silent and calm; language displays its power in a more clear and incisive way; justice is the voice of reason and counseling; language moves the passions of the soul... Those who master a powerful word become leaders of men...[9]

Finally – and this is by far his most important contribution to the history of humanistic dialectics – Vives led the revival of medieval topical literature initiated by Agricola to its ultimate conclusion.[10] In the contest between categories and topics, Vives did not hesitate for a moment to declare the supremacy of the latter. Besides excluding the categories from dialectics as an invasion of metaphysics, Vives dedicated two short essays exclusively to the study of the topics, *De instrumento probabilitatis* and *De explanatione cuiuscumque essentiae*.[11] Unfortunately, Vives' own

---

[7] M, III, 42; R, II, 296 b. Vives writes: "The grammarian does not impose the rules, he recognizes them... The same is the case with dialectical rules, which are not executory. The rules existed before dialectic was ever invented. The dialectician teaches what the use of language prescribes." (*Adv. ps-d.*).

[8] *Ibid.*, III, 47; II, 300 b.

[9] M, VI, 152; R, II, 453. "Humanae omnes societates duabus potissimum rebus vinciuntur ac continentur, justitia ac sermone; quarum si alterutra desit, difficile sit coetum et congregationem ullam sive publicam sive privatam diutius consistere ac conservari. Neque enim vel cum iniquo possit quis habitare... vel cum eo velit vivere, quem non intelligit; itaque duo sunt velut clavi, quibus conventus hominum reguntur, justitia et sermo; sed justitia tacitas habet vires et lentas, sermo vero praesentiores et magis celeres, quod altera rationis et consilii vim admonet, alter animi motus excitat... qui vero plurimum potest sermone... hunc volunt ductorem." (*DD.*, I, 4, 1).

[10] Ong, *Ramus*, pp. 55-72, gives a clear account of the importance of Peter of Spain's *Summulae logicales* in shaping the thought of Agricola. Like most Humanists of Northern Europe, Vives was extremely unfair to Petrus Hispanos, whom he blamed for all the wasteful subtleties of terministic logic. (M, III, 49; R, II, 303 b. *Adv. ps-d.*).

[11] M, III, 82-121, 122-142; R, II, 979-1040, 1040-1057.

version of topical dialectics was, by his own admission, "a mixed and muddled jungle of instruments," not much better than Aristotle's own attempt.[12] In any case Vives made absolutely clear that the study of invention, which had been "stolen by the rhetoricians," belongs exclusively to dialectics as its most important part.[13] One might feel tempted to ask why Vives failed to see that the topics, no less than the categories, were bridges between the purely formal aspect of discourse and the material content of the discourse itself. The answer to this question leads us to consider the relationship between Vives' conception of dialectics and his theory of knowledge.

In the *Organon* Aristotle presented the categories as the bridge between reality and the formal rules of the syllogism, whereas the topics mediate between the material sources of information and the forms of probable discourse which lack the apodictic necessity and certainty of scientific demonstration. Agricola's insistence upon the topics blurred the distinction between a dialectic of probabilities and scientific demonstration. In Vives this process went one step further: all discourse striving for certitude is assimilated to less scientific forms of discourse. Vives' emphasis upon the topics was perfectly fitting with his own theory of knowledge. Philosophy "is all based on probability and verisimilitude" because the Aristotelian process of apodictic demonstration from first and necessary principles is seldom possible. Vives had no objection against the syllogism itself. He called it "the most perfect form of argumentation." [14] However, the vital problem Vives wanted to consider was the "finding" (*inventio*) of the best available premises from which the syllogism starts. The categories are of little help in finding material premises; the formal rules of inference are seldom questioned by the human mind, once it has understood them. The practical problem in the quest for truth is to accumulate evidence in order to reach that degree of persuasion which makes possible a free but prudent choice; the main task of dialectics is to reduce to an art – a set of precepts – the different approaches and sources of argumentation. If we compare the attitudes of Agricola, Vives, and Ramus with Aristotle – who made a fundamental distinction between categorical logic and topical dialectics – we shall be able to telescope into a general scheme the history of humanistic logic from the second half of the fifteenth century to the end of the sixteenth century. Agricola amalgamated the logic of science and the logic of probability

---

[12] M, III, 83; R, II, 982 b.
[13] M, VI, 154-155; R, II, 454-456. (DD., I, 4, 1).
[14] *Ibid.,* III, 169; II, 1030 a. "Germana et perfecta argumentatio," (*De censura,* II).

under the general concept of teaching. Vives assimilated the scientific ideal of valid and certain inference to the notion of prudent and practical persuasion. Ramus believed that all forms of discourse need to follow the pattern of scientific methodology. If Vives' books are the expression of a rhetorical conception of logic as a dialectic of persuasion, an art of discourse, and a theory of human communication, Ramus' popular writings symbolize the early shift toward logic conceived as an art of reason, a tool of scientific discovery and of the study of the thought-processes.

It is hard to specify concretely the role of Vives in these developments. Ramus' dependence upon Agricola is generally attributed to the mediation of Johan Sturm, a disciple of the latter and a teacher of the former at the University of Paris. However, it is fair to suppose that Ramus himself was familiar with Vives' books which were at that time extremely popular in Paris. On the other hand Sturm was clearly under the influence of his personal acquaintance, Juan Luis Vives. Although he failed to acknowledge Vives' merits in his writings, this was probably due to his own religious partisanship.[15] The influence of Vives upon English Logicians and Rhetoricians throughout the sixteenth and seventeenth centuries is evidenced by the frequent mention of his name by such writers as Gabriel Harvey and Robert Sanderson.[16] In Germany, the name of Melanchthon overshadows, of course, any competitor, but Vives is still frequently mentioned in the works of such German Ramists as J. H. Alsted, B. Keckermann, J. Althusius, J. T. Freige, and Comenius.[17]

Vives' conception of logic as an art of persuasion through cumulative evidence was based upon a theory of philosophical certainty, which is highly significant in the history of European thought because it represents a middle position between the Ockhamistic criticism of late medieval philosophy and the radical rationalism of seventeenth century Cartesianism. In Vives' case, it appeared as a personal reaction against the epistemology of Durandus whose influence he strongly felt during his studies at Paris.[18] Because of its compromising and its tense equilibrium, Vives'

---

[15] Lange, *Vives*, p. 166. On Johan Sturm, see L. Kúckelhann, *Johan Sturm* (Leipzig, 1872).

[16] See Howell, *Logic and Rhetoric in England*, pp. 198, 199, 251, 302.

[17] A. Nebe has explored the relations between Vives and Alsted, see above, p. 10, note 33. According to Estelrich (*Vivés*, p. 149) the logical treatises of B. Keckermann, especially his *Gymnasium logicum* (Hannover, 1605), "donnent l' impression d' avoir lu Vives a fond." T. Freige recommends the *Exercitatio linguae latinae* of Vives as one of the best available texts to learn Latin.

[18] Vives was probably impressed by Durandus' denial of cognitive species and of the active intellect. The clearly Augustinian trend of Durandus' epistemology prepared Vives for a better understanding of the *Civitas Dei*. On Durandus' popularity in Paris in the first decades of the XVI century, see Renaudet, *Préréforme et Humanisme*, pp. 470, 518.

thought cannot fairly be related to the Pyhrronian scepticism of Sánchez or Pierre Bayle. On the other hand, one has to recognize that Vives' philosophical attitudes were opposed to the main stream of continental rationalism in the seventeenth century. Mystics and visionaries were equally remote from Vives' zone of influence. If we want to find Vives' intellectual heirs among post-Renaissance European philosophers, we should search among men of strong but independent mind, warm and unsystematic thinkers strongly inclined to find a compromise between the destructive but undeniable pressure of sceptical doubt and the irrepressible practical demands of man's material and ethical life.

The first name to be mentioned is that of Michel de Montaigne, whose relationship with Vives has been strongly suggested by Professor Américo Castro.[19] Montaigne shared with Vives not only a common Iberian and Jewish heritage, but also the same conception of philosophy as personal wisdom which transcends the inarticulate passions of man but never reaches the recipe-methods of the exact sciences. We know that Montaigne used Vives' critical remarks to Saint Augustine's *Civitas Dei*, a fact which suggests a more comprehensive knowledge of Vives' ideas.[20]

Another intellectual heir might be Mersenne, the pragmatic scientist of the seventeenth century who saw in man's limited knowledge of nature a sound and reliable practical basis of scientific knowledge.[21] More significant but yet unexplored are the affinities between Vives and Pascal. Vives' apologetical work *De veritate fidei Christianae* and Pascal's *Pensées* are both based upon the same "strategy": the act of faith is not a necessary conclusion from evident premises but a free persuasion which must be carefully encouraged and invited. Vives' proof of the immortality of the soul is a masterpiece in this direction; the last book of Vives' apologetical treatise, which deals with the intrinsic human values of Christian ethics, has a strong resemblance to the last part of the *Pensées*.[22] There is no concrete evidence of Vives' direct influence upon Pascal. However, Vives' close relationship with other French apologists, such as Duplessis-

[19] A. Castro, "Un aspecto del pensar Hispano-Judío," p. 160.
[20] Montaigne himself quotes Vives in *Essays*, XXI, "Of the power of the imagination." (*The Complete Essays of Montaigne*, tr. D. M. Frame, 3rd ed. [Stanford, 1965], p. 73). On the sources of Montaigne, see P. Villey, 2 vols., 2nd revised ed., *Les Sources et l'évolution des Essais de Montaigne* (Hachette, 1933).
[21] On Mersenne's "constructive scepticism," see R. Popkin, *The History of Scepticism from Erasmus to Descartes*, revised ed. (New York, 1964), pp. 132-148. Mersenne believed that "even if the claims of the sceptics could not be refuted, nonetheless we could have a type of knowledge which is not open to question, and which is all that is requisite for our purposes in this life." (p. 133).
[22] M, VIII, 428-454; R, II, 1642-1669 (*De VFC*.).

Mornay might be evidence enough of an indirect, but significant, impact upon Pascal himself.[23]

Last but not least, we have to mention the importance of Juan Luis Vives in the history of the Scottish School of Common Sense. Vives' insistence upon the common notions of mankind as a reliable starting point of human inquiry was greatly appreciated by the leaders of that School. William Hamilton, who quoted Vives several times in his works, reacted very sharply against the attempt of James Mackintosh to elevate Hobbes above Vives; moreover, writing about memory's laws of association, Hamilton did not hesitate to write that "Vives' observations comprise in brief nearly all of principal moment that has been said upon this subject, either before or since." [24] Dugald-Stewart wrote about Vives:

> In point of good sense and acuteness . . . he yields to none of his contemporaries; and in some of his anticipations of the future progress of science he discloses a mind more comprehensive than any of them.
>
> Of all the writers of the sixteenth century Luis Vives seems to have had the liveliest and most assured foresight of the new career which the human mind was about to enter.[25]

Ironically enough, one of the most significant revivals of Vives' thought in his own country was the result of the influence of this Scottish School of Common Sense upon the Barcelonese group of Martí de Eixala, Pedro Codina, José Joaquin de Mora, and Francisco Javier Llorens y Barba.[26]

b. Medicine and "Art"

The century which followed Vives' death was characterized by a growing tension between the methodologists of the arts and the methodologists of the sciences. To the first group belonged the educational reformers who drew their inspiration from humanist ideals. The second trend was carried out by the partisans of a strict *methodus scientificus*. The pedagogues

[23] P. Graf in his doctoral dissertation "Luis Vives als Apologet," proves with several parallel quotations the plagiarisms of the French Apologist. (pp. 145-147).

[24] Hamilton (*Lectures on Metaphysics and Logic* [Boston, 1868]) quotes Vives among the leading logicians of the XVI century (p. 198), and defends him against the accusations of Scaliger (p. 481). Furthermore, Hamilton calls our Humanist "the great Vives" (p. 134) and recommends him for having pointed out the dangers of an excessive study of mathematics (p. 290). In *Discussions on Philosophy and Literature* (New York, 1856) Hamilton sympathyzes with Vives' insistence upon humility as "a virtue of human reason" (p. xlviii, Introduction) and quotes Vives on the importance of training the deaf (p. 177). For other quotations of Vives, see Hamilton's remarks and footnotes in *The Works of Thomas Reid*, 2 vols. (Edinburgh, 1863), II, 896 a, 902 a, 908, 946, 893b.

[25] Dugald Stewart, *The Collected Works*, 2 vos. (Edinburgh, 1854), I, 28, 58.

[26] Bonilla, *Luis Vives*, II, 338-339.

were concerned primarily with communicating knowledge; the scientists were oriented toward research and investigation. The former relied upon attractive and orderly persuasion and were inclined to subordinate all human achievements to a high and noble ideal of moral perfection and wisdom. The latter were being pressed by a quickly expanding bourgoisie to perfect the tools of trade and domination. The educators were prone to include under the headline of "philosophy" the study of empirical disciplines and thus to assimilate the method of natural research into the methods of rhetorical persuasion. The scientists, on the other hand, advocated an ethically and metaphysically "neutral" study of nature based primarily on the quantification of physical forces and the application of geometrical logic to the very process of inquiry.

History tells us unequivocally that the scientific trend gained the upper hand, and that humanist ideals of individual wisdom and moral perfection were gradually relegated to a secondary position. The *methodus scientificus* reached its most radical expression in the continental rationalism of the seventeenth century. The Cartesian method was a drastic attempt to categorically eliminate the false in every process of thought. After all, the uncompromising self-defense of Galileo had abundantly proved that commonly accepted theories could be nothing but fantastic self-deceptions.

In spite of the fact that humanists championed a cause which was doomed to at least a partial defeat, their gallant defense of individual wisdom helped to maintain noble thoughts in a context of exact geometrical reasoning. There is indeed a profound stream of humanism in Descartes' concern with morality and human passions.[27] Later in this same chapter, we shall deal with this contribution of humanism in general, and Vives more in particular, to the preservation of ethical ideals in modern European thought. Here, however, we want to raise a different and probably less expected claim in favor of Renaissance Humanism. I contend that some humanists at least, and Vives more eloquently and convincingly than any of his contemporaries, made important positive contributions to the final success of the scientific revolution. This claim goes beyond the recognized positive influence of Renaissance scholarship. There is no doubt that humanists brought a growing sense of history and a more critical attitude toward the past into European culture; clearly they widened the horizons and raised the standards of accuracy and textual criticism. Their translations of classical sources provided a wealth of new information. Ptolemy, Galen, and Hippocrates – to mention only

---

[27] See, for instance, R. Lefèvre, *L'Humanisme de Descartes* (Paris, 1957).

the most important – were translated, printed, and widely read. In every one of these areas (except that of translations) Vives was truly exceptional, not only because he was able to include them in the most philosophical defense humanism ever attained, but also because he embodied those lessons in a clear educational program.

However, Vives' most decisive service to the cause of science was his vision of a practical learning in which theory and skill balance each other in perfect harmony. The dilemma between the two has never been more acute than it was in the days of the Renaissance. Vives attacked with equal fervor the false science of the medical practitioners and the visionary dreams of the Rosicrucians or the disciples of Paracelsus. Unfortunately, we have to recognize that for some strange reason Vives seems to have entirely ignored the most promising speculation of the age and the most amazing performances of the great scientists who were his contemporaries.

During the years of Vives' life, scholastic speculation on nature had embarked on exciting adventures. The nominalist physicists of the University of Paris – some of them, like Dullard, Vives' professor at Montaigu – were leading a significant attack against the Aristotelian theory of motion, and were preparing for the application of the mathematical method to the study of physical forces. Their speculation was based upon the amazing results obtained by Buridan, Oresme, and Albert of Saxony at the end of the fourteenth century, and by Domingo de Soto in the first half of the sixteenth century. The humanists, however, ignored or misunderstood the significance of this movement. Instead, the rich tradition of Paris found a sympathetic echo in the schools of medicine, especially in Padua, which showed a surprising understanding of numbers and proportions, probably because of a closer relationship with Platonic philosophy.[28]

Copernicus, Tartaglia, Leonardo da Vinci, and Dürer were Vives' contemporaries, but their names fail to appear in his otherwise encyclopedic works. The Spanish Humanist was much more impressed by the performances of the artisans of his days, and, most of all, by the impressive recovery of medicine.[29] In medicine Vives saw the ideal case of practical learning, the model of all "Arts."

[28] See P. M. M. Duhem, Le Système du monde; histoire des doctrines cosmologiques de Platon a Copernic, 5 vols. (Paris, 1913-1917); J. H. Randall, "The Development of Scientific Method in the School of Padua," Journal in the History of Ideas, I (1940), pp. 177-206. For a different point of view on the Parisian influence upon Padua, see E. Garin, La Cultura filosofica del Rinascimento Italiano (Firenze, 1961), "Il Problema della Fonti del pensiero di Leonardo da Vinci," pp. 388-401.

[29] Donald Campbell gives detailed information on the role of Galen in his article "The Medical Curriculum of the Universities of Europe in the Sixteenth Century,"

Modern scholars have emphasized the extraordinary importance of this Renaissance concept of "Art" as the transitional stage between medieval speculation on nature and modern science.[30] By substituting the notion of "Art" for the Aristotelian idea of science, the humanists prepared – probably unconsciously – the scientific revolution of Galileo's generation. In the quest for a happy medium between unlearned skill and impractical speculation, Vives and the other humanists looked up to medicine as the ideal solution. This humanistic trend had a long history. In the *Phaedrus*, Plato had already introduced the method of Hippocrates as a pattern to be applied to every τέχνη.[31] This Platonic doctrine remained alive in the Stoic school through a definition of "Art" which included a materialistic theory of knowledge: "Art is a set of *percepts* exercised together for some useful end in life." [32] Medieval Latin commentators and translators changed the word "percept" for "precept" thus producing the epistemologically neutral defintion of Art which Vives used in his own books: "Art is the complex of precepts oriented toward the execution of a certain goal." [33] The immediate source of this generally accepted defintion of Art was the writing of Galen, especially the *Methodus medendi* translated into Latin in 1519 by a personal friend of Vives, Thomas Linacre.[34] The eclectic character of Galen, who was able to merge Aristotle's theory of science with Platos' dialectical method and Hippocrates' wise observations, was probably highly appealing to the Spanish Humanist. In any case, the μέθοδος of Galen presented itself to Vives as the model of an art both practical and learned, based both on the *experimentum* which Thessalus' dogmatism ignored and on the *judicium* which quacks and medical practicioners scorned.

The use of the word *experimentum* by Vives should not suggest, however, a theory of experimentation, not even in its most primitive form. *Experimentum* in Vives' vocabulary means no more than empirical observation. Vives' only contribution to the progress of inductive methods was his occasional, although firm, recommendation to avoid the hasty gener-

---

Science, Medicine and History: Essays on the Evolution of Scientific Thought and Medical Practice, 2 vols. (Oxford, 1953) I, pp. 357-367.

[30] For the study of the subject I have greatly depended upon N. Gilbert's brilliant study *Renaissance Concepts of Method.*

[31] 265 d-277 c.

[32] Gilbert, *Renaissance Concepts,* pp. 11-12.

[33] M, VI, 252; R, II, 534. "Quare definiatur nobis ars: Collectio universalium praeceptorum parata ad cognoscendum, agendum vel operandum, in certa aliqua finis latitudine." (*DD.,* II, 1, 3).

[34] The translation was published in Paris (1519) under the title *Galeni methodus medendi, vel de moribus curandis.*

alizations of Aristotle through a careful, patient, and more qualified observation of nature itself.[35]

This harmonious balance of theory and practice which Vives eloquently advocated positively enhanced the possibility of the scientific revolution which was about to come. First of all, it involved the rejection of a metaphysical speculation on nature. Since such speculation was mainly Aristotelian, Vives' attitude resulted in a rejection of Aristotle's authority as a sacred criterion of truth. Probably more convincingly than Erasmus' sarcasm or the exaggerations of other humanists, Vives' judicious but firm criticism of Aristotelian physics helped serious scholars to emancipate themselves from the tyranny of such authority. In two particular cases, at least, Vives' direct influence can be ascertained. The first is Rabelais, whose practically oriented and iconoclastic program of education was clearly affected by Vives' ideas.[36] The second is much more important in the history of the scientific movement. In his book *Exercitationes paradoxicae adversus Aristoteleos,* Gassendi recognized Vives as the author who helped him to liberate himself from the Aristotelian bondage.[37]

Last but not least, Vives' orientation of all human knowledge toward the guidance of action, both on the ethical and the material levels of life, was obviously a significant component of the "great restoration" which has been symbolically attributed to Francis Bacon. Without repeating the obvious exaggerations of some biographers of Vives, who see in Bacon almost a disciple of Vives, and without even pretending to claim a direct influence of the Spanish scholar upon the British genius, I think it is fair to say that the message of Francis Bacon might have been impossible without the modest but significant suggestions of other people, among whom Juan Luis Vives has a distinctive claim.

c. Jurisprudence and Moral Wisdom

The third and most important part of philosophy, according to Vives, deals with the study of morals, *de moribus.* This special concern with the ethical life of man echoed the social, intellectual, and religious trends of the day. The civic enthusiasm of early Italian humanists, and the social

[35] See *De disciplinis,* part I, book 5, chapter 1. (M, VI, 181-185; R, II, 475-479).
[36] Compayré (*Histoire critique,* p. 411) does not hesitate to mention Vives' name among the immediate predecessors of Rabelais' thought.
Rousselot and Estelrich also consider Vives a leader of women education in France. See Estelrich, *Vives,* p. 124.
[37] *Exercitationes Paradoxicae Adversus Aristoteleos,* ed. B. Rochot (Paris, 1959), p. 7: "Verum nihi animos adjecit timoremque omnem detulit et Vivis et mei Charronis lectio" (preface). See also pp. 87, 103 (I, 3, 12; I, IV, 6).

awareness of English and Flemish reformers reflected the worldliness of an increasingly powerful bourgoisie, committed more and more to the secular delights of profit-making and to the manipulation of natural resources. Classical scholars, at the same time, rediscovered and printed the writings of Roman Stoicism with their special Latin accent upon the useful and prudential aspect of human knowledge. Cicero and Seneca strongly competed with Greek speculation; sixteenth century philology especially in northern Flanders, completed the revival of classical Stoicism, a fact of decisive momentum in the history of baroque civilization. Finally, the secularized Christian kerygma of Erasmus of Rotterdam and his tight circle of disciples and friends adapted medieval dogmas and canons to the more practical demands of the trader and the diplomat.

Vives' racial heritage and personal dispositions concurred and harmonized with this historical environment. A strong sense of involvement with communal responsibilities and issues marked his Jewish heritage.[38] More concretely, Vives learned from his maternal ancestors the lofty ideals and strict requirements involved in the administration of the law. We have already mentioned that as a child Vives studied the *Institutiones* of Justinian under the auspices of his uncle, Enrique March. We can assume that more than once Vives witnessed the processes of the Water-Tribunal, the unique Valencian jury set up by the farmers themselves to regulate the irrigation of the rice fields.[39] Vives' early interest in law and jurisprudence was further enhanced by his closest friends. Budé was an outstanding specialist in Roman law; Cranevelt, a successful and brilliant city-attorney; Thomas More, the right hand of Henry VIII as a mediator in trade disputes.

Vives' sapiential and legal writings reveal that his basic conception of wisdom as a prudent choice between moral alternatives sprang from a thoughtful reflection upon the judicial process. According to Vives, the wise philosopher and the prudent judge are very much alike in many respects. The judge decides according to the law, the procedural regulations, and the evidence of the case. His final sentence, however, involves a personal decision which is not exactly like the conclusion of syllogism or the result of a mathematical inference. Such a decision is made upon the basis of some interpretation of the law and according to the degree of credibility granted to the alleged evidence. In the final moment of this process, the judge is left alone in front of his case. The law is not self-

---

[38] See above, p. 20, note 17.
[39] Roger B. Merriman, *The Rise of the Spanish Empire in the Old World and in the New*, 3 vols., 2nd ed. (New York, 1962), I, pp. 452-475, gives a good description of the characteristic features of Aragonese government and administration.

explanatory, there are no rules for the interpretation of the rules. "Laws are straight and right, but they are also deaf and mute." [40] The evidence must be weighed according to the norms of that evasive and undefinable virtue which Aristotle called ἐπιείχεια and which neither Cicero and Boethius was able to translate into Latin. The personal choice of the judge is a moral choice. A prudent judge needs to be a good man, free from uncontrolled passions. Ethical perfection is a condition of prudence. In the same way, the evidence offered to human reason as motivation for ethical behavior is never mathematically compelling, but yields only a reasonable conjecture. The rules of the syllogism are like forensic procedural law: reason has to abide by them, but the rules alone do not guarantee the truth of the premises. The credibility of the conclusion depends on the credibility of the premises, and this, in most cases, is only a matter of prudent choice. Paradoxically, reason presupposes ethical perfection: only the pure man is inclined to understand the evidence which motivates right and pure behavior. Moral perfection, then, is not only the goal, but also the condition of all human knowledge. To be wise is to be virtuous enough to understand the reasons to be virtuous. Wisdom then can be defined either as a prudent judgment which leads to a virtuous choice, or as the virtue which makes possible a prudent judgment. This apparent circularity reflects the very core of the Stoic identification of ethics and epistemology, which Vives, among others, helped to revive in the sixteenth century. This eclectic defintion of virtue placed Vives in the very center of the complicated process of secularization and derationalization which began with Petrarch and culminated in Charron's masterpiece *De la sagesse* (1601).[41] With Colet and Lefèvre d'Etaples, Vives retained the noetic foundation of moral wisdom; but his insistence upon the final orientation of all knowledge to probity in action and moral behavior brought him close to Petrarch and Salutati. Although in his dialogue *Praelectio in Sapientem* Vives still identified wisdom with the knowledge of the Son of God, two years later (1524), in his much better known *Introductio ad Sapientiam*, wisdom was defined as the right evaluation of things earthly. However, as a whole, Vives appears much closer to those who insist upon the moral and natural character of wisdom, than to those who emphasize its noetic and revelatory aspects. Vives' influence seems to appear in the eclectics Budé and Cardan, in the naturalism of Conrad Celtis and

---

[40] M, V, 483; R, I, 685. (*Aedes legum*).
[41] E. F. Rice, *The Renaissance Idea of Wisdom* (Cambridge, 1958) gives a brilliant account of this process.

Thomas Elyot, and, especially, in the strong moralism of Justus Lipsius, Guillaume du Vair, Montaigne, and Charron.

There is, however, one particular aspect of knowledge which is directly relevant to morality, knowledge about man himself. Vives' treatise *De anima* belongs to a long and rich humanist tradition which began roughly with Petrarchs' attention to man's interiority, and found its classical statement with Ficino's *Theologia Platonica* and Pico della Mirandola's *De hominis dignitate*. Vives' special significance in this tradition is that he approached the study of man from an entirely new perspective.[42] Vives' concern was not to give a defintion of man's position in the cosmos nor to discuss the great themes of freedom and immortality, but to observe the internal mechanism of man's operations, and to derive from such observations practical rules of behavior and education. Dilthey was probably the first to notice the enormous importance of this new trend inaugurated by Vives, and to make clear its continuity in the works of Telesio, Cardano, Scaliger, Lipsius, Montaigne, and even Spinoza and Hobbes.[43] There is convincing evidence that both Cardano and Scaliger were familiar with Vives' ideas. Vives' description of human passions as a system of attractions and aversions governed by the principle of self-conservation became the center of Telesio's thought, and through Telesio, the guiding principle of Hobbes' political philosophy. Dilthey made a thorough comparison of Vives' and Spinoza's theory of passions, pointing to the almost literal parallelism between Vives' introduction to the third book of the treatise *De anima* and Spinoza's well-known preface to the third book of *Ethics*.[44] As in the case of Montaigne, the racial affinity of Vives and Spinoza adds a special touch to the relationship between the two men. Lipsius' long residence in Louvain (1592-1606), only fifty years after Vives' death, justifies the assumption that he read some of Vives' most popular books. Vives' *Introductio ad Sapientiam* was printed twelve times in the Low Countries alone during Lipsius' life.[45] Recently some scholars have added Descartes to those who felt Vives' influence by point-

[42] N. Lenkeith's translation of Vives' *Fabula de homine* (*The Renaissance Philosophy of Man*, ed. E. Cassirer, P. O. Kristeller, J. H. Randall [Chicago, 1948] "may well illustrate the interdependence of the cutural movement of the Renaissance" (*ibid.*, p. 386) and Pico's pervasive influence among Northern Humanists, but fails to give an accurate idea of Vives' more creative and mature thought.

[43] Dilthey, "Die Funktion des Anthropologie in der Kultur des 16. and 17. Jahrhunderts," *Weltanschauung und Analyse des Menschen seit Renaissance und Reformation*, pp. 416-439.

[44] Dilthey writes: "Das berühmte Vorwort Spinozas zu seiner Affektenlehre ... welche die Notwendigkeit seiner neuer Bearbeitung hervorhebt, hat seinen vorlaufer in dem Anfang des dritten Buches [*De anima*], das von den Affekten handelt." (*Ibid.*, p. 424).

[45] See Appendix I, pp. 299-305.

ing to the striking similarities between Descartes *Traité des passions* and Vives' *De Anima*.[46] For these reasons, such scholars as Lange, Foster Watson, Dilthey, Dugald-Stewart, Menéndez y Pelayo, Sciacca, and many others, have not hesitated to call Juan Luis Vives ,the forgotten Humanist from Valencia, "the father of modern psychology." [47]

Vives' concern with man was also an eloquent proof of a profound naturalism. An educational reform planned upon the solid basis of self-knowledge indicates that the melioration of the individual depends primarily on the right use of human resources. Man can be corrected insofar as he is known. Man's relations to himself and to other men have to be solidly founded upon natural principles which reason can discover and men of all races and religions are able to embrace. Progress and peace cannot be made dependent upon dogmatic differences or institutional polarization. In fact, Vives claimed that religion is only the climax of moral wisdom.[48] Although Vives never made a formal distinction between natural and supernatural religion, his constant tendency was to reduce the latter to the former. Like Erasmus, Vives was much more interested in the ethical dimension of religion than in its revelatory or institutional character. Vives' name deserves much more to be linked to that of Grotius or Herbert of Cherbury than to that of Ignatius of Loyola. I must admit, however, that this judgment about Vives' religiosity is not a popular one. Catholic and Spanish scholars generally have not only denied Vives' apparent naturalism, but maintained the unspoiled Catholic orthodoxy of the Spanish Humanist.[49] Protestant critics, on the other hand, present Vives as a sympathizer of the Reformation, or even

[46] Lefèvre (*L'Humanisme de Descartes*, p. 53, note 1) quotes Vives as the first possible source of Descartes' *Traité des Passions*. See also, G. Lewis, "Une source inexplorée du *Traité des Passions*," *Revue philosophique de la France et del'Etranger*, VII (1948).

F. M. Sciacca (*Le Filosofia di Tomasso Reid* [Napoli, 1935]) writes: "... per la psicologia Cartesio deve molto allo Spagnuolo Vives, da lui spesse volte citato." (p. 124, note 1).

[47] F. M. Sciacca (*ibid.*): ("Vives)e il fondatore della psicologia empirica contra quella razionale."

Dilthey, "Funktion der Anthropologie," p. 423, "So bezeichnet Vives den Übergang aus der metaphysischen Psychologie zu der beschreibenden und zergliedernden."

On Dugald-Steward, see above, note 25. Watson wrote a book entitled *Vives, el padre de la psicología moderna* (Madrid, 1916).

M. y Pelayo writes: "Vives es el gran pedagogo del Renacimiento, el escritor más completo y enciclopédico de aquella época portentosa... En él comienza la escuela moderna... Rodeado de eruditos que filosofaban sin grande originalidad... invocó el testimonio de la razón y no el de los antiguos, y formuló por vez primera los cánones de la ciencia experimental..." (*Ensayos de crítica filosófica*, pp. 167-168).

Lange, *Vives*, p. 114 calls Vives "el mayor reformador de la filosofía de su época."
[48] M, VI, 386; R, II, 645 a. (*DD.*, II, 5, 1).
[49] This is the typical attitude of Bonilla, Menéndez y Pelayo, and their followers.

as a covert Lutheran.[50] Others have insisted on Vives' profound Erasmianism.[51] Since the last opinion has previously been corrected and qualified in chapter seven, here I must deal with the others, which I consider to be even further from the mark.

If Juan Luis Vives is judged by post-Tridentine standards, we cannot find in him a convincing Catholic. His faith in the Church as an institution was totally inoperative and practically nonexistent in spite of some routine verbal protestations of loyalty.[52] He practically ignored the fundamental teaching that the Sacraments are the ordinary channel of sanctifying grace.[53] He never attempted to justify nor to defend the "divine right" of the Papacy. Further, Vives betrayed some attitudes which, at least in that century, were highly suspicious. He was absolutely uninterested in the theological disputes of the day, disputes which appeared fundamental tests of loyalty to the faithful servants of the Church. In fact, Vives truly despised the fanaticism of both sides and bitterly criticised the abuses of the clergy and the Pope.[54] Vives also rejected the superstitious aspects of Catholic piety, and was convinced that philology was more important than patristic tradition in the interpretation of the Holy Writ.[55] For all these reasons the Jesuits attacked him, and some of his books were filed in the *Index*; the simple fact that his devotional books were completely acceptable to Protestants, Socinians, Anglicans, Erasmians, and Catholics proves beyond any doubt their dogmatic neutrality. Some Protestant scholars have gone to the point of claiming Vives as their own, a claim which would be totally absurd if Vives had been a freelancing, secular Jesuit, as some Spanish scholars have described him.[56]

---

[50] Besides Osiander and Brücker (see above, p. 3, note 11) we should mention Lange, who in his essay on Vives insists frequently on the fact that "from a Protestant point of view Vives' writings do not contain anything truly unacceptable." (*Vives*, p. 71).

[51] Specially Marcel Bataillon. (See above, Chapter 7).

[52] M, VIII, 177; R, II, 1469 a. Vives professes to abide by the ecclesiastical interpretation of the Bible. (*De VFC.*, II, 9). See also, *ibid.*, 22; 1342. (*De VFC.*, I, 3).

These solemn declarations of obedience to the Church appear frequently in the writings of those writers of the sixteenth century whose orthodoxy was most questionable. For Telesio, e.g., see N. Abbagnano, *B. Telesio* (Milano, 1941), p. 40.

[53] See above my comments on the un-sacramental character of Vives' *Introductio ad Sapientiam*, p. 205.

[54] Vives' apologetical treatise *De veritate fidei Christianae*, a posthumous book written in the middle of the Lutheran controversy, does not even mention the divine right of the Papacy. One of the most eloquent and passionate criticism of Catholic priesthood is the last part of book 2, *De concordia*. (M, V, 227-229); R, II, 129-132).

[55] In spite of Vives' admiration for Erasmus' amazing work in editing the Fathers of the Church, his own intellectual activities disclose a surprising detachment from the Patristic tradition.

[56] Vives' contribution to the Erasmian campaign in favour of an ecumenical council has often been misrepresented as one of the initial steps toward the Counter-reformation. See, e.g., J. B. Gomis, *Vives pro Concilio de Trento* (Madrid, 1945).

Unfortunately for the Reformation, Vives was far from being a Protestant. In spite of his religious tolerance and liberal ecumenism, Vives had no sympathy for Luther, and much less for the religious mission of Henry VIII. Vives could not share Luther's conviction of the innermost corruption of man through Adam's sin; on the contrary, Vives' life was passionately dedicated to those human values which the divine punishment had spared. Luther's Christ was the great expiator, Vives' Christ was the enlightened teacher. Luther believed that Christ covers up the miseries of man with his own redeeming blood, while Vives was convinced that Christ's teaching helps man to bring his passions under the control of his own reason. Lutheranism meant for Vives the destruction of European unity. By some kind of historical inertia, Vives was inclined to prefer a weakened and less dogmatic form of Catholic unity than Lutheran disruption and chaos.[57]

Vives' ecumenical Christian spirit sprang from a hidden but profound trend toward natural religion. Christ's teaching and guidance, Vives claimed, basically coincide with the inborn moral sense of all mankind. The pages of De veritate Fidei which deal with the truths of Christianity and their fitness to the needs of human nature, are the most eloquent of the book. Vives maintained that the fundamental truths of God's existence and the immortality of the soul are "common notions" of all mankind which human reason can reach with a degree of prudent persuasion sufficient to base upon them a firm moral decision. Christ himself appeared to Vives as the glorious confirmation and ideal of moral virtue. Christ as the Son of God or the Founder of a Church was not Vives' Christ. As for the Church and its dogmas, he felt the same indifference he had experienced toward the subtleties of scholasticism: they had nothing to do with life. Vives' religion was much more Christian than Catholic, much more theocentric than it was Christian. Without a profound faith in God, the Creator and the Supreme end of man, Vives cannot be understood; but sacrament, dogmas, and canons were no part of him.

d. Vives' Position in the History of Education

Vives arrived in the Low Countries in a critical moment for the history of modern European education. Dilthey's thesis that Dutch and Flemish humanists were mainly responsible for the conversion of Italian humanist

[57] Such is the interpretation of Lange (Luis Vives, p. 74) with whom I basically agree. In a way, the whole Erasmian movement can be seen as an attempt to save Europe's religious unity.

ideals into a revolutionary system of pedagogy can be accepted today with only minor qualifications.[58] The first decades of the sixteenth century were the climax of a long process which Dilthey divides into steps. In the fourteenth century the Brethren of the Common Life initiated a Hieronymian reformation which urged a solid instruction in classical Latin as a means of understanding the Bible. In the fifteenth century the genius of Rudolph Agricola blended into a harmonious ideal the pietistic goals of the Brethren and the Humanistic values of Theodore Gaza and Battista Guarino, his Ferrara masters. Agricola and Reuchlin spread through the Rhineland their own version of humanism; Hegius in Deventer and Rudolph von Langen in Münster began to update educational policies according to the new principles. Erasmus, a disciple of Hegius, exported the new spirit to England, where Colet, Lily, Linacre, and Grocyn were actively dedicated to the transformation of medieval education.

At this precise moment Vives arrived in Flanders, after his frustrating experience in Paris. In contact with the Louvain humanists of the College Trilingue, and as a member of Erasmus' circle, Vives began a calm but exhaustive criticism of medieval education together with a constructive projection into the future of Renaissance ideals and values. His masters were Cicero, Quintilian, and Plutarch; Saint Jerome, Erasmus' favorite, takes only a secondary place for Vives.

Vives' educational books incorporate all the lasting values of Renaissance pedagogy: the principle of a secular education for all with special emphasis upon women and the poor, the professional character of teaching, the need of supervision, the respectability of the vernacular, the orientation of education to the practical needs of life, the ethical responsibility of the educator, the importance of style and diction. Vives, obviously, belongs to the mainstream of sixteenth century pedagogy. His influence upon later educators is more social than individual, as a representative of a set of new ideas rather than as an original innovator. Nevertheless, I think it is fair to say that within the tradition of Renaissance pedadogy Vives holds a central and leading position. His name and his suggestions appeared in almost every book on the subject written in Europe up to the days of the Cartesian revolution. Vives' biographers have pointed to his impact upon such educators as Rabelais, Sturm, and Baduel in France; Thomas Elyot, Mulcaster, and Roger Ascham in England; Melanch-

---

[58] These qualifications have to do with the role of Italian educators, such as Guarino de Verona and Vittorino da Feltre and their influence upon Rudolph Agricola. See, e.g., Garin, La cultura filosofica, "Motivi della cultura filosofica Ferrarense nel Rinascimento," pp. 402-432.

thon, Verripe, Neander, and Trotzendorf in Germany; and finally, the creators of the Jesuit *ratio studiorum* in Italy and Spain.[59]

Vives' personal contribution to Renaissance pedagogy consists, first of all, in the mature philosophical statement of the new educational principles. In the second place, Vives rose above his contemporaries in the judicious and wise eclecticism of his program. Vives corrected the two main excesses of sixteenth century educators: the exaggerated pietism of Erasmus, Melanchthon, and other confessional pedagogues, and the overemphasis of diction and style which characterized the pedagogy of Johan Sturm in Strassburg and of Thomas Elyot in the Court of Henry VIII.[60] These two points deserve further consideration. Vives denied that the aim of education is the understanding of the Holy Writ or of scholastic theology, although he believed in the final subordination of all worldly education to a religious interpretation of life. The ultimate purpose of all school activities is to achieve a prudent evaluation of human pursuits in the light of man's final goal. However, dogmatic considerations remain totally strange to Vives' pedagogy. Vives' educational reform was completely independent from the German protestant schools and from the Jesuit schools in the lands of the counter-Reformation, although both relied heavily upon Vives' methods and drafts. The second excess Vives helped to quell was the banality of the Ciceronians and of those humanists who took Quintilian's rhetorical ideals as a mere glorification of beautiful words. Vives encouraged a return to Latin and Greek classicism, but warned against the dangers of literature and the limitations of *imitatio*. Finally, Vives' unique contribution to the history of educational theory lay in the farsightedness of some of his visions. A clear proof of this is the intensive study which German scholars have made of the undeniable relationship between Vives and Comenius, the pedagogue of the Cartesian age. The similarities here are certainly striking. Like the Spanish Humanist of the sixteenth century, Comenius stressed a balanced harmony of knowledge, virtue and piety. Education prepares for life by fostering an

---

[59] On Vives' relations to Rabelais, see above, pp. 183-184. Lange, *Vives,* pp. 162-166, makes a comparison between Vives' pedagogy and Sturm.

On Baduel's relations to Vives, see M. J. Gaufrés, *Claude Baduel et la Reforme des etudes au XVI siècle* (Paris, 1880), pp. 30-33. The author narrates the visit of Baduel to Vives in Louvain, after the long talks of the French pedagogue with Melanchthon in Wittenberg.

Parmentier has made a comprehensive study of Vives' influence upon the English pedagogues (See above p. 11): Nonetheless the best authority on the subject is Foster Watson. (See above, p. 12). Lange (*Vives,* pp. 47-171) explores the relations of Vives with German educators. On the influence of Vives upon the Jesuits, see Bonilla, *Vives,* III, 121.

[60] See Woodward, *Studies in Education,* pp. 268-321.

industrious character, a refined virtue, a "sweet conversation," and fear of God. Like Vives before him, Comenius based his educational theory upon self-knowledge and observation of human operations. Comenius' insistence upon temperamental differences and personal talents, memory training, and the importance of sense perception in the educational process was obviously inspired by Vives' works.[61] If Comenius is rigthly praised as "a prophet of modern principles and methods," Vives is certainly entitled to share part of this glory.

e. A Final Word

The basic contention of this book has been that Vives deserves an important place in the intellectual history of Europe. Vives' merits in the past have been either ignored or exaggerated. He was certainly not what Spanish scholars, or most of them, have tried to make out of him; he was different and in many ways better. A partial distortion of Vives' thought is easily excusable. After all, his highly complex, encyclopedic, and eclectic work includes a variety of ingredients which do not seem compatible with each other. Vives is known as a Humanist, but he despised the world of poety and fiction – "full of evil and lust" – and called man "a monster worse than beasts." He is supposed to be a characteristic figure of the classical revival, although he considered Plato and Aristotle the products of a childish and immature civilization. The author of revolutionary books on pedagogy, he personally hated the noble art of teaching and was one of the few humanists who never guided a rich Prince in the foundation of a new school or in the reform of an old institution. His personal pessimism contrasts with an unwavering faith in the endless resources of nature which in time correct all the mistakes of the individual. He believed in God and his providence but he was contented with a reasonable persuasion about His existence. He wrote a summary of Aristotelian metaphysics, but he was convinced that knowledge was primarily an instrument to master nature rather than a tool for theoretical speculation. He believed that all the secrets of human behavior could be explained by a combination of black and yellow bile, but he was the first to observe and describe with dispassionate concentration the emotional mechanism of man. He thought that the time to overhaul the physics of Aristotle had arrived, but he tried to find a biblical proof of the essential difference between the heavenly and the sublunar universe. He called himself a logician, but he diluted the study of formal inference into a

[61] See above, p. 10, note 33.

rhetorical manual of dialectical argumentation. Modern and intuitive as he was, his work was still imprisoned by typically medieval patterns of thought. He never understood the role of mathematics in the world of physics nor the importance of economics in the body politic. He never questioned the morality of colonialism and failed to see the true position of women in a modern society. He was unable to enjoy poetry because of its moral risks, and condemned sex as an enemy of enlightened reason.

In spite of these apparent contradictions and limitations Vives was a great thinker. In the midst of a loud generation lost in sectarian controversy or in the worship of pure form, he stood alone, aware that human culture had reached a crossroad where fundamental decisions had to be made. Although Vives was a privileged witness to the mental trends of his contemporaries, in many ways he was superior to them. Firstly, because he concerned himself with the basic issues rother than with the detail, with the problems rather than with the form. Secondly, because he resisted the temptation to be radical in an era of change where it was still possible to dream a constructive synthesis of the old and the new. Thirdly, because in an age of polarization he managed to live in peace with all, *sine querela,* alone with his conscience and his thoughts.

Vives asked himself, first of all, what philosophical knowledge itself should be. The issue transcended questions of "method." The very conception of human culture depended upon the solution. Vives' answer came out to be a total indictment of Aristotelian and medieval intellectualism. Knowledge for Vives was not an end in itself, a contemplation of reality, a theory, a rational verbalization of our vision of things. Vives rejected the Peripatetic notion of *episteme,* the scientific conclusion from first principles through an almost mechanical and mathematical inference based on formal rules of validity. Vives scorned medieval speculation on God, nature, and man, based upon metaphysical notions and deductive processes, as useless and proud. In his opinion Aristotle could be reduced to a general metaphysical frame of reference without detail or controversy, and to a simplified manual of syllogistic rules. This rejection of Aristotle, however, did not entail a conversion to Plato or an attempt to reconcile the two great masters of classical thought. Vives was persuaded that both Plato and Aristotle had to be transcended. Vives' conception of philosophical knowledge was rather a modern interpretation of that eclectic, practical, and moralizing form of Roman Stoicism which Latin humanists found in the writings of Cicero, Seneca, and Quintilian.

Knowledge for Vives was primarily an instrument of man *qua* moral being. Knowledge has been given by God to man only in direct proportion to his needs as a morally responsible creature. Through knowledge man reaches enough motivation for moral behavior. The standard of that motivation is not a theoretical and naked criterion of truth and evidence, but the degree of moral persuasion generated in man by his cognitive faculties. Theoretical rationality is reduced to practical persuasion and prudence. Even the "arts," or the rules to master nature in order to satisfy man's physical needs, cannot reach their goal without a prudent evaluation of facts. The inductive process does not generate more than a strong belief, the validity of which has to be accepted in proportion to the practical results it yields. The general rules derived from induction do not pretend to be an interpretation of nature in the Aristotelian sense of science, but only practical guiding lines in the use of nature for the sake of man.

Vives' Stoic conviction that knowledge was above all an implement of man's ethical equipment led him to the naturalistic belief that the Stoic sage was a perfect Christian. Vives was convinced that Christianity was nothing more than a glorified form of that natural wisdom which consists in living according to right reason. Nature itself has impressed upon the conscience of man an innate moral sense and some theoretical common notions which guide man in the application of knowledge to the purpose and in the measure God wanted it be used.

Without this basic conception of philosophical knowledge Vives' educational program cannot be understood. Vives turned to education because he was convinced that in man himself, in nature itself, one could find the powers and the means to reform the individual and the society. Vives' treatise *De anima* in a brilliant study of man's internal mechanism for the sake of educational reform.

Vives' influence upon European thought was surely significant because his books were found in all the libraries of the continent. It had to be vague because he suggested more than he explicitly said. It was rather impersonal because he reflected, more than he caused, the mental achievements of the age. It is safe to say that the moderate scepticism of Montaigne cannot be well understood without the growing criticism of the powers of reason which is mirrored in Vives' books. Ramus' popularity had something to do with Vives' concern about the usefulness of Peripatetic logic. Gassendi lost any respect for the Aristotelian "sect" by reading the books of our Humanist. Grotius followed Vives' steps and found in the laws of nature what medieval Europe had tried to find in ecclesiastical legislation. Telesio's naturalistic reductionism was only a radical replica of Vives' powerful naturalism. Melanchthon complemented Vives in Luther's zone of influence, although the Spanish scholar never succumbed to the fascination of any religious leader. Sturm, Baduel, and Comenius reproduced most of Vives' pedagogical ideas. Bacon substituted the more baroque and pretentious *instauratio* for Vives' idea of natural growth, but coincided with Vives in proclaiming the pragmatic purposiveness of all human knowledge.

The prudent choice of Vives' judgment and the cautious wager of Pascal reduce the rationale of faith to a dim form of fideistic voluntarism, probably still acceptable before the Vatican Council, but certainly far removed from Thomistic theology. In any case, Vives' skin-deep faith in the Church as an institution contrasted sharply with his profound conviction that the vital part of religion is within the grasp of natural reason – a teaching which, from Herbert of Cherbury, led to all the deistic forms of religious naturalism in the two generations following Vives' death. Vives' Stoic ideal of wisdom through the control of our passions reappeared in another peninsular Jew, the great Spinoza. Finally, Reid, Hamilton, and Dugald-Stewart proclaimed Vives as one of the most convincing crusaders in the cause of common sense.

Vives is still significant today because he can help us to understand better the crisis of his age, a crisis which modern man has not yet entirely overcome. The lesson of Vives' moderate eclecticism is not completely out of place in a world divided by radical views to the right and to the left. His emphasis upon the moral values of the individual can only increase the awareness of the younger generations that the main problem of our advanced industrial society is man himself. A breeze of calm and noble humanism can only be welcomed in an age when it is difficult to decide what is more awful and imposing: the power of the machines which man has put together or the stupidity of the human beings who use them.

APPENDIX I

EDITIONS OF VIVES' MAIN WORKS
FROM 1520 TO 1650

This catalogue contains all the editions of Vives' most popular works up to the middle of the seventeenth century, as they are mentioned by the authors whose abbreviated names appear below. Since the only purpose of this appendix is to prove the popularity of Vives' books, the reference to the editions is reduced to a shortened title of the book, date and place of publication, the name of the Library where the book is found today, and, finally, (whenever this datum is available) the order of the different editions. In the case of translations I will further give the language and (when possible) the name of the translator. The titles of the books are given in alphabetical order.

Signs and abbreviations

A) Authors
- (B): A. Bonilla y San Martín, *La Filosofía del Renacimiento*, III, 181-241.
- (K): F. Kaiser, *J. L. Vives Paedagogische Schriften, passim.*
- (L): A. Lange, "Luis Vives," *Enzyklopaedie des gesamten Erziehung,* IX, *passim.*
- (M): G. Mayans y Síscar, *J. L. Vives Vita,* Vivis *Opera Omnia,* I, 1-220.
- (N): A. J. Naméche, *Mémoire sur la vie et les ecrits de J. L. Vives, passim.*
- (P): M. Paquot, *Mémoires,* II, *passim.*
- (V): E. Vanden Bussche, *J. L. Vives. Eclaircissements et rectifications bibliographiques, passim.*
- (E): Estelrich, J., *Vivés.*

B) Libraries
- BB: Bibliotheque de Besançon
- BC: Bibliotheque de Chartres
- BE: Biblioteca del Escorial
- BMa: Bibliotheque Mazarine

BM: British Museum
BN: Biblioteca del Noviciado de Madrid
BNM: Biblioteca Nacional de Madrid
BNP: Bibliotheque Nationale de Paris
BRP: Biblioteca Real de Palacio
BUB: Biblioteca de la Universidad de Barcelona
BUP: Bibliotheque de l'Université de Paris
BUV: Biblioteca de la Universidad de Valencia
MP: Musée Pedagogique de Paris
Lib.: Library

Adversus Pseudo-Dialecticos
    1520   Paris   BNM, BM   (B)
           Louvain   BNM   (B)
    1538   Basel   (V)

Commentaria Sancti Augustini
    1522   Basel   BM   (B)
    1529   Basel   BN   (N)
    1532   Paris   BNM   (B)
    1544   Paris   (K)
    1551   Venice   (K)
    1555   Paris   (K)
    1563   Lyon   BM   (N)
    1570   Basel   (K)
    1574   French by G. Hervet   (E)
    1580   Lyon   BM   (K)
    1585   French, Hervet, 2nd   (E)
    1600   Antwerp   (K)
    1610   London   English by Hyrde   (B)
    1613   Paris   (K)

    1635   Alcalá   BN   (B,M)
De Anima et vita
    1538   Basel   BUB   (B)
    1555   London   BM   (B)
           Lyon   BNP   (B)
    1556   Lyon   BM   (B)
    1563   Tiguri   (N)
    1569   Zürich   BNM   (B)

De concordia et discordia
    1526   Bruges   BM, BUV   (B)
           Antwerp   (M)
    1529   Antwerp   BNM, BM   (B)

1532	Lyon			(N)
1536	Cologne	BC		(B)
1538	Basel	BN		(B)

De Disciplinis

1532	Cologne	BNM	(B)
1551	Lyon	BN	(M)
1612	Oxford	BM	(B)
1636	Lyon	BM	(B)

De officiis mariti

1538	Basel	BN		(B)
1540	Basel	Lib. of Rodez		(B)
1541	Basel	BNP		(B)
1553	London	BM	English by Pynell	(B)

De subventione pauperum

1526	Bruges	BM		(B)
1530	Paris	BN		(B)
1532	Paris	BNP		(B)
	Lyon	BUV		(B)
1533	Strassbourg	BM	German by?	(K)
1545	Venice		Italian by?	(B)
1583	Lyon			(N)

De Veritate Fidei

1543	Basel		(B)
1551	Basel	BNM	(N)
1555	Lyon		(B)
1564	Cologne		(N)
1639	Lyon	BNM	(B)

Exercitatio Linguae Latinae

1538	Basel	Lib. of Gray	(B)
	Breda		(K)
	Cologne		(K)
1539	Paris	BM	(B)
	Lyon	BM	(B)
	Lyon	Lib. of Dole	(B)
	Basel	BNP	(B)
1541	Bruges		(V)
1542	Lyon	BUB	(B)
1543	Lyon	BNM	(B)
1544	Paris	BUP	(B)
	Cologne	Lib. of Nancy	(B)
1545	Lyon	BB	(B)

	Paris	Lib. of Vesoul		(B)
1547	Paris	BMa		(B)
	Paris	Lib. of Bayaux		(K)
	Aberdeen			(B)
1548	Avignon			(K)
1550	Paris	BC		(B)
1553	Lyon	Lib. of Rodez		(B)
1555	Paris	BMa		(B)
1556	Antwerp	Lib. of Anvers		(B)
1557	Lyon	Lib. of Mende		(B)
1558	Cologne			(K)
1560	Lyon	BMa	French by Housteville	(B)
1564	Lyon	Lib. of Toulouse		(B)
	Venice			(K)
	Paris	BNP	Housteville, 2nd	(B)
	Augsburg			(L)
1568	Lyon	Lib. of Carpentras		(V)
	Florence	MB	Italian by Mancini	(B)
	Lyon	Lib. of Avignon	Housteville, 3rd	(B)
1569	Venice	BNM	Mancini, 2nd	(B)
1571	Nüremberg			(M)
	Anvers	BNP	Housteville, 4th	(B)
1573	Paris	BNP	French by Jamin	(B)
	Nancy	BNP	Housteville, 5th	(B)
1574	Zaragoza		Spanish by Anton	(M)
	Augsburg			(L)
1575	Anvers	Lib. of Vesoul	Housteville, 6th	(B)
1576	Madrid	BNM	Spanish by Coret	(B)
1577	Valencia	BNM		(B)
1578	Valencia			(M)
	Paris	Lib. of Abbeville	Housteville, 7th	(M)
1582	Nüremberg		Spanish by Navarro	(B)
1585	Lyon	BNP		(M)
	Nüremberg			(B)
1587	Lyon	Lib. of Auxerre		(B)
1593	Leipzig	Lib. of Perpignan		(L)
	Alcalá			(B)
1597	Madrid	BN		(B)
1607	Zaragoza			(K)
1612	Venice			(M)
	Venice	Lib. of Mende		(B)
1615	Barcelona			(M)
1618	Bremen			(M)

1620	Edinburg	BNM		(B)
1622	Nüremberg			(B)
	Antwerp	Lib. of Anvers		(B)
1625	Aberdeen	BM		(B)
	Wittenberg			(N)
1627	Zaragoza			(M)
1641	Leewarden	BM		(B)
1643	Barcelona	BNM		(B)
1649	Madrid	BNM		(B)

Institutio feminae Christianae

1524	Antwerp	BM, BRP		(B)
1528	Valencia	BM, BE	Spanish by Justiniano	(B)
	Alcalá	BN	Justiniano, 2nd	(B)
	Valencia		Justiniano, 3rd	(B)
1537	Basel			(B)
1538	Basel			(B)
1539	Zaragoza	BNM, BN	Justiniano, 4th	(B)
	Zamora	BNM	Justiniano, 5th	(B)
1540	Basel	BB		(B)
	London	BM	English by Hyrde	(B)
1541	Basel	BNP		(B)
	London	BM	Hyrde, 2nd	(B)
1542	Paris	BNP	French by Changry	(N)
1543	Paris	BNP	Changry, 2nd	(B)
1544	Augsburg	BM	German by Bruno	(B)
1545	Zaragoza		Justiniano, 6th	(B)
	Paris		Changry, 3rd	(B)
	Lyon		Changry, 4th	(B)
	Paris		Changry, 5th	(B)
	Poitiers		Changry, 6th	(B)
1546	Venice	BM	Italian by Vangris	(B)
1548	Paris		Changry, 7th	(B)
1555	Zaragoza	BNM	Justiniano, 7th	(B)
1557	London	BM	Hyrde, 3rd	(B)
1566	Frankfurt	BM	Bruno, 2nd	(B)
1579	Paris	BM	French by Tyron	(B)
	Anvers	BMa	Changry, 8th	(B)
	Lyon		Changry, 9th	(B)
1583	Valladolid	BNM	Justiniano, 8th	(M)
1587	Paris	BNP	French by Lemocier	(B)
1592	London	BM	Hyrde, 4th	(B)
1614	Paris		Changry, 12th	(B)
1641	Basel			(B)

Introductio ad Sapientiam

1524	Louvain			(V)
	Paris	BM		(B)
1526	Paris	BUB		(B)
1530	Lyon			(K)
1531	Paris	BUB		(B)
	Bruges			(K)
1532	Lyon	BNP		(B)
1535	Leyden	BNP		(B)
1536	Leyden			(K)
1539	Basel	BMa		(B)
	Leipzig		German by Bruno	(L)
	Leyden	MP		(K)
	Cologne			(K)
1540	London	BM	English by Morrison	(B)
	Basel		Bruno, 2nd	(L)
1541	Paris			(B)
1543	Paris	Lib. of Rodez		(B)
	Basel			(M)
1544	Burgos			(M)
	Sevilla	BN	Spanish by Salazar	(B)
	London	BM	Morrison, 2nd	(B)
1544	Bruges			(B)
1545	Ingolstadt	Lib. of Ingolstadt	Bruno, 3rd	(K)
1547	Lyon	Lib. of Aurillac		(B)
	Alcalá	BN	Salazar, 2nd	(B)
	Paris	BC		(B)
1548	Cologne			(P)
	Ingolstadt			(K)
1550	Paris		French by Paradin	(B)
1551	Medina	BN		(B)
	Leyden			(K)
1553	Antwerp	BMa	Paradin, 2nd	(B)
1555	Basel	Lib. of Dijou		(B)
	Antwerp	Lib. of Anvers		(B)
1556	Oporto	BUB		(B)
	Berna	Lib. of Carcassone		(B)
	Leyden			(K)
	Lyon	BMa		(B)
1561	Anvers	BNM	Spanish by Astudillo	(B)
1562	Cologne	MP		(B)
1565	Lyon	BN		(B)
1566	Cologne			(K)

1572	Salamanca			(M)
1586	Cologne			(M)
	Prague			(K)
1589	Cologne			(K)
1593	Leipzig			(M)
	Antwerp			(M)
1599	Basel			(K)
1604	Sevilla	BN	Astudillo, 2nd	(B)
1615	Helmstadt			(K)
	Leyden			(K)
1637	Helmstadt			(K)
1643	Cambridge	BM		(B)
1646	Cologne			(K)
1649	Hamburg			(K)

Preces et Meditationes generales

1520	Louvain	BNM		(B)
1535	Antwerp	BM		(B)
1538	Antwerp			(N)
1539	Basel	BMa		(B)
	Burgos	BNM	Spanish by Ortega	(B)
1552	Avignon		French by L'Eucreau	(B)
1578	Paris		French by Buly	(V)
1593	Burgos	BNM	Ortega, 2nd	(M)

Satellitium

1524	Louvain			(V)
	Paris	BM		(B)
1547	Frankfurt	BM		(L)
1548	Cologne	BM	French by?	(P)

APPENDIX II

CHRONOLOGICAL LIST OF VIVES' BOOKS

1514,	Paris.	*Christi Jesu Triumphus. Virginis Dei-Parentis Ovatio*
1514,	Paris.	*Veritas fucata*
1518,	Louvain.	*Meditationes in septem psalmos quos vocant poenitentiae*
1518,	Louvain.	*Fabula de Homine*
1518,	Louvain.	*Praelectio in Georgica Vergilii*
1518,	Louvain.	*Anima senis*
1518,	Louvain.	*Genethliacon Jesu Christi*
1518,	Louvain.	*De tempore quo, id est, de pace in qua natus est Christus*
1518,	Louvain.	*Clypei Christi Descriptio*
1518,	Louvain.	*De initiis, sectis et laudibus philosophiae*
1519,	Louvain.	*Liber in pseudo-dialecticos*
1520,	Paris.	*Praefatio et Vigilia in Somnium Scipionis Ciceroniani*
1520,	Paris.	*Aedes legum*
1520,	Louvain.	*In leges Ciceronis Praelectio*
1520,	Louvain.	*Declamationes quinque Syllanae*
1521,	Louvain.	*Declamatio qua Quintiliano respondetur pro noverca contra caecum*
1521,	Louvain.	*Commentaria in XXII libros De Civitate Dei Divi Aurelii Augustini*
1521,	Louvain.	*Praelectio in convivia Francisci Philelfi*
1522,	Louvain.	*Praelectio in quartum Rhetoricorum ad Herennium*
1522,	Louvain.	*In Suetonium quaedam*
1522,	Louvain.	*In sapientem praelectio: Dialogus qui sapiens inscribitur*
1522,	Louvain.	*De Europae statu ac tumultibus*
1523,	Louvain.	*Veritas fucata sive de licentia poetica: quantum poëtis liceat a Veritate abscedere*
1523,	Louvain.	*De institutione feminae Christianae*
1523,	Oxford, Londres.	*De ratione studii puerilis*
1523,	Oxford, Londres.	*Liber de consultatione*

1523, Oxford,
     Londres.   *Isocratis Oratio Areopagitica*
1524, Bruges.   *Satellitium animi*
1524, Bruges.   *Introductio ad Sapientiam*
1525, Oxford.   *De Francisco Galliae Rege a Caesare capto*
1525, Oxford.   *De pace inter Caesarem et Franciscum Galliarum Regem deque optimo regni statu*
1526, Bruges.   *De subventione pauperum*
1526, Bruges.   *De Europae disidiis et bello Turcico*
1526, Bruges.   *De conditione vitae Christianorum sub Turca*
1528, Bruges.   *De officio mariti*
1529, Bruges.   *Sacrum Diurnum de Sudore Domini nostri Jesu Christi*
1529, Bruges.   *Concio de sudore nostro et Christi*
1529, Bruges.   *Meditatio de Passione Christi in psalmum XXXVII*
1529, Bruges.   *De concordia et discordia in humano genere*
1529, Bruges.   *Liber de pacificatione*
1531, Bruges.   *De disciplinis*
1532, Bruges.   *De ratione dicendi*
1534, Bruges.   *Descriptio Temporum et Rerum populi Romani*
1535, Bruges.   *De communione rerum ad germanos inferiores*
1535, Bruges.   *Excitationes animi in Deum*
                (Praeparatio animi ad orandum. Preces et meditationes quotidianae. Preces et meditationes generales. In precationem Dominicam comentarius.)
1536, Paris?   *Poeticon Astronomicon, de Julio Higinio*
1536, Paris?   *De conscribendis epistolis*
1537, Breda.   *Bucolicarum Vergilii interpretatio*
1538, Breda.   *Censura de Aristotelis operibus*
1538, Bruges.   *De anima et vita*
1538, Bruges.   *Linguae Latinae Exercitatio*
1543, Bruges.   *De Veritate Fidei Christianae*

BIBLIOGRAPHY

a. Primary Sources

Bacon, Francis. *The Works of F. Bacon*, eds. J. Spedding and R. L. Ellis, London, 1887.

Baduel, Claudé. *De ratione vitae studiosae ac litteratae in matrimonio collocandae ac degendae*. Lyon, 1544.

Budé, Guillaume. *Annotationes . . . in quattuor et viginti Pandectarum libros*. Paris, 1535.

—. *Répertoire analytique et chronologique de la correspondence de G. Budé*, ed. L. Delaruelle. Toulouse, 1907.

Cano, Melchor. *Opera omnia*. Bassano, 1776.

Coronel, Antonio. *In Posteriora Aristotelis commentaria*. Paris, 1510.

Dullaert, Jean. *Questiones super octo libros Physicorum Aristotelis*. Paris, s.d.

Erasmus. *Opera Omnia*. Leyden, 1703.

—. *Opus Epistularum Des. Erasmi Roterodami*, eds. Ps. and H. M. Allen, 12 vols., Oxford, 1906-1958.

Freige, John Thomas. *Paedagogus*. Basel, 1582.

García Matamoros, Alfonso. *De asserenda Hispanorum eruditione*. Alcalá, 1553.

Gassendi, Pierre. *Exercitationes paradoxicae adversus Aristoteleos*. The Hague, 1656.

Gesner, Conrad. *Bibliotheca Universalis*. Tiguri, 1545.

Horn, Georg. *Historiae philosophiae libri septem*. Louvain, 1765-1770.

Keckermann, Bartholomew. *Gymnasium logicum*. Hannover, 1605.

Luther, Martin. *Luther's Werke*, ed. O. Clemen, 7 vols., 5th ed., Berlin, 1959.

Melanchthon, Philip. *De dialectica libri quatuor*. Wittenberg, 1536.

Montaigne, Michel. *The Complete Essays of Montaigne*, trans. D. M. Frame, 3rd. ed., Stanford, 1965.

Hutten, Ulrich von. *Opera Omnia*, ed. E. Bocking, 7 vols. Osnabrück, 1966.

More, Thomas. *The English Works*, ed. W. E. Campbell. London, 1931-1939.

Morhof, Georg. *Polyhistor*. Lubeck, 1708.

Nicolás, Antonio. *Bibliotheca Hispana Nova.* Rome, 1672.

Nizolio, Mario. *De veris principiis et vera ratione philosophandi contra pseu-dophilosophos libri quattuor,* ed. Q. Breen, 2 vols., Rome, 1956.

Possevino, Antonio. *Apparatus sacer.* Cologne, 1608.

Rabelais, Francis. *Oeuvrès de F. Rabelais,* ed. A. Lanfranc, 3 vols., Paris, 1922.

Ramus, Peter. *Aristotelicae animadversiones.* Paris, 1543.

——. *Ramus and Talon Inventory,* ed. W. Ong. Cambridge, 1958.

Sturm, Johan. *Institutionis litteratae . . .* Thorn, 1586.

——. *Partitionum dialecticarum libri duo.* Strasbourg, 1539.

Vives, Juan Luis.

a) Complete works

——. *J. L. Vivis Valentini Opera.* Basel, 1555.

——. *J. L. Vivis Valentini Opera Omnia,* ed. Gregorio Mayans y Síscar. 8 vols., Valencia, 1782.

——. *Juan Luis Vives. Obras completas,* ed. Lorenzo Riber, 2 vols., Madrid, 1947.

b) Correspondence

——. "Clarorum Hispaniensium epistolae ineditae," ed. Adolfo Bonilla y San Martin, *Revue Hispanique.* VIII (1901), 263-264.

——. *Litterae virorum eruditorum ad Franciscum Craneveldium,* ed. Henry de Vocht, Louvain, 1929.

c) Translations

1. Spanish Translations

——. *Diálogos Latinos,* trans. C. Fernández, Barcelona, 1940.

——. *Diálogos,* trans. C. Coret, Buenos Aires, 1940.

——. *Introduccion a la Sabiduría,* trans. Francisco Alcayde Vilar, Madrid, 1944.

——. *Instruccion a la mujer cristiana,* trans. Fernandez Ramirez, Madrid, 1936.

——. *Las Quexas y Llanto de Pompeyo,* trans. J. Martin Cordero, Anvers, 1556.

——. *Introduccion a la Sabiduría,* trans. Juan Alventosa, Valencia, 1930.

——. *Pensamientos,* ed. L. Garner, Madrid, 1940.

——. *Antología,* ed. and trans. José Corts y Grau, Madrid, 1943.

2. French Translations

——. *Saint Augustin de la Cité de Dieu, illustrée des Commentaires de J. L. Vivès,* trans. G. Hervet, Paris, 1578.

——. *L'institution de la femme chretienne,* trans. Pierre Changy, Paris, 1543.

——. *Divine Philosophie de Vivès,* trans. G. Paradin, Paris, 1553.

—. *Les Dialogues,* trans. G. Cotier, Lyon, 1560.

—. *Les Dialogues,* trans. G. de Housteville, Anvers, 1571.

—. *Les Dialogues,* trans. B. Iamin, Paris, 1573.

—. *De l'assistance aux pauvres,* trans. R. A. Casanova and L. Caby, Bruxelles, 1943.

3. English Translations

—. *Of the Citie of God: with the learned Comments of J. L. Vives,* trans. John Healey, London, 1620.

—. *Vives on Education* (*De disciplinis*), trans. Foster Watson, Cambridge, 1913.

—. *On Poor Relief,* trans. Margaret H. Shwerwood, New York, 1928.

—. *The Fable of Man,* trans. N. Lenkeith, in *The Renaissance Philosophy of Man,* ed. E. Cassirer et al., Chicago, 1948.

b. Secondary Sources

Adams, Robert P. *The Better Part of Valor.* Seattle, 1962.

Alcayde Vilar, Francisco et al. *Coleccion de artículos.* Ofrenda en el IV centenario de la muerte de Luis Vives. Cátedra de Luis Vives en la Facultad de Filosofía y Letras de la Universidad de Valencia, Valencia, 1940.

Allen, Percy Stafford and H. M. "Ludovicus Vives at Corpus," *Pelican Record,* December, 1902, 156 ff.

Arnauld, Carolus. "Quid de pueris instituendis senserit L. Vives," doct. diss., Paris, 1883.

Atkinson, William C. *Luis Vives and Poor Relief.* Dublin, 1935.

Barbera, M. "G. L. Vives e la pedagogia dei Gesuiti," *Civitta Cattolica,* I (1923), 522-532; II (1923), 130-137.

Baron, Hans. *The Crisis of the Early Italian Renaissance. Civic Humanism and Republican Liberty in an Age of Classicism and Tyranny.* Princeton, 1955.

Baroux, M. Robert. *Pierre de la Ramée: son influence philosophique.* Paris, 1922.

Bataillon, Marcel. *Erasmo y España,* trans., Antonio Alatorre. 2 vols., México, 1950.

—. "Du nouveau sur J. L. Vives," *Bulletin Hispanique,* XXXII (1930), 97-114.

Batle, Vázquez M. *Introduccion, programa y bibliografía sobre J. L. Vives.* Murcia, 1942.

Battistesa, Angel. "Juan Luis Vives," *Nosotros,* Buenos Aires, L-LI (1940).

Blanco, Ricardo. *Luis Vives: la Pedagogía científica y la instruccion de la mujer.* Madrid, 1935.

Blanco y Sánchez, Rufino. *Paidología y paidotecnia . . . Los diálogos escolares de la época del Renacimiento y extracto amplio de los de Luis Vives.* Madrid, 1920.

Böhmer, Ermund. *Spanish Reformers.* 3 vols., Strassbourg–London, 1874–1904.

Bohatec, Joseph. *Budé and Calvin. Studies in the World of Early French Humanism.* Kraz, 1950.

Bohlen, Jan Lucken. "Die Abhängigkeit J. A. Comenius von seinen Vorgängern," doct. diss., Erlangen, 1906.

Bonet-Maury, Gaston. *Gerard Groote, un precursor de la Reforme.* Paris, 1856.

Bonilla y San Martín, Adolfo. *Luis Vives y la filosofía del Renacimiento.* 2 vols., Madrid, 1929.

Book, Emil. *J. L. Vives, en reformator inom den pedagogiske vetenskapen.* Helsingfors, 1887.

Bordoy-Torrents, Pablo. "Del summe equilibri de Lluis Vives," *Quaderns d'Estudi,* 1919, 321-339.

Bosch-Kemper, Jan de. *J. L. Vives geschetst als Christelijk philantroop der 16de eeuw. met eenige plaaten uit zijne godsdienstige geschriften.* Amsterdam, 1851.

Braam, Henry. "Dissertatio Theologica exhibens J. L. Vives Theologiam Christianam," doct. diss., Groningen, 1853.

Bröring, Julius. *Commentario de los diálogos de Vives.* Oldenburg, 1897.

Brücker, Jacobus. *Historia critica Philosophiae.* 6 vols., Leyden, 1746.

Buisson, Ferdinand. *Répertoire des ouvrages pedagogiques du XVI siècle.* Paris, 1886.

Bullon, E. *Los precursores españoles de Bacon y Descartes.* Salamanca, 1905.

Bürger, Otto. *Erasmus von Rotterdam and der Spanier Vives.* Kempsten, 1914.

Busch, Douglas. *The Renaissance and English Humanism.* Toronto, 1939.

Busson, Henry. *Le rationalisme dans la literature francaise de la Renaissance.* 2nd. ed., Paris (Vrin), 1957.

Calatayud, Boades. *Luis Vives, Feijoo y Panduro.* Madrid, 1925.

Calmette, Joseph. *L'élaboration du monde moderne.* 3rd. ed., 3 vols., Paris, 1949.

Carcat, Luis. "Introducción al estudio de Luis Vives," *Revista de Indias* (Bogotá, Colombia), VI (1940), 5-20.

Carreras y Artau, Tomás. *Historia de la Filosofía española.* 2 vols., Madrid, 1939.

—. *La Filosofía moral y jurídica de Luis Vives.* Barcelona, 1911.

—. *Luis Vives, philosophe de l'humanisme.* Louvain, 1962.

Carriazo, José María. *Las ideas sociales de J. L. Vives.* Madrid, 1927.

Casanova, Ricardo Aznar. *Soixante lettres de Juan Luis Vivès, traduites du latin.* Paris, 1943.

Casas, José Mariá. "Luis Vives y sus comentarios a la 'Civitas Dei,' " *La Ciudad de Dios.* CLXVIII (1957), 615–619.

Cassirer, Ernest et al. *The Renaissance Philosophy of Man.* Chicago, 1948.

Chabod, Federico. *Machiavelli and the Renaissance.* London, 1958.

Chambers, Robert W. *Thomas More.* London, 1935.

Chatelain, Emile. *Essai d'une bibliographie de l'ancienne Université de Paris.* Paris, 1891.

Codina, Arturo. *Los orígenes de los Ejercicios espirituales de San Ignacio.* Barcelona, 1926.

Compayré, Gabriel. *Histoire critique des doctrines de l'education en France depuis le seizième siècle.* 3 vols., Paris, 1879.

Corts y Grau, José. *Breviarios del pensamiento español. J. L. Vives.* (Antología). Madrid, 1943.

—. "Luis Vives y nosotros," *El Escorial.* Madrid (I), 1940, 53–69.

—. "La dignidad humana en Juan Luis Vives," *Archivo de Derecho Público.* III (1950), 73–89.

Crespo de Lartigua, Blanca. "Vives y su influjo en la pedagogía," *Anales del Instituto de Investigaciones pedagógicas.* III (1954), 49–51.

Crévier, Maurice. *Histoire de l'Université de Paris depuis son origine jusqu'à l'année 1600.* 2 vols., Paris, 1761.

Cuevas, Santiago. *Luis Vives. Fox Morcillo y Gómez Pereira.* Habana, 1897.

Daly, Walter. "The Educational Psychology of Juan Luis Vives," doct. diss., Washington, 1924.

Delaruelle, Louis. *Guillaume Budé.* Paris, 1907.

Denifle, Heinrich. *Die Entstehung der Universität des Mittelalters bis 1400.* Graz, 1956.

—. and Chatelain E. *Chartularium Universitatis Parisiensis.* 4 vols., Paris, 1889–1897.

Denk, O. *Vives.* Donanwoerth, 1892.

Díaz Jimenez, Enrique. *Los fundamentos éticos, religiosos y psicológicos de la Pedagogía de Juan Luis Vives.* Madrid, 1929.

Dilthey, Wilhelm. *Pädagogik. Geschichte und Grunlinien des Systems,* ed. Otto F. Bollnow. Gesammelte Schriften, Band IX. Stuttgart (Teubner Verlag), 1960.

—. *Weltanschauung und Analyse den Menschen seit Renaissance und Reformation,* ed. George Misch. Gesammelte Schriften, Band II. 3rd. ed., Leipzig, 1923.

Du Dezert, George Desdevisses. "Bonilla sur L. Vives," *Revue Hispanique.* XII (1905), 373–412.

Du Pin, E. *Nouvelle bibliothèque des auteurs ecclesiastiques.* Paris–Amsterdam, 1697–1715, vol. 8.

Edelbluth, Johan. *Johann Ludwig Vives, pedagogische Hauptshriften.* Paderborn, 1912.

Einstein, Lewis. *The Italian Renaissance in England.* New York, 1913.

Enciclopedia italiana, di scienze, lettere ed arti, Roma, 1937, vol. XXXV.

Enciclopedia manual de pedagogía y ciencias auxiliares. Barcelona, 1928.

Encyclopädie des gesamten Erziehungs- und Unterrichtswesens. Leipzig, 1887, t. 9, 776–851.

Ensayo de un diccionario biográfico-cronológico de los siglos XV al XX. Madrid, 1942, 771–773.

Enzyklopädisches Handbuch der Padagogik. Rhein, 1909.

Escolano, Caspar. *Década primera de la historia de la insigne y coronada ciudad de Valencia.* Valencia, 1610.

Escosura, Pablo de la. "La beneficencia en el siglo XVI; consideraciones sobre el opúsculo de Juan Luis Vives, '*Del socorro de los pobres,*' " *Revista de España,* IX (1876), 193–210; 339–356; 462–481.

Estelrich, Juan. *La mission de l'Espagne: Au Méxique sur les traces de Vives.* Paris, 1941.

—. *Luis Vives. Exposition organisée a la Bibliothèque Nationale.* Paris, 1941.

Eulitz, Adolphus. *Der Verkehr zwischen Vives und Budeus.* Chemnitz, 1897.

Ferguson, Wallace. *The Renaissance in Historical Thought.* Cambridge, 1948.

Fernandez Almuzara, Eugenio. "Influencia de España en la restauracion de la Universidad de Coimbra. Vives y Juan III," *Hispania* (Madrid), 1940 (I), 71–82.

Ferrer, José, and Garrido, Ricardo. *Luis Vives y la psicología educativa.* Valencia, 1944.

Fitzmaurice-Kelly, Julia. "Vives and the *Carros de las Donas,*" *Revue Hispanique,* LXXXI (1933), 305–344.

Fornet, Asensi de. *Blanca March y Valencia. Las madres de Luis Vives.* Madrid, 1942.

Fowler, Thomas. *The History of Corpus Christi College.* Oxford, 1893.

Francken, W. *J. L. Vives de vriend van Erasmus in zijn leven en als merkwaardig christelijk theoloog en philanthroop der 16de eeuw.* Rotterdam, 1853.

Fuente, Vicente de la. "Luis Vives," *Semanario pintoresco español.* III (1841), 1–2, 11–12.

Garin, Eugenio. *La cultura filosófica del Rinascimento Italiano,* ed. G. C. Sansoni. Firenze, 1961.

—. *L'Umanesimo Italiano: Filosofía e vita nel Rinascimento.* Bari, 1952.

—. *Interpretazioni del Rinascimento.* Firenze, 1950.

Garmendia de Otaola, A. "Luis Vives: ensayo de pedagogía comparada," *Razón y Fé,* CXIX (1940), 130–139.

—. "La Universidad de Lovaina conmemora el IV centenario de la muerte de Luis Vives," *Razón y Fé,* 1940, 120–125.

Garrido, Ramon. *Luis Vives y la Psicología educativa.* Valencia, 1944.

Gaufrés, Mathieu J. *Claude Baduel et la Reforme des études au XVI siècle.* Paris, 1923.

Geiger, Ludwig. *Renaissance und Humanismus in Italien und Deutschland.* Berlin, 1882.

Gerard, Jacques. "Vives et l'organisation de l'enseignement," *Revue de l'Université de Bruxelles,* XLIV (1938), 69–85.

Getino, Alonso L. *Vitoria y Vives.* Madrid, 1931.

Gilbert, Neal W. *Renaissance Concepts of Method.* New York, 1960.

Gilmore, Myron P. *The World of Humanismus.* New York, 1952.

Gil y Calpe, José. "Iconografía de J. L. Vives," *Cultura Valenciana,* 1927, 2–23.

Gómez, H. "Los fundamentos filosóficos del Humanismo de Luis Vives," *Verdad y Vida,* XII (1954), 339–385.

Gomis, J. B. *Bibliografía vivista, "De Subventione pauperum," nuevo ejemplar de la edicion de 1526.* Madrid, 1943.

—. *Criterio social de Luis Vives.* Madrid, 1946.

—. *Luis Vives, forma de la Hispanidad.* Valencia, 1941.

—. *El Nuevo Mundo en Luis Vives.* Madrid, 1943.

—. *Balmes y Vives: El Criterio y el Tratado del Alma.* Madrid, 1948.

—. *Vives pro Concilio de Trento.* Madrid, 1945.

Gonzalez de la Calle, P. "Luis Vives y España: Datos y sugerencias para un ensayo biográfico," *Revista de Indias,* V (1940), 431–441.

Gonzalez-Múzquiz, Ricardo. *Vindicacion del ilustre filósofo español Juan Luis Vives, primer reformador de la Filosofía en Europa.* Valladolid, 1789.

Gordon, J. *Luis Vives.* Madrid, 1945.

Graf, Paul. "Ludwig Vives als Apologet." Inaugural Dissertation der Theologischen Fakultät der Universität Freiburg i Br., Freiburg, 1932.

Graves, Frank P. *Peter Ramus and the Educational Reformation of the XVI century.* New York, 1912.

Green, Otis H. "Additional data on Erasmus in Spain," *Modern Language Quarterly,* X (1949), 47-58.

Grypdonck, Marcel. *Juan Luis Vives in zijn beteekenis voor de paedagogiek,* VOT, 1940 (21), 433-444.

Guerrero, Eustaquio. "Para el IV centenario de la muerte de Luis Vives," *Razón y Fé,* CXX (1940), 30–47.

Günther, R. *Invieweit hat Ludwig Vives die Ideen Bacons von Verulan vorbereitet,* doct. diss., Leipzig, 1912.

Hamilton, William. *Lectures on Metaphysics and Logic,* ed. Henry L. Mansel and J. Veitch, Boston (Harper), 1868.

—. *Discussions on Philosophy and Literature,* with an introd. essay by R. Turnbull. New York, 1856.

Hartfelder, Karl. *Philip Melanchthon als Praeceptor Germaniae,* 2nd. ed., Nieuwkoop, 1964.

Hause, Paul. "Die Pädagogik des Spaniers Luis Vives und sein Einfluss auf Amos Comenius," doct. diss., Erlangen, 1890.

Heine, Heinrich. "Vives Schriften über Erziehung und Unterricht," *Pädagogische Bibliothek*, ed. by Karl Richter, Berlin, 1905.

Hernández, Gil, A. "Etica, Derecho, en la doctrina de Luis Vives," *Revista de la Facultad de Derecho*, XII (Madrid, 1943).

Höfer, J. C. *Nouvelle biographie generale, t. XLVI.*

Hofer, J. M. "Die Stellung des Erasmus und J. L. Vives zur Pädagogik Quintilians," doct. diss., Erlangen, 1910.

Hoppe, Gerhard. *Die Psychologie des J. L. Vives.* Berlin, 1901.

Horas, Plácido. "Ubicacion de J. L. Vives en la historia de la psicología," *Anales del Instituto de Investigaciones psico-pedagógicas.* V (1957-1958), 259-266.

Howell, Wilbur Samuel. *Logic and Rhetoric in England, 1500-1700.* New York, 1961.

Huizinga, Johan. *Erasmus*, trans. by Werner Kaegi, 4th. ed., Basel, 1951.

Hyma, Albert. *The Youth of Erasmus.* Ann Arbor, 1930.

—. *From Renaissance to Reformation.* Michigan, 1951.

Ilg, Paul. "Die Selbstätigkeit als Bildungsprinzip bei J. L. Vives," doct. diss., Langensalza, 1931.

Jung, G. "Das Methodenproblem bei Vives," *Congres Descartes*, V, 1937, 134-139.

Kaiser, Franz. *Juan Luis Vives Pädagogische Schriften.* Freiburg, 1896.

Kalkoff, Paul. *Die Anfänge der Gegenreformation in den Niederlanden.* 2 vols., Halle, 1903-04.

Kater, Theodor G. A. "J. L. Vives und seine Stellung zu Aristoteles," doct. diss., Erlangen, 1909.

Kristeller, Paul O. *Augustine and the Early Renaissance.* New York, 1943.

Kückelhahn, Ludwig. *Johan Sturm.* Leipzig, 1872.

Kuypers, Franz. *Vives in seiner Pädagogik.* Leipzig, 1897.

Lange, A. *Luis Vives,* trans. Menéndez y Pelayo. Madrid, 1894.

Lara, Tomás de. *Ubicacion de J. L. Vives en el Renacimiento español,* Buenos Aires, 1943.

Lecigne, Chanoine C. "Quid de rebus politicis senserit J. L. Vives," doct. diss., Paris, 1898.

León Tello, F. J. "Vives y la estética del Renacimiento," *Revista de Filosofía*, XXI (1965), 27-54.

Leroux, E. "Quid de puellis instituendis senserit Luis Vives," doct. diss., Paris, 1888.

Lewis, G. "Une source inexplorée du Traité des Passions," *Revue Philosophique de la France et de l'étranger.* VII (1958), 341-381.

Lexikon der Pädagogik in 3 Bänden. Bern, III, 1952.

Lexikon der Pädagogik. Freiburg, 1921.

Llorente, Juan A. *Histoire critique de l'Inquisition d'Espagne.* 2nd. ed., 4 vols., Paris, 1818.

Losada, Angel. "Luis Vives en la actualidad internacional," *Revista de Filosofía,* XI (1952), 149-167.

Mallaina, Carlos. *Estudio biográfico de Luis Vives.* Burgos, 1872.

Mann, Margarete. *Erasme et les débuts de la Reforme francaise, (1517-36).* Paris (Bibliotheque de la Renaissance), 1934.

Manzari, Bina. "La prospettiva de l'educazione secondo L. Vives e G. G. Rousseau," *Rassegna di Scienze philosophische.* XVIII (1965), 27-54.

Marañon, Gregorio. *Españoles fuera de España.* 5th ed., Madrid, 1961.

Marc'Hadour, Germain. *L'Univers de Thomas More.* Paris, 1963.

Marticorena, Octavio. "Filósofos españoles: Luis Vives," *Revista de España,* V (1872), 60-80.

Massabieau, Louis. *Les Colloques escolaires du XVI siècle.* Paris, 1878.

Mateu y Llopis, Eduardo. *Vives, el expatriado.* Barcelona, 1941.

Mestwerdt, Paul. *Die Anfänge des Erasmus Humanismus und Devotio Moderna.* Leipzig, 1917.

Meuwissen, B. *De Spaans-Nederlandse pedagoog Jan Louis Vives (1492-1540).* (Opvoedkundige Brochurenreeks, 110). Tilburg, R.K. Jongensweeshuis, 1940.

Michaud, G. L. "L'influence de Vives sur Rabelais," *Revue du seizième siècle,* XII (1925).

—. "Luis Vives and Rabelais' pedagogy," *Publications of the Modern Languages of America* (New York), XXXVIII (1923).

Millás Vallicrosa, J. M. "La apologética de Luis Vives y el judaismo," *Sefarad.* Madrid, II (1942), 293-323.

Monsegú, Bernardo. *Filosofía del humanismo de Juan Luis Vives.* Madrid (Consejo Superior de Investigaciones Científicas), 1961.

—. "La doctrina cristológica de Luis Vives," *Estudios franciscanos,* LVI (1955), 43-70.

Montoya, Delia O. de. *Juan Luis Vives y la Madurez de la conciencia pedagógica moderna.* Santa Fé, 1941.

Muñoz, Alonso. *Expresion filosófica y literaria de España.* Barcelona, 1956.

Namèche, Alexander J. "Mémoire sur la vie et les écrits de J. L. Vives," *Memoires couronneés par l'Academie Royale des sciences et belles-lettres de Bruxelles,* XV, Prémière Partie (1841), 3-126.

Nebe, August. "Vives, Alsted und Comenius in ihrem Verhältniss zu einander," doct. diss., Elberfeld, 1891.

Nulli, Siro Attilio. *Erasmo e il Rinascimento.* Roma, 1955.

Oliveros, W. Gonzalez. *J. Luis Vives, "De Communione rerum ad Germanos inferiores."* Trad. española. Valladolid, 1938.

Ong, Walter J. *Ramus, Method, and the Decay of Dialogue.* Cambridge, 1958.

—. *Ramus and Talon Inventory.* Cambridge, 1958.

Oroz, R. *Juan Luis Vives y los humanistas de su tiempo, ante la enseñanza del Latin.* Santiago de Chile, 1935.

Ortega y Gasset, José. *Vives-Geothe,* ed. by *Revista de Occidente,* obras inéditas, conferencias. Madrid (*Revista de Occidente*), 1961.

Pade, N. "Die Affektenlehre des J. L. Vives," doct. diss., Münster, 1893.

Palacio, J. M. "Luis Vives y la propiedad," *La Propiedad.* (Madrid), 1935, 112-136.

Pappagallo, A. "La pedagogia di G. L. Vives," doct. diss., Torino, 1955.

Paquot, Jean Noel. *Mémoires pour servir a l'histoire des Pays-Bas.* 3 vols., Louvain, 1765-70.

Parmentier, Jacques. "J. L. Vives: De ses theories sur l'education et de leur influences sur les pedagogues anglais," *Revue Internationale de l'enseignement,* XXV (1893), 441-455.

Piazzi, A. "Luis Vives, pedagogista del Rinascimento," *Revista Italiana di Filosofia,* IX (1891), 113-179.

Pineau, Jean Baptiste. *Erasme, sa pensée religieuse.* Paris, 1924.

Pinta y Llorente, Miguel, and José M. de Palacio. *Procesos Inquisitoriales contra la familia judía de Luis Vives.* Madrid (Consejo Superior de Investigaciones Científicas), 1964.

Pín y Soler, Joseph. *Juan Luis Vives.* Barcelona, 1914.

Popkin, Richard. *The History of Scepticism from Erasmus to Descartes.* Van Gorcum, Assen, The Netherlands, 1960.

Prantl, Karl. *Geschichte der Logik im Abendland.* 2nd. ed., 2 vols., Graz, 1955.

Probst, Jean-Henri. *Le Lullisme de Raymond de Sebonde.* Toulouse, 1912.

Puigdollers. Mariano. *La filosofía española de Juan Luis Vives.* Barcelona, 1940.

Ram, Pierre. *Analects pour servir a l'histoire de l'Université de Louvain.* Louvain, 1838-1859.

Rashdall, Hastings. *The Universities of Europe in the Middle Ages.* 2nd. ed., 3 vols., Oxford (University Press), 1936.

Raumer, Karl. *Geschichte der Pädagogik.* 3 vols., Berlin, 1841-42.

Read, Conyers, *Bibliography of British history; Tudor period.* Oxford, 1933.

Reid, Thomas. *Essays on the Intellectual Powers of the Human Mind.* 2nd. ed., London, 1827.

Remusat, Charles de. *Bacon sa vie, son temps, sa philosophie.* 3rd. ed., Paris, 1877.

Renan, Ernest. *Averroes et l'Averroisme.* 2nd. ed., Paris, 1861.

Renaudet, Augustin. *Préréforme et Humanisme à Paris pendant les premières guerres d'Italie.* 2nd. ed., Paris (Librairie d'Argences), 1951.

—. "Jean Standonck, un reformateur catholique avant la Réforme," *Bulletin de la societé d l'histoire du Protestantisme francais.* January-February, 1908.

Rey Altuna, Luis. "La ética del Renacimiento (Luis Vives)," *Revista de Filosofía,* V (1946).

Riba, García Carlos. *Luis Vives y el Pacifismo.* Leccion inaugural del año académico 1933-34 en la Universidad de Zaragoza. Zaragoza, 1933.

Ríos, Amador de los. *Historia social, política y religiosa de los judíos de España y Portugal.* Madrid, 1875.

Rivari, Enrico. *La sapienza psicologica e pedagogica di Giovanni Ludovico Vives da Valenza.* Bologna, 1922.

Saitta, Giuseppe. *Marsilio Ficino e la filosofia del Umanesimo.* Firenze, 1943.

Sánchez, Amador. *El humanista Luis Vives,* Universidad de Antioquia (Medellín), 53–54.

Sánchez, L. J. *La psicología profética de J. L. Vives.* Universidad Nacional de Colombia, 1953.

Sancipriano, Mario. "Il sentimento dell' Europa in G. L. Vives," *Humanitas,* XII (1957), 629–634.

—. *Il pensiero psicologico e morale di G. L. Vives.* Firenze, 1957.

Schmidt, Carl. *La vie et les travaux de Jean Sturm, premier recteur du Gymnase et de l'Academie de Strasbourg.* Paris, 1855.

Serrano, Serrano. "Doctrina de J. L. Vives sobre la propiedad y el trabajo y su repercusion en las Instituciones sociales contemporáneas," *Salmaticensis,* 1965 (XII), 57–107.

Simpson, Peter. "Tamquam explorator," *Modern Language Review,* Il (1907), 201–210.

Thibaut, Franciscus. "Quid de puellis instituendis senserit J. L. Vives," doct. diss., Paris, 1888.

Thode, Heinrich. *Franz von Assisi und die Anfänge der Kunst der Renaissance in Italien.* Berlin, 1885.

Thorndike, Lynn. *Science and Thought in the XV Century.* New York, 1929.

—. "John Louis Vives," *Essays Dedicated to James Harvey Robinson.* New York, 1929.

Thurlemann, Ines. *Erasmus von Rotterdam und Ludovicus Vives als Pazifisten.* Freiburg, 1932.

Thurot, Charles. *De l'organization de l'enseignement dans l'Université de Paris au Moyen-Age.* Paris, 1850.

Toffanin, G. *La fine dell Umanesimo.* Torino, 1920.

—. *Il Cinquecento.* Storia letteraria d'Italia. Milano, 1929.

Tomás y Sampere, R. *Juan Luis Vives, ilustre español.* Notas para una leccion escolar. Madrid, 1940.

Torre del Cerro, Antonio. *La Universidad de Alcalá. Estado de la enseñanza según las visitas de cátedra de 1524–25 a 1527–28.* Homenaje a Menéndez Pidal, vol. III, 361–378.

Torró, Antonio. *La pedagogía científica según Luis Vives.* Barcelona, 1932.

Urmeneta, Fermin de. "Senequismo y Vivismo," *Augustinus.* X (1965), 409–417.

—. "Referencias a las Bellas Artes en las obras pedagógicas de Luis Vives," *Revista española de pedagogía*. VI (1948), 233–244.

—. "Luis Vives como precursor de Suárez y Balmes," *Revista de Filosofía*. VII (1948).

—. "Ramón Lull y Luis Vives," *Estudios Franciscanos*, XXXI (1950).

—. "San Augustin ante su comentarista Luis Vives," *Augustinus*. VIII (1963), 519–533.

Vadier, Berthe. *Un moraliste du XVI siècle. Jean Louis Vives et son livre de l'education de la femme chretiènne*. Berne, 1892.

Valdés, Francisco. "Un intelectual del siglo XVI," *Accion Española*, IV (1932), 639–647.

Valentini, M. E. *Erasmo y Vives*. Buenos Aires, 1934.

Valle, F. del. "La mendicidad y el paro en el '*Socorro de los pobres*' de Juan Luis Vives," *Razón y Fé*, CXXV (1942), 78–95.

Vasoli, Cesare. "G. L. Vives e la polemica antiscolastica nello '*In pseudo-dialecticos*,'" *Miscelanea de estudios a Joaquín Carvalho*. VII (1961), 679–686.

—. *J. L. Vives e un programma umanistico di riforma della Logica*. Firenze, 1961.

Villey, Pierre. *Les sources et l'evolution des Essays de Montaigne*. 2 vols., Paris (Fondation Thiers), 1912.

Villoslada, R. G. *L. Vives y Erasmo, Cotejo de dos almas*. (Humanidades), vol. V, Univ. Pont. de Comillas, 1953.

—. "Erasmo y Vitoria," *Razón y Fé*. XXXV (1935), 19–38.

—. *La Universidad de Paris durante los estudios de Francisco de Vitoria, 1507–1522*. Rome, 1938.

—. "Luis Vives y Erasmo, coloquio de dos almas," *Humanidades*, X (1955), 159–177.

Vocht, Henry de. *Monumenta Historia Lovaniensia*. Louvain, 1934.

Voight, George. *Die Wiederlebung des classischen Althertums*. Berlin, 1859.

Watson, Foster. *Vives on Education*. Cambridge, 1913.

—. *Vives and the Renascence Education of Women*. New York, 1912.

—. *Vives, padre de la Psicologia moderna*. Madrid, 1916.

—. "The Influence of Valencia on Vives," *Aberystwyth Studies*. XI (1927), 47–103.

—. "J. L. Vives and Saint Augustine's *Civitas Dei*," *Church Quarterly Review*. LXXVI (1913), 154–157.

—. *J. L. Vives: A Scholar of the Renascente, 1492–1540*. London, 1920.

—. *Luis Vives*. Oxford, 1922.

—. *Luis Vives, el Gran Valenciano*. Valencia, 1923.

Weismann, Gerhard. *Die Soziale Bedeutung des Humanisten Vives*. Berlin, 1905.

Werner, Karl. *Geschichte der apologetischen und polemischen Literatur*. 5 vols., Shaffhausen, 1861.

Wightman, William. *Science and the Renaissance*. An Introduction to the Study of the Emergence of Science in the XVI Century. New York, 1962.

Woodward, William Harrison. *La pedagogia del Rinascimento*. Firenze, 1923.

Würkert, Gerog. *Ludwig Vives Schrift von der Armenpflege*. Pirna, 1901.

Wychgram, Jacob. *Johan Ludwig Vives: Pädagogische Schriften*. Wien, 1891.

Xirao, J. *El pensamiento vivo de J. L. Vives*. Buenos Aires, 1944.

Zaragüeta, Bengoechea, J. *Las directrices de la pedagogía de Juan Luis Vives*. Madrid, 1945.

Zeller, Eduard. *Outlines of the History of Greek Philosophy*. trans. by L. R. Palmer, 13th ed., Cleveland, 1950.

INDEX OF NAMES